商业环境与人力资源管理

主　编◎徐艳辉　全毅文　田　芳

副主编◎刘海娟　张　燕　赵凤英　陶玉婷

吉林大学出版社
JILIN UNIVERSITY PRESS

图书在版编目（CIP）数据

商业环境与人力资源管理 / 徐艳辉, 全毅文, 田芳
主编.—长春 : 吉林大学出版社, 2019.6
ISBN 978-7-5692-4958-3

Ⅰ.①商… Ⅱ.①徐… ②全… ③田… Ⅲ.①商业环
境 ②人力资源管理 Ⅳ.①F71 ②F243

中国版本图书馆CIP数据核字（2019）第119122号

书　　名	商业环境与人力资源管理
	SHANGYE HUANJING YU RENLI ZIYUAN GUANLI
作　　者	徐艳辉　全毅文　田　芳　主编
策划编辑	刘明明
责任编辑	高欣宇
责任校对	赵　莹
装帧设计	中尚图
出版发行	吉林大学出版社
社　　址	长春市人民大街4059号
邮政编码	130021
发行电话	0431-89580028/29/21
网　　址	http://www.jlup.com.cn
电子邮箱	jdcbs@jlu.edu.cn
印　　刷	河北盛世彩捷印刷有限公司
开　　本	787mm×1092mm　1/16
印　　张	29
字　　数	600千字
版　　次	2019年6月　第1版
印　　次	2019年6月　第1次
书　　号	ISBN 978-7-5692-4958-3
定　　价	88.00元

Business Environment and Managing People（《商业环境与人力资源管理》）是根据我院中外合作办学项目专业教师的双语教学实际，结合新时期中外合作办学项目高职学生的专业需求编辑出版。

内蒙古商贸职业学院自2007年起分别与英国桑德兰城市学院、英国南埃塞克斯学院开展联合办学项目，合作培养具有专业视角的国际化商务人才。根据这一要求，联合办学项目学生既要掌握本专业理论知识，又要具备运用国际商务知识的能力。为此，作为中外合作办学项目一线教师，本着"立足高职、服务高职，培养国际商务人才"的宗旨，编写本教材。本书根据中外合作办学项目专业人才培养目标，以国际商务环境、人才管理的基本理论为出发点，旨在把中外合作办学项目学生培养成为既具有系统的专业理论知识，又具有实际工作经验与能力、了解相关商务环境、人力资源管理知识的国际商务人才。

本书具有以下特点：

1.实用性强：本书根据中外合作办学项目各专业培养目标，以商务环境、人力资源管理基本理论为出发点，既培养学生系统的专业理论知识，又注重培养学生的实际分析、解决问题的能力。为其他相关专业课的学习及未来实际工作奠定基础。

2.逻辑性强：本教材根据商务环境、人力资源管理各知识点之间的逻辑关系，由易到难，由浅到深进行设计编写。各章节之间循序渐进，有效衔接。

3.简明扼要：本教材使用通俗易懂的语言，简明扼要地阐述商务环境及人力资源管理的基本理论、原理，并辅以相关案例，力求使学生更容易理解掌握国际商务专业理论及术语。

由于时间仓促，加之编者水平有限，本书难免有错漏和不足之处，恳请读者和同行批评指正。本书在编写过程中，得到了相关教师以及出版社专家的指导和帮助，在此深表谢意。

编　者

2019年3月

CONTENTS
目 录

Part 1
Business Environment

Introduction to the Book

Description

The purpose of the book is to introduce learners to the institutions and influences which constitute the economic and broader environment in which businesses operate and to develop an understanding of how businesses adjust their behaviour to changes in the environment, both nationally and internationally.

Learners are encouraged to identify the objectives of organizations and the influence of stakeholders and to investigate the operation of organizations in relation to the local, national, and global environments.

It is expected that learners will develop an understanding of the nature and purpose of political and economic institutions, underpinned by a knowledge of how basic economic theory works in different types of economy. Learners will also be expected to develop a basic understanding of economic, social and technological forces and be able to compare China with other countries.

Details of Contents

1.Objectives and Responsibilities of An Organization

Categories of organizations	Size, sector/type-private, public, voluntary, charitable; activity-primary, secondary, tertiary
Mission, values and objectives of organizations	Concept of corporate mission or vision, underlying values/philosophy, profit, market share, return on capital employed (ROCE), sales, growth, levels of service, customer/user perceptions and audits
Stakeholders	Identification of stakeholders, stakeholder groups, conflict of expectations, attitude, power-influence matrix; satisfying stakeholder objectives, measuring performance
Responsibilities of organizations	Responsibilities to stakeholders, key legal responsibilities e.g. consumer, employment, disability discrimination and equal opportunities, stakeholder pensions; wider responsibilities including ethical and environmental; ethical practice

2. Economic, Social and Global Environment

Resource issues and types of economic system	Basic economic problem, effective use of resources; type of economic systems-command, free enterprise, mixed, including transitional economies, public and private sector initiatives; private finance initiatives
Government policy	Fiscal policy and monetary policy in China, stakeholder and interest groups, the influence of the global economy-trends, uncertainties, growth, impact on the economy, UK and Chinese multinationals, World Bank

3. Behavior of Organizations and the Market Environment

Market types	Perfect competition, monopoly, monopolistic competition, oligopoly, duopoly; competitive advantage, behaviour/strategies adopted by firms; role of the Competition Commission in the UK and regulatory bodies such as OFTEL, OFGAS, OFWAT
Market forces and organizational responses	Supply and demand, elasticity, customer perceptions and actions, issues relating to supply, cost and output decisions short run and long run, economies of scale, growth of organizations: reasons, methods, financing, Multi-National Corporations/Trans-National Corporations (MNCs/TNCs), joint ventures, outsourcing; core markets/skills, technology and innovation, labour market trends, cultural environment

4. International Trade and the European and Asian Dimensions

The benefit of international trade	To the UK and Chinese economy, businesses, balance of payments, patterns and trends in international trade, World Trade Organization (WTO), UK and Chinese trade with the European Union (EU), USA and other countries, trading blocks throughout the world (including APEC and ASEAN), introduction of the EU etc.

Summary of learning outcomes and assessment criteria:

No.	Outcomes	Assessment criteria Learners should be able to:
1	Identify the objectives, stakeholders and responsibilities of an organization within its environment	★ Identify the mission, vision, values and key objectives of organizations ★ Assess the influence of stakeholders and identify the responsibilities that an organization should have
2	Investigate the business environment in which an organization operates	★ Identify the local, national and global business environment ★ Undertake the business environment analysis
3	Investigate the behaviour of organizations and the market environment	★ Identify the demand and supply, cost and price ★ Analyse the factors that can affect market forces ★ Identify the four market types and for a business analyse how to have competitive advantages
4	Explore the significance of international trade and international strategies applied by businesses	★ Discuss the importance of international trade; ★ Analyse how to set up international strategies in international environment ★ Analyse the economic implication for China and UK

Teaching/ Learning Strategies

The book will be delivered through a combination of lectures, seminars, small group tutorials as well as guided self-study. A topic will be introduced via a lecture. In the days following the lecture students will be invited to undertake related research which will then be discussed, reinforced, extended and enhanced via group seminars which may be tutor or student-led. The strategy will be underpinned and formatively assessed by small group tutorials.

Chapter 1   Organizations and Their Objectives

Introduction

A great number of organizations with many different types, forms and usually with various objectives can be encountered in our lives. The business organizations we come into contact vary from huge organizations, employing thousands all over the world and with a turnover lager than some nations' gross national product, to modest business organizations hiring only a few people and operating in a small locality.

So what is the purpose of all organizations? Why were they set up, and why some of them cannot continue and some can operate successfully? In this chapter we are going to consider the advantages and disadvantages of different forms of businesses, like sole traders, partnerships, and limited liability companies. We also identify the differences between the public and private sectors, and explain the functions of three levels of economic activities, including primary, secondary and tertiary industries.

In this chapter, we will mainly identify and discuss the mission, vision, values and various objectives of an organization. An organization should have its mission—the guiding idea behind the organization's all activities. Vision is a kind of intention of an organization that is expected to be realized in the future. Values can be a set of principles or ideas that influence the activities of an organization. Objectives of an organization are used to fulfil the mission, which also explain the organization's mission to a number of different client groups or stakeholders, who all have an interest in the organization's activities.

The objectives of this chapter:

(1)The size and types of organizations

(2)The nature of the public and private sectors

(3)The three levels of economic activities

(4) Business objectives

1.1 Categories of Organizations

An organization is an arrangement of people, pursuing common goals, achieving results and standards of performance. There are many different types of organizations that are set up to serve a number of different aims and to meet a variety of needs. They come in all forms, shapes and sizes. All businesses try to achieve their goals so that they can be operated successfully.

Any business has people and resources to do one of two following things.

A. To produce or make items or goods to be sold, like shoe factory, furniture maker, jeans factory, computer maker.

B. To provide services to be sold including banks, police, hospitals and insurance.

Here are some possible differences between organizations.

Factor	Example
Ownership (public or private)	Public sector: owned by the government Private sector: owned by private owners
Control	By the owners themselves, by people working on behalf, or indirectly by government-sponsored regulators
Profit or non-profit purpose	Business exists to make a profit. On the other hand, some are not profit orientated, like police, the army
Legal status	Partnership, limited company, sole trader, or public company
Size	Size can be measured in many ways, e.g. staff number, number of branches, sales revenue each year, market share and number of customers
Source of finance	Government funding, borrowing and share issues
Technology	Some organizations need to have a high technology usage, e.g. mobile telephone manufacturers
Activity (what they do)	Manufacturing, healthcare

All organizations are affected by the environment both nationally and internationally and by the government. So the nature and type of organizations will be constantly changing and developing in reaction to environmental changes; A business that starts as a sole trader may develop into a partnership, then a limited company, then maybe a group of companies.

1.1.1 The Forms of Organizations

Depending on how it is legally constituted an organization may have a legal existence separating from that of its owners and of its numbers. Following are three kinds of organizations with different nature.

Sole trader

Sole traders are single individuals carrying on a business on their own. Such businesses are usually small, although large ones with some managerial delegation do exist. The sole trader earns the profit or covers the losses of his or her venture. Legally, the business affairs of a sole trader are not distinguished in any way from their personal affairs. If there is a debt in their business dealings and the earnings of that business are not enough to pay the debt then the creditor can require payment out of the trader's non-business property. There are both advantages and disadvantages of being a sole trader, which are as follows.

The advantages:

(1) No formal procedures needed to begin trading.

(2) Independence and self-reliance—the owner has no need to consult with others about his or her decisions, except for tax purposes, nature of the business is not required to issue trading results.

(3) Commitment and motivation are encouraged by the solely accountable nature of the business.

(4) Being close to their customers and respond quickly to market changes.

The disadvantages:

(1)The owner has total personal liability to the full extent of the private assets for the business debts. A sole trader can lose his or her home and all possessions as a result of business failure.

(2) There are financial problems including difficulties in raising finance and expansion is only possible by ploughing back profits. Borrowed capital for expansion is often limited by lack of collateral.

(3) The individual usually has one skill, e.g. an inventor or a good salesperson but the sole trader needs to be adequate in all areas (e.g. advertising, purchasing and maintaining accounts).

(4) Lack of cover in the case of illness and lack of succession in the case of death are two major problems.

Partnership

Legally, partnership is two or more associated for the purpose of a business or profession. It is one stage beyond the sole trader and often arises from the need to introduce more capital or to combine skills, e.g. a garage proprietor may introduce a marketing partner. Each partner contributes an agreed amount of capital and there is an agreed method of sharing profits, salaries and interests. Like a sole trader, the partners have considerable influence over the business and are fully liable to outside parties in the event of financial failure. Sole traders who develop into a partnership often find difficulty in adapting to the need to consult others before any major decisions can be taken.

Can you find out the advantages and disadvantages of being a partnership?

Companies or corporations

Companies or corporations are distinct artificial "person" created in order to separate legal responsibility for the affairs of a business from the personal affairs of the individuals who own or operate it. Since a company exists only to establish legal responsibilities, it can only be created, operated, dissolved in accordance with the legal rules governing it. Consequently, the business debts are those of the company and not those of its members. In other words, if the assets owned by the business are not enough to pay off the debts incurred by the business, the owners can not be forced to make up the deficit from their private resources. The point is that the debts are not the owners' responsibility, but the business'. The debts belong to the company, which is regarded as a separate person in its own right.

The Company Acts distinguished between:

(1) Public limited company which is traded on an official stock market. Public limited company tends to be owned by a wide range of investors.

(2) Private limited company whose shares are only transferable by direct contact and purchase from the shareholders. It must include "Ltd" or "Limited" in their title. Because there is no natural place for its shares. Private limited company tends to be owned by a small number of shareholders.

The benefits of limited liability encouraged companies register as "limited" or "plc", which attracts investors who needn't pay the further capital to meet company's debts. But limited liability can only exists where the company is a separate legal entity and the two fundamental factors—limited liability and separate legal entity distinguish companies from other forms of organizations.

Ltds & Plcs are owned by shareholders—Ltds are generally still run by the owners and not quoted on the stock market. Plcs tend to have a board of directors and are often owned by insurance companies and are mostly quoted on the stock market.

1.1.2 The Size of Organizations

Depending on the staff number, volume of output, volume of sales, assets employed, profits earned or net worth in real terms, we can classify organizations into three different sizes: small, medium and large.

Small businesses are usually owned and run by one person (a sole trader) or by a few people (partnership) and tend to sell their goods or services locally. They normally employ no more than 50 people. Businesses of this type can include:

Small/ medium-sized shops

Computer trainers

Solicitors and accountants

Bicycle repair shops

Small businesses usually have following advantages:

A. They are likely to operate in competitive markets, in which prices will tend to be lower and the most efficient firms will survive at the expense of inefficient.

B. They are more likely to be risk takers, investing venture capital in projects that might make high rewards. Innovation and entrepreneurial activity are important ingredients for economic recovery or growth.

C. Management-employee relations are more likely to be co-operative, with direct personal contacts between managers at the top and all the employees.

D. They tend to specialize and so can contribute efficiently towards the division of labour in an economy.

E. The structure of a small business may allow for greater flexibility.

F. Small businesses often sell to a local market, so there is relatively low cost, e.g. the cost of transport.

Can you find out the disadvantages of being a small business?

Medium-sized businesses are usually owned and run by one or more people and tend to sell their goods or services locally or nationally. They normally employ no between 50~250 people. Businesses of this type can include:

Manufacturers, e.g. clothing, furniture, household goods

Theatres, insurance companies

Can you find out the advantages and disadvantages of being a medium-sized business?

Large businesses normally have factories or offices and outlets in more than one city and even in more than one country. They may have following typical examples:

Car manufacturers: e.g. Ford, Nissan, Das-Auto

Rail food outlets: e.g. Tesco, Victory

Oil companies: e.g. Esso, BP, Petro-China

Finance company/ banks: e.g. Bank of China

Most national businesses have household names, are easily recognized by their logos, are large in size. They usually employ a workforce of more than 250 people, and have branches/ factories in major cities. Well-known national business include Haier, Yili, Galanz and so on.

Multinational businesses sell goods or services all over the world and operate in more than one country. Some well known multinational businesses are Ford, McDonalds, Shell and Esso.

Advantages of large businesses are:

A. They can have a good chance to have access to sufficient resources to hold a significant market share, which in turn will influence prices in the market so as to ensure continuing profitability.

B. A large organization can provide for greater division of work and specialization. Specialization and the development of a wider range of products or customer services should enable the business to attract continuing customer support and market shares. In contrast, a small or medium-sized business will require greater competence and versatility from its top management, because they will not have the benefits of support from functional specialists, which are available to the top managers of large organizations.

C. A large organization having a wide range of products or customer services can offer an attractive career to prospective employees, and the talented people may be likely to work for the large business, which in turn will enable it to recruit and develop high-quality personnel for future top management position.

D. A large business can have the ability to have the specialization providing expert services at a relatively low cost to the customers. It can make good use of the advantages of efficient large-scale equipment such as advanced computer systems or manufacturing equipment. Just for this reason, economies of scale in the use of resources can be achieved by an large business. Cheap costs in turn mean either lower prices for customers or higher profits for the business.

E. The continuity of goods or services, management philosophy, customer relations and so on are likely to be provided by large organizations than a smaller organization.

In a word, large organizations usually have more ability to overcome the risks or difficulties in the process of operation.

The disadvantages of a large organization are as follows:

A. It is relatively easier to develop management hierarchy in different levels. The more management levels there are, the greater the problem of communication between top and bottom, and the greater the problem of control and direction by management at the top.

B. A large organization might become so widely diversified in the range of products or services it offers that it becomes difficult, if not impossible, for management to integrate all the organization under a common objective and within a single management philosophy and culture.

C. There might be too much time in maintenance of the organization by top management. That's to say there is difficulty managing the whole organization. Therefore, the primary aims and future plans of the organization can be hard to realize.

D. There is a tendency of top management in large organization to become "ingrown and inbred, smug and self-satisfied".

E. There may be other problems like co-ordination, planning policy, and effective control. And in a large business many of the tasks of junior management might be routine and boring.

The size of organizations cannot remain the same forever. Organizations grow where economies of scale encourage the success of large businesses in a market at the expense of small organizations. In some markets, being large essential. In other situation, small organizations may be better. Small, medium or large are all necessary in the market.

1.2 Three Levels of Economic Activity

The type of activity which businesses are involved in varies according to their products or services. There are three levels of economic activity.

The primary sector: this industry consists of industries that produce raw materials, such as crops and minerals. Examples of this type of business activity would include oil extraction, wood felling, or a coal mining company.

The secondary sector: this sector of industry consists of industries that use the raw materials produced by the primary sector, for example, processing oil to produce petrol, chemicals, gas etc. Businesses taking part in secondary production either involve in manufacturing or in construction. They manufacture the finished articles, or parts for further assembly and manufacture. They construct buildings such as houses and shops as well as roads building.

The tertiary sector: this sector consists of distribution and service industries. They are involved in passing the goods from the producer to consumer. Services include such various activities as banking, tourism, hairdressing, teaching, office cleaning and the media.

Classification of Industry

In order to know this part clearly, here we need to talk about the word—industry.

Industry is the production of a good or service within an economy. Manufacturing industry became a key sector of production and labour in European and North American countries during the Industrial Revolution, upsetting previous mercantile and feudal economies. This occurred through many successive rapid advances in technology, such as the production of steel and coal. Following the Industrial Revolution, perhaps a third of the world's economic output is derived from manufacturing industries. Many developed countries and many developing/semi-developed countries (People's Republic of China, India etc.) depend significantly on manufacturing industry. Industries, the countries they reside in, and the economies of those countries are interlinked in a complex web of interdependence.

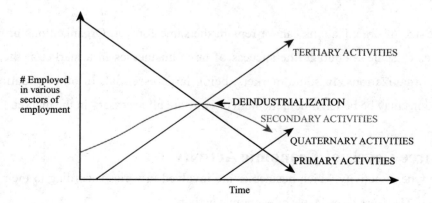

Figure 1-1 Clark's Sector Model

Industries can be classified in a variety of ways. At the top level, industry is often classified into sectors: Primary or extractive, secondary or manufacturing, and tertiary or services. Some authors add quaternary (knowledge) or even quinary (culture and research) sectors. Over time, the fraction of a society's industry within each sector changes.

Sector	Definition
Primary	This involves the extraction of resources directly from the Earth; this includes farming, mining and logging. They do not process the products at all. They send it off to factories to make a profit.
Secondary	This group is involved in the processing products from primary industries. This includes all factories—those that refine metals, produce furniture, or pack farm products such as meat.
Tertiary	This group is involved in the provision of services. They include teachers, managers and other service providers.
Quaternary	This group is involved in the research of science and technology and other high level tasks. They include scientists, doctors, and lawyers.
Quinary	Some consider there should be a branch of the quaternary sector called the quinary sector, which includes the highest levels of decision-making in a society or economy. This sector would include the top executives or officials in such fields as government, science, universities, non-profit, healthcare, culture, and the media.

There are many other different kinds of industries, and often organized into different classes or sectors by a variety of industrial classifications. Market-based classification systems such as the Global Industry Classification Standard and the Industry Classification Benchmark are used in finance and market research. These classification systems commonly divide industries according to similar functions and markets and identify businesses producing related products. Industries can also be identified by product, such as: chemical industry, petroleum industry, automotive industry, electronic industry, meatpacking industry, hospitality industry, food industry, fish industry, software industry, paper industry, entertainment industry, semiconductor industry, cultural industry, and poverty industry.

Primary industries include farming, forestry, fishing, mining, quarrying and oil supply. They are the starting point for nearly all production. Mined raw materials include coal, iron ore and copper as well as diamonds, platinum and gold.

There is an important distinction between farming, forestry, fishing and mining, quarrying and oil production. If carefully managed, crops, trees and animals (including fish) can be renewed and replaced. Mineral deposits, however, cannot. This makes it extremely important to use them wisely. Some (e.g. most metals) are highly recyclable. Others, like coal, are not.

These characteristics make the mining, oil and gas and quarrying industries particularly challenging, both for governments and the people who wish to manage them responsibly.

This presents challenges, especially when economic growth drives the usage of raw materials, e.g. iron ore which is used in the manufacture of steel for use in cars and many other products. World iron ore consumption has grown and is forecast to continue growing this decade.

This growth is driven by China, the second largest economic entity of the world, having the biggest population over the world. The primary sector has been the basis of China's economy. China's rapid industrialization and construction boom means over the coming years China may grow to account for up to 50% of demand.

Every country needs to consider how a business that depletes natural resources can contribute to sustainable development. Sustainable development includes passing on to future generations a stock of "capital" that is at least as big as the one that our own generation inherited. Capital in this sense means the world's assets, these include money, buildings and less tangible assets such as the stoke of skills and social systems, as well as natural resources. Responsible use of all natural resources benefits both the next generation and companies (because the costs are reduced). It includes reducing the amount of resources that are used (input—e.g. iron and coal) for the amount of product (output—e.g. steel).

The United Nations set out the Millennium Development Goals for the year 2015. These include:

A. Developing a global partnership for sustainable development

B. Halving the numbers of people living on less than $1 a day or suffering from hunger

C. Ensuring all children complete primary schooling

D. Halting the spread of AIDS and other major diseases

Many businesses accept they have a responsibility to work with international bodies (e.g. the United Nations or the World Bank), governments, Non-Governmental Organizations (e.g. Sightsavers International, Oxfam or Save the Children) and communities worldwide to work towards sustainable development. In mining, this typically involves using natural capital (the rewards from extracting raw materials) to build social and human capital (e.g. schools, hospitals and worthwhile jobs and skills).

The secondary sector of the economy or industrial sector normally grows rapidly during early stages of economic development. It includes those economic sectors that create a finished, tangible product: production and construction. This sector generally takes the output of the primary sector and manufactures finished goods. These products are then either exported or sold to domestic consumers and to places where they are suitable for use by other businesses. This sector is often divided into light industry and heavy industry. Many of these industries consume large amounts of energy and require factories and machinery to convert the raw materials into goods and products. They also produce waste materials and waste heat that may pose environmental problems or cause pollution.

The tertiary sector or service sector is the third of the three economic sectors of the three-sector theory. The service sector consists of the production of services instead of end products. Services (also known as "intangible goods") include attention, advice, access, experience, and affective labor. The production of information has long been regarded as a service, but some economists now attribute it to a fourth sector, the quaternary sector.

Businesses in the tertiary sector provide a service, such as banking, transportation or retailing. They do not extract the raw materials or make products themselves. As economies develop the primary sector becomes less important and the secondary and tertiary sectors take over.

For example, the service sector is the dominant sector of the UK economy, and contributes around 80.2% of GDP in 2016, which is by far the biggest proportion of the economy.

China's phenomenal economic growth in recent years was primarily due to growth in the secondary and tertiary sector of the economy. In fact, the primary sector (which is mainly the agriculture) grew only slightly since 1996 (changes in the proportions between primary, secondary and tertiary sector). Among economists there is a debate about the true values of China's GDP growth.

Table 1-1　Nominal GDP Sector Composition, 2017 (in percentage and in billions of dollars)

No.	Country	Total GDP (billions of U.S.$)	Agri. %	Indus. %	Service %	Agri. B$	Indus. B$	Service B$
1	the United States	19,362	0.90%	18.90%	80.20%	174.26	3,659.42	15,528.33
2	China	11,938	8.20%	39.50%	52.20%	978.92	4,715.51	6,231.64
3	Japan	4,884.5	1.00%	29.70%	69.30%	48.85	1,450.70	3,384.96
4	Germany	3,651.9	0.60%	30.10%	69.30%	21.91	1,099.22	2,530.77
5	France	2,574.8	1.60%	19.40%	78.90%	41.20	4,99.51	2,031.52
6	the United Kingdom	2,565.1	0.60%	19.00%	80.40%	15.39	487.37	2,062.34

From: "World GDP Ranking 2017 | GDP by country | Data and Charts—knoema.com". Knoema.

It is sometimes hard to define whether a given company is part and parcel of the secondary or tertiary sector. And it is not only companies that have been classified as part of that sector in some schemes; government and its services such as police or military, and non-profit organizations such as charities or research associations can also be seen as part of that sector. In order to classify a business as a service, one can use classification systems such as the United Nations' International Standard Industrial Classification standard, the United States' Standard Industrial Classification (SIC) code system and its new replacement, the North American Industrial Classification System (NAICS), the Statistical Classification of Economic Activities in the European Community(NACE) in the EU and similar systems elsewhere. These governmental classification systems have a first-level hierarchy that reflects whether the economic goods are tangible or intangible.

All economic activities can involve public or private sector organizations. The main differences between public and private sector may be summarized as follows:

Public sector: organizations are set up and owned by the government for the benefit of general public. They are established in the interests of the community and are funded wholly or partly by the government from public funds and are answerable to a government department.

The essential feature of a public organization is that the assets of the industry have been taken over by the state so that the industry is owned, managed and controlled by and on behalf of the state. Objectives of public sector organizations reflect not only a desire on the part of management to provide goods and services efficiently and achieve a target return on capital invested but also the wider economic and social objectives.

Private sector: organizations are usually set up for personal gain and are funded by shares issued, loans from banks, overdrafts etc. These private organizations are owned by individuals, not by the state and can be small, or large.

Besides the above two kinds of organizations, there is another one, which can be defined as non-profit driven, non-statutory, autonomous and run by individuals who do not get paid for running the organization. That's voluntary organizations—organizations with objectives other than purely profit include various types of mutual and voluntary organizations:

A. Co-operatives and other mutual organizations such as building societies.

B. Charities, which have specific charitable objectives.

C. Trade unions, employers associations, professional associations.

D. Various other voluntary societies, clubs and associations

Not for profit: co-operative or mutual organizations exist to provide services which are paid for by their customers, who share in any surplus that is made. Charities have normally been set up to achieve specific goals.

1.3 Objectives of Organizations

In order to survive or develop successfully, businesses need have well-designed strategies. A business strategy is the means by which it sets out to achieve its desired ends (objectives). It can simply be described as a long-term business plan. Typically a business strategy will cover a period of about 3~5 years (sometimes even longer), which is concerned with major resource issues, e.g. raising the finance to build a new factory or plant. And strategies are also concerned with deciding on what products to allocate major resources to.

An essential requirement for a meaningful strategic plan is the establishment of a set of goals and objectives for the organization. The process of developing these can be shown as a progression or hierarchy of aims or purposes.

1.3.1 Strategic Planning—Mission and Vision

According to Johnson & Scholes (1999), strategy "is the direction and scope of an organization over the long-term: which achieves advantage for the organization through its configuration of resources within a changing environment, to meet the needs of markets and to fulfil stakeholder expectations".

A strategic plan starts with a clearly defined business mission. Mintzberg defines a mission as follows:

"A mission describes the organization's basic function in society, in terms of the products and services it produces for its customers".

The Mission Statement is a crucial element in the strategic planning of a business organization. Creating a mission is one of the first actions an organization should take. This can be a building block for an overall strategy and development of more specific functional strategies. By defining a mission an organization is making a statement of organizational purpose.

A clear business mission should have each of the following elements (Figure 1-2):

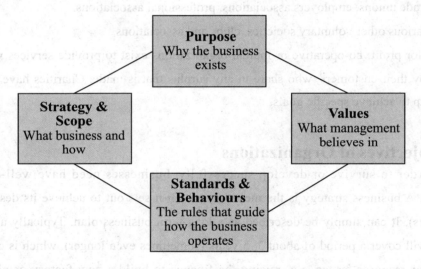

Figure 1-2　Business Mission Elements

Taking each element of the above diagram in turn, what should a good mission contain?

(1) A Purpose

Why does a business exist? Is it to create wealth for shareholders? Does it exist to satisfy the needs of all stakeholders (including employees, and society at large?)

(2) A Strategy and Strategic Scope

A mission statement provides the commercial logic for a business and so defines two things:

① The products or services it offers (and therefore its competitive position)

② The competences through which it tries to succeed and its method of competing

A business' strategic scope defines the boundaries of its operations. These are set by management. For example, these boundaries may be set in terms of geography, market, business method, product etc. The decisions management make about strategic scope define the nature of the business.

(3) Policies and Standards of Behavior

A mission needs to be translated into everyday actions. For example, if the business mission includes delivering "outstanding customer service", then policies and standards should be created and monitored that test delivery.

These might include monitoring the speed with which telephone calls are answered in the sales call centre, the number of complaints received from customers, or the extent of positive customer feedback via questionnaires.

(4) Values and Culture

The values of a business are the basic, often un-stated, beliefs of the people who work in the business. They are a set of ethical or operating principles and beliefs that guide decision-making. These would include:

• Business principles (e.g. social policy, commitments to customers)

• Loyalty and commitment (e.g. are employees inspired to sacrifice their personal goals for the good of the business as a whole? And does the business demonstrate a high level of commitment and loyalty to its staff?)

• Guidance on expected behavior—a strong sense of mission helps create a work environment where there is a common purpose

What role does the mission statement play in marketing planning?

In practice, a strong mission statement can help in three main ways:

• It provides an outline of how the marketing plan should seek to fulfil the mission

• It provides a means of evaluating and screening the marketing plan; Are marketing decisions consistent with the mission?

• It provides an incentive to implement the marketing plan

In general, the corporate mission plays three important roles for business organization. These roles are:

Direction: The corporate mission can point the organization in a certain direction, by defining the boundaries within which strategic choices and actions must take place. By specifying the fundamental principles on which strategies must be based, the corporate mission limits the scope of strategic options and sets the organization on a particular heading.

Legitimization: The corporate mission can convey to all stakeholders inside and outside the company that the organization is pursuing valuable activities in a proper way. By specifying the business philosophy that will guide the company, it is hoped that stakeholders will accept, support and trust the organization.

Motivation: The corporate mission can go a step further then legitimization, by actually inspiring individuals to works together in a particular way. By specifying the fundamental principles driving organization actions, there will be powerful capacity to motivate people over a prolonged period of time.

Problems with mission:

Ignored in practice: official goals often do not correspond with the end that seems to be pursued.

Public relations: sometimes, of course, mission is merely for public consumption, not for internal decision-making.

Missions are sometimes produced to rationalize the organization's existence to particular audiences. In other words, mission does not drive the organization, but what the organization actually does is assumed to be mission.

Full of generalizations: "best" "quality" "major" is just a wish list.

A concept that is often confused with mission is vision. Individuals or organizations have a vision if they picture a future state of affairs they wish to achieve. While the corporate mission outlines the basic points of the departure, a corporate vision outlines the desired future at which the company hopes to arrive. In other words, vision provides a business aim, while mission provides a business philosophy.

A vision is a motivating summary of what an organization hopes to achieve. It links the objectives with the core values of the business.

The entrepreneurial school of strategy believes that vision is the most central concept. It may be viewed as a mental representation of strategy, created or at least expressed in the head of the leader. That vision serves as both an inspiration and a sense of what needs to be done—a guiding idea, if you like. True to its label, vision often tends to be a kind of image more than a fully articulated plan (in words and numbers). That leaves it flexible, so that the leader can adapt it to his or her experiences. This suggests that entrepreneurial strategy is both deliberate and emergent: deliberate in its broad lines and sense of direction emergent in its details so that these can be adapted en route.

But how to distinguish real vision? Perhaps the simplest answer is that true vision is something you can see in your mind's eye. Being the biggest or earning 42% return on investment would hardly count. A vision has to distinguish an organization, set it apart as a unique institution.

Warren Bennis perhaps put it best with the comment that "if it's really a vision, you'll never forget it". In other words, you don't have to write it down. In their book on leadership, Bennis and Namus devote a good deal of attention to vision:

• To choose a direction, a leader must first have a developed a mental image of a possible and desirable future state of the organization. This image, which we call a vision, may be as vague as a dream or as precise as a goal or a mission statement. The critical point is that a vision articulates a view of a realistic, credible, attractive future for the organization, a condition that is better in some important ways than what now exists.

• A vision always refers to a future state, a condition that does not presently exist and never existed before. With a vision, the leader provides the all important bridge from the present to the future of the organization.

• By focusing attention on a vision, the leader operates on the emotional and spiritual resources of the organization, on its values, commitment and aspirations. The manager, by contrast, operates on the physical resources of the organization, on its capital, human skills, raw materials, and technology.

• If there is a spark of genius in the leadership function at all, it must lie in the transcending ability, a kind of magic, to assemble—out of the variety of images, signals, forecasts and alternatives—a clearly articulated vision of the future that is at once simple, easily understood, clearly desirable, and energizing.

Generally a company vision is a type of goal that is less specific than an objective. Vision is usually defined as a broad conception of a desirable future state, of which the details must still be determined (e.g. Senge, 1990). As such, corporate vision can play the same type of roles as corporate mission. A corporate vision can point the firm in a particular direction, can legitimize the organizations existence and actions, and can motivate individuals to work together towards a shared end. So successful organizations/leaders strive to:

- Develop a clear vision consistent with the organizations overall purpose and direction
- Translate the vision into objectives for the organization
- Encourage staff to take ownership of the vision
- Use the vision to inspire others
- Review and update the vision as circumstances change

The best visions are:

- Different or innovative
- Closely related to the work of the organization
- Easily understood by others
- Believed and lived by the leader of the organization
- Adopted by the whole workforce

Mission and vision are sometimes used interchangeably but are different things. Developing a mission statement can be a very difficult process. Drohan says that when creating a mission statement it should be done as part of the strategic planning process for the organization (Drohan, 1999). This process should be started with environmental analysis, followed by development and prioritizing goals and objectives (Drohan, 1999). After this process is finished, the mission of the company becomes clearer and an effective mission statement can be created.

1.3.2　Strategic Planning—Setting Objectives

From mission and vision, goals are derived. Mintzberg (1997) defines goals as "the intentions behind decisions or actions, the states of mind that drive individuals or collectives of individuals called organizations to do what they do ". Aims are the long-term goals of an organization, for example, "to ensure customer satisfaction" or "to deliver shareholder value". Objectives are medium term targets that act as stepping stones to achieve the aims, for example, "to achieve a return on equity of 16%" "to increase profits by 10% in 2012". Aims and objectives often relate to:

- Survival
- Profit
- Growth
- Providing a service
- Market share

- Customer satisfaction
- Ethics and sustainability

The main aims or objectives of a business:

- To provide goods or services to the local community
- To provide goods or services to the wider community (nationally or internationally)
- To provide a charitable or voluntary service
- To improve the quality of a product or service
- To provide a highly competitive service

Other aims include:

- To expand
- To be environmentally friendly
- To survive as a business
- To make a profit or surplus
- To maximize sales

Changing objectives: Organizations may change their objectives over time because of the following reasons:

- They may have achieved their original objectives
- The business has grown
- The competitive environment changes
- The market changes
- Technology changes

Conflicting objectives: Some objectives may conflict. For example:

- Profit and growth-expansion can increase costs, especially in the short-term
- Providing a service and growth-smaller firms may know their customers better than large firms and therefore be able to provide a more personalized service

Purpose of aims and objectives:

- To provide direction for the organization
- To form a basis for allocating resources
- To be motivational
- To monitor performance
- To measure success

Setting objectives:

The objectives that organizations set will depend on several factors:

• The overall aims

• Analysis of business performance, e.g. SWOT analysis

• Ownership—public sector objectives are more likely to focus on providing a service whereas private sector firms may focus on profit and growth

Objectives set out what the business is trying to achieve, which can be set at two levels.

(1) Corporate level

Examples of corporate objectives might include:

• Aim for a return on investment of at least 15%

• Aim to achieve an operating profit of over £10 million on sales of at least £100 million

• Aim to increase earnings per share by at least 10% every year for the foreseeable future

(2) Functional level

Objectives concern the business or organization not as a whole, instead, they focus on specific aspects of organizations, e.g. specific objectives for marketing activities.

Examples of functional marketing objectives might include:

• Aim to build customer database of at least 250,000 households within the next 12 months

• Aim to achieve a market share of 10%

• Aim to achieve 75% customer awareness of our brand in our target markets

Both corporate and functional objectives need to conform to the commonly used **SMART** criteria.

The **SMART** criteria (an important concept which you should try to remember and apply in exams) are summarized below:

Specific—the objective should state exactly what is to be achieved

Measurable—an objective should be capable of measurement—so that it is possible to determine whether (or how far) it has been achieved

Achievable—the objective should be realistic given the circumstances in which it is set and the resources available to the business

Relevant—objectives should be relevant to the people responsible for achieving them

Time Bound—objectives should be set with a time-frame in mind

Objective examples

There are a number of business objectives which an organization can set:

Market share objectives: Objectives can be set to achieve a certain level of market share within a specified time, for example:

To obtain 3% market share of the mobile phone industry by 2010

To increase sales by 10% from 2008—2014

To grow by 15% year on year for the next five years

To increase brand awareness over a specified period of time should also be one of business objectives

Corporate and units objectives

Corporate objectives are different from unit objectives which are specific to individual units of an organization. Corporate objectives concern the firm as a whole, for example:

- Growth and profitability
- Market share
- Cash flow
- Return on capital employed
- Sales
- Customer satisfaction

- Quality
- Industrial relations
- Added value
- Earnings per share
- Risk
- Brand loyalty

Examples of unit objectives

- Increase the number of customers by 10% (an objective of the sales department)
- Reduce the number of rejects by 30% (an objective of the production department)
- Produce monthly reports quickly, within 5 working days of the end of each month (an objective of the management accounting department)
- Increase the market share by 5% (an objective of the marketing department)
- More efficient employee training (an objective of the human resources department)

Objectives of public sector activity

- Access—available to all regardless of location or income
- Quality—high quality services that do not cut corners
- Affordability—services offered at prices that are cheaper than private sector or free at the point of use
- Equity—available to anyone whatever their background, status, income, class, race, religion, etc.

Can you tell what the objectives of **Private Sector Activity** are?

Primary and secondary objectives

Usually in a business, some objectives are more important than others, for example, to grow and survive can be regarded as the primary objective, which is normally more important and is the basic thing in the process of the development of a business. Secondary objectives may refer to sale, innovation, customer services and so on.

An organization's objectives typically include growth, profitability and return on investment (ROCE). Companies failing to achieve their goals will either go out of business or else. So setting suitable mission, vision and objectives is necessary and essential to all the organizations.

Exercises

1. Why are objectives important to an organization? List some of the objectives of private-sector businesses.

2. Define mission.

3. List some advantages of being a sole trader.

4. What are the primary objectives of a business?

5. What are the main features of a best corporate vision?

Glossary

Turnover: Volume of business, revenue 成交量；营业额

Sole trader: A person who owns their own business and does not have a partner or any shareholders 个体经营者

Partnership: A relationship in which two or more people, organizations, or countries work together as partners; a contract between two or more persons who agree to pool talent and money and share profits or losses 合伙人身份；合作关系

Limited liability: The liability of a firm's owners for no more than the capital they have invested in the firm 有限责任

Tertiary industry: The industry mainly providing services like banks, insurances, retails 第三产业

Proprietor: Someone who owns (is legal possessor of) a business 所有人，业主；地主；业主

Dissolve: Stop functioning or cohering as a unit 解散

Deficit: The amount by which something is less than what is required or expected, especially the amount by which the total money received is less than the total money spent 赤字，亏损，逆差

Division of work: The practice of dividing a job, task, assignment, or contract into smaller tasks 分工

Specialization: The act of specializing; making something suitable for a special purpose 专业化

Versatility: Having a wide variety of skills 多才多艺；多用途

Hierarchy: The organization of people at different ranks in an administrative body 等级系统

Sustainable development: A mode of human development in which resource use aims to meet human needs while ensuring the sustainability of natural systems and the environment 可持续性发展

Overdraft: A draft in excess of the credit balance 透支；透支额

Statutory: Relating to or created by statutes 法定的

Customer satisfaction: When customers are pleased with the goods or services they have bought, you can refer to customer satisfaction 客户满意度

Chapter 2 Businesses Stakeholders

Introduction

The goals of an organization and its structure are influenced by particular individuals and groups. In order to understand organizations better we need to examine this influence.

All enterprises, whether in the public or private sectors, whether they are profit or non-profit, have stakeholders, who have this or that kind of interest in how the organization performs because it affects them in some way—that is they have a stake in the organization. All organizations affect and are affected by different stakeholders. The aim of management with regard to stakeholders is to try to satisfy the majority of them for the most of time.

The objectives of this chapter:

(1) The identification of stakeholders

(2) The analysis of stakeholders

(3) The types of stakeholders

(4) The conflicting objectives of stakeholders

(5) Stakeholder mapping

2.1 The Identification of Stakeholders

Stakeholders can be person, group, or organization that has direct or indirect stake in an organization because it can affect or be affected by the organization's actions, objectives, and policies. Traditionally, the owners of a business were seen as the most important stakeholders. And meeting their requirements was the sole reason for the existence of the enterprises. But currently, it is widely accepted that there is a broad range of stakeholders, all of whose requirements must be met in order for an enterprise to succeed.

Can you tell which of the following can be the stakeholders in an organization?

owners, shareholders, banks, lenders / creditors, suppliers / buyers, customers, managers, competitors, employees, trade unions, the community, the local or national government and its agencies, media, directors, public interest groups, parties, religions, strategic and collaborative partners

What can we learn from the above information?

The answer can be that such a wide range of stakeholders demonstrates that businesses operate in a complex system of often conflicting interests and influences.

Characteristics of Stakeholders

Different stakeholders have different characteristics.

Owners and Shareholders:

- The number of owners and the roles they carry out differ according to the size of the firm

- In small businesses there may be only one owner (sole trader) or perhaps a small number of partners (partnership)

- In large firms there are often thousands of shareholders, who each owns a small part of the business

Managers:

- Organize
- Make decisions
- Plan
- Control
- Be accountable to the owner(s)

Employees or Staff:

- A business needs staff or employees to carry out its activities
- Employees agree to work a certain number of hours in return for a wage or salary
- Pay levels vary with skills, qualifications, age, location, types of work and industry and other factors

Customers:

- Customers buy the goods or services produced by firms

• They may be individuals or other businesses

• Firms must understand and meet the needs of their customers, otherwise they will fail to make a profit or indeed survive

Suppliers:

• Firms get the resources they need to produce goods and services from suppliers

• Businesses should have effective relationships with their suppliers in order to get quality resources at reasonable prices

• This is a two-way process, as suppliers depend on the firms they supply

Community:

• Firms and the communities they exist in are also in a two-way relationship

• The local community may often provide many of the firm's staff and customers

• The business often supplies goods and services vital to the local area

• But at times the community can feel aggrieved by some aspects of what a firm does

Government:

• Economic policies affect firms' costs (through taxation and interest rates)

• Legislation regulates what business can do in areas such as the environment and occupational safety and health

• Successful firms are good for governments as they create wealth and employment

2.2　The Analysis of Stakeholders

Why is it necessary to carry out a stakeholder analysis? The reasons can be as follows:

(1)Draws out the interests of stakeholders in relation to the problems which the project is or you are seeking to address.

(2)Identifies conflicts of interest and potential conflicts

(3)Identifies viability other than in pure financial terms (e.g. includes social not just economic factors)

(4)Helps provide an overall picture

(5)Helps identify relationships between different stakeholders—helps possible coalition.

To be more specific, stakeholder analysis serves to:

(1)Be helpful in creating solutions that are appropriate to the business context.

This is important for making sure that user experience moves with the rest of the company.

(2)Build into plans and the actions that will help win support for the project / change.

(3)Helps gain greater acceptance of solutions.

(4)The biggest benefit of stakeholder analysis is that change recommendations are more likely to gain acceptance. By conducting stakeholder analysis early in the process, and getting some feedback on the recommendations, the stage is set for the recommendations to gain acceptance.

(5)By spending time understanding stakeholder perspectives, recommended solutions are more likely to be in tune with business requirements and goals.

Stages in stakeholder analysis:

Identify organizational stakeholders

Prioritize stakeholders (stakeholder mapping)

Understand stakeholder perspectives

Incorporate stakeholder perspectives into design

Stakeholder Analysis Table/grid—4 alternative versions

(1) Simple version

Stakeholder Who they are	What's their perspective/ viewpoint?	Impact Likely impact/affect on the project

(2) Stakeholder Analysis Table—Alternative version

Stakeholder	Priority VH/H/M/L/VL	Stakeholder's perspective	Action

(3) Stakeholder Analysis—Another version

Stakeholder	Importance	Relative influence	Risks/assumptions	Action

(4) Stakeholder table—An alternative example

Stakeholder	Interest	Importance	Influence	Priority

Stakeholder Analysis—How to use alternative example tables

(1)Draw up a stakeholder table identifying who the stakeholders are.

(2)Assess each stakeholder's importance and their relative power/influence.

E.g. high importance but low influence, or low importance but high influence.

Can rank/rate each stakeholder's importance from 0 (zero importance) to 10 (vital).

(3)Identify risks and assumptions which will affect the project's success.

What do we assume each stakeholder's response is if the project is successful?

Are these assumptions realistic?

Are there negative responses?

What impact will negative responses have?

Importance, influence and priority can all be ranked numerically. The actual figures are not important, but ranking allows a better indication of the importance of something.

The aim of management about stakeholders is to prioritise their objectives so as to satisfy the majority of them most of the time. Stakeholders can have the following stakes in a business:

(1) An interest—when a person or group will be affected by a decision, they have an interest in that decision.

(2) A right—when a person has a legal claim or moral right to be treated in a particular way, or has a particular right to be protected.

(3) Ownership—when a person/group has a legal title to an asset or property.

All stakeholders are not equal. Different stakeholders are entitled to different considerations. For example, a firm's customers are entitled to fair trading practices but they are not entitled to the same consideration as the firm's employees. Shareholders' consideration/stake can be company's survival, return on investment, dividends or capital growth. Meanwhile, there is one thing which needs to be pointed out. Remember that different groups of stakeholders have different effects on a business. Employees will have influence on internal matters such as working conditions, whereas external stakeholders, such as environmental groups, will affect location and pollution decisions.

2.3 The Types of Stakeholders

There are many different individuals or groups who affect or are affected by an organization. They are called stakeholders of the organization. Stakeholders are individuals or groups who have an interest in a particular organization. Note that this is different from shareholders who are one of the stakeholder groups. Shareholders own the organization—they have a financial stake in the company.

Different stakeholders can have more power or influence than others and so can have a bigger influence on the strategic intent of the organization. Even within a particular group there can be differences in the amount of influence, for example there may be particular shareholders own have a bigger share of the organization. In analysing the stakeholders of an organization we may separate out particularly dominant ones from the others. The owners or particular leaders can have a considerable influence on setting the direction. However, strong staff groups could work to oppose changes desired.

Other stakeholders include: customers who buy from the organization; lenders, including banks, who help to fund the organization's activities; suppliers who trade with the organization; competitors who are in the same industry as the organization; local communities in which the organization operates.

Different Stakeholders in Organizations

As we have seen earlier in this unit, organizations may have a variety of stakeholders, who have an interest in the way the organization is operated, its success, failure, strategy, and financial outcomes. A stakeholder is any person or organization likely to be affected directly or indirectly by a change in an organization. Examples of stakeholders are:

- Shareholders: institutions and individuals who own a stake in a company
- Employees: those who work for an organization
- Directors and managers: those who lead organizations
- Communities: those who are affected by the organization, e.g. by living near the workplace
- Government: which imposes regulations and collects taxes
- Customers: who buy the products or services
- Suppliers: who provide raw materials and services
- Financiers: for example banks who lend organizations money
- Unions: who provide support to employees

Shareholders

Shareholders are interested in the organization and how it is run in order to determine whether their investment is safeguarded and the resources given to the managerial team have been used effectively. Shareholders will be in a powerful position to influence the path of the organization in that if they choose to withdraw their financial support for the management of the organization, the business may fall into decline through lack of funds.

Employees

Employees are primarily interested in job security and may also be shareholders. This group is a vital resource of the organization, as such, without their continued efforts the organization would not be able to survive. They contribute to the wealth of the organization and are key to its success.

They also react to the environment in which they work. For example, the Royal Bank of Scotland opened new headquarters in August 2005 on the outskirts of Edinburgh. In order to maintain good working conditions for the staff, some of whom had moved from the centre of town where they enjoyed many facilities which were not readily available at the new site, the new building incorporates a swimming pool and gym, an onsite nursery for employees' children, a Tesco, a hairdresser, a pharmacy, a dentist, coffee shops and bistros. There has obviously been a great deal of investment in employees and the bank hopes that this will identify to their staff that they are worth investing in.

Directors and Managers

Directors and managers are likely to be interested in how best to maximise profits and generate wealth both for themselves and others, or to meet other targets which have been set by the organization, such as maximising market share.

Whatever the aims, without the skill and efforts of the directors and management of the organization, the resources of it would not be used to best advantage. By having a good team in this role all other stakeholders will benefit: employees will have a job for the foreseeable future; the communities in which they live and work, along with the unions, will benefit; customers and suppliers will share in the continued success of the organization; financiers will have a satisfactory return for the risk they have taken in financially supporting the organization and their own wealth will be increased; shareholders are likely to benefit from the continuing success of the organization by the reward of dividends.

Communities

Communities tend to be interested in the impact of the organization operating in their own neighbourhood and how it may affect the environment. They may have an interest in local employment and the charitable contribution that the organization may make towards any community projects.

Local pressure groups can bring to bear any objections to the plans of the organization by blocking planning permission and demonstrating against the organization's activities. They may involve outside pressure groups such as Greenpeace or Campaign for Nuclear Disarmament if they feel it will further their cause.

The Government

The government imposes taxes and regulations on organizations, which may be costly to implement and abide by. It is not generally interested in the day-to-day running of the organization unless it is in breach of statute or laws are being broken. The payment of taxes on a regular basis is of great importance to this group. The government has the power to force the organization to cease operations if it is in breach of any of its statutory duties, e.g. health & safety, payment of taxes (whether they are in the form of VAT or income or corporation taxes and national insurances).

Customers

Customers are generally interested in receiving value for money in the form of a good service or product, which is fit for purpose. They are likely to show an interest in the long-term future of the organization if there is a warranty agreement with the product they have purchased. If the customer is also an organization rather than an individual they may wish to continue a good working relationship with the organization in the interests of their own organization and its profitability. The two are likely to have a mutually beneficial relationship. Without customers the business would have no source of income.

In the case of public sector organizations, customers may not be a source of income themselves but provision of a service may attract government funding.

Suppliers

Suppliers, similar to customers, are likely to wish to maintain a good relationship with the organization since there may be a monetary reward involved.

Up until the 1990s Marks & Spencer was famed for its excellent relationships with its suppliers. Firms would go to great lengths in order to become a supplier. Since then, it has changed the way in which it deals with suppliers, and a few established firms whose main client was Marks & Spencer have ceased to trade, leading to redundancies. This publicity has not been good and it has often decided to seek supplies from abroad rather than from within the UK, which was one of its original selling points. This is one of the reasons that

Marks & Spencer is currently suffering from a decline in fortunes. The long-term success of the business may impact on suppliers' success. Similarly, without suppliers the organization would not have its supplies to continue in operation.

Financiers

Financiers look at an organization as a potential money-earning instrument. Financiers can include organizations such as large banks, insurance companies or other institutions and private venture capitalists. They are unlikely to invest if they do not think that there will be any financial gain or reward for themselves. They may also be in an advisory position and wish to advise their own clients of a potentially lucrative investment.

Unless financiers consider that they can improve their own wealth they are unlikely to risk providing the organization with additional funding by lending money. If the organization can find alternative sources of funds they will survive, but they may be limited in any plans they may have for expansion. This is relevant only to organizations operating in the private sector.

Unions

Unions will be primarily interested in the security of their members' jobs. They are likely to be interested in the organization's profitability, which will give them leverage to enter into bargaining for wage increases. Their members may also be shareholders and members of the local community.

The unions need to feel that they are a valuable ally of the organization and continue to work with the organization and be consulted at every stage of the organization's life-cycle. If they are not included in planning the organization may well find itself in direct conflict with the unions, which may prove to be costly. If the union perceives that it is not included in the decision-making team it may object to plans put forward for changes in working patterns or wage and salary amendments. This could lead to industrial action in the form of work-to-rule or strikes, and the organization losing money through downtime.

The above is not an exhaustive list of the reasons for the interest in the organization taken by various stakeholders. It may be apparent from all of this information that some groups of stakeholders may find their interests conflicting with those of other groups.

Some stakeholder groups are likely to be more influential than others and will have more power to steer the organization along a particular path to suit their own needs. This can lead to conflict.

Stakeholders of businesses also can be classified as internal, external and connected.

Internal—Owner, Management, Staff/ Employees

In many cases the company is owned by shareholders—some of whom may be external to the company and will not have much influence on its day-to-day running. However, the owners will be interested in a return on their investment and possibly the long-term growth and development of the business.

Management is appointed to act in the interests of the owner and will seek to ensure the survival, growth and development of the business. One of its main aims will be to ensure that the business is profitable (in the case of private sector organizations) or run efficiently (in the case of public sector organizations).

Staff will want job security and good payment (remuneration) for their work. They may also want opportunities for training and progression. Staff may form groupings such as trade unions or have staff committees who will act on their behalf to protect their interests.

Management and employees are so intimately connected with the company. Their objectives are likely to have a strong and immediate influence on how it is run. They are interested in the organization's continuation and growth. Employees have a major effect on the success of a business as it is they who are responsible for all aspects of work. "Employees are the most important of all factors of production." When they are motivated, employees will usually be more productive.

Connected—Bankers, Customers, Suppliers

Bankers are interested in an organization's overall condition. From the point of view of the security of any loan they make, a bank is keen to minimize the risk of interest not being paid, or of its security being eroded.

Customers want to buy products or services at a relatively low price. Large customers have significant power over prices and procedures. They ultimately determine what is produced, what quality is needed, what price is charged and what development is needed. Failure to listen to customers finally leads to no sales and no market. The businesses can get feedback, suggestions, even complaints to improve the customer satisfaction.

Suppliers expecting to be paid on time and hoping the business dealings can continue in the future.

External—Government, Local Authorities, Professional Bodies, Pressure Groups

Government:

- Passing laws or policies to protect workers and customers
- Collecting taxes
- Supporting businesses in socially or economically deprived areas
- Subsidizing activities (subsidize)
- Aiding exporters

Local authorities:

- Bring local employment
- Affect local environment (pollution/traffic)

Professional bodies:

- Members work for companies comply with professional ethics and standards
- Having diverse objectives and have ability to ensure their demand is met

Pressure groups:

- To influence government policy or business activity to secure the interests of their members and supporters
- Have interest in particular issues

2.4 The Conflicting Objectives of Stakeholders

The objective of an organization is a formal statement of stakeholders' expectation. The expectation of some stakeholders may clash and conflict with the interests of other stakeholders. For example, employers seeking higher wages might conflict with the desire by management to cut costs to boost profit and thus satisfy their own ambitions and meet the needs of the shareholders.

It's important for an organization to balance the claims of the various directly interested groups. There are a number of issues that need to be considered when examining the stakeholders of an organization:

- Differences in aims/expectations
- Differences in perception—how "facts" are interpreted
- How to identify and establish priorities
- Relationships and relative power
- Negotiation/conflict resolution mechanisms.

As can be seen from above, many of the groups interested in an organization will have their own "agenda" for what they wish to gain from the organization. This can lead to conflicts where groups with differing needs exert influence on the managers setting goals. Groups often exert influence by putting forward representatives with their interest at heart to become members of the board of directors. This has been an issue in British politics for a number of years. Certain members of parliament are paid salaries by organizations as board members, and "encouraged" to vote in a way beneficial to the organization they work for. The conflicts can arise if the organization they are paid by is at odds with the community in which it operates. This is just one example of where conflicts can arise.

Conflicts in Objectives

There are generally three main objectives of a profit-making business organization:

To continue in existence (survival)

To maintain growth and development

To make a profit

All of the objectives are linked. It is a matter of debate whether an organization survives and develops in order to make a profit or makes a profit so that it can survive and develop!

We could consider that survival is the ultimate objective of the organization and this will require a steady and continuous profit.

A reduction in short-term profitability is likely to be required to provide for future investments and to maintain growth and development.

The objectives of customer satisfaction (which can be included in growth and development) and profit can be seen as in conflict, or incompatible, because they pull in different directions. Customer satisfaction is likely to involve some element of cost to the organization, eating into the profits.

Survival is not an end in itself. Most organizations would want to reach a performance level which is better than just "hanging on" and if this was not attainable then shareholders might not want to have the business survive. When setting objectives the shareholders are a major group to be taken into account. In order to answer the question "why does a company want to survive", we will look at long-term prospects.

In order to resolve the conflict here the organization must decide that if profit is its main objective should it pursue at any cost? Why does the company wish to have satisfied customers unless to make a profit?

Another possible area for conflict comes in short-term and long-term planning. An organization may be able to improve its profit in the long-term by sacrificing some profit in the short-term, such as spending money on product development. If the organization concentrated on short-term profitability it would more than likely find itself in an unhealthy position in the long-term as lack of investment in products take their toll.

2.5　Stakeholder Mapping

Stakeholders all have power, whether it is the formal power invested in a position of authority or it is social power of being able to persuade others to support or oppose the change.

Those with higher power are likely to be your most useful supporters or most dangerous opponents—thus power analysis helps you prioritize your focus on stakeholders.

Identify Your Stakeholders:

- Who are they?
- What do they want?
- How satisfied are they?
- How much/what sort of power do they possess?
- What conflicts exist?
- How to response to their concerns?

The first step in your stakeholder analysis is to brainstorm who your stakeholders are. As part of this, think of all the people who are affected by your work, who have influence or power over it, or have an interest in its successful or unsuccessful conclusion.

The table below shows some of the people who might be stakeholders in your job or in your projects:

Your boss	Shareholders	Government
Senior executives	Alliance partners	Trades associations
Your coworkers	Suppliers	The press
Your team	Lenders	Interest groups
Customers	Analysts	The public
Prospective customers	Future recruits	The community
Your family		

Remember that although stakeholders may be both organizations and people, ultimately you must communicate with people. Make sure that you identify the correct individual stakeholders within a stakeholder organization.

Prioritize Your Stakeholders

You may now have a long list of people and organizations that are affected by your work. Some of these may have the power either to block or advance. Some may be interested in what you are doing, others may not care.

Map out your stakeholders on a Power/Interest Grid on our free template as shown in Figure 1-3, and classify them by their power over your work and by their interest in your work.

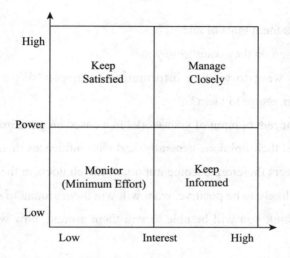

Figure 1-3 Power/Interest Grid for Stakeholder Prioritization

For example, your boss is likely to have high power and influence over your projects and high interest. Your family may have high interest, but are unlikely to have power over it.

Someone's position on the grid shows you the actions you have to take with them:

● High power, interested people: these are the people you must fully engage and make the greatest efforts to satisfy.

● High power, less interested people: put enough work in with these people to keep them satisfied, but not so much that they become bored with your message.

● Low power, interested people: keep these people adequately informed, and talk to them to ensure that no major issues are arising. These people can often be very helpful with the detail of your project.

● Low power, less interested people: again, monitor these people, but do not bore them with excessive communication.

Understand Your Key Stakeholders

You now need to know more about your key stakeholders. You need to know how they are likely to feel about and react to your project. You also need to know how best to engage them in your project and how best to communicate with them.

Key questions that can help you understand your stakeholders are:

• What financial or emotional interest do they have in the outcome of your work? Is it positive or negative?

• What motivates them most of all?

• What information do they want from you?

• How do they want to receive information from you? What is the best way of communicating your message to them?

• What is their current opinion of your work? Is it based on good information?

• Who influences their opinions generally, and who influences their opinion of you? Do some of these influencers therefore become important stakeholders in their own right?

• If they are not likely to be positive, what will win them around to support your project?

• If you don't think you will be able to win them around, how will you manage their opposition?

• Who else might be influenced by their opinions? Do these people become stakeholders in their own right?

A very good way of answering these questions is to talk to your stakeholders directly—people are often quite open about their views, and asking people's opinions is often the first step in building a successful relationship with them.

You can summarize the understanding you have gained on the stakeholder map, so that you can easily see which stakeholders are expected to be blockers or critics, and which stakeholders are likely to be advocates and supporters or your project. A good way of doing this is by colour coding: showing advocates and supporters in green, blockers and critics in red, and others who are neutral in orange.

Activity: Read the Following Two Organizations to Complete the Tasks as Required

This activity helps embed your understanding of the characteristics of stakeholders and how they are affected by and can affect business organizations. Working in small groups, students are given the following information. The groups should carry out the following tasks:

• Identify as many stakeholders as possible

- Distinguish between the internal and external stakeholders
- Select one group of stakeholders and suggest the positive and negative aspects of their relationship with the business
- Write notes on the likely characteristics of stakeholders in the second business organization listed below
- Present your findings to the whole group

Organization 1:

Melchester F.C. are an English Premiership football club with an annual revenue of over £800 million. After winning the Premiership for four out of the last five years, Melchester won the UEFA Champions League last season. The club is a Public Limited Company, with its shares listed on the London Stock Exchange. It has more than 400 full-and part-time staff, including players and officials.

More than 50,000 supporters can attend home games at Melchester, but several thousand people apply unsuccessfully for tickets for every match. Among its facilities, the club has hospitality boxes, a conference hall, hotel accommodation, shopping centre, TV station and website. But the club's relations with its local residents are suffering, with locals raising their concerns to the club over the noise, traffic congestion and pollution that they say blights their lives.

The football club's manager, Malik Merguson, is widely seen as the main reason for the club's international success and worldwide popularity, but he is quick to acknowledge the work of the many managers who run different areas of what is not just a football club, but an international business.

Organization 2:

The City Nightclub Lasers' nightclub is an established business. In recent years, it has expanded and taken over more building space above a shopping centre in the heart of the city. It prides itself on attracting some of the country's big-name DJs to its events.

Lasers employs a full-time staff of 12, but part-time workers push this figure up to 25 on weekend nights. It employs staff in catering, bar work, dancing, resident DJs, door security, accounts and finance, and cleaning. There have been problems over physical assaults on staff in the past year. On a busy weekend, Lasers can attract as many as 500 customers through its doors. A "foam party" this summer helped the club set its record for bar takings.

This event also attracted the attention of the Environmental Health Officers in the area, after several customers developed skin rashes following the party. Local residents are few and far between in this central part of the city, but the club has been accused lately by the local media of being the source of anti-social behaviour, damage and pollution in surrounding areas.

Exercises

1. What are stakeholders of an organization? List three types of stakeholders.

2. How can stakeholders influence an organization's decisions?

3. What are internal stakeholders?

4. What interest do connected stakeholders have?

5. To find a business and identify its main stakeholders (group work).

Glossary

Accountable: Liable to account for one's actions 有责任的；有解释义务的

Stakeholder: Someone entrusted to hold the stakes for two or more persons betting against one another; must deliver the stakes to the winner 利益相关者

Aggrieve: Infringe on the rights of 侵害；伤害

Perspectives: A way of regarding situations or topics etc. 看法；视角

Prioritize: Assign a priority to 把……区分优先次序

Trading practices: A customary way of operation or behaviour while trading 贸易惯例

Managerial: Of or relating to the function or responsibility or activity of management 管理的；经理的

Private venture: Businesses not owned by government 私营企业

Capitalist: Someone who owns a business which they run in order to make a profit for themselves 资本家

Lucrative: Producing a good profit 获利多的，赚钱的；合算的

Investment: An amount of money that you invest, or the thing that you invest it in; the activity of investing money 投资额；投资

Chapter 3 Responsibilities of Organizations

Introduction

Organizations are part of human society, and like people, are subject to rules that govern their conduct towards others. Some of these rules are laws and enforced by legal sanction. Other rules belong to ethics or morality and are enforced only by the strength of society's approval or disapproval. Social responsibility and ethical issues relate to many aspects of the organizations—its environment, its culture and its management practice.

This chapter mainly introduces the social, environmental responsibilities of organizations and their responsibilities towards different stakeholders like employees, suppliers, customers and shareholders, etc.

From this chapter, we can see that an organization's main responsibility is to make as much money as possible. Meanwhile, It also should establish codes of conduct to ensure that such responsibility is properly realized.

The objectives of this chapter:

(1)Management responsibilities

(2) Social responsibilities

(3) Responsibility to the environment

(4) Ethics and corporate image

3.1 Management Responsibilities

Management responsibilities mainly refer to the responsibilities that management of the organizations should have to the owners (shareholders), employees, customers, suppliers, competitors, the local community and the general public.

3.1.1 The Responsibilities to Shareholders

To shareholders, businesses have a responsibility to manage funds so as to return a fair profit to investors. Loss of investor confidence restricts a firm's ability to meet future capital needs.

Example: Casio and its shareholders

Casio considers the maintenance and expansion of returns for all of its shareholders an important management issue, and constantly strives to improve its business performance and financial structure. The company's dividend policy calls for maintaining stable dividends, and Casio determines the allocation of profit by taking into account all factors such as profit levels, financial position, the dividend payout ratio, and future business development and forecasts. Considering this policy, Casio paid dividends of ¥ 20 per share in fiscal 2013. This was an increase of ¥ 3 over the previous fiscal year. Starting in fiscal 2014, Casio will also pay interim dividends, returning profits to shareholders more frequently than the year-end dividend system used to date.

3.1.2 The Responsibilities to Employees

Employees are the most important of all factors of production. They are intimately connected with company and are interested in organization's continuation and growth. They also have a strong and immediate influence on the company. If motivated, employees can be more productive. Meanwhile employees have their individual interests and goals:

(a) Income security

(b) Increases in income

(c) Safe & comfortable working condition

(d) A sense of community

(e) Interesting work

(f) Skills and career development

(g) A sense of doing something worthwhile

(h) Health and welfare

(i) Job satisfaction

The responsibilities to employees range widely from paying workers appropriately to making a business as safe as possible. Following can be some of the responsibilities to employees. Organizations should respect the rights and innate worth of the individuals, promote and preserve the health and safety of employees, provide good working conditions and good training and development schemes, etc.

(1)Wages or Salary

Businesses have a responsibility to pay employees of your business at least the minimum hourly wage and to pay each employee money owed from working per pay period, including overtime, sick leave and vacation wages. Paychecks should always be on time and without delay so your workers can meet individual financial obligations. Government also requires you to pay Medicare, Social Security for each employee.

(2)Workplace Safety Standards

Businesses need maintain a safe working environment for their employees the proper standards. You must also make employees aware of areas in your business that have a high risk for injury and train your employees in safety procedures to minimize the risk of injury. Ensuring each employee is using tools and equipment safe for your small business's particular industry is also your responsibility as a business owner. Continual inspection of your facilities and employee knowledge of safety standards is necessary to make certain your workplace remains as safe as possible.

(3)Workers' Compensation Insurance

Despite the best efforts to maintain a safe working environment, accidents will happen. When injuries occur through no fault of employees, it's your responsibility to file a claim with your workers' compensation insurance provider. This coverage provides for medical care and wage replacement for your injured employee. You must treat your injured employee with respect and file the claim without attempting to (cause a delay in processing) or attempting to deter the worker from filing a claim at all. This is illegal and can cost you hefty fines and possible jail time if you refuse to honor your commitments and requirements as a business owner.

(4)Positive Working Climate

Employees of your small business don't have to be cheery, but the environment shouldn't encourage workers to harass each other in any way. It is your responsibility as a small business owner to create a working climate that develops respect and fair treatment of every employee regardless of age, race, gender, ethnicity, country of origin, disability or religion. Never ignore employees who come to you with problems of harassment. Confronting these issues directly can help you avoid a costly civil lawsuit from allowing a climate of harassment in your workplace.

Example 1: Mitsubishi Electric' s responsibility to its employees

Mitsubishi Electric, a global corporation, has many specific measures to show its responsibilities to its employees.

Workforce Diversity and Equal Opportunity:

As a global corporation, Mitsubishi Electric seeks to hire a diverse workforce with respect for human rights in mind and without regard for gender, age, nationality or race. Hiring a diverse array of people with respect for human rights and without discrimination by gender, age, nationality or race is essential to the ongoing business development of a global company.

In order to pass on the skills possessed by highly experienced employees to younger technicians at Japan production sites accompanying the company's generational shift, they have developed a training program that allows the skills of accomplished employees to be learned in one-on-one settings. Technical skills are also passed on to young technicians through various measures such as the use of "technical help desks", where newer employees can consult with highly experienced employees through the company's intranet.

In Japan, Mitsubishi Electric instituted a multi-track personnel system in fiscal 2002, which makes diverse employment formats possible by allowing employees aged 50 and over to choose from among a variety of options. The options include financial assistance for an employee's "second life" following retirement, a "second life" support program that provides two years of paid vacation, and extending employment up to the age of 65 through a re-employment program.

Mitsubishi Electric works to promote the employment of people with disabilities and to create barrier-free workplaces at its business sites throughout Japan to make it easy for people with disabilities to work at the company.

Creating a Fulfilling Workplace:

Mitsubishi Electric aims to develop a corporate culture in which employees recognize organizational targets as well as their own roles, work to increase their own value, and take on the responsibilities associated with challenging goals.

Maintaining a Favorable Working Environment:

Mitsubishi Electric endeavors to develop workplace conditions that allow employees to both excel in their careers and meet the duties of raising families.

Respecting Human Rights:

The Mitsubishi Electric Group understands that its business operations are interrelated with a wide range of peoples and societies throughout the world, and implements and enforces a code of conduct that fosters respect for human rights.

Supporting Career Development:

Mitsubishi Electric provides a human resources development system that supports the careers of employees, a self-development support program and transfer opportunities for willing employees.

Ensuring Occupational Safety & Health:

Mitsubishi Electric promotes the management of occupational safety and health, measures to prevent lifestyle-related diseases, the support of mental health care and initiatives to achieve and maintain workplace environment standards.

Example 2: Motorola's responsibility to its employees

Motorola makes its Chinese employees enjoy health care, retirement and unemployment protection. During working hours, which will allow employees enjoy extra welfare like a free lunches and housing, at the same time, Motorola has always respected the privacy of each employee and makes confidential documents include the case, counseling records for each employee.

When is an employer required to pay a severance payment to an employee?

An employer should pay a severance payment when an employee, who has been employed under a continuous contract for not less than 24 months, is dismissed due to redundancy or is laid off. (Note: A series of short contracts of employment of less than 24 months may still be treated as a single contract. More details are stated on the last two paragraphs.)

Meaning of Redundancy

An employee is considered to be dismissed due to redundancy if the dismissal is due to the fact that:

• The employer closes or intends to close the business;

• The employer has ceased, or intends to cease, the business in the place where the employee was employed;

• The requirement of the business for employees to carry out work of a particular kind, or for the employee to carry out work of a particular kind in the place where the employee was employed, ceases or diminishes or is expected to cease or diminish.

Meaning of Lay-off

If an employee is employed on such terms and conditions that the remuneration depends on the amount of work provided by the employer, the employee will be considered to be laid off if the total number of days on which no work is provided or no wage is paid exceeds:

— half of the total number of normal working days in any four consecutive weeks; or

— one-third of the total number of normal working days in any 26 consecutive weeks.

Rest days, annual leave and statutory holidays should not be counted as normal working days during the above periods.

Employees who wish to claim for severance payments should serve written notice to their employers within three months after the dismissal/lay off takes effect. The deadline for serving such notice may be extended if approved by the Commissioner for Labour. The employers must make the severance payments to their employees not later than two months from the receipt of such notice.

3.1.3 The Responsibilities to Customers

According to Smith (1998), "A customer is an individual or group of individuals to whom you provide one or more products or services". The responsibilities to customers means that businesses provide a product or service of a quality as customers expect and deal honestly and fairly with customers.

Example: Casio and its customers

Casio is recognized by the market for its commitment to treating customers' right. The company constantly strives to ensure its business management is worthy of customer confidence. Casio focuses on daily improvement in order to provide customers with reliability and peace of mind, and to meet customer demands with speed and integrity.

Casio believes it is important not only to provide products and services that delight customers, but also to win acceptance from the whole of society and achieve mutual prosperity. Toward this end, Casio Quality includes everything from the quality of individual products, to environmental protection and recycling. The role of quality assurance is to deliver quality that satisfies customers in every possible way. Casio's production plants carry out plan-do-check-act (PDCA) cycles using the ISO 9001 Quality Management System in order to deliver reliability and peace of mind to customers that use Casio products.

3.1.4 The Responsibilities to Suppliers

The responsibilities of a business to its suppliers are expressed mainly in terms of trading relationships.

Example: Casio and its suppliers

Casio procures various materials from a large number of suppliers in and outside Japan. In order to develop long-term business relationships, Casio has established Procurement Policies to conduct fair and equitable transactions throughout the supply chain. The policies cover matters including legal compliance, respecting human rights, labor, safety, and health, as well as environmental protection such as biodiversity preservation and risk control of chemical contents and information security. Casio constantly improves its socially responsible procurement by obtaining the understanding and support of suppliers for the policies and building strong partnerships.

■ Fair and equitable transactions

Casio carries out fair and equitable transactions by providing equal opportunities to all suppliers (and candidates) in and outside Japan in accordance with its internally established procedures.

■ Compliance with laws and social norms

Casio's procurement activities comply with all relevant laws, social norms, standards and treaties worldwide, including the protection of human rights, the prohibition of child labor, forced labor and discrimination, and avoiding the use of conflict minerals, and respect for freedom of association, the right to associate, and the right to collective bargaining, as well as ensure that absolutely no contact is made with organized criminal elements. Therefore, Casio requires its suppliers to observe the same legal and social requirements.

■ Environmental protection

Casio helps to protect the global environment through environmentally friendly procurement, which is based on the Casio Environmental Vision and Casio's Environmental Declaration, in cooperation with suppliers.

■ Strengthening partnership with suppliers

Casio builds up relationship of trust with its suppliers through reciprocal efforts, such as merging and complementing mutual technological development abilities, supply chain cooperation, compliance with laws and social norms and protection of the global environment, which will benefit both parties.

■ Policies on supplier selection and transaction continuation

Casio initiates and continues transactions with suppliers based on comprehensive evaluation criteria, which include compliance with laws and social norms, environmental protection, proper information security, respect for intellectual property, sound and stable corporate management, superior technological development ability, right price and quality, stable supply capabilities and electronic transaction systems.

■ Securing right price and quality

Casio endeavors to secure right price and quality in order to provide its customers with stable supply of optimal products, which ensures that Casio gains the full confidence of customers around the world.

3.1.5　The Responsibilities to Competitors

The responsibilities of a business to its competitors are expressed mainly in terms of fair competition. Responsibilities regarding competition are more or less directed by ethics. There is also a great deal of law surrounding the conduct of fair trading anti-competitive practices, abuses of a dominant market position and restrictive trade practices.

3.1.6　The Responsibilities to the Community

A business is a part of the community that it serves, and it should be responsible for the following things:

(1) Upholding the social and ethical values of the community.

(2) Contributing to the well-being of the community, e.g. by sponsoring local events and charities, or providing facilities for the community to use.

(3) Responding constructively to complaints from local residents about the problems caused by the business.

3.2　Social Responsibilities

Corporate Social Responsibility is "concerned with the ways in which an organization exceeds its minimum obligations to stakeholders specified through regulation", according to Johnson & Scholes (2008).

More and more firms are committing themselves to socially responsible actions and doing their business in an ethical way. Why? We will explore the social responsibility and managerial ethics.

"Today, corporate social responsibility goes far beyond the old philanthropy of the past—donating money to good causes at the end of the financial year—and is instead an all year round responsibility that companies accept for the environment around them, for the best working practices, for their engagement in their local communities and for their recognition that brand names depend not only on quality, price and uniqueness but on how they interact with companies workforce, community and environment. Now "we need to move towards a challenging measure of corporate responsibility, where we judge results not just by the input but by its outcomes: the difference we make to the world in which we live, and the contribution we make to poverty reduction". (Gordon Brown, 2004)

- The business philosophy emphasises that business should behave as good citizens.

- The business should consider the effects of their activities on society as a whole on the stakeholders.

- While making decisions, organizations should adopt a moral code—identifying what is "right" and what is "wrong" and act accordingly.

Businesses should consider the following points:

- Profits versus higher wages
- Expansion versus development
- Production versus pollution
- Supplier benefits versus consumer prices/lower costs
- Survival of the business versus needs of stakeholders

CSR should again apply the principles of:

- Fairness
- Honestly
- Trust
- Respect

Example 1: Casio and its social responsibilities

Striving to be a model corporate citizen, Casio makes the most of its unique know-how and management resources to fulfil its various social responsibilities.

Philosophy on Social Contribution:

Casio's social contribution initiatives aim to help build a healthy, spiritually rich society. The five priority areas are education of the next generation, study and research, environmental conservation, community service, and culture and arts.

Casio takes a proactive approach to these initiatives, seeking to communicate with various stakeholders in order to determine how it can be most helpful as a good corporate citizen. In this process, Casio seeks to make innovative social contribution, leveraging its unique expertise and management resources as well as the broad range of knowledge and experience possessed by its employees. Going forward, Casio will continue to provide assistance to people suffering in the aftermath of the Great East Japan Earthquake. Casio also plans to make sure that its social contribution initiatives target global challenges.

CASIO Education Scholarship Foundation

Casio (Shanghai) Co., Ltd., set up the CASIO Scholarship Foundation at Peking University, Shanghai International Studies University, Fudan University, East China University of Politics and Law, Beijing Foreign Studies University, Tianjin Foreign Studies University, and East China Normal University. The foundation provides scholarships for outstanding students and teachers who have produced high quality research. Through the establishment of the scholarship foundation, Casio aims to support the long-term development of these universities, which have a key role as institutions for the development of human resources.

Looking to the future, Casio will provide support for scholarship across a diverse array of subject areas including languages, international finance and trade, international business administration, the mass media, law, and international education as it contributes to the development and revitalization of academic research.

Example 2: NIKE and its social responsibility

"Nike has zero tolerance for under-age labour" ——Nike CEO Phil Knight
1.Forced Labour: The manufacturer does not use forced labour in any form——prison, indentured, bonded or otherwise. 2.Child labour: The manufacturer does not employ any person below the age of 18 to produce footwear. The manufacturer does not employ any person below the age of 16 to produce apparel, accessories or equipment. Where local standards are higher, no person under the legal minimum age will be employed. 3.Compensation: The manufacturer provides each employee at least the minimum wage, or the prevailing industry wage, whichever is higher; provides each employee a clear, written accounting for every pay period; and does not deduct from worker pay for disciplinary infractions, in accordance with the Nike Manufacturing Leadership Standard on financial penalties. 4.Benefits: The manufacturer provides each employee all legally mandated benefits. Benefits vary by country, but may include meals or meal subsidies; transportation or transportation subsidies; other cash allowances; health care; child care; emergency, pregnancy or sick leave; vacation, religious, bereavement or holiday leave; and contributions for social security and other insurance, including life, health and worker's compensation.

5.Hours of Work/Overtime: The manufacturer complies with legally mandated work hours; uses overtime only when each employee is fully compensated according to local law; informs each employee at the time of hiring if mandatory overtime is a condition of employment; and on a regularly scheduled basis, provides one day off in seven, and requires no more than 60 hours of work per week, or complies with local limits if they are lower.

6.Management of Environment, Safety and Health (MESH): The manufacturer has written health and safety guidelines, including those applying to employee residential facilities, where applicable; has a factory safety committee; complies with Nike's environmental, safety and health standards; limits organic vapour concentrations at or below the Permissible Exposure Limits mandated by the U.S. Occupational Safety and Health Administration (OSHA); provides Personal Protective Equipment(PPE) free of charge, and mandates its use; and complies with all applicable local environmental, safety and health regulations.

Example 3: Starbucks and its social responsibility

Ever since the first store in 1971, Starbucks dedicated themselves to striking a balance between profitability and social conscience. They are committed to offering the highest-quality, ethically purchased and responsibly produced products. Through their responsible purchasing practices they invest in our farmers, suppliers and their communities. They've always believed that businesses can and should have a positive impact on the communities they serve. They believe in helping communities thrive. In April 2012, Starbucks accomplished more than 2,100 community service projects and more than 230,000 hours of service contributed in just 30 days.

3.3 Responsibility to the Environment

Businesses are profit-driven, but meanwhile, they have also produced the deep impact on the surroundings. Some of environmental concern may refer to the impact that businesses' actions have on natural resources. Some consequent problems may be water pollution, air pollution, land pollution, chemical pollution, noise pollution, disposal of waste and land erosion, etc.

Every small step of a business makes a difference towards environmental sustainability and some businesses remain committed to conducting their business in an environmentally-conscious manner by employing solutions or supporting causes that minimise the environmental impact of the businesses.

Example 1: Alliance Bank Malaysia Berhad and its responsibilities to environment

Alliance Bank Malaysia Berhad is a dynamic, integrated banking group offering end-to-end financing solutions through its consumer banking. The banking group is involved in the provision of financial services through its principal subsidiaries. It provides easy access to its broad base of customers. Following is what Alliance Bank does to show its responsibilities to environment:

(1)Reducing IT carbon footprint

While it places priority on investing in information technology infrastructure to deliver the best service to our customers, it continuously strives to reduce the overall energy usage to minimise its impact on the environment. It achieve this by constantly updating its network of servers and computers, implement virtualisation technologies, and consolidating its data centres. These have resulted in an overall reduction in energy consumption and real estate footprint.

It also made it a priority to contract an IT-waste disposal specialist to dispose obsolete machinery in compliance with processes approved by the Department of Environment under the purview of the Ministry of Natural Resources and Environment.

(2)Energy and paper conservation

From the time it launched an awareness campaign for employees back in 2008, it has since taken positive steps to conserve energy and paper usage.

All air-conditioning units at its premises are automatically switched off at 5:45 p.m. and are only restarted at 8:45 a.m. to conserve energy. Employees are also encouraged to use double-sided printing and copying as a standard practice, and to reduce their overall usage of paper.

Example 2: Nokia and its environmental responsibilities

Over the last decade Nokia has reduced the greenhouse gas footprint of their phones by 50%. In 2012 Nokia banned the use of radioactive substances in all products, packaging, and internal production processes. This is the latest in a long line of substance and material management policies. For example, the use of perfluorooctanoic acid (PFOA) was restricted, and in 2010 all Nokia products were free from bromine and chlorine compounds related to flame retardants.

In 2012 Nokia retail packaging material used 18,875 tonnes of paper (on average 52% recycled) and a further 9,569 tonnes of paper (on average 89% recycled) in transport packaging material. Over the last 10 years Nokia has reduced the no-load consumption of its chargers by 73% (i.e. charger plugged in, but not being actively used for charging). The best-in-class chargers have seen a 90% reduction. The average no-load power consumption on Nokia chargers shipped in 2012 was 0.098W, a reduction of 13% from the previous year. In

2012 all new Nokia devices are being shipped with four or five star charger.

40% of the electricity used by Nokia comes from renewable sources. Nokia aims to reduce CO_2 emissions by a minimum of 30% by 2020 (from a 2006 baseline). The 2013 emissions figure was down 29% from 2006. Nokia reduced CO_2 emissions from air travel by 54% from 2011 to 2012 in total, and by 39% when calculating reductions per employee. In part this was due to the installation and greater use of new video conferencing facilities.

Case Study 1: Corporate Responsibility to the Environment and Society—How Nestlé Does It

Corporate Social Responsibility is defined as a concept whereby companies incorporate social and environmental concerns in their business operations and in their interactions with their stakeholders on a voluntary basis (European Commission n.d.). As most corporations are profit-driven, social obligations such as are often neglected, resulting in negative impacts on the society and environment (Shah, 2009). Nestlé, a Swiss multinational corporation is the largest food group in the world, trading in almost every country (Simonian, 2006). In relation to that, the society and media expect large companies to surpass the minimum regulations that the government sets on the work situations and ecological impact. In addition, society expects large corporations that rake in massive earnings annually to contribute to the community, employees, and environmental causes (Clapper, 2007). This paper will review the social performance of Nestlé in terms of the impacts on Nestlé's stakeholders. It will review Nestlé's involvement in the infant formula controversy and their efforts with the establishment of The Cocoa Plan, displaying both positive and negative sides in their operations and their impact on stakeholders.

Case against Nestlé

One of the biggest cases Nestlé has starred in is the infant formula controversy. It all started in the late 1800s when Henri Nestlé and the company created and marketed infant formula as a substitute to human milk for mothers who do not breast feed. However, due to profit motive reasons, Nestlé also began irresponsibly marketing the infant formula to mothers perfectly capable of breastfeeding. Nestlé managed to persuade a large proportion of mothers in the Third World that infant formula was better for their babies than human milk. But the fact is that breast milk is essential for babies because it provides them with certain nutrients and antibodies that cannot be substituted (Mokhiber, 1987). Nestlé has deeply impacted the lives of numerous stakeholders, especially the consumers and their family by the irresponsible marketing of the infant formula causing deaths and suffering to infants. Besides that, an economic impact can be seen to negatively affect the society's lifestyle because as more women in the Third World do not practice breast feeding, the demand for infant formula imports from other countries increases which causes a decline in national and household economies (Pettigrew, 1992).

The results of more infants being fed with infant formula were severe. Approximately 1.5 million infant deaths were recorded annually throughout the world due to infants being inadequately breastfed(Global Strategy for Infant and Young Child Feeding, 2001). The deaths occur not only because of the lack of natural nutrients, but also because people were trying to prolong the supply of infant powder by diluting it and some of the consumers were not educated enough, leading to the misuse of infant formula (Baker, 1985). For example, in Tanzania it was reported that although the mothers know their native language, Nestlé's Lactogen, a type of infant formula largely marketed in the community, only had instructions in English, which mothers could not read. Other than that, as boiled water is considered lavish to Third World women, the water used to prepare the milk is often contaminated and the bottle they use are not properly sterilized (Mokhiber, 1987). In relation to that, WHO estimated that annually, ten million cases of malnutrition or disease could be the result of improper use of infant formula and one tenth of the babies die (Baker, 1985).

Following that, a boycott towards Nestlé products was announced by the Infant Formula Action Coalition (INFACT) in 1977 to protest the marketing of infant formula in the Third World (Akhter, 1994). It has been reported that Nestlé violated the rules set by the World Health Organization (WHO) which was aimed at providing a safe and adequate nutrition for infants with the promotion of breastfeeding and the proper use of milk substitutes. A notion supported by the WHO was that the marketing of breast milk substitutes required suitable marketing practices appropriate for infant formula. However, Nestlé broke 25 WHO recommendations in 56 countries within a year in 1990 to 1991 (Pettigrew, 1992). For example, in Singapore, Nestlé hired women to dress up as nurses and convince mothers that infant formula was a modern and better way of feeding their infants. Besides that, in 1983, INFACT cited Nestlé for taking no notice of the important sections of the WHO International Code of Marketing of Breastmilk Substitutes (1981), for the company had given out excessive amounts of free infant formula to a hospital in Malaysia (Mokhiber, 1987). The Nestlé boycott stretched beyond its area of operations. This could be seen through the incident where when the American Public Health Association was to take place in Ohio. After realizing that the hotel was owned by one of Nestlé's subsidiary, the conference was called off, resulting in a loss of 6,000 convention room rentals. In efforts to deal with the boycott, Nestlé reported a severe loss in earnings in 1980 and 1981.

To cushion the blow of the boycott, Nestlé came up with a few strategies in 1981. One of the major strategies undertaken by Nestlé which was to formally support the WHO code finally progressed in 1982 to prevent further loss. Another move which is arguably the best move made by Nestlé was to launch the Infant Formula Audit Commission (IFAC) to go over claims that Nestlé violated WHO or national codes. A report submitted by IFAC included a detailed plan that included dissuasion of the promotion of infant formula by promoters, an agreement to give out free or cheaper infant formula specifically to those infants that are unable to breastfeed and applying the WHO Code to infant formula for all use by children. After a few more of such reports, the boycott was finally lifted in 1984 due to the fulfillment of the Code (Baker, 1985). Overall, although Nestlé did not deliberately violate laws, there were many social costs. Many deaths and suffering of infants have occurred throughout the world because of Nestlé's infant formula. The fact remains, those lives cannot be replaced and all Nestlé can do is minimize the impact by being more socially responsible. Nestlé's sincerity in their cleaning up efforts are questionable because a about decade later, the Advertising Standards Authority lodged a complaint to Nestlé about unethical advertising of infant formula in the newspaper (Ferriman, 1999).

Case for Nestlé

On the other hand, Nestlé has also shown great concern for the society. This is shown through the launch of their concept of Corporate Social Responsibility in 2006, Creating Shared Value (CSR). A statement made in the report was that business and society are interdependent, one fails to survive without the other (Kramer, 2006). Since the launch of CSR, Nestlé has undertaken many projects to help the society. One particular project that has brought upon significant change to the society is The Cocoa Plan. Being one of the biggest buyers of cocoa beans, Nestlé launched the Cocoa Plan project to facilitate African cocoa farmers and the society take advantage of mounting market prices by increasing their productivity (Media Club South Africa, 2009). Furthermore, on top of the 60 million Swiss francs invested in cocoa sustainability projects over the last 15 years, Nestlé has planned to invest 110 million Swiss francs over a decade in Côte d'Ivoire and Ghana which produce over half of the world's cocoa supply (Bhatti, 2009). The investments include distributing 12 million disease-resistant plantlets to the cocoa farmers which is claimed to be able to produce up to double the amount of trees being used in several plantations in Côte d'Ivoire and Ghana. Since the launch of the Plan in 2009, Nestlé has funded farmer schools in West Africa so that farmers can learn more efficient up-to-date ways which could enable them to produce better quality cocoa and increase their income. Besides that, Nestlé also set up a research and development centre in Côte d'Ivoire that worked in hand with Nestlé's plant science base in Tours. The result of the collaboration is the allocation of one million high-yield cocoa plantlets every year starting 2012 (The Cocoa Plan: Nestlé and sustainable cocoa, 2010).

As a result of the Cocoa Plan initiatives, many have benefited. Nestlé, as a partner of International Cocoa Initiative and the World Cocoa foundation tackled problems such as child labour and lack of excess to health and education. For example, sending farmers to field schools not only educates the farmer on methods to increase cocoa productivity, but they are also educated on diseases and prevention methods. Also, because of the boost in the production of cocoa, household incomes have increased. This is shown through the increase in income by more than 20% for 80,000 West African households, thus improving their lifestyles (The Cocoa Plan: Nestlé and sustainable cocoa, 2010). Besides that, the boost in production of cocoa could also increase their exports and in turn reduce their foreign debt. By setting up the research centre in Côte d'Ivoire, the locals sent to work and learn there could gain new skills, study the technology and share the information with the other locals towards having useful technological advances of their own. Needless to say, Nestlé has demonstrated that they are corporately responsible towards their stakeholders, particularly the farmers who supply them with cocoa and their families, impacting their lives positively.

With all that, the social performance of Nestlé in relation to their consumers and workers has scraped both negative and positive results. In a positive light, Nestlé impacted the lives of many by introducing the Cocoa Plan. Several communities in Côte d'Ivoire and Ghana have been given many opportunities and advantages towards a more sustainable development. It shows that Nestlé has upheld its part of the social contract by giving back to the society that supplies them with resources to produce their goods. In contrast, Nestlé started the infant formula controversy by irresponsibly marketing infant formula and it had caused unnecessary death and suffering to millions of babies. Their greed and inability to take action earlier resulted in irreversible consequences. Although they cleaned up their act a few years later, the damage had been done; those dead babies cannot be brought back to life. Regardless of the corporation's efforts, it is obvious that they have not withheld their part of the social contract. Their actions clearly do not meet the expectations of the society and up till now, they are dealing with more controversies. The business power invested in them could go a long way towards affecting peoples' lives positively, but instead is sometimes being misused.

Discussion: What can you learn from the above case?

Case Study 2: External Influences: Coca-Cola

Most businesses have to consider the impact of their activities on stakeholders. Coca-Cola is no exception but their operations in the southern Indian state of Kerala have caused widespread concern and a string of claims and counter-claims by residents of the local community and the company.

The Story

In 1998, Coca-Cola set up a bottling plant in Perumatti in the southern state of Kerala. Since it opened, local villagers have complained about the fall in the amount of water available to them and have blamed the fall in supplies on Coca-Cola who they claim, use up a million litres per day at the plant. Coca-Cola claims that the shortage in the water is due to the lack of rains in the region. Coca-Cola even sends round tankers of water to the region to help the local community. Local farmers are claiming that their livelihood has been destroyed since the building of the plant and that the number of people working on the land has dropped considerably because they cannot survive.

Following the cleaning of the bottles, a waste sludge is produced that Coca-Cola have been disposing of on the land of local farmers, claiming it was a useful fertilizer. Following a BBC Radio 4 program, samples of the sludge were analyzed by scientists at Exeter University in the south-west of England and found to contain toxic chemicals including lead and cadmium—both of which can be harmful to humans—and further suggested that there was little or no benefit of the sludge as a fertilizer. Recent tests by the local state laboratories find that the levels of toxic chemicals are within safety levels but that it should not be used as a fertilizer.

In a separate development, sales of Coca-Cola have been hit by suggestions that its drinks produced in India contained higher levels of pesticide residues than was healthy! A large number of bodies have joined in the local community's campaign demanding the plant be closed down and that tests be carried out on Coca-Cola to assess its safety. A lawsuit to this effect was thrown out in August, which prompted Coca-Cola to issue an angry comment claiming that the reports were scurrilous, unnecessarily scared large numbers of Coca-Cola's customers and put thousands of jobs in its plants throughout India at risk. Coca-Cola claims to employ in excess of 5,000 people in the country, not to mention the many thousands that are linked in some way to the product.

Analysis

There are a number of issues relating to this incident that demonstrate the ethical and moral issues surrounding the business.

Coca-Cola has become one of the most popular drinks in India.

Coca-Cola's business in India leads to a wide range of direct and indirect employment related to the business as a result of $1 billion worth of investment by the company.

Coca-Cola claims that its activities are entirely legal.

- How honest are the claims that Coca-Cola is making?

- How reliable are the claims made by those who oppose Coca-Cola's activities?

- What conflicts arise between the responsibilities that Coca-Cola has to the environment and the local community, and to its shareholders, suppliers and employees?

- How much pressure would local council officials be under to give Coca-Cola a clean bill of health, as some would suggest?

3.4 Ethics and Corporate Image

3.4.1 Ethics of Organizations

Ethics according to the *Collins Dictionary* are: Moral principle(s) or set of moral values held by an individual or a group.

Ethics are the standards of right or wrong that influence behaviour, while ethical behaviour is behaviour that is accepted as "right" according to those standards. Businesses need to understand ethics, values, the four approaches to ethical dilemmas, and how to promote ethics.

An ethical dilemma is a situation in which you have to decide whether to pursue a course of action that may benefit you or your organization but that is unethical or even illegal.

Values are the relatively permanent and deeply held underlying beliefs and attitudes that help determine a person's behaviour. Ethical dilemmas can take place when a firm's value system is challenged.

The four approaches to deciding ethical dilemmas

(1) According to the utilitarian approach, ethical behaviour is guided by what will result in the greatest good for the greatest number of people.

(2) Under the individual approach, ethical behaviour is guided by what will result in the individual's best long-term interests, which ultimately is in everyone's self-interest.

(3) According to the moral-rights approach, ethical behaviour is guided by respect for the fundamental rights of human beings.

(4) Ethical behaviour under the justice approach is guided by respect for impartial standards of fairness and equity.

How can organizations promote ethics?

Firms can promote ethics in three ways:

(1) Top management needs to support a strong ethical climate.

(2) Companies can adopt a code of ethics—a formal written set of ethical standards guiding an organization's actions

(3) Companies can promote ethical behaviour by rewarding whistleblowers—employees who report organizational misconduct to the public

Social responsibility is a business' duty to take the actions that will benefit the interests of society as well as the organization, while ethical responsibility focuses on being a good individual citizen, social responsibility focuses on being a good organizational citizen. In the past, social responsibility was an afterthought for companies, but today, many firms believe it is critical to success.

Milton Friedman argues that firms need to focus on making a profit, not on social responsibility. He claims that firms that focus on social responsibility get distracted from their real purpose. However, Paul Samuelson suggests that firms need to be concerned for the welfare of society as well as corporate profits. Samuelson claims that since firms create problems like pollution, they should help solve them.

Two issues linked to social responsibility are sustainability and philanthropy. Sustainability is defined as economic development that meets the needs of the present without compromising the ability of future generations to meet their own needs. Philanthropy involves making charitable contributions to benefit humankind.

How does being good pay off?

■ Customers prefer to buy products from companies that are ethically and socially responsible even if the products cost more.

■ Managers consider a company's social and ethical track record when considering joining and staying with companies.

■ A poor record of ethical and social responsibility can have a negative effect on profits.

■ Managers at companies where dishonesty is common tend to see misconduct.

■ People prefer to buy stock in companies they perceive as being ethical.

■ Profitability is enhanced by a reputation for honesty and good citizenship.

What do you think are ethical business issues?

■ Sexism, racism issues of inequality

■ Power use/abuse

■ Pollution/environmental damage

■ Advertising and promotion for manipulation

■ Anti-competitiveness

■ Manufacturing in developing countries

■ Poor work life balance

■ Staff perks/theft

■ Obscene profit

■ Out sourcing

3.4.2 Corporate Image

Corporate Image is a mental picture that springs up at the mention of a firm's name. It describes the public attitude towards a company, or the image of the company in the mind of the general public, potential customers and the society.

It is a composite psychological impression that continually changes with the firm's circumstances, media coverage, performance, pronouncements, etc. Similar to a firm's reputation or goodwill, it is the public perception of the firm rather than a reflection of its actual state or position.

A corporate image refers to how a corporation is perceived. It is a generally accepted image of what a company "stands for". The creation of a corporate image is an exercise in perception management. It is created primarily by marketing experts who use public relations and other forms of promotion to suggest a mental picture to the public. Typically, a corporate image is designed to be appealing to the public, so that the company can spark an interest among consumers, create share of mind, generate brand equity, and thus facilitate product sales.

The reasons why an organization might attempt to build up a corporate image? The main reasons could be:

(1) Strengthen customer loyalty: the businesses try to produce good products and services and show concern for the customers' interests to build and strengthen customer loyalty.

(2) Create customer awareness: the businesses try to give a public identity by establishing a good image in society in front of their customers to make them realize the existence of some businesses.

(3)Strengthen employees' loyalty: the businesses try to show concern for the employees' interests to build and strengthen employees' loyalty.

(4) Develop a corporate image of social responsibility: the businesses try to develop a corporate image by undertake some social responsibilities, which will help businesses to prevent adverse publicity or prevent pressure from stakeholders, e.g. a coal company or oil company may try to establish an image of caring for the environment and for the future needs of society; TV companies may promote an image of quality programme-makers.

(5)Win public and political support.

(6)A good image has a variety of benefits for management if there is good public relations. The purpose is the survival, reputation and finally success of the businesses.

Image of Large Corporations

Corporations must consider not only sensitivity to newly budget conscious consumers; they must also consider the increasing sustainability/green movement by some consumers and a greater sense of nationalism by other consumers. The economic and political environment has greatly influenced the new corporate image. Given the crushing blows to corporate image that have occurred in the recent past, BP provides an excellent example, corporations should be in a state of constant vigilance to ensure their image is at worst non-impactful at best an important aspect of brand loyalty.

Corporations could learn a great deal from disastrous blows to image, such as Monsanto, Cargill and ADM when looked at through the lens of individuals concerned about genetically modified organisms and monoculture crop production. These corporations are now considered nearly evil on many people's radar and are an immediate turn off to many consumers and investors.

Small Companies and Image

Image likely influences smaller corporations more intensively than larger corporations who can be more dependent on the image of individual brands under the corporation. Smaller corporations, such as Harley Davidson Motorcycle, can be nearly entirely dependent on the image of the corporation for their success. Harley Davidson makes a particularly good example of the importance of image. They have been masterful at exploiting the American ideal of freedom and autonomy, when a consumer purchases a Harley Davidson product they are purchasing a "fantasy" experience and buying into the iconic image of that corporation.

Failures are also more impactful to small corporations, when GAP recently decided to change its iconic GAP logo it traded in its image "capital" and entirely left behind the positive connotations associated with its GAP brand. This is an excellent example of an image failure and GAP very quickly returned to its original GAP logo.

The Future Lies in Corporate Image

The short-term future (for the next 3~5 years) of the economy will be highly dependent on image and iconic branding. Failure to have a strong image demonstrating a progressive attitude, an understanding of issues related to a sustainable future including consideration to environment, social and economic factors, and compassion for consumers will result in economic downfall for corporations. Savvy marketing analysts understand the need to have a strong image or at least an image that doesn't hurt the company. Once your image has been tainted by something like BP's environmental disaster in the way of the massive, unprecedented oil spill, there is very little a corporation can do to overcome that damage.

However, given consumer apathy and cynicism a corporation must now go to very great lengths to establish a positive image. Corporations who have managed to establish a positive image and have successfully maintained their image capital will have exponentially greater success than even very large corporations like Monsanto, Cargill and ADM who have damaged their image capital irreparably. At the end of the day, the consumer demand will create the image of the corporations.

How to Start Corporate Image Building

Have you recently started a business corporation? It is never too early to start corporate image building. There are many great ideas out there that will help you with the corporate image building process.

The first step to take is to identify a simple key idea you want to convey to your potential customers. Try to come up with a positive association with your business that can be easily summarized in three words or less, like "cutting edge technology" or "kid-friendly service".

Now think of some images and ideas that will help you associate your company with the ideas. For example, if you own a software company and you want people to think of "cutting edge technology", you will want your advertising to look very sleek and modern. You will want to use modern, sans serif fonts in your marketing materials, and have a logo that people associate with the latest and greatest websites or gadgets. On the other hand, if you are a restaurant that wants to cater to families with small children, your corporate image building could consist of bright, colorful decor and a cartoon mascot.

The next step after you have done your initial branding and advertising is community outreach. Try to stick with your theme. The high tech software company may want to get in the paper for providing services for the website of an award-winning documentary filmmaker whose work focuses on Silicon Valley, so it may be worthwhile to provide services to such a person at a discount. The kid-friendly restaurant owner may want to do volunteer work at a local children's hospital.

Another important aspect of building your corporate image is "damage control" if something bad happens. For example, if a factory has an environmental accident, such as a chemical spill, the corporation that owns the factory should take quick steps to reassure the public that the problem is being contained, and to show support for environmental causes.

Another aspect of corporate image management is to appeal to new audiences. If you are opening a restaurant in a new state, take the time to determine how local tastes may differ from the tastes of people where you are already operating. You don't want your new restaurant to be so different from your others as to be unrecognizable or sacrifice economies of scale, but it doesn't hurt to tweak your brand here and there. For example, a sports bar that has Yankees paraphernalia on the walls in New York may want to have Orioles paraphernalia on the walls in Baltimore. A steak house that expands to California may want to consider adding a vegetarian option to the menu at its new location, like a marinated portabella mushroom with mashed potatoes and onion gravy. That kind of menu item would be in keeping with the "meat and potatoes" theme, but would enable a different kind of local diner to also enjoy the experience. The steakhouse may not want to add an item like vegetable stir fry, which would stray too far from its original branding.

To build corporate image, it's necessary for organizations to have good public relations.

Public relations are designed to create and maintain a favourable public image for the organization. For example, they might write press releases or sponsor corporate events to help maintain and improve the image and identity of the company. They also help to clarify the organization's main issues (avoiding scandal). They observe social, economic, and political trends that might ultimately affect the firm, and they make recommendations to enhance the firm's image on the basis of those trends. In order to have good public relations, a business should necessarily have a smooth communication.

Communication is a process that allows speakers to exchange information by several methods. Communication requires that all parties understand a common language that is exchanged with each other. Exchange requires feedback. The word communication is also used in the context where little or no feedback is expected such as broadcasting, or where the feedback may be delayed as the sender or receiver use different methods, technologies, timing and means for feedback.

Corporate communications is the process of having information and knowledge exchanges with internal and key external groups and individuals that have a direct relationship with an enterprise. It is concerned with internal communications : sharing knowledge and decisions from the enterprise with employees, suppliers, investors and partners. Primary Communications: the communications effects of products, services, management, staff and corporate behaviour. Secondary Communications: controlled forms of communications such as advertising.

Tools of Communications

Financial Reports

Investors

Analysts

Newsletters

Advisory boards

Intranets

Employees

Vendors

Advisory boards

Business and Ethics

Creating ethical, high-integrity organizations

Business practices

Moral standards

Why does a business need to show that it has social responsibilities?

It can enhance the corporate image of the company. This can lead to increased sales, customer loyalty, and desirable shares. Let's have a look at the following case—cases of bribery.

To take just one example, the Chrysler Corporation, third largest of the U.S. car manufacturers, revealed that it made questionable payments of more than $2.5 million between 1971 and 1976. By announcing this, it joined more than 300 other U.S. companies that had admitted to the U.S. Securities and Exchange Commission that they had made payments of one kind or another — bribes, extra discounts, etc.

For discussion purposes, we can divide these payments into three broad categories.

The first category consists of substantial payments made for political purposes or to secure major contracts. For example, one U.S. corporation offered a large sum of money in support of a U.S. presidential candidate at a time when the company was under investigation for possible violations of U. S. business laws. This same company, it was revealed, was ready to finance secret U.S. efforts to throw out the government of Chile.

In this category, we may also include large payments made to ruling families or their close advisers in order to secure arms sales or major petroleum or construction contracts. In a court case involving an arms deal with Iran, a witness claimed that £ 1 million had been paid by a British company to a "negotiator" who helped close a deal for the supply of tanks and other military equipment to that country. Other countries have also been known to put pressure on foreign companies to make donations.

The second category covers payments made to obtain quicker official approval of some project, to speed up the wheels of government. An interesting example of this kind of payment is provided by the story of a sales manager who had been trying for some months to sell road machinery to the Minister of Works of a country. Discovering that the minister collected rare books, he bought a rare edition of a book, slipped $20,000 within its pages, then presented it to the minister.

This man examined its contents, then said: "I understand there is a two-volume edition of this work" The sales manager, who was quick-witted, replied: "My company cannot afford a two-volume edition, sir, but we could offer you a copy with a preface!" A short time later, the deal was approved.

The third category involves payments made in countries where it is traditional to pay people to help with the passage of a business deal. Some Middle East countries would be included on this list, as well as certain Asian countries. Is it possible to devise a code of rules for companies that would prohibit bribery in all its forms? The International Chamber of Commerce (ICC) favours a code of conduct that would ban the giving and seeking of bribes.

This code would try to distinguish between commissions paid for real services and exaggerated fees that really amount to bribes. A council has been proposed to manage the code. Unfortunately, opinions differ among members of the ICC concerning how to enforce the code. The British members would like the system to have enough legal power to make companies behave themselves.

However, the French delegates think it is the business of governments to make and impose law; the job of a business community like the ICC is to say what is right and wrong, but not to impose anything. In a well-known British newspaper, a writer argued recently that "industry is caught in a web of bribery" and that everyone is "on the take". This is probably an exaggeration. However, today's businessman, selling in overseas markets, will frequently meet situations where it is difficult to square his business interests with his moral conscience. (Taking or seeking to take bribes or illegal income)

Exercises

1. Which would you like to choose, if you can, working for the government or working for a company? Why?

2. List some ways in which a business can demonstrate its responsibilities to different stakeholders.

3. List several types of direct ecological impact on a business.

4. Why public image is important to an organization? How to set up a good public image?

Glossary

Legal sanction: Justice 法律制裁

Harass: Annoy continually or chronically使困扰；使烦恼

Code of Ethics: 道德准则

Conventional: Following accepted customs and proprieties(礼仪，礼节); conforming with accepted standards 传统的；常见的；惯例的

Ethical Dilemmas: 道德困境，伦理困境

Philanthropy: Voluntary promotion of human welfare 博爱，慈爱；慈善事业

Proactive approach: (of a policy or person or action) Controlling a situation by causing something to happen rather than waiting to respond to it after it happens 有前瞻性的

Social responsibility: 社会责任

Sustainability: The property of being sustainable 持续性；永续性

Values: Beliefs of a person or a social group in which they have an emotional investment(either for or against something) 价值观念；价值标准

Chapter 4　Business Environment Analysis

Introduction

Aside from the company's internal resources and industry factors, there are several other macro-economic factors that can have a profound impact on the performance of a company. In particular situations such as new ventures or product launch ideas, these factors need to be carefully analyzed in order to determine how big their role in the organization's success would be. One of the most commonly used analytical tools for assessing external macro-economic factors related to particular situation is **PEST Analysis** that can help you understand the macro-economic business environment.

The political factors account for all the political activities that go on within a country and if any external force might tip the scales in a certain way. They analyze the political temperament and the policies that a government may put in place for some effect. For example, the fiscal policy, trade tariffs and taxes are those things that a government levies on traders and organizations and they greatly alter the revenue that is earned by those companies.

The economic factors take into view the economic condition prevalent in the country and if the global economic scenarios might make it shift or not. These include the inflation rates, foreign exchange rates, interest rates etc. All these can affect the supply and demand cycle and can result in major changes of the business environment.

Social factors have to do with the social mindset of the people that live in a certain country. This sums up the aspect of culture, age demographics, gender and its related stereotypes, at times this analysis has to include the religious factors (when pertaining to products or services of a different kind).

Technological factors take into consideration the rate at which technology is advancing and how much integration does a company needs to have with it.

Legal factors have to do with all the legislative and procedural components in an economy. Also, this takes into account certain standards that your business might have to meet in order to start production/promotion.

Environmental factors have to do with geographical locations and other related environmental factors that may influence upon the nature of the trade you're in. For example, agri-businesses hugely depend on this form of analysis.

Objectives of this chapter:

(1) To identify the changing global business environment.

(2) To identify the business environment.

(3) To evaluate the business environment by using SWOT and PESTLE Analysis.

4.1 The Changing Global Business Environment

The world is becoming smaller. More and more countries get close contact with the development of globalization. As globalization continues, businesses will be presented with opportunities and face challenges.

Globalization is a process that widens and deepens the interactions between each country and the rest of the world. In general, these interconnections refer to the institutions associated with the flows of goods, services, people, information, and cultural traits in a worldwide context. In particular, economic globalization refers to the institutions associated with the flows of traded goods and services, financial and direct capital, migrant labour and tourism, and economic information and ideas, within a global arena of cultural institutions and traits.

The global business environment can be defined as the environment in different sovereign countries, with factors exogenous to the home environment of the organization, influencing decision-making on resource use and capabilities. This includes the social, political, economic, regulatory, tax, cultural, legal, and technological environments. The political environment in a country influences the legislations and government rules and regulations under which a foreign firm operates. The economic environment relates to all the factors that contribute to a country's attractiveness for foreign businesses. Every country in the world follows its own system of law. A foreign company operating in that particular country has to abide with its system of law as long as it is operating in that country. The technological environment comprises factors related to the materials and machines used in manufacturing goods and services. Receptivity of organizations to new technology and adoption of new technology by consumers influence decisions made in an organization.

As firms have no control over the external environment, their success depends upon how well they adapt to the external environment. A firm's ability to design and adjust its internal variables to take advantage of opportunities offered by the external environment, and its ability to control threats posed by the same environment, determine its success.

When transacting business in a geographic market, companies must comply with all applicable laws and regulations of that particular jurisdiction, including insurance and tax. No two countries are the same. These regulations vary significantly from one country to another. The penalties of non-compliance can be severe.

With Chinese enterprises expanding into other countries, they need to actively research and forecast all types of cross-border operating risks and take steps to mitigate those risks.

Credit risk. It is well understood within a domestic context. When going abroad, Chinese companies will face customers that may operate on different credit, payment and enforcement principles. They can insure against these credit risks by engaging in a program that evaluates counterparty risks and insures against counterparty defaults.

Political risk. This is related to trade restrictions, civil disorder, political stalemates, infrastructure bottlenecks and corruption. Political risk may seem bewildering and unmanageable. The first step is trying to understand how such risks could trouble a large investment project. When these risks are outlined, a well-planned insurance program can mitigate these risks.

Interconnectivity Risk. This emerges as businesses cross borders, contract and outsource, and expand their geographic footprint. Supply chain management presents a significant area of risk, especially in emerging markets where firms may have more limited visibility of their suppliers and distributors. The majority of risks that have the potential to disrupt a supply chain originate from suppliers. These include delays or incomplete deliveries, quality control issues and working capital constraints.

With the first announcement of "One Belt, One Road" by President Xi Jinping in 2013, the "One Belt, One Road" concept has expanded immensely as a vision that connects China to Asia, Europe and Africa in trade, development and culture. About 5.5 trillion *yuan* (U.S. $900 billion) will be invested in 900 projects over two transcontinental Silk Roads to connect 60 countries in just two years. This also means that Chinese companies have more opportunities to have global business. So we need to clearly identify the complicated global environment.

4.2 Identification of Business Environment

The term Business Environment is composed of two words "Business" and "Environment". In simple terms, the state in which a person remains busy is also known as business. The word "Business" in its economic sense means human activities like production, extraction or purchase or sales of goods that are performed for earning profits. So we can see "Business" is an organization or economic system where goods and services are exchanged for one another or for money. Every business requires some form of investment and enough customers to whom its output can be sold on a consistent basis in order to make a profit.

Businesses can be privately owned, not-for-profit or state-owned. An example of a corporate business is PepsiCo, while a mom-and-pop catering business is a private enterprise. Businesses may focus on goods, services, or both to consumers or tertiary business in exchange for money. Generally, a business has internal and external environment in which businesses operate. Elements of internal business environment may include:

(1) Key business drivers (e.g. market indicators, competitive advances, product attractiveness, etc.);

(2) The organization's strengths, weaknesses, opportunities and threats;

(3) Internal stakeholders;

(4) Organization structure and culture;

(5) Assets in terms of resources (such as people, systems, processes, capital etc.);

(6) Intellectual assets like patents/ process knowledge;

(7) Goals and objectives and the strategies already in place to achieve them.

Elements of external business environment include conditions, entities, events, and factors surrounding an organization that influence its activities and choices, and determine its opportunities and risks. Also called operating environment , which are the major external and uncontrollable factors that influence an organization's decision-making, and affect its performance and strategies. These factors include the economic factors; demographics; legal, political, and social conditions; technological changes; and natural forces. Specific examples of macro-environment may influences include competitors, changes in interest rates, changes in cultural tastes, disastrous weather, or government regulations.

4.3 SWOT and PESTLE Analysis

SWOT refers to strengths, weaknesses, opportunities and threats, which is used to identify the internal and external environment of a business.

PESTLE, which is sometimes referred as PEST analysis, is a concept in marketing principles. Moreover, this concept is used as a tool by companies to track the environment they're operating in or are planning to launch a new project, product or service etc.

PESTLE is an effective tool to analyze macro-environment. It not only can analyze external environment, but also can identify all factors which can effect an organization. Each letter represents a factor, "P" for Political, "E" for Economic, "S" for Social, "T" for Technological, "L" for Legal and "E" for Environmental. It gives a bird's eye view of the whole environment from many different angles that one wants to check and keep a track of while contemplating on a certain idea or plan.

The framework has undergone certain alterations, as gurus of marketing have added certain things like an "E" for Ethics to instill the element of demographics while utilizing the framework while researching the market.

4.3.1 SWOT Analysis

There are certain questions that one needs to ask while conducting this analysis, which give them an idea of what things to keep in mind. They are:

- What is the political situation of the country and how can it affect the industry?
- What are the prevalent economic factors?
- How much importance does culture has in the market and what are its determinants?
- What technological innovations are likely to pop up and affect the market structure?
- Are there any current legislations that regulate the industry or can there be any change in the legislations for the industry?
- What are the environmental concerns for the industry?

All the aspects of this technique are crucial for any industry a business might be in. More than just understanding the market, this framework represents one of the vertebras of the backbone of strategic management that not only defines what a company should do, but also accounts for an organization's goals and the strategies stringed to them.

The importance of each of the factors may be different to different kinds of industries, but it is imperative to any strategy a company wants to develop that they conduct the **PESTLE analysis** as it forms a much more comprehensive version of the **SWOT analysis**.

SWOT analysis is a situational analysis carried out for different purposes, usually but not necessarily by businesses. This analysis is used to assess four different factors related to any situation:

- **Strengths**
- **Weaknesses**
- **Opportunities**
- **Threats**

(1) **Identification of Strength**: The analysis of the internal environment helps to identify strength of the firm. For instance, if the company has good personal policies in respect of promotion, transfer, training, etc. than it can indicates strength of the firm in respect of personal policies. This strength can be identified through the job satisfaction and performance of the employees. After identifying the strengths the firm must try to consolidate its strengths by further improvement in its existing plans & policies.

(2) **Identification of Weakness**: The analysis of the internal environment indicates not only strengths but also the weakness of the firm. A firm may be strong in certain areas; where as it may be weak in some other areas. The firm should identify weakness so as to correct them as early as possible.

(3) **Identification of Opportunities**: An analysis of the external environment helps the business firm to identify the opportunities in the market. The business firm should make every possible effort to grab the opportunities as and when they come.

(4) **Identification of Threats**: Business may be subject to threats from competitors and others. Therefore, environmental analysis helps to identify threats from the environment identification of threats at an earlier date is always beneficial to the firm as it helps to defuse the same.

All these factors can be about a situation, an organization or an individual's career; there are very few limits regarding where SWOT can be applied. Here, we will be discussing what is SWOT analysis, and its importance for organizations.

What Is SWOT Analysis for Organizations?

For an organization, this analysis is a framework that helps them analyze all internal and external factors that might impact their current plans. These plans can be regarding a new product, project or a strategy that the company is going to undertake currently. In a very precise and simple manner, a SWOT helps a company understand what the dynamics of everything related to the situation being contemplated are. Over the years, this analysis has been adopted by a number of different firms and there is a large number of successful SWOT analysis examples that can be used as guides.

In this analytical model, strengths and weaknesses are considered as the internal factors, completely controllable by the organization itself. Opportunities and threats, on the other hand, are regarded as external factors that might or might not be controllable by the organization. The model states that after thoroughly analyzing every element lying in these categories, an organization should work towards managing and developing further the strengths and opportunities while weaknesses and threats should be eradicated.

A company's resources and their quality of performance are usually factors that become their strengths or weaknesses. Opportunities and threats are market factors and trends that can either benefit or harm the company's current plans. This analysis is usually carried out before a company is in the process of developing a new product, project or strategy to determine whether there resources are matched against the competitive market to make the situation a success.

Based on the results, organizations can determine whether a new project is worth pursuing or not, and if yes, what additional resources or actions would be required to make it successful. An organization's physical, financial and human resources, its processes, past experiences, reputation, competitors, the market movements for the product/service company is offering, the movement of their complimentary and substitute products and other micro- and macro-economic factors are all included in this analysis.

Example: SWOT Analysis of Starbucks

Strengths

Starbucks Corporation, the most famous chain of retail coffee shops in the world, mainly benefits from roasting and selling special coffee beans, and other various kinds of coffee or tea drinks. It owns about 4,000 branches in the whole world. As of 2018, the company operates 28,218 locations worldwide. Moreover, it has been one of the most rapid growing corporations in America as well. The reasons why Starbucks is popular worldwide are not only the quality of coffee, but also its customer service and cosy environment. It is a global coffee brand built upon a reputation for fine products and services.

Starbucks was one of the Fortune Top 100 Companies to Work For in 2005. The company is a respected employer that values its workforce. The organization has strong ethical values and an ethical mission statement as follows, "Starbucks is committed to a role of environmental leadership in all facets of our business."

Weaknesses

Starbucks has a reputation for new product development and creativity. However, they remain vulnerable to the possibility that their innovation may falter over time.

The organization has a strong presence in the United States of America with more than three quarters of their cafes located in the home market. It is often argued that they need to look for a portfolio of countries, in order to spread business risk.

The organization is dependant on a main competitive advantage, the retail of coffee. This could make them slow to diversify into other sectors should the need arise.

Opportunities

Starbucks are very good at taking advantage of opporunties. In 2004, the company created a CD-burning service in their Santa Monica (California, USA) cafe with Hewlett Packard, where customers create their own music CD.

New products and services that can be retailed in their cafes, such as fair trade products. The company has the opportunity to expand its global operations. New markets for coffee such as India and the Pacific Rim nations are beginning to emerge.

Co-branding with other manufacturers of food and drink, and brand franchising to manufacturers of other goods and services both have potential.

Threats

Who knows if the market for coffee will grow and stay in favor with customers, or whether another type of beverage or leisure activity will replace coffee in the future?

Starbucks are exposed to rises in the cost of coffee and dairy products.

Since its conception in Pike Place Market, Seattle in 1971, Starbucks' success has led to the market entry of many competitors and copycat brands that pose potential threats.

If a business wants to understand and evaluate its macro-environment, it is very critical for one to understand the complete depth of each of the letters of the **PESTLE**. It is as below.

Political: These factors determine the extent to which a government may influence the economy or a certain industry. For example, a government may impose a new tax or duty due to which entire revenue generating structures of organizations might change. Political factors include tax policies, fiscal policy, trade tariffs etc. that a government may levy around the fiscal year and it may affect the business environment (economic environment) to a great extent.

Economic: These factors are determinants of an economy's performance that directly impacts a company and have resonating long-term effects. For example, a rise in the inflation rate of any economy would affect the way companies' price their products and services. Adding to that, it would affect the purchasing power of a consumer and change demand/supply models for that economy. Economic factors include inflation rate, interest rates, foreign exchange rates, economic growth patterns etc. It also accounts for the FDI (foreign direct investment) depending on certain specific industries who're undergoing this analysis.

Social: These factors scrutinize the social environment of the market, and gauge determinants like cultural trends, demographics, population analytics etc. An example for this can be buying trends for Western countries like the U.S. where there is high demand during the holiday season.

Technological: These factors pertain to innovations in technology that may affect the operations of the industry and the market favourably or unfavourably. This refers to automation, research and development and the amount of technological awareness that a market possesses.

Legal: These factors have both external and internal sides. There are certain laws that affect the business environment in a certain country while there are certain policies that companies maintain for themselves. Legal analysis takes into account both of these angles and then charts out the strategies in light of these legislations. For example, consumer laws, safety standards, labour laws etc.

Environmental: These factors include all those that influence or are determined by the surrounding environment. This aspect of the PESTLE is crucial for certain industries particularly for example tourism, farming, agriculture etc. Factors of a business environmental analysis include but are not limited to climate, weather, geographical location, global changes in climate, environmental offsets etc.

PESTLE Analysis Template

This is a **template** that allows a company to understand what basics are required to conduct the analysis onto the environment. It combines all the representative factors in one table, and then you need to analyze based on the current market situation.

Here is a comprehensive list of headings that one must look toward while carrying out the analysis on a market.

(1) Political factors:

- Trading policies
- Government changes
- Shareholder and their demands
- Funding
- Governmental leadership
- Lobbying
- Foreign pressures
- Conflicts in the political arena
- Political instability in a foreign partner country

(2) Economic factors:

- Disposable income
- Unemployment level
- Foreign exchange rates
- Interest rates
- Trade tariffs
- Inflation rate
- Foreign economic trends
- General taxation issues
- Taxation changes specific to product/services
- Local economic situation and trends

(3) Social factors:

- Ethnic/religious factors
- Advertising scenarios
- Ethical issues
- Consumer buying patterns
- Major world events
- Buying access
- Shifts in population
- Demographics
- Health
- Consumer opinions and attitudes

- Views of the media
- Law changes affecting social factors
- Change in lifestyle
- Brand preferences
- Working attitude of people
- Education
- Trends
- History

(4) Technological factors:

- Technological development
- Research and development
- Trends in global technological advancements
- Associated technologies
- Legislations in technological fields
- Patents
- Licensing
- Access into the technological field
- Consumer preferences
- Consumer buying trends
- Intellectual property and its laws
- How mature a certain technology is
- Information technology
- Communication
- Innovation

(5) Legal factors:

- Employment law
- Consumer protection
- Industry-specific regulations
- Competitive regulations
- Current legislation
- Future legislation
- Regulatory bodies and their processes

- Environmental regulations
- Discrimination laws
- Health and safety laws
- Copyright and patent laws

(6) Environmental factors:

- Ecological
- Environmental issues
- International
- National
- Stakeholder/ investor values
- Staff attitudes
- Management style
- Environmental regulations
- Customer values
- Market value
- Changes in weather and climate
- Laws regarding pollution and recycling
- Waste management
- Use of green or eco-friendly products and practices

4.3.2　PESTLE Analysis

The PESTLE Analysis is a common approach for examining the general business environment in order to manage the future opportunities and threats from probable changes in the environment (Mullins, 2002) by analyzing the political and legal conditions, economic conditions, social and cultural conditions, technological conditions and environment related issues. In the following we will execute a PESTLE Analysis on the e-commerce sector of the Chinese market.

Example 1: A PESTLE analysis on Chinese market (E-commerce sector)

Political and legal analysis

Political factors include government regulations and legal issues and define both formal and informal rules under which a firm must operate. And it is claimed that the political force is probably the most turbulent force in the environment (Fahey & Narayanan, 1986). In the past one decade, the Chinese government attaches great importance and focus to the development of e-commerce in the most populous country, for example, on issuing the Summaries of the Middle/Long Term Science and Technology Development Plans of China and the Development of Information Industry Plans in the Eleventh Five-year and Long Plan in 2020 Years in the Ministry of Information Industry, the "application of e-commerce platform technology" has been listed as a key point (Li, 2010, p.260).

In term of the legal system, the Chinese legal framework for e-commerce is still in its nascent stage and has already experienced several problems. China has limited experience with drafting e-commerce legislation for issues such as transactional security, intellectual property rights protection and tax. And regulations supporting areas critical to the development of e-commerce such as the privacy, consumer rights, and validation of electronic contracts and recognition of digital signatures have yet to be written (Kariyawasam, 2011, p.270). But the legal system of China does develop quickly to meet the needs of the e-commerce.

Economic analysis

Any development in the economic part of a country's environment could have significant impacts on the SMEs and their activities. These factors include the total GNP trend, GDP per head, inflation rate, exchange rate, energy and raw materials availability and cost, employment level, interest rate, monetary and fiscal policies, banking policies an investment and so on (Analoui & Karami, 2003, p.75).

Some economists have argued that China's economic growth rates are actually much lower than reported by the National Bureau of Statistics. However, in the context of rural and regional development it is more important that the relative contribution of agriculture to China's GDP has declined significantly. China is clearly moving from an agricultural society to an industry and services based society—even in many rural areas.

Social and cultural analysis

To understand the social and cultural environment involves close analysis of the society. Demographic changes such as population growth, movements and age distribution will be important, as will changes in cultural values and social trends such as family size and social behaviors (Dransfield, 2005, p.60). Such factors could include: consumer lifestyles, environmental issues, demographic issues, education, immigration/emigration and religion.

With the rapid economic growth, there are growing people having Internet access and use the Internet to do shopping. Many people have called themselves the Taobaoer by spending much of their monthly expenditure on Taobao, the largest B2C e-commerce website. In 2010, China's online shopping industry had a turnover of $80bn, and grew 87% year-on-year. China's 420 million Internet users spend around a billion hours each day online and last year, 185 million made at least one online purchase. According to Boston Consulting Group, the volume is expected to increase fourfold by 2015. And e-commerce has already been changing the way Chinese consumers think about shopping: online, it is more social than a hard sell. It's a new engaging experience to savour (bbc.co.uk, 2011). But like many other physical shopping, cheating and fake products are common in the online shops though the most populous shops tend to sell quality and price competitive products to the customers or will state clearly the possible quality problems of the products in the introduction of the products in the pages. And also according to Patricia Ordóñez de Pablos and Miltiadis D. Lytras (2009, p.406), in Chinese business there is often a need and expectation for face to face contact to exist in order to build up a sense of trust which is related to the Hofstede's notion of individualism—collectivism in which the Chinese culture is considered as having a high collective scores (Hofstede, 1997).

Technological analysis

Technological factors include areas such as new products being developed, new purchasing mechanisms (intranet, extranet), new production technology, new distribution mechanisms (the Internet) and new methods of working (e.g. mobile telecommunications) (Botten, 2009, p.39). One technological problem that hinder the development of the Chinese B2C industry is the lack of a stable and secure online payment systems and this problem is further strengthened by the Chinese consumers' preference for high Uncertainty Avoidance Index (UAI) and high Long-Term Orientation (LTO) (Hofstede, 1997). What is more, based on the perspective of Ortolani (2005), there had been only 1 percent credit card penetration in China suggesting that the most widely used payment method had low acceptance in China and the payment system to support online credit card transaction is also facing low usage. And the lack of safe online credit card payment system is one of the key reasons behind this low usage and penetration.

Environmental analysis

Environmental factors refer to all the factors directly related, influenced or determined by the surrounding environment. This includes, but is not limited to weather, climate, geographical position, climate change and even insurance (Heldman, 2011). Despite the fact that the environmental protection work is still low in China because the majority of focus and priority had been attributed to the alleviation of poverty and economic development which result in the low public participation in the environmental protection work, in the recent years, with the substantial economic advancement and raised living standard, income level and also the degradation of environment in the country, the Chinese government has started educate the public about the environmental protection. And with a joint effort from the non-governmental organizations (NGOs) and media such as newspapers, radio and TV, we are witnessing an increasing environmental awareness in the public resulting in changes in the consumer behaviors to put environment protection in a higher importance level (Heggelund, 2004, p.157).

Conclusion

As proposed by Bjorn Moller (2010, p.6), with the help of the PESTLE, companies would have the possibility to understand the external macro-environment in which they operate and might operate in the future. Here based on the analysis we have above, we are able to draw some conclusions. Firstly, very stable political conditions and rapid economic growth has made the e-commerce industry in China attractive to investors and the increasing awareness of environment protection also promote the way of e-commerce as it creates less pollution and damage to the environment; secondly, there are also risks such as lack of trust, stable and secured online payment systems and lack of legal protection that create challenges and uncertainties to the players in the industry.

Example 2: The PESTLE analysis of Lenovo

In the society with a fast economic development, it's getting very competitive in the market, if a company wants to exist and develop, a good strategic plan is very important to help the company win in the competitive marketing. But how to make a good strategic planning for a company? PESTLE analysis is very helpful for analyzing the external environment of a business. The following will explain what PESTLE analysis is and focus on analyzing the Lenovo Corporation's external environment which likely influences their business environment to be faced in the next five to ten years.

As is known, the six letters stand for six words. The letter "P" stands for political factor which contains freedom of press, rule of law and level of bureaucracy, regulation and de-regulation trends and tax policy, trade and tariff controls. The letter "E" stands for economic factor which is about current and project economic growth, inflation and interest rates, labour supply, labour cost and levels of disposable income and impact of globalization. "S" stands for social culture, which contains population growth rate and age profile, population health, education and social mobility and attitudes, lifestyle choice and attitudes, job marketing freedom and attitudes to work. "T" stands for technological factor which is about impact of energy technologies, interest, reduction in communications costs and increased remote working, research and development activities and impact of technology transfer. The letter "L" stands for legal factor and it means legal structure in private and public sector, firms' legal structure and joint ventures. "E" stands for ethical factor and it means how the ethical standards of the environment will affect the business and how the organization will be affected by current or planed changes to environment standards (Chris B. & Lan W., 2003).

In 1984, Liu Chuanzhi and ten scientists who worked in Chinese Academy of Science, built the Legend Company and in 2004 Legend changed their name to Lenovo. In 2005, they finished purchase IBM. Then the head office was set in America and they have branch offices in 66 countries and conduct business scope in 166 countries (Lenovo, 2005). So as a global corporation, making clear the external environment is very important to help make the strategic planning, and the following will focus on Lenovo's PESTLE analysis.

For the political, from the last century, computers come into people's life, it was used in business and other industries and helps the industries increase the production and interest. But at the same time, some new problems come with computers such as energy consumption, health and pollution of the environment. Considering these problems, in China, the government encourage the green IT that means lower noise pollution and lower energy consumption. So in Lenovo groups, the isopsophic index of "Kai Tian S" (a brand of Lenovo) was lower than 30 dB. In noise pollution section, Lenovo meets the standards (Lenovo, 2005). Since China joined WTO, the export tariff of IT industry has decrease to 9.1% in 2005 (Global M&A Research Center, 2006). So some policies concerned tend to encourage business organizations like Lenovo to develop globally.

For economic, influenced by the 2008 economic crisis, the world economy tends to go down. But in the worst time, Chinese government published the new economic policy which was positive financial policy and loose and comfortable monetary policy. The government also offered four-hundred million RMB stimulates economic development (The Marketing Surveillance Center of China, 2008). For China's IT industry, this is a great opportunity to develop. In 1950, the total trades of China include import and export was 11.3 hundred million dollars, but in 2008, it enhanced 25,616 hundred million dollars. Also at home, the GDP increased with a high speed. China's GDP has achieved satisfactory level and the disposable personal income has increased too. So the demand of products will increase with the economic enhancing. In the other words, the IT market becomes bigger and Lenovo also has strength to compete the market share because Lenovo not only produces computers but also other products, like mobile phones.

For social culture, the population growth, lifestyle choice and attitudes, population health, education, social mobility and attitudes all influence the demand of high technology products. 60 years ago, 80% people in China were illiteracy, but nowadays it is clearly that the education level has increased and the demand of high technology products is also enhancing. This situation offers a huge market for Lenovo. On the other hand, because the globalization and influenced by the developed countries' lifestyle, the Chinese people also become more international which live with a high level life and influenced by the education level, the lifestyle of Chinese people become more out-going and open enough. So the consumption custom of modern Chinese people offers a good developing environment to Lenovo. In the next five to ten years, this situation will be increased. At the same time, the social culture of China has changed from traditional feudalism to modern lifestyle which has more science and high technology in life.

For technological, Lenovo was set by 11 scientists who worked in Chinese Academy of Science which is a governmental organization. So this situation offered a good technology support. In 2005, Lenovo has finished the purchase IBM, the technology transfer from IBM also helps Lenovo make the Research & Development activities and produce high quality products with high technology (Lenovo, 2005). At the same time, with the technology development, the communications costs and increased remote work can help the different corporations share their techniques. So all of these technological factors can help Lenovo increase their competitive ability.

For the legal section, here two articles are mentioned ,which can support Lenovo. Firstly, in light of article 6, People's Republic of China Consumer Protection, the government encourages and supports every person and organization supervise the illegal action which damages the consumers' legal power (National People's Congress, 1993). So this law can reduce other organizations use illegal method to compete in the marketing and it's also a protection for Lenovo. On the other hand, in light of article 6, *People's Republic of China Law on Product Quality*, the government encourages to apply scientific management method, advanced science and technology to support the products achieved or beyond the industry standard or international standard, and give the award to the organizations whose products achieved or beyond the international standard (National People's Congress, 1993). So as an international corporation, Lenovo links the technology of IBM, they will produce the high quality products and receive the government supports from the legal.

Finally, for the ethical, because of the increased education level, the people's diathesis also enhanced. Protecting the legal power has become normal in the modern society. Then if the organization make illegal actions, it will be ejected from the market by customers, such as never buy their products. Also for an organization, the ethical problems are faith, fair and good service. As Lenovo, their values are serve consumers, innovation, faith and fair (Lenovo, 2005), so this entire ethical development tendency is good for Lenovo's business environment in the next five to ten years.

In conclusion, the policies about green IT from Chinese government are good for Lenovo's improvement; at the same time, the economic development of China and the increased disposable personal income also offer a big market to Lenovo's development in the future; in the modern society, the population of the world has achieved 67-hundred million in 2007 (Unctad Report, 2008). It offers a huge number of customers; also because the education increases, the modern lifestyle tends to make customers to use high technology and high quality products. On the other hand, the purchase of IBM also offers the technology transfer and the development mechanics of communication saved the communications costs and it's good for international Research & Development activities and international cooperation. So based on the above analysis, in the next five to ten years, the likely major influences in Lenovo's business environment are environment protection, international cooperation, the economic development, technology communication and Research & Development, legal protection and ethical problems. But all of these tend to be good for Lenovo in the future. So if the strategy department managers base on the external environment to make the strategic planning, Lenovo will take a great leap for their business in the following five to ten years.

Example 3: PESTLE analysis on Coca-Cola

As we all know, the Coca-Cola is today's one of the biggest corporation that offers different refreshment in form of a soft-drink. These carbonated drinks are consumed at the rate of more than one billion drinks per day. But aside from their historical success, the Coca-Cola Company is still a typical business that is affected and at the same time affecting the different type of communities.

Political

Political analysis examines the current and potential influences from political pressures. The non-alcoholic beverages falls in the category under the FDA and the government plays a role within the operation of manufacturing these products. In terms of regulations, the government has the power to set potential fines for the companies that did not meet their standard law requirement.

The changes in laws and regulations, such as accounting standards, taxation requirements and environmental laws and foreign jurisdictions might affect the book of the company as well as their entry in foreign country. Other than that, the changes in the nature of business as non-alcoholic beverages can gain competitive product and pricing pressures and the ability to improve or maintain the share in sales in global market as a result of action by competitors.

The political conditions of the country are also basis of the study, especially in internal markets and other government changes that affects their ability to penetrate the developing and emerging markets that involves the political and economic conditions. However, Coca-Cola continuously monitoring the policies and regulations set by the government.

Economical

Economic analysis examines the local, national and world economy impact which is also includes the issue of recession and inflation rates. The non-alcoholic beverage industry has high sales in countries outside the U.S. According to the Standard and Poor's industry surveys, "For major soft-drink companies, there has been economic improvement in many major international markets such as Japan , Brazil, and Germany." These markets will continue to play a major role in the success and stable growth for a majority of the non-alcoholic beverages industry. There is a low growth in the market for carbonated drinks, especially in Coca-Cola's main market, North America. The market growth recorded at only 1% in 2004 for North America.

Social

This analyzes the ways in which changes in society affect the organization such as changing in lifestyles and attitudes of the market. Consumers from the ages of 37 to 55 are also increasingly concerned with nutrition. There is a large population of the age range known as the baby boomers. Since many are reaching an older age in life they are becoming more concerned with increasing their longevity. This will continue to affect the non-alcoholic beverages industry by increasing the demand for carbonated drinks decreased and this pulled down the revenues of Coca-Cola.

Technological

Technology is the main focus of the analysis where the introduction and the emerging technological techniques are valued. This creates opportunities for new products and product improvements in terms of marketing and production. As the technology advances, new products are introduced into the market. The advancement in technology has led to the creation of cherry coke in 1985 but consumers still prefers traditional taste of the original coke.

Legal

Legal aspect focuses on the effect of the national and world legislation. The Coca-Cola Company receives all the rights applicable in the nature of their business and every inventions and product developments are always going into the patented process.

Environmental

Environment Analysis examines the local, national and world environment issues. According to the data of the Coca-Cola Company, all of the facilities are strictly monitored according to the environmental laws imposed by the government.

Summary

With the intensive study of the PESTEL, the company will continue to emerge and develop if they manage to find solutions in different challenges that the entire organization might face.

Exercises

1. What is business environment?
2. What does PESTLE analysis stand for?
3. Why does a business need to undertake its macro-environment analysis? How?
4. What is the economic factor while giving a business pestle analysis?
5. To use SWOT analysis model to evaluate a business' external influential factors.

Glossary

Mindset: A habitual or characteristic mental attitude that determines how you will interpret and respond to situations 心态；倾向；习惯

Demographics: The quantifiable statistics of a given population. Demographics is also used to identify the study of quantifiable subsets within a given population which characterize that population at a specific point in time. 人口统计资料

Capability: The ability or the qualities that are necessary to do something 能力；性能

Legislation: The act of making or enacting laws; law enacted by a legislative body 立法；法律

Receptivity: Willingness or readiness to receive (especially impressions or ideas) 接受能力

Framework: A structure supporting or containing something 框架；结构

Utilize: Put into service; make work or employ (something) for a particular purpose or for its inherent or natural purpose 利用

Consolidate: Strengthen; unite into one 巩固；联合

Beneficial: Promoting or enhancing well-being 有益的，有利的

Defuse: Remove a dangerous or tense situation 平息；使除去危险性

Eradicate: Destroy completely, as if down to the roots 根除，根绝；消灭

Lobbying: The act of attempting to influence decisions made by officials in the government, most often legislators or members of regulatory agencies. Lobbying is done by many different types of people and organized groups, including individuals in the private sector, corporations, fellow legislators or government officials, or advocacy groups (interest groups) 游说

Regulatory body: Management , administration section 监察机构；管理部门

Chapter 5 Market Forces

Introduction

Market forces describe the interaction between supply and demand within a market. An organization's response to market forces is a key in any circumstance as it will have a direct impact on the company's profits and reputation. In terms of supply and demand the most successful companies will have appropriate market research and analysis in place to ensure that they are able to supply a product or service to meet the demands of its customers. If a company has judged the market demand for their product correctly then they will keep their customers happy by ensuring they supply the product or service requested by their customers in the appropriate quantities. It will also increase profits as the company will have judged their margins correctly to be able to supply and sell as much of their product as possible, without over stocking, bringing added finances to the business. Poor judgment could lead to a misinterpretation of market forces, either leaving customers empty handed as not enough product has been supplied, or leave their business overstocked as customers do not want the quantities supplied. In both scenarios a company's profits would be greatly affected, and the organization's reputation may be tarnished. The relationship between market forces and organization response is therefore paramount in terms of business success and customer satisfaction. It is important to continue in monitoring market forces to ensure that an organization can respond to any changes in market conditions. More or less product may be needed to match customer demand during different market seasons.

The objectives of this chapter:

(1) Market demand and supply

(2) The Factors affecting market demand and supply

(3) Cost and price

(4) Competitive advantage of businesses

5.1 Market Demand and Supply

Supply and demand is perhaps one of the most fundamental concepts of economics and it is the backbone of a market economy. Demand refers to how much (quantity) of a product or service is desired by buyers. The quantity demanded is the amount of a product people are willing to buy at a certain price; the relationship between price and quantity demanded is known as the demand relationship. Supply represents how much the market can offer. The quantity supplied refers to the amount of a certain good producers are willing to supply when receiving a certain price. The correlation between price and how much of a good or service is supplied to the market is known as the supply relationship. Price, therefore, is a reflection of supply and demand.

The relationship between demand and supply underlie the forces behind the allocation of resources. In market economy theories, demand and supply theory will allocate resources in the most efficient way possible. How? Let us take a closer look at the law of demand and the law of supply.

The Law of Demand

The law of demand states that, if all other factors remain equal, the higher the price of a good, the less people will demand that good. In other words, the higher the price, the lower the quantity demanded. The amount of a good that buyers purchase at a higher price is less because as the price of a good goes up, so does the opportunity cost of buying that good. As a result, people will naturally avoid buying a product that will force them to forgo the consumption of something else they value more.

The Law of Supply

Like the law of demand, the law of supply demonstrates the quantities that will be sold at a certain price. But unlike the law of demand, the supply relationship shows an upward slope. This means that the higher the price, the higher the quantity supplied. Producers supply more at a higher price because selling a higher quantity at a higher price increases revenue.

Time and Supply

Unlike the demand relationship, however, the supply relationship is a factor of time. Time is important to supply because suppliers must, but cannot always, react quickly to a change in demand or price. So it is important to try and determine whether a price change that is caused by demand will be temporary or permanent.

Let's say there's a sudden increase in the demand and price for umbrellas in an unexpected rainy season; suppliers may simply accommodate demand by using their production equipment more intensively. If, however, there is a climate change, and the population will need umbrellas year-round, the change in demand and price will be expected to be long-term; suppliers will have to change their equipment and production facilities in order to meet the long-term levels of demand.

Supply and Demand Relationship

Now that we know the laws of supply and demand, let's turn to an example to show how supply and demand affect price.

Imagine that a special edition CD of your favourite band is released for $20. Because the record company's previous analysis showed that consumers will not demand CDs at a price higher than $20, only ten CDs were released because the opportunity cost is too high for suppliers to produce more. If, however, the ten CDs are demanded by 20 people, the price will subsequently rise because, according to the demand relationship, as demand increases, so does the price. Consequently, the rise in price should prompt more CDs to be supplied as the supply relationship shows that the higher the price, the higher the quantity supplied.

If, however, there are 30 CDs produced and demand is still at 20, the price will not be pushed up because the supply more than accommodates demand. In fact after the 20 consumers have been satisfied with their CD purchases, the price of the leftover CDs may drop as CD producers attempt to sell the remaining ten CDs. The lower price will then make the CD more available to people who had previously decided that the opportunity cost of buying the CD at $20 was too high.

Equilibrium

When supply and demand are equal (i.e. when the supply function and demand function intersect) the economy is said to be at equilibrium. At this point, the allocation of goods is at its most efficient because the amount of goods being supplied is exactly the same as the amount of goods being demanded. Thus, everyone (individuals, firms, or countries) is satisfied with the current economic condition. At the given price, suppliers are selling all the goods that they have produced and consumers are getting all the goods that they are demanding.

In the real market place equilibrium can only ever be reached in theory, so the prices of goods and services are constantly changing in relation to fluctuations in demand and supply.

Disequilibrium

Disequilibrium occurs whenever the price or quantity is not equal to P^* or Q^*.

(1) Excess Supply

If the price is set too high, excess supply will be created within the economy and there will be allocated inefficiency.

The suppliers are trying to produce more goods, which they hope to sell to increase profits, but those consuming the goods will find the product less attractive and purchase less because the price is too high.

(2) Excess Demand

Excess demand is created when price is set below the equilibrium price. Because the price is so low, too many consumers want the good while producers are not making enough of it.

Shifts vs. Movement

For economics, the "movements" and "shifts" in relation to the supply and demand curves represent very different market phenomena:

(1) Movements

A movement refers to a change along a curve. On the demand curve, a movement denotes a change in both price and quantity demanded from one point to another on the curve. The movement implies that the demand relationship remains consistent. Therefore, a movement along the demand curve will occur when the price of the good changes and the quantity demanded changes in accordance to the original demand relationship. In other words, a movement occurs when a change in the quantity demanded is caused only by a change in price, and vice versa.

(2) Shifts

A shift in a demand or supply curve occurs when a good's quantity demanded or supplied changes even though price remains the same.

5.2 Factors Affecting Market Demand and Supply

Supply chain managers should have a clear understanding of the different factors that can influence supply and demand. Managers should be able to capitalise on increased demand and look for cost savings and opportunities provided by increased supply. Failing to understand supply and demand will make it difficult to anticipate and manage supply shortages and may increase the negative impact of a reduction in demand.

Supply is the amount of a product that suppliers would like to produce at a given price. It can be negatively affected by factors totally outside of the control of organizations further down the supply chain. For example, a factory that supplies raw materials to a manufacturing plant is badly damaged in a fire and is unable to operate for two weeks. The manufacturing firm that relies totally on their supplier has no contingency plan in place and as a result, they have to close for two weeks. As a manager at a retail store, you run out of products to sell, are unable to replenish your inventory and your sales are badly affected.

This example highlights the risks of total reliance on a single supplier. Ideally, managers should aim to source products from more than one supplier to reduce their risk, or alternatively, they should have an agreement with a backup supplier in case of emergencies.

There are also factors that can negatively affect the demand for an organizations products and services. An example of this would be a downturn in economic conditions. Customers have less money to spend, resulting in them purchasing less and impacting on demand for products and services. As supply chains become more global, variable economic conditions continue to have a greater impact on the effective management of supply chains. It can often be difficult to address factors resulting in reduced demand, however, you can use marketing, competitive pricing and product diversification to maximize your profit-making potential during difficult times.

Demand can be impacted by either independent or dependent factors. Independent demand is the demand for a primary product, for example a car. Dependant demand is the demand for a secondary product related to the primary product, for example car tyres. The demand for the secondary product is dependent on the demand for the primary product.

During periods of increased demand, it is vital that managers are able to work towards maximizing the profit earning potential of their organization. Demand may be increased due to favourable economic conditions, seasonal changes or emerging and popular trends. Positive changes in supply can be caused by new suppliers entering the market, beneficial environmental factors or even through changes in government policy. An increase in supply should provide managers with an opportunity to reduce costs through new agreements and seek opportunities with new suppliers.

Some main determinants of market supply:

- The price obtainable for the product
- The price of other products
- Costs of production
- Profitability of alternative products (substitutes in supply)

- Profitability of goods in joint supply
- Nature and other random shocks
- Aims of producers
- Expectations of producers
- Changes in technology

Activity: Think of a specific example of products whose supply has been affected by the weather, a natural disaster or a strike.

Some main determinants of market demand:

Demand is the willingness and ability of a consumer to purchase a good under the certain circumstances; Price of the products will affect demand, and any circumstance that affects the consumer's willingness or ability to buy the good or service can be a non-price determinant of demand. As an example, weather could be a factor in the demand for beer at a baseball game. Therefore, non-price determinants of demand are those things that will cause demand to change even if prices remain the same—in other words, the things whose changes might cause a consumer to buy more or less of goods even if the goods' own price remained unchanged. Non-price determinants of demand include:

- Prices of related goods (both substitutes and complements)
- Disposable income
- Population size and composition
- Expectations of customers
- Changes in tastes and preferences
- Advertising and other social factors

Most products have alternatives which are known as substitute products, and increase in demand for one of them should result in a decrease in demand for another, e.g.:

tea and coffee / car travel & rail travel

Coca-Cola & Pepsi-Cola / plays & films

Complementary products: Goods tend to be bought and used together, e.g. cups and saucers/ bread & butter. And, the increase in demand for any one of substitute products should result in a decrease in demand for another, but for its complementary products goes up or falls?

Relationship between supply and price: In the other conditions remain unchanged, a rise in commodity prices, supply will increase; prices fall, supply will be reduced, that is, supply and other commodity prices into changes in the same direction.

- As price rises, firms supply more.
- It is worth incurring the extra unit costs.
- Firms switch from less profitable goods.
- In the long run, new firms will be encouraged to enter the market.

Relationship between demand and price:

What will a fall in demand for a good result in? Which of the followings is right?

- A rise in the price of the good and a fall in the price of factors used to make it.
- A rise in the price of the good and a rise in the price of factors used to make it.
- A fall in the price of the good and a fall in the price of factors used to make it.
- A fall in the price of the good and a rise in the price of factors used to make it.

5.3 Cost and Price

Price refers to the amount of money that consumers have to give up to acquire goods or service. Cost refers to the amount paid to produce goods or service. The cost represents the sum of the value of the inputs in production—land, labour, capital and enterprise. Production is carried out by firms using the factors of production .The cost of production is the cost of the factors employed. A cost incurred by a business when manufacturing a good or producing a service. Production costs combine raw material and labour. To figure out the cost of production per unit, the cost of production is divided by the number of units produced. A company that knows how much it will cost to produce an item, or produce a service, will have a clearer picture of how to better price the item or service and what will be the total cost to the company. Let's take a bar of chocolate for example to see how the price is charged.If the price for a chocolate bar we pay is £1.30. Then what is the price of this chocolate bar is made up of? It will involve raw materials, capital, labor and profit.

The raw materials will include the cocoa, sugar, milk, honey, flavoring and color that are used to make the chocolate bar.

The capital will include all the buildings and factories that make up the business, the machinery, equipment used in the manufacture of the bar as well as all the vehicles and so on involved in the distribution of the finished product and the offices and administration buildings that support the business.

Labor includes not only those who are involved directly in the making of the bars but all the sales staff, administration staff, management, marketing teams and so on that are employed by the business.

The profit is the reward for enterprise. It is the amount left over when all the costs have been paid. The profit is equal to total revenue minus total cost of any level of output.

"If a business increases the cost, the profits will rise. "

"If the business wants to increase its profits, it could increase its costs and hope to sell more."

Which one do you agree? Why?

Now let's have a detailed look at costs of production.

Production is carried out by firms using the factors of production which must be paid for their use. The costs of production are the costs of the factors used.

Fixed and variable costs

Fixed costs are those that do not vary with output and typically include rents, insurance, depreciation, set-up costs, and normal profit. They are also called *overheads*.

Variable costs are costs that do vary with output, and they are also called *direct costs*. Examples of typical variable costs include fuel, raw materials, and some labour costs.

Plotting this gives us total cost, total variable cost, and total fixed cost.

Total costs

The total cost (TC) is found by adding total fixed and total variable costs. Its position reflects the amount of fixed costs, and its gradient reflects variable costs.

Average fixed costs

Average fixed costs are found by dividing total fixed costs by output. As fixed cost is divided by an increasing output, average fixed costs will continue to fall.

Average variable costs

Average variable costs are found by dividing total fixed variable costs by output.

Average total cost

Average total cost (ATC) is also called average cost or unit cost. Average total costs are a key cost in the theory of the firm because they indicate how efficiently scarce resources are being used. Average variable costs are found by dividing total fixed variable costs by output.

Areas for total costs

Total fixed costs and total variable costs are the respective areas under the average fixed and average variable cost curves.

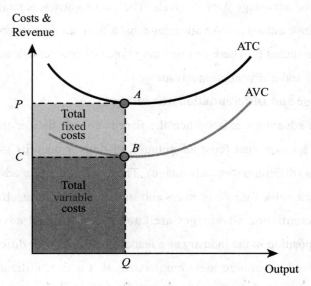

Figure 1-4 Average Fixed and Variable Cost Curves

Marginal costs

Marginal cost is the cost of producing one extra unit of output. It can be found by calculating the change in total cost when output is increased by one unit. It is important to note that marginal cost is derived solely from variable costs, and not fixed costs.

ATC and MC

Average total cost and marginal cost are connected because they are derived from the same basic numerical cost data. The general rules governing the relationship are:

(1) Marginal cost will always cut average total cost from below.

(2) When marginal cost is below average total cost, average total cost will be falling, and when marginal cost is above average total cost, average total cost will be rising.

(3) A firm is most productively efficient at the lowest average total cost, which is also where average total cost (ATC) = marginal cost (MC).

Total costs and marginal costs

Marginal costs are derived exclusively from variable costs, and are unaffected by changes in fixed costs.

5.4 Competitive Advantage of Businesses

When a firm sustains profits that exceed the average for its industry, the firm is said to possess a competitive advantage over its rivals. The goal of business strategy is to achieve a sustainable competitive advantage. An advantage that a firm has over its competitors, allowing it to generate greater benefits. There can be many types of competitive advantages including the firm's advantage and differentiation advantage.

Cost Advantage and Differentiation Advantage

A competitive advantage exists when the firm is able to deliver the same benefits as competitors but at a lower cost (cost advantage), or deliver benefits that exceed those of competing products (differentiation advantage). Thus, a competitive advantage enables the firm to create superior value for its customers and superior profits for itself.

Cost and differentiation advantages are known as positional advantages since they describe the firm's position in the industry as a leader in either cost or differentiation.

A resource-based advantage view emphasizes that a firm utilizes its resources and capabilities to create a competitive advantage that ultimately results in superior value creation.

Resources and Capabilities

According to the resource-based view, in order to develop a competitive advantage the firm must have resources and capabilities that are superior to those of its competitors. Without this superiority, the competitors simply could replicate what the firm was doing and any advantage quickly would disappear.

Competencies

Competencies refer to the firm's ability to utilize its resources effectively. An example of a capability is the ability to bring a product to market faster than competitors. Such capabilities are embedded in the routines of the organization and are not easily documented as procedures and thus are difficult for competitors to replicate.

The firm's resources and capabilities together form its distinctive competencies. These enable innovation, efficiency, quality, and customer, all of which can be leveraged to create a cost advantage or a differentiation advantage.

Competitive advantage is created by using resources and capabilities to achieve either a lower cost structure or a differentiated product. A firm positions itself in its industry through its choice of low cost or differentiation. This decision is a central component of the firm's competitive strategy.

Another important decision is how broad or narrow a market segment to target. Porter formed a matrix using cost advantage, differentiation advantage, and a broad or narrow focus to identify a set of generic strategies that the firm can pursue to create and sustain a competitive advantage.

Value Creation

The firm creates value by performing a series of activities that Porter identified as the value chain. To achieve a competitive advantage, the firm must perform one or more value creating activities in a way that creates more overall value than do competitors. Superior value is created through lower costs or superior benefits to the consumer (differentiation).

Exercises

1. What is the market demand?

2. What's the relationship between demand and price?

3. What are the main factors affecting demand and supply?

4. What are costs of production?

5. What is competitive advantage? How does a business get and maintain its competitive advantage?

Glossary

Market forces: The interaction of supply and demand that shapes a market economy 市场力量

Misinterpretation: Putting the wrong interpretation on 误解；误释

Allocation: The act of distributing by allotting or apportioning; distribution 分配，配置

Equilibrium: Equality of distribution; balance 均衡

Determinant: Something causes it to be of a particular kind or to happen in a particular way 决定因素

Profitability: The quality of affording gain or benefit or profit 赢利能力

Complementary: Acting as or providing a complement (something that completes the whole) 补足的，补充的

Fixed cost: A periodic charge that does not vary with business volume (as insurance or rent or mortgage payments etc.) 固定成本

Variable cost: Cost that varies directly with output 可变成本

Total cost: Fixed costs plus variable costs 总成本

Marginal cost: The increase or decrease in costs as a result of one more or one less unit of output 边际成本

Chapter 6 Market Structure and Competitive Forces

Introduction

In this chapter we will discuss the implication for the firms of different market structures. We also look at the competitive environment of businesses.

Both economists and marketers define market structure, but each defines the term a bit differently. Economists look at the overall market structure with the goal of defining and predicting consumer behavior. Marketing managers seek to define market structure to create competitive strategies as part of an overall marketing plan. In both cases, managers define market structure with the understanding that market structure is fluid. What the market looks like today, and what it looks like tomorrow, may be two completely different pictures. In economics, there are four general market structures.

Monopoly: A monopoly exists when one company only provides services in a particular industry, or one company dominates and consumers cannot substitute anything that comes close.

Oligopoly: An oligopoly consists of only a handful of companies selling similar products. Consumers can substitute products, but only one company's offerings for another.

Monopolistic Competition: It occurs when a large number of firms sell closely related, but not homogenous products.

Perfect Competition: In markets with perfect competition, there are no barriers to entry, and many offering different goods. Consumers often shop on price differences alone.

Some businesses operate in very competitive market structures where there are many businesses competing for customers. At the opposite end of the spectrum some businesses operate in markets where they are the only business and competition is non-existent. Other businesses operate in markets that fall somewhere between these two extremes. In each case, the consequences for businesses and their customers will vary. Anyhow there are different degrees of competition in an industry.

The objectives of this chapter:

(1) To identify four market structures

(2) To understand the differences between different market types

(3) To understand the five basic competitive forces

6.1 Market Types of Market Structure

Economists assume that there are a number of different buyers and sellers in the marketplace. This means that we have competition in the market, which allows price to change in response to changes in supply and demand. Furthermore, for almost every product there are substitutes, so if one product becomes too expensive, a buyer can choose a cheaper substitute instead. In a market with many buyers and sellers, both the consumer and the supplier have equal ability to influence price.

In some industries, there are no substitutes and there is no competition. In a market that has only one or few suppliers of a good or service, the producer(s) can control price, meaning that a consumer does not have choice, cannot maximize his or her total utility and has have very little influence over the price of goods.

In economics, market structure is the number of firms producing identical products which are homogeneous. The elements of market structure include the number and size distribution of firms, entry conditions, and the extent of differentiation. Type of market structure influences how a firm behaves:

(1) Pricing

(2) Supply

(3) Barriers to entry

(4) Efficiency

(5) Competition

Market structure is used to describe:

(1)The numbers of buyers and sellers in a market.

(2) The extent to which the market is concentrated in the hands of a small number of buyers and /or sellers.

(3) The degree of competition between buyers and /or sellers of different market types.

Here four market types are introduced—monopoly, oligopoly, perfect competition, and imperfect competition (monopolistic competition).

A monopoly is a market structure in which there is only one producer or seller for a product. In other words, the single business is the industry. Entry into such a market is restricted due to high costs or other impediments, which may be economic, social or political. For instance, a government can create a monopoly over an industry that it wants to control, such as electricity. Another reason for the barriers against entry into a monopolistic industry is that oftentimes, one entity has the exclusive rights to a natural resource. For example, in Saudi Arabia the government has sole control over the oil industry. A monopoly may also form when a company has a copyright or patent that prevents others from entering the market. Pfizer, for instance, had a patent on Viagra.

In an oligopoly, there are only a few firms that make up an industry. This select group of firms have control over the price like a monopoly, and an oligopoly has high barriers to entry. The products that the oligopolistic firms produce are often nearly identical, therefore, the companies, which are competing for market share, are interdependent as a result of market forces. Assume, for example, that an economy needs only 100 widgets. Company X produces 50 widgets and its competitor, Company Y, produces the other 50. The prices of the two brands will be interdependent, therefore, similar, if Company X starts selling the widgets at a lower price, it will get a greater market share, thereby forcing Company Y to lower its prices as well.

There are two extreme forms of market structure: monopoly and its opposite, perfect competition. Perfect competition is characterized by many buyers and sellers, many products that are similar in nature, as a result, many substitutes. Perfect competition means there are few, if any, barriers to entry for new companies, and prices are determined by supply and demand. Thus, producers in a perfectly competitive market are subject to the prices determined by the market and do not have any leverage. For example, in a perfectly competitive market, should a single firm decide to increase its selling price of goods, the consumers can just turn to the nearest competitor for a better price, causing any firm that increases its prices to lose market share and profits. Wal-Mart may be viewed as a purely competitive company within the grocery industry for its super centers that offer lower prices than competing grocery chains.

Monopoly

Monopoly is a term used by economists to refer to the situation in which there is a single seller of a product (i.e., a good or service) for which there are no close substitutes.

Governmental policy with regard to monopolies (e.g., permitting, prohibiting or regulating them) can have major effects not only on specific businesses and industries but also on the economy and society as a whole. Today, very few industries are monopolies. Utility companies such as water companies or electric companies may be considered monopolies. Consumers can't exactly substitute something else for electricity from the local provider, unless they switch to firewood or candles!

Two Extreme Cases

It can be useful when thinking about monopoly to look at two extreme cases. One is a pure monopoly, in which one company has complete control over the supply or sales of a product for which there are no good substitutes. The other is pure competition or perfect competition, a situation in which there are many sellers of identical, or virtually identical, products.

There are various degrees of monopoly, and rarely does anything approaching pure monopoly exist. Thus, the term is generally used in a relative sense rather than an absolute one. For example, a company can still be considered a monopoly even if it faces competition from (1) a few relatively small scale suppliers of the same or similar product(s) or (2) somewhat different goods or services that can be substituted for the product(s) supplied by the monopolist. A business that produces multiple products can be considered a monopoly even if it has a monopoly with regard to only one of the products.

A company with a product that is just slightly different from other companies' products (e.g., a unique brand of food or clothing) could be considered to have a monopoly for that narrow range of product (assuming that it could not be copied due to protection by a patent, copyright, trademark, etc.). However, it might have very little monopoly power within the broader product category that includes both its and its competitors' products (e.g., food or clothing as a whole). In contrast, a company with exclusive rights to sell a product for which there are few if any good substitutes (e.g., steel or table salt) would have tremendous monopoly power.

For a product characterized by perfect competition (or nearly perfect competition), each supplier or seller must set its price equal to (or very close to) those of its competitors. This equilibrium price tends to be close to the cost of producing the product due to price competition among its many sellers. It is difficult for any seller to charge a higher price than its competitors because it would be easy for buyers to purchase from other sellers instead. It is likewise difficult for a seller to charge a lower price, because profit margins (i.e., revenue minus cost) are already thin.

Naturally, all businesses, regardless of their degree of monopoly power, generally want to be as successful as possible, and thus they attempt to maximize their profits. However, it is much easier for a monopolist to make large profits through profit maximizing behaviour than it is for a firm in a highly competitive industry. The reason is that the former has much greater flexibility in setting prices than does the latter, which has little if any control over prices.

The monopolist has this flexibility because there is little or no direct competition to force the price down close to the cost of production. Of course, the monopolist will be acutely aware of the fact that the higher the price it charges, the smaller will be the number of units sold. This is because at higher prices some purchasers will just decide to buy fewer units or no units at all. A reduction in the number of units sold will eventually occur when the price rises to a sufficiently high level, regardless of how much buyers think they want the product, because buyers are ultimately limited by their incomes and savings.

Assuming (unrealistically, but for the sake of simplification) that a monopolist could only charge a single price for a product, and it would find the unique price that maximizes its profits. Raising the price above that level would reduce profits because the negative effect of the reduction in the number of units sold due to the higher price would more than offset the positive effect from the higher price. This profit maximizing price would generally be substantially higher than the product's cost of production, and it would thus also be substantially higher than the equilibrium price that would exist for the product if it were instead supplied by a number of competitive firms. Likewise, the volume of output and sales would be substantially lower than in a competitive situation.

The monopoly power of a company for a product is commonly thought of in terms of its market share for that product. However, it can also be measured by the ability that a company has to set the price for the product. In fact, this is the measure of monopoly used by some government agencies when studying competition in various industries.

Oligopoly

An oligopoly is a market dominated by a few large suppliers. The degree of market concentration is very high (i.e. a large percent of the market is taken up by the leading firms). Firms within an oligopoly produce branded products (advertising and marketing is an important feature of competition within such markets) and there are also barriers to entry.

Another important characteristic of an oligopoly is interdependence between firms. This means that each firm must take into account the likely reactions of other firms in the market when making pricing and investment decisions. This creates uncertainty in such markets—which economists seek to model through the use of game theory. An example would be the three big American car companies of today: Ford, GM and Chrysler.

Key Features of Oligopoly

- A few firms selling similar products.

- Each firm produces branded products.

- Likely to be significant entry barriers into the market in the long run which allows firms to make supernormal profits.

- Interdependence between competing firms. Businesses have to take into account likely reactions of rivals to any change in price and output.

Theories about Oligopoly Pricing

There are four major theories about oligopoly pricing:

(1) Oligopoly firms collaborate to charge the monopoly price and get monopoly profits.

(2) Oligopoly firms compete on price so that price and profits will be the same as a competitive industry.

(3) Oligopoly price and profits will be between the monopoly and competitive ends of the scale.

(4) Oligopoly prices and profits are "indeterminate" because of the difficulties in modelling interdependent price and output decisions.

Price Leadership in Oligopoly Market

When one firm has a dominant position in the market, the oligopoly may experience price leadership. The firms with lower market shares may simply follow the pricing changes prompted by the dominant firms. We see examples of this with the major mortgage lenders and petrol retailers.

Perfect Competition

The degree to which a market or industry can be described as competitive depends in part on how many suppliers are seeking the demand of consumers and the ease with which new businesses can enter and exit a particular market in the long run.

The spectrum of competition ranges from highly competitive markets where there are many sellers, each of whom has little or no control over the market price—to a situation of pure monopoly where a market or an industry is dominated by one single supplier who enjoys considerable discretion in setting prices, unless subject to some form of direct regulation by the government.

In many sectors of the economy markets are best described by the term oligopoly—where a few producers dominate the majority of the market and the industry is highly concentrated. In a duopoly two firms dominate the market although there may be many smaller players in the industry.

Competitive markets operate on the basis of a number of assumptions. When these assumptions are dropped—we move into the world of imperfect competition. These assumptions are discussed below.

Assumptions behind a Perfectly Competitive Market

(1) Many suppliers each with an insignificant share of the market—this means that each firm is too small relative to the overall market to affect price via a change in its own supply—each individual firm is assumed to be a price taker.

(2) An identical output produced by each firm—in other words, the market supplies homogeneous or standardized products that are perfect substitutes for each other. Consumers perceive the products to be identical.

(3) Consumers have perfect information about the prices all sellers in the market charge—so if some firms decide to charge a price higher than the ruling market price, there will be a large substitution effect away from this firm.

(4) All firms (industry participants and new entrants) are assumed to have equal access to resources (technology, other factor inputs) and improvements in production technologies achieved by one firm can spill-over to all the other suppliers in the market.

(5) There are assumed to be no barriers to entry & exit of firms in long run—which means that the market is open to competition from new suppliers—this affects the long run profits made by each firm in the industry. The long run equilibrium for a perfectly competitive market occurs when the marginal firm makes normal profit only in the long term.

(6) No externalities in production and consumption so that there is no divergence between private and social costs and benefits.

Short Run Price and Output for the Competitive Industry and Firm

In the short run the equilibrium market price is determined by the interaction between market demand and market supply. In the following diagram, price P_1 is the market-clearing price and this price is then taken by each of the firms. Because the market price is constant for each unit sold, the AR curve also becomes the Marginal Revenue curve (MR). A firm maximises profits when marginal revenue = marginal cost. In the diagram below, the profit-maximising output is Q_1. The firm sells Q_1 at price P_1. The area shaded is the economic (supernormal profit) made in the short run because the ruling market price P_1 is greater than average total cost.

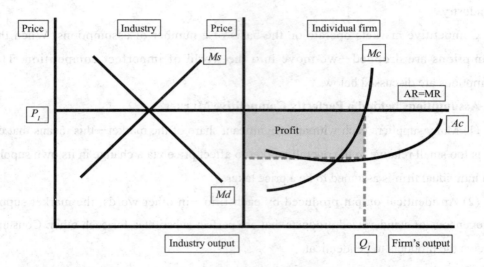

Figure 1-5 Price and Output for the Competitive Industry and Firm

Not all firms make supernormal profits in the short run. Their profits depend on the position of their short run cost curves. Some firms may be experiencing sub-normal profits because their average total costs exceed the current market price. Other firms may be making normal profits where total revenue equals total cost (i.e. they are at the break-even output). In the diagram, the firm shown has high short run costs such that the ruling market price is below the average total cost curve. At the profit maximising level of output, the firm is making an economic loss (or sub-normal profits).

Monopolistic Competition

In monopolistic competition, many sellers sell different products. It's very similar to competition, with the exception that the products themselves are a bit different from one another, so consumers look for those differences rather than price differences. An example is the restaurant industry. Anyone can obtain the proper permits, licenses and open a restaurant offering any cuisine or food in the world. Whether the restaurant is successful or not depends upon whether or not consumers like the food, service, decor, location, and all the other factors that make restaurants successful.

Monopolistic competition resembles perfect competition in three ways:

(1)There are many buyers and sellers.

(2)Entry and exit are easy.

(3)Firms take other firm's prices as given.

The distinction is that products or services are identical under perfect competition while under monopolistic competition they are differentiated, and as a result, a firm can raise its price without losing all its customers. Petrol stations, builders, restaurants, books, shampoos, frozen foods, piano lessons and hairdressers are all examples of monopolistic competition.

The Comparison of the Four Market Structures:

• Monopolistic competition, also called competitive market, where there is a large number of firms, each having a small proportion of the market share and slightly differentiated products.

• Oligopoly, in which a market is run by a small number of firms that together control the majority of the market share.

• Monopoly, where there is only one provider of a product or service. Natural monopoly, a monopoly in which economies of scale cause efficiency to increase continuously with the size of the firm. A firm is a natural monopoly if it is able to serve the entire market demand at a lower cost than any combination of two or more smaller, more specialized firms.

• Perfect competition, a theoretical market structure that features no barriers to entry, an unlimited number of producers and consumers, and a perfectly elastic demand curve.

The imperfectly competitive structure is quite identical to the realistic market conditions where some monopolistic competitors, monopolists, oligopolists, and duopolists exist and dominate the market conditions. These somewhat abstract concerns tend to determine some but not all details of a specific concrete market system where buyers and sellers actually meet and commit to trade. Competition is useful because it reveals actual customer demand and induces the seller (operator) to provide service quality levels and price levels that buyers (customers) want, typically subject to the seller's financial need to cover its costs. In other words, competition can align the seller's interests with the buyer's interests and can cause the seller to reveal his true costs and other private information. In the absence of perfect competition, three basic approaches can be adopted to deal with problems related to the control of market power and an asymmetry between the government and the operator with respect to objectives and information: (a) subjecting the operator to competitive pressures, (b) gathering information on the operator and the market, and (c) applying incentive regulation.

Table 1-2　Quick Reference to Basic Market Structures

Market Structure	Seller Entry Barriers	Seller Number	Buyer Entry Barriers	Buyer Number
Perfect Competition	No	Many	No	Many
Monopolistic Competition	No	Many	No	Many
Oligopoly	Yes	Few	No	Many
Monopoly	Yes	One	No	Many

The correct sequence of the market structure from most to least competitive is perfect competition, imperfect competition, oligopoly, and pure monopoly.

The main criteria by which one can distinguish between different market structures are: the number and size of producers and consumers in the market, the type of goods and services being traded, and the degree to which information can flow freely.

6.2　Competitive Forces of Businesses

There is a fierce competition among different businesses in an industry, and even among different industry competition also exists. The competitive environment consists of five forces: competitive rivalry, power of suppliers, power of buyers, threats of substitutes and threat of new entrants. These are Porter's five forces model, which is an excellent model to analyze a particular industry. It looks at the five main factors that affect a particular industry. It is useful to find out about these factors before you enter an industry or if you are wondering why your business industry is not doing well.

Competitive Rivalry

Competitive rivalry is a good starting point of analyzing a particular industry. If entry to an industry is easy then competitive rivalry is likely to be high. If it is easy for customers to move to substitute products for example from coke to water then again rivalry will be high. Generally competitive rivalry will be high if:

- There is little differentiation between the products sold by competitors.

- Competitors are approximately the same size of each other.
- If competitors have similar strategies.
- It is costly to leave the industrys (exit barriers)

Power of Suppliers

Suppliers are also essential for the success of an organization as they provide businesses with the resources they need to produce their products and services. Supplier power can come from:

- If there is one or just a few suppliers that can provide the resources a business needs.
- If it is expensive to move from one supplier to anothers (known also as switching cost).
- If there is no other substitute for the product provided by the supplier.

Power of Buyers

Buyers or customers can exert influence and control over an industry in certain circumstances. This happens when:

- There is little differentiation over the product and substitutes can be found easily by customers/buyers.
- Buyers/customers are sensitive to price fluctuations.
- Switching to another product is not costly for customers/buyers.

Threat of Substitutes

Are there alternative products that customers can purchase instead of yours? Alternative products that offer the same benefit as your products? The threat from substitute (competitor) products is high when:

- The price of the substitute (competitor) product falls.
- It is easy for consumers to switch from one substitute product to another.
- Buyers are willing to substitute products from different competitors.

Threat of New Entrants

The threat of new organizations entering the industry is high when it is easy for an organization to enter the industry, e.g. entry barriers are low. When a new business is deciding whether to enter an industry it will look at:

- How loyal customers are to existing products?
- How quickly it can achieve economy of scales?
- Would it have access to suppliers?
- Would government legislation prevent them or encourage them to enter the industry?

Summary

Porter's five forces model is an essential analysis tool if you want to understand an industry. All five of Porter's forces affect the strength of an industry and the prices that an industry can charge.

Example: Competitive analysis of Chinese e-commerce industry with Porter's five forces model (1980)

Around 1980, Michael Porter (1985) introduced his highly influential concepts of the five forces model and the value chain and the five forces model according to him could determinate an industry's attractiveness by looking into five external forces:

1. Competitive rivalry within an industry

2. Bargaining power of suppliers

3. Bargaining power of customers

4. Threat of new entrants

5. Threat of substitute products

The five forces are also the five key players in most business markets. The interaction and bargaining between these five forces are believed to be critical and of great importance to the determination of the competitive extent of an industry or market. Below we will implement a competitive analysis using the Porter's five forces model (1980) to see how intense the competition would be in the Chinese B2C market.

Competitive rivalry within an industry—medium level

Competitive rivalry among the existing firms in an industry is the extent to which firms respond to competitive moves of other incumbent firms (Stahl & Grigsby, 1997, p.147). Various data and new reports suggest that with the further spread of Internet applications, B2C and other e-commerce model are in the booming in these few years in term of a dramatic growth. Based on the analysis think tank that recently released, "the third quarter of 2011, China's B2C market quarterly monitoring" data demonstrating that during the third quarter of 2011, the Chinese B2C market transactions grew by 137%. Strong demand results in even stronger supply growth, based on the CNZZ data which suggested that during the calendar year of 2010 the number of B2C website grew in a surprising speed from 10,100 in early of December to 1.18 million, the growth rate of 20.45%, a growth rate that exceeds the overall industry growth speed of the e-commerce. What is more the CNZZ June data also shows that, B2C industry, the total number of sites had totaled 12,200 and still with a more than 200 per month rate of growth (IXWebhosting, 2011).

Another factor that increases the intensity of the internal competition in the B2C industry is the existence of the large B2C websites such as the largest Taobao Mall, QQ Mall, Jingdong, Amazon and Dangdang. For example, so far in 2011, many of the existing B2C websites have already raise campaign to compete with each other. The first moves of the QQ Mall launched the "million marketing resources in the run", commitment to the business community to provide "an efficient, high quality, low-cost e-commerce platform", and only pay 20,000 *yuan* deposit costs, eliminating fees for technical services. Dangdang is committed to continue to maintain the industry platform for business charges a lower level, such as business management platform to maintain about $500 per month, the same proportion of sales commissions, etc. Just on the line items together near grand network is launched at one go 12 incentives, including fee-free three-year technical services (5888 *yuan* per year), donated 50,000 *yuan* platform advertising resources (nikedeluxe.com, 2011).

But still two factors contribute to the medium level of rivalry within the exiting companies in the B2C market in China rather than a seeming high level of competition: the first factor is the ongoing increase of the B2C market size. According to iResearch's data, each segment of China online shopping market has the growth of different level and the fastest growth rate belongs to the B2C sector (including tmall.com and shop.qq.com) which has a growth rate of 19.5% (iresearchchina.com, 2011). With an enlarging market size, it is expected that many B2C companies will focus on getting the attention of the new customers rather than gaining the competitors' share by intense marketing efforts which means that the direct fierce competition among the existing players will be lowered to some extent; the second factor contributing to the medium level of rivalry rather than a high level within the exiting companies in the B2C market in China is the differentiation of the B2C business model. In a growth stage of the B2C industry, we can see that there are different models of B2C such as the raise of the D2C (designer to customer) model. When this sub-market appears, differentiation will help avoid direct price competition because product are marketed and positioned differently.

Bargaining Power of Suppliers—Low

The bargaining power of the suppliers can be shown in their ability to charge a high price in the supply demand relationship with the B2C companies. Based on the perspective of Robert P. Greenwood (2002, p. 128) since the suppliers wish to charge the highest prices for their products, a power struggle arises between organizations and their suppliers, the advantage accruing to the side which has more choices or less lose if the relationship ends. To the B2C market in China, the supplier bargaining power is in a low level for the following three reasons. First of all, the input contributed by the suppliers is not indefensible to the B2C platforms. Most people who go to the B2C website are looking for products with similar functions and they probably would not name a specific brand which means the input offered by the suppliers is not a must to the B2C websites. The second reason is that there is little switching cost for B2C companies to change to other product suppliers since the products are not sold in a physical store, changing the suppliers would in most case equals to the changes of pictures and description in the websites. What is more, the fact that there are usually no substantial warehouses held by the B2C companies actually minimize the switching cost of the B2C companies and hence reduce the bargaining power of the suppliers. Thirdly, the B2C companies are very important customers of the suppliers. Because of the usual large scale of the B2C companies in term of large volume of purchasing such as Taobao Mall, the importance of these B2C companies have at the same time reduced the bargaining power of the suppliers.

Bargaining Power of Customers—Medium

Buyers or customers have a great power if buyers are concentrated and there are few of them or if the product from the organization is not clearly differentiated from the product from other suppliers (Berger, 2010). In the B2C market, the customers are the individual customers who tend to have medium bargaining power for the following four reasons. First of all, the individual customers are scattered in different places and they purchase products online via the B2C website in different times and also they tend to have little communications with each other so that they are in most time alone and thus have little bargaining power with the large B2C websites. Secondly, the units purchased by the individual customers each time tend to be small in volume. As according to my online shopping experience and also some of my friends' experiences, many individual customers go to the Internet time by time when they are looking forward for some products but the each time purchasing volume would not be large in most time because the demand are individual needs rather than group needs. Thirdly, the individual customer could have increased their bargaining power by choosing a different B2C websites since the switching cost would not be high either, the threat of changing to the competing websites will be strengthened by the current trend that the B2C websites are growing in numbers, there would be more choices to the individual customers; fourthly, the individual customer could have increased their bargaining power by using group purchasing which could be traced to China where group buying or team buying was executed to get discount prices from retailer when a large group of people and it has becoming more and more popular in the recent years. And with this trend, many B2C websites have already supported the group purchasing function and it will leverage the power of collective bargaining to provide incredible online deals that offer huge savings for consumers while also promising spectacular sales numbers to participating merchants (Tomuse.com, 2010).

Threat of New Entrants—High

Threat of the new entrants depends for instance on the extent to which entry barriers are present in an industry (e.g. economies of scale, capital requirements, access to distribution channels and so on) (Lebel, Lorek & Daniel, 2010, p.181). The threat of the new entrants in the B2C market in China will be in a high level for the following reasons. First of all, the capital requirements to open a B2C website are relatively low. B2C websites could be in large scale or in a smaller scale depending on the visiting volume of the customers, for example, the investment of a large scale B2C website could begin with a smaller scale one because in the beginning the visitors are small in numbers. And to many companies that have their own products, they could also enter into the B2C market by adding the B2C functions into their official websites. Secondly, many exiting successful C2C website with the current popularity could easily enter into the B2C market using their existing customer base. For example, Taobao has long been China's large C2C website but its growth into the B2C experiences a rapid process. As an independent B2C platform, Taobao Mall (Tmall) on April 10, 2008 on the line, now attracts more than 70,000 brands to enter, the highest single-day turnover reached 936 million *yuan*. Research released in April 2010, top 30 online retailers, B2C rankings, Taobao Mall 30 billion in annual trade among the first in the absolute superiority over the other 29 combined turnover of B2C website. Last year, Taobao Mall occupies nearly 50% of China's B2C market share, Jingdong Mall is ranking second, the market share is 18.1%, Dangdang is only 2.2% (taobaotrading.com, 2011). Thirdly, the distribution channel is not proprietary to the existing players. The distribution channels are the pathways that companies use to sell their products to end-users. Both B2C and B2B companies can sell through a single channel or through multiple channels that may include: direct/sales team, the Internet, value-added reseller and dealers and etc. (marketingmo.com, 2009) And to most B2C websites, the

Internet will be the major distribution channel. What is more the logistic service is also open for all B2C companies and C2C shops.

Threat of Substitute Products—High

Substitute products refer to products in other industries. The threat of substitutes is higher, the stronger the supply of substitute goods affects the price elasticity. If the supply of substitute goods leads to a great change in demand and price of the substituted good, because the customer can switch easily to the other good, the threat form substitutes becomes very high (Mateo, 2010, p. 36). Customers have several other choices when they do not choose to visit the D2C websites. First of all, they could choose to use the C2C platforms in which there could be thousands of online shops operated unofficially by the individual merchants and these merchants could usually provide even cheaper price than the product manufacturers because the manufacturers need to protect the wholesalers' interest and keep the online retail price in a certain level. Secondly, the customers could straightly go to the physical stores and other various retailers to purchase the products rather than buying online through which the customers could only view by pictures and descriptions but cannot touch the product by their hands.

When talking about the choice between narrow market scope or broad market scope, one theory that we must mention is Michael E. Porter's (1985) Generic Competitive Strategies. According to Porter's (1985, p. 11) Generic Competitive Strategies, positioning determines whether a company's profitability is above or below the industry average which is one of the two central questions relating to the company's competitive strategy which is one of the focuses of Porter's studies and researches. Based on his view, there are two main types of competitive advantage as cost advantage and differentiation. In developing and maintaining their competitive advantage, companies have the option to adopt one of the three generic strategies: cost leadership, differentiation or focus. A company pursuing a cost leadership business model chooses strategies that do everything possible to lower its cost structure so that the company can make and sell goods or services at a lower cost than its competitors. These strategies include functional strategies designed to improve its operating performances, and competitive strategies intended to influence industry competition in its favor. Using the cost leadership model, a company will seek to achieve a competitive advantage and above-average profitability by developing a model that positions it on the value creation frontiers as close as possible to the lower costs/lower prices axis (Hill & Jone, 2010, p. 168). The differentiation strategy refers to the provision of exceptional outputs at higher prices to broadly based buyers. The outputs of the differentiation strategy are meant to be distinguishable from the outputs of the competitors. Both the low cost strategy and the differentiation strategy have a broad approach to the market (Wright, Nazemzadeh, Parnell & Lado, 1991). In comparison, focus strategy means concentrating on a particular group of customers, geographic markets or on particular product-line segments in order to serve a well-defined but narrow market better than competitors who serve a broader market (publishyourarticles.org, 2010).

The horizontal axis across the top of the graph shows the type of competitive advantage the company has, whilst the vertical axis relates to the scope of the competition, either broad and company-wide or narrow and limited to a market segment (lmcuk.com, 2009). In his famous book, *Competitive Advantage*, the author Michael E. Porter (1985, p. 12) pointed out, "each of the generic strategies involves a fundamentally different route to competitive advantage combining a choice about the type of competitive advantage sought with the scope of the strategic target in which competitive advantage is to be achieved." The cost leadership and differentiation strategies seek competitive advantage in a broad range of industry segments while focus strategies aim at cost advantage (cost focus) or differentiation (differentiation focus). With the assumption that competitive advantage is the core of any strategy, a company must make a choice among these three generic strategies and covering all fields would mean no competitive advantage at all.

Criticism over the Porter's Generic Competitive Strategies

Despite the widespread enthusiasm for Porter's generic strategies, some critics have voiced opinions that may point towards important deficiencies and limitations in the paradigm. Firstly, it is a primary focus of criticism that Porter is too concerned with the narrow context of established big businesses. Mature and saturated industries are prioritized over niche and fragmented ones, and this obviously imposes certain limitations upon the supposedly universally applicable generic strategy framework. While it is clear that Porter's research is very much founded on hard data, which is naturally easier to obtain in mature industries, there have been some critics holding that Porter's Generic Competitive Strategies framework cannot be applied reliably to the more dynamic and evolving industries (Andersen & Poulfel, 2009). Also, secondly some argued that some business environments such as national macro-business environmental conditions had not been taken into consideration in this model and these conditions could have significant impacts over the profitability of the chosen generic strategies and hence the Porter's generic strategies may not be appropriately used universally. Thirdly, while Porter's generic competitive strategies mainly talk about company's competitive position and based on which a company should make decisions, as a matter of fact there are many situations in which a company will not make decisions merely based only on the competition considerations. For example, a company which may already enjoy a market leadership position by adopting a differentiation strategy in the industry could still use a low pricing strategy in order keep off the potential entry of the new competitors or for other strategic intensions.

The generic strategies remain useful to characterize strategic positions at the simplest and broadest level. In his later work, Porter (1996) introduces the three basics of positioning——varieties, needs and access in order to enhance the understanding of generic strategies to a greater level of specificity. Based on his view, IKEA and Southwest are both focused on cost, but IKEA's focus is based on all the home furnishing needs of its targets consumer group (price sensitive young family) while Southwest's is based on offering a particular service variety (Moon, 2009, p. 10).

Variety-based positioning refers to the produce a subset of an industry's products or services. It is based on the choice of product or service varieties rather than customer segments. It is economically feasible only when a company can best produce particular products or services using distinctive sets of activities. And needs-based positioning involves serving most or all the needs of a particular group of customers. It is based on targeting a segment of customers. It arises when there are a group of customers with differing needs, and when a tailored set of activities can serve those needs best (maaw.info, 2002). Access-based positioning focus on customers that is accessible in different ways, which can be based on geography, the Internet or other similar conditions (scribd.com, 2007). Amazon.com is an example of access-based positioning, accessing customers exclusively through the Internet. The addition of these three generic strategies had made the original model more mature and practical though there are still difference voices and ideas.

Whirlpool's Competitive Strategy

Whirlpool produces and markets three well-established pan-European brands: Bauknecht, a premium upscale product; Whirpool, for the broad middle segment of the white-goods market; and IGNIS, its low-price "value" brand aimed at price-sensitive consumers. This comprehensive product strategy allows Whirlpool to fully utilize its European production facility and distribution system and markets its goods to Europeans at all income levels. It will be recommended that the company should not abandon any of these well established brands, it could actually adopt a variety based positioning strategy which refers to the produce of a subset of an industry's products or services and it is based on the choice of product or service varieties rather than customer segments as mentioned above. There are two major reasons for these choices: first of all, the abandon of any of these three brands could be a great loss for the company; secondly, the above theoretical reviews actually support a variety based strategy rather than "must choose among the three generic strategies", therefore the company could provide a variety of choices to the customers. And when the EU consumers think about buying any white goods, the majority of them could think of Whirlpool because of its variety of offerings.

Exercises

1. What are the advantages and disadvantages of monopoly, oligopoly, monopolistic competition and perfect competition?

2. What are the conditions for perfect competition?

3. Describe the barriers to entry.

4. What does the competitive environment include?

5. Identify the differences between competition and imperfect competition?

Glossary

Market structure: In economics, market structure is the number of firms producing identical products which are homogeneous. 市场结构

Spectrum: A range of a particular type of thing 范围

Homogenous: All of the same or similar kind or nature 同质的；同类的

Barriers to entry: In theories of competition in economics, barriers to entry, also known as barrier to entry, are obstacles that make it difficult to enter a given market. The term can refer to hindrances a firm faces in trying to enter a market or industry—such as government regulation, or a large, established firm taking advantage of economies of scale—

or those an individual faces in trying to gain entrance to a profession—such as education or licensing requirements. 进入壁垒；进入障碍

Marketplace: The world of commercial activity where goods and services are bought and sold 市场

Monopoly: Exclusive control or possession of something; (economics) a market in which there are many buyers but only one seller 垄断

Oligopoly: (economics) A market in which control over the supply of a commodity is in the hands of a small number of producers and each one can influence prices and affect competitors 寡头买主垄断

Perfect competition: In economic theory, perfect competition (sometimes called pure competition) describes markets such that no participants are large enough to have the market power to set the price of a homogeneous product. Because the conditions for perfect competition are strict, there are few if any perfectly competitive markets. 完全（自由）竞争

Supernormal : Exceeding the normal or average 非凡的；异于寻常的

Rival: Competitor 竞争者

Assumption: A hypothesis that is taken for granted 假定；设想

Divergence: A difference between conflicting facts or claims or opinions 分歧

Monopolistic competition: A type of imperfect competition such that many producers sell products that are differentiated from one another as goods but not perfect substitutes (such as from branding, quality, or location). In monopolistic competition, a firm takes the prices charged by its rivals as given and ignores the impact of its own prices on the prices of other firms. 垄断性竞争

Chapter 7 The International Business Environment

Introduction

A fundamental shift is occurring in the world economy. We are moving away from a world in which national economies were relatively self-contained entities, isolated from each other by barriers to cross-border trade and investment; by instance, time zones, and language; and by national differences in government regulation, culture, and business systems. And we are moving toward a world in which barriers to cross-border trade and investment are declining; perceived distance is shrinking due to advances in transportation and telecommunications technology; material culture is starting to look similar; and national economies are developing into an interdependent, integrated global economic system. The process by which this is occurring is commonly referred to as globalization.

With the development of globalization, more and more companies begin to go into international markets, which deeply influences the companies' decision-making. And some international organizations also appear or grow stronger which influence the development of multinational companies, too. Meanwhile, international markets are getting more competitive, so every global firm needs to be familiar with the environment in which they operate and adopt suitable actions to meet the challenge.

The objectives in this chapter:

(1) The international business environment

(2) International trade

(3) Global institutions

(4) The strategy of international business

7.1 The International Business Environment

A fundamental shift is occurring in the world economy. We are moving away from a world in which national economies were relatively self-contained entities, isolated from each other by barriers to cross-border trade and investment; by instance, time zones, and languages; and by national differences in government regulations, cultures, and business systems. And we are moving toward a world in which barriers to cross-border trade and investment are declining; perceived distance is shrinking due to advances in transportation and telecommunications technology; material culture is starting to look similar the world over; and national economies are developing into an interdependent, integrated global economic system. The process by which this is occurring is commonly referred to as globalization.

In this interdependent global economy, an American might drive to work in a car designed in Germany that was assembled in Mexico by DaimlerChrysler from components made in the United States and Japan that were fabricated from Korean steel and Malaysian rubber. She or he may have filled the car with gasoline at a BP service station owned by a British multinational company. The gasoline could have been made from oil pumped out of a well of the coast of Africa by a French oil company that transported it to the Unites States in a ship owned by a Greek shipping line. While driving to work, the American might talk to her or his stockbroker on a Nokia cell phone that was designed in Finland and assembled in Texas using chip sets produced in China that were designed by Indian engineers working for Texas Instruments.

This is the world in which we live. It is a world where the volume of goods, service, and investment crossing national borders has expanded faster than world output consistently for more than half a century. It is a world where more than $1.2 billion in foreign exchange transactions are made every day, where $10.41 trillion of goods and $2.41 trillion of services were sold across national borders in 2005. It is a world in which international institutions such as the World Trade Organization and gathering of leaders from the world's most powerful economies have called for even lower barriers to cross border trade and investment. It is a world the symbols of material and popular culture are increasingly global: from Coca-Cola and Starbucks to Sony PlayStation, Nokia cell phones, MTV shows, Disney film, and IKEA stores.

For businesses, this process has produced many opportunities. Firms can expand their revenues by selling around the world and reduce their costs by producing in nations where key inputs, including labor, are cheap. At the same time, globalization has created new threats for business accustomed to dominating their domestic markets. Therefore, globalization is not only an opportunity for every enterprise but also a big challenge.

What is globalization?

Globalization refers to the trend towards a more integrated global economic system. In 2000, the International Monetary Fund (IMF) identified four basic aspects of globalization: Trade and transactions, capital and investment movements, migration and movement of people, and the dissemination of knowledge. further, environmental challenges such as global warming, cross-boundary water air pollution, and over-fishing of the ocean are linked with globalization. Globalizing processes affect and are affected by business and work organization, economics, socio-cultural resources, and the natural environment. Academic literature commonly subdivides globalization into three major areas: economic globalization, cultural globalization, and political globalization. Current globalization trends can be largely accounted for by developed economies integrating with less developed economies by means of foreign direct investment, the reduction of trade barriers as well as other economic reforms, and in many cases,e.g. immigration.

Economic globalization is the increasing economic interdependence of national economies across the world through a rapid increase in cross-border movement of goods, services, technology, and capital. Whereas the globalization of business is centered around the diminution of international trade regulations as well as tariffs, taxes, and other impediments that suppresses global trade, economic globalization is the process of increasing economic integration between countries, leading to the emergence of a global marketplace or a single world market.

Two key facets of globalization are:

- The globalization of markets

The globalization of markets refers to the meaning of historically distinct and separate national markets into one huge global marketplace. Falling barriers to cross-border trade have made it easier to sell internationally. It has been argued for some time that the tastes and preferences of consumers in different nations are beginning to converge on some global norm, thereby helping to create a global market. Consumer products such as Citigroup credit cards, Coca-Cola soft drinks, Sony PlayStation video games, McDonald's hamburgers, Starbucks coffee, and IKEA furniture are frequently held up as prototypical examples of this trend. Firms such as those just cited are more than just benefactors of this trend; they are also facilitators of it. By offering the same basic product worldwide, they help to create a global market.

• The globalization of production

The globalization of production refers to the sourcing of goods and services from locations around the globe to take advantage of national differences in the cost and quality of factors of production (labour energy, land, and capital).

By doing this, companies hope to lower their overall cost structure or improve the quality or functionality of their product offering, thereby allowing them to compete more effectively.

The Global Economy in the 21st Century

• A more integrated global economy

• New opportunities for firms

• Political and economic disruptions can throw plans into disarray

7.2 International Trade

International trade is the exchange of goods and services between countries. An import is the purchase of a good or service made overseas and an export is the sale of a good or service made at home.

Reasons for International Trade

There are a variety of reasons why nations trade, but most importantly, there are two reasons: Domestic non-availability of resources and the principle of comparative advantage. In a simple world, a nation trades because it lacks the climate, raw materials, specialist labour, capital, technology, etc. needed to manufacture a particular good or a service. A nation also trades because it wants to maximize its economic wellbeing even if it has the reasons for the goods and services they need.

Resource Reasons

Generally speaking, wealth is produced with three main resources, natural resources, capital and labor. Natural resources include land, raw materials, water, and other natural things, such as living species in air, in sea, and on land. It is not difficult to see that these resources are distributed unevenly around the world, and this uneven distribution of resources is one of the basic reasons why nations began and continue to trade with each other.

• Climatic conditions and terrain

Climatic conditions and terrain are very important for agriculture product. The difference in these factors enables some countries to grow certain plants and leaves other countries with the only choice to import the produce they consume. Colombia and Brazil have the ideal climate for growing coffee beans and therefore have the opportunity to export coffee beans and coffee to other countries worldwide.

- Natural resources

The middle east for example, has rich oil reserves and is the main source of oil supply to the world, it has close to 70% of the world's total reserves and products about 40% of the world total output, over 2/3 of the oil that Western Europe and Japan consume is imported from the Middle East, and the U.S. military oil consumption in Europe and Asia is largely purchased from that area, too.

- Technologies and labor

The U.S, Japan and many European countries have strong research and development capabilities and advanced technology. They also have skilled workers who are able to manufacture sophisticated equipment and machinery such as jet aircraft. Other countries, who do not have enough number of well-trained engineers and workers, must import equipment from these countries.

Economic Reasons (International Trade Theory)

In addition to getting the products they need, countries also want to gain economically by trading with each other. This is made possible by varied prices for the same commodity around the world, reflecting the differences in the cost of production.

- The principle of absolute advantage

In his work *The Wealth of Nations*(1776), Adam Smith assumed that each country could produce one or more commodities at a lower real cost than its trading partners. It then follows that each country will benefit from specialization in those commodities in which it has an "absolute advantage", exporting them and importing other commodities which it produces at a higher real cost than another.

Table 1-3 Absolute Cost Example

	Days of Labor Required to Produce	
Country	Cloth(1 bolt)	Wine(1 barrel)
Scotland	30	120
Italy	100	20

From this chart, we can see clearly that Scotland should specialize in the production of cloth on which it has a cost advantage. Instead of spending 120 days of labor to produce a barrel of wine, Scotland should import wine from Italy where a barrel of wine is produced with only 20 days of labor. Similarly, Italy should concentrate on the production of wine and import cloth from Scotland.

- The principle of comparative advantage (David Ricardo)

David Ricardo, in his work *On the Principles of Political Economy and Taxaion*(1817), showed that absolute cost advantages are not a necessary condition for two nations to gain from trade with each other. Instead, trade will benefit both nations provided only that their relative costs, that is, the ratio of their real costs measured by labor-hour or another commodity, are different for two or more commodities. In short, trade depends on differences in comparative cost or opportunity cost, and one nation can profitably trade with another even though its real costs are higher(or lower) in every commodity.

A country has a comparative advantage if it can make a product relatively more cheaply than other countries. A countries should make the product that yields it the greatest advantage or the least comparative disadvantage. This theory is the basis of specialization and trade.

Table 1-4 Comparative Cost Example 1

Country	Total Output		Ratio of Costs within the Country
	Rice (R)	Copper(C)	
A	2	4	1R : 2C or 1/2R : 1C
B	1	1	1R : 1C

Assuming that both countries spend the same amount of labor for both products, we can see clearly that country A is more efficient in both products than country B, however, as we see, the price of one product in terms of the other or the opportunity costs of rice and copper are different in A and B. In such a case, there should be a gain for both countries if they trade with each other.

Suppose that country A concentrates on producing copper and country B on rice, country A produces eight units of copper and country B two units of rice, further assume that they will use half of their output to exchange for the other commodity they need but do not produce. If we look at the costs of each country, it seems both of them, as the following table shows, can get twice as much as they can produce themselves.

Table 1-5 Comparative Cost Example 2

Country	Quantity Owned After Trading		Exchange Rates Used
	Rice (R)	Copper(C)	
A	(4)	4	1R : 1C
B	1	(2)	1R : 2C or 1/2R : 1C

But a second look reveals that the transaction can not be concluded since these two countries are using two different rates of exchange. It is likely that a buyer wants to pay $50 for a watch while the seller asks for $100. However, the trade can still be meaningful as long as the following is achieved.

Table 1-6 Comparative Cost Example 3

Country	Quantity Owned After Trading	
	Rice	Copper
A	$2<X<4$	4
B	1	$1<Y<2$

And in order to conclude the deal, there should be one common rate:

$X/4=1/Y$ or $XY=4$

Other Reasons

• Political reasons

• Different tastes and preferences

Benefits of International Trade

• Cheaper goods

For one thing, countries trade because there is a cost advantage from production efficiency as demonstrated in the principle of comparative advantage. Further, the prices fall because trade allows firms to produce further down along the average cost curve and that means a lower per unit cost of production. This implies that each product is being produced more efficiently. In addition, competition in the world market remains strong and constant and it forces profit to zero for each firm and implies that efficiency improvements are passed along to consumers in the form of lower prices.

• Greater variety with goods coming from more countries

Anyone who has experienced China's trade development in the past decades can tell the changes in the variety of both capital goods and consumer goods. These changes have not only increased the productivity of our industries but also improved the quality of our life. Consumers have a more satisfying collection of goods and services from which they can choose and consumption efficiency is thus improved.

- Wider market with increasing number if trading partners

Indeterminable trade can greatly expand the market. The expansion enables manufacturers to take advantage of economies of scale in both research and production. Besides, since markets around the world are often in different development stages, newly expanded markets can help extend the life of products. A product outdated in one market may be sold like hot cakes in another.

- Growth of economy

Foreign trade has become more and more important for many countries as it creates jobs that have economic, social, and political significance. Thus, countries have attached increasing importance to foreign trade. For economies that are highly dependent on foreign trade, it is crucial for them to keep foreign trade growing to ensure the development of the economies, the creation of jobs, and the stability of political situation.

7.3　Global Institutions

As markets globalize and an increasing proportion of business activity transcends national borders, institutions are needed to help manage, regulate, and police the global marketplace, and to promote the establishment of multinational treaties to govern the global business system. Over the past half century, a number of important global institutions have created to help perform these functions, including the *General Agreement on Tariffs and Trade* (*GATT*) and its successor, the World Trade Organization(WTO); the International Monetary Fund(IMF) and its sister institution, the World Bank; the United Nations(UN); Asia-Pacific Economic Cooperation (APEC) and the Association of Southeast Asian Nations (ASEAN). All these institutions were created by voluntary agreement between individual nation-states, and their functions are enshrined in international treaties.

The World Trade Organization (WTO)

The World Trade Organization(like the GATT before it) is primarily responsible for policing the world trading system and making sure nation-states adhere to the rules laid down in trade treaties signed by WTO member states. As of 2010, 154 members accounted for 97% of world trade, thereby giving the organization enormous scope and influence. The WTO is also responsible for facilitating the establishment of additional multinational agreements between WTO member states. Over its entire history, and that of the GATT before it, the WTO has promoted the lowering of barriers to cross-border trade and investment. In doing so, the WTO has been the instrument of its member states, which have sought to create a more open global business system unencumbered by barriers to trade and investment between countries. Without an institution such as the WTO, the globalization of markets and production is unlikely to have proceed as far as it has.

The WTO as a negotiation forum:

The WTO provides a platform that allows member governments to negotiate and resolve trade issues with other members. The WTO was created through negotiation, and its main focus is to provide open lines of communication concerning trade between its members. For example, the WTO has lowered trade barriers and increased trade among member countries. On the other hand, it has also maintained trade barriers when it makes sense to do so in the global context. Therefore, the WTO attempts to provide negotiation mediation that benefits the global economy. Once negotiations are complete and an agreement is in place, the WTO then offers to interpret that agreement in the event of a future dispute. All WTO agreements include a settlement process whereby the organization legally conducts neutral conflict resolution.

The WTO as a set of rules:

No negotiation, mediation or resolution would be possible without the foundational WTO agreements. These agreements set the legal ground rules for international commerce that the WTO oversees. When a member country signs an agreement, that country's government is bound to a set of constraints that it must observe when setting future trade policies. These agreements protect producers, importers and exporters while encouraging world governments to meet specific social and environmental standards.

China became a member of the World Trade Organization (WTO) on 11 December 2001. The admission of China to the WTO was preceded by a lengthy process of negotiations and required significant changes to the Chinese economy. It signified China's deeper integration into the world economy. When China joined the WTO, it agreed to considerably harsher conditions than other developing countries. After China joined the World Trade Organization (WTO), the service sector was considerably liberalized and foreign investment was allowed; restrictions on retail, wholesale and distribution ended. Banking, financial services, insurance and telecommunications were also opened up to foreign investment. Furthermore, China had to deal with certain concerns linked to transparency and intellectual property that the accession to WTO underlined.

The International Monetary Fund and the World Bank

The International Monetary Fund (IMF) and the World Bank were both created in 1944 by 44 nations that met at Bretton Woods, New Hampshire. The IMF was established to maintain order in the international monetary system; the World Bank was set up to promote economic development. In the 60 years since their creation, both institutions have emerged as significant players in the global economy. The World Bank is the less controversial of the two sister institutions. It has focused on making low-interest loans to cash-strapped governments in poor nations that wish to undertake significant infrastructure investments (such as building dams or roads).

The IMF is often seen as the lender of last resort to nation-states whose economies are in turmoil and currencies are losing value against those of other nations. Repeatedly during the past decade, for example, the IMF has lent money to the governments of troubled states, including Argentina, Indonesia, Mexico, Russia, the Republic of Korea, Thailand, and Turkey. IMF loans come with strings attached, however, in return for loans, the IMF requires nation-states to adopt specific economic policies aimed at returning their troubled economies to stability and growth.

The United Nations

The United Nations was established October 24, 1945, by 51 countries committed to persevering peace through international cooperation and collective security. Today nearly every nation in the world belong to the United Nations (UN); membership by the end of 2012 totals 193 countries. When states become members of the United Nations, they agree to accept the obligations of the UN Charter, an international treaty that establishes basic principles of international relations. According to the charter, the UN has four purposes: to maintain international peace and security, to develop friendly relations among nations, to cooperate in solving international problems and in promoting respect for human rights, and to be a centre for harmonizing the actions of nations.

Although the UN is perhaps best known for its peacekeeping role, one of the organization's central is the promotion of higher standards of living, full employment, and conditions of economic and social progress and development—all issues that are central to the creation of a vibrant global economy. As much as 70% of the work of the UN system is devoted to accomplishing this mandate. To do so, the UN works closely with other international institutions such as the World Bank. Guiding the work is the belief that eradicating poverty and improving the well-being of people everywhere are necessary steps in creating conditions for lasting world peace.

Asia-Pacific Economic Cooperation (APEC)

The Asia-Pacific Economic Cooperation (APEC) was founded in 1989 at the suggestion of Australia that seeks to promote free trade and economic cooperation throughout the Asia-Pacific region. APEC currently has 21 member states, including such economic powerhouses as the United States, Japan, and China. Collectively the member states account for about 57 percent of the world's GNP, 46 percent of world trade, and much of the growth in the world economy. The stated aim of APEC is to increase multilateral cooperation in view of the economic rise of the Pacific nations and the growing interdependence within the region. The U.S. support for APEC was also based on the belief that it might prove a viable strategy for heading off any moves to create Asian groupings from which it would be excluded. It was in response to the growing interdependence of Asia-Pacific economies and the advent of regional trade blocs in other parts of the world; to fears that highly industrialized Japan would come to dominate economic activity in the Asia-Pacific region; and to establish new markets for agricultural products and raw materials beyond Europe. APEC works to raise living standards and education levels through sustainable economic growth and to foster a sense of community and an appreciation of shared interests among Asia-Pacific countries. APEC includes newly industrialized economies, although the agenda of free trade was a sensitive issue for the developing NIEs at the time APEC founded, and aims to enable ASEAN economies to explore new export market opportunities for natural resources such as natural gas, as well as to seek regional economic integration by means of foreign direct investment. Members account proximately 54% of the world's gross domestic product and about 44% of world trade.

An annual APEC Economic Leaders' Meeting is attended by the heads of government of all APEC members. The location of the meeting rotates annually among the member economies, and a famous tradition, followed for most summits, involves the attending leaders dressing in a national costume of the host country.

To meet the Bogor Goals, APEC carries out work in three main areas:

1. Trade and Investment Liberalisation

2. Business Facilitation

3. Economic and Technical Cooperation

Association of Southeast Asian Nations (ASEAN)

The Association of Southeast Asian Nations is a political and economic organization of ten countries located in Southeast Asia, which was formed on 8 August 1967 by Indonesia, Malaysia, the Philippines, Singapore and Thailand. Since then, membership has expanded to include Brunei, Burma (Myanmar), Cambodia, Laos, and Vietnam. Its aims include accelerating economic growth, social progress, cultural development among its members, protection of regional peace and stability, and opportunities for member countries to discuss differences peacefully. ASEAN covers a land area of 4.46 million km², which is 3% of the total land area of the Earth, and has a population of approximately 600 million people, which is 8.8% of the world's population. The sea area of ASEAN is about three times larger than its land counterpart. In 2012, its combined nominal GDP had grown to more than U.S. $ 2.3 trillion. If ASEAN were a single entity, it would rank as the eighth largest economy in the world.

The European Union (EU)

The European Union (EU) is an economic and political union of 28 member states that are located primarily in Europe. The EU operates through a system of supranational independent institutions and intergovernmental negotiated decisions by the member states. Institutions of the EU include the European Commission, the Council of the European Union, the European Council, the Court of Justice of the European Union, the European Central Bank, the Court of Auditors, and the European Parliament. The European Parliament is elected every five years by EU citizens. Brussels is the capital of the union.

The EU traces its origins from the European Coal and Steel Community (ECSC) and the European Economic Community (EEC), formed by the inner six countries in 1951 and 1958, respectively. In the intervening years the community and its successors have grown in size by the accession of new member states and in power by the addition of policy areas to its remit. The *Maastricht Treaty* established the European Union under its current name in 1993. The latest major amendment to the constitutional basis of the EU, the *Treaty of Lisbon*, came into force in 2009.

The EU has developed a single market through a standardized system of laws that apply in all member states. Within the Schengen Area (which includes 22 EU and 4 non-EU states) passport controls have been abolished. The EU policies aim to ensure the free movement of people, goods, services, and capital, enact legislation in justice and home affairs, and maintain common policies on trade, agriculture, fisheries, and regional development.

The monetary union was established in 1999 and came into full force in 2002. It is currently composed of 18 member states that use the euro as their legal tender. Through the Common Foreign and Security Policy the EU has developed a role in external relations and defence. The union maintains permanent diplomatic missions throughout the world and represents itself at the United Nations, the WTO, the G8, and the G20.

The EU is considered by many to be a potential superpower. With a combined population of over 500 million inhabitants, or 7.3% of the world population, the EU in 2012 generated a nominal gross domestic product (GDP) of 16.584 trillion U.S. dollars, constituting approximately 23% of global nominal GDP and 20% when measured in terms of purchasing power parity, which is the largest nominal GDP and GDP (PPP) in the world. The EU was the recipient of the 2012 Nobel Peace Prize.

7.4 The Strategy of International Business

Our primary concern in this book is the aspects of the larger environment in which international businesses complete. As we have described it in the preceding chapters, this environment has included the different political, economic, and cultural institutions found in nations, the international trade and investment framework, and the international monetary system. Now our focus shift from the environment to the firm itself and in particular, to the actions managers can take to compete more affectively as an international business. In this chapter, we discuss the different strategies that firms pursue when competing internationally. We consider the pros and cons of these strategies.

Before we discuss the strategies that managers in the multinational enterprise can pursue, we need to review some basic principles of strategy. A firm's strategy can be defined as the actions that managers take to attain the goals of the firm. For most firms, the preeminent goal is to maximize the value of the firm for its owners, its shareholders. To maximize the value of a firm, managers must pursue strategies that increase the profitability of the enterprise and its rate of profit growth over time.

Pressures for local responsiveness imply that it may not be possible to leverage skills and products associated with a firm's core competencies wholesale from one nation to another. Concessions often have to be made to local conditions. Despite being depicted as poster boy for the proliferation of standardized global products, even McDonald's has found that it has to customize its product offerings to account for national differences in taste and preferences.

How do the pressures for cost reductions and local responsiveness influence a firm's choice of strategy?

There are four basic strategies to compete in the international environment.

¤ Global standardization strategy

¤ Localization strategy

¤ Transnational strategy

¤ International strategy

When does a global standardization strategy make sense?

¤ **A global standardization strategy** focuses on increasing profitability and profit growth by reaping the cost reductions that come from economies of scale, learning effects, and location economies.

¤ The goal is to pursue a low-cost strategy on a global scale.

¤ Makes sense when there are strong pressures for cost reductions and demands for local responsiveness are minimal.

When does a localization strategy make sense?

¤ A localization strategy focuses on increasing profitability by customizing the firm's goods or services so that they provide a good match to tastes and preferences in different national markets.

¤ It makes sense when there are substantial differences across nations with regard to consumer tastes and preferences, and where cost pressures are not too intense.

When does a transnational strategy make sense?

¤ A transnational strategy tries to simultaneously

- achieve low costs through location economies, economies of scale, and learning effects;

- differentiate the product offering across geographic markets to account for local differences;

- foster a multidirectional flow of skills between different subsidiaries.

¤ It makes sense when there are both high cost pressures and high pressures for local responsiveness.

When does an international strategy make sense?

¤ An international strategy involves taking products first produced for the domestic market and then selling them internationally with only minimal local customization.

¤ It makes sense when there are low cost pressures and low pressures for local responsiveness.

Localization may give a firm a competitive edge, but if it is simultaneously facing aggressive competitors, the company will also have to reduce its cost structure, and the only way to do that may be to shift toward a transnational strategy. Thus, as competition intensifies, international and localization strategies tend to become less viable, and managers need to orient their companies toward either a global standardization strategy or a transnational strategy.

Strategic Alliances

Strategic alliances—cooperative agreements between potential or actual competitors.

¤ Examples:

- Formal joint ventures
- Short-term contractual arrangements

¤ The number of international strategic alliances has risen significantly in recent decades.

Advantages of Strategic Alliances

Strategic alliances are attractive because they

¤ facilitate entry into a foreign market;

¤ allow firms to share the fixed costs (and associated risks) of developing new products or processes;

¤ bring together complementary skills and assets that neither partner could easily develop on its own;

¤ can help establish technological standards for the industry that will benefit the firm.

Disadvantages of Strategic Alliances

¤ Strategic alliances can give competitors low-cost routes to new technology and markets.

¤ Unless a firm is careful, it can give away more in a strategic alliance than it receives.

Exercises

1. Tell the influences of globalization on the Chinese economy in these recent years.

2. The reasons why so many nations take part in the global trade.

3. Describe the advantages and disadvantages of global trade.

4. Take an example to show how the global standardization strategy is used.

5. How do the international institutions influence the development or the actions of international businesses?

Glossary

Globalization 经济全球化

Globalization of markets 市场全球化

Globalization of production 生产全球化

Foreign direct investment 国外直接投资

Multinational enterprise 跨国公司

Absolute advantage 决定优势

Comparative advantage 比较优势

General Agreement on Tariffs and Trade (GATT) 关贸总协定

World Trade Organization(WTO) 世界贸易组织

International Monetary Fund(IMF) and World Bank 国际货币基金组织

The United Nations(UN) 联合国

Asia-Pacific Economic Cooperation (APEC) 亚太经济合作组织

Association of Southeast Asian Nations (ASEAN) 东南亚国家联盟

The European Union (EU) 欧盟

Global standardization strategy 全球标准化战略

Localization strategy 本地化战略

Transnational strategy 跨国战略

International strategy 国际战略

Appendix

Module Guide of Business Environment

Description of the Module:

Introduction

The module on the Business Environment aims to provide students with an introduction to the complex nature of leading organizations within the context of their environment. It will explore the objectives of organizations and the influence of stakeholders as well as investigate the operation of organizations in relation to the local, national and global environment. The module looks at how organizations react to the market environment by evaluating market forces and determining competitive advantage. Through this module the student will understand the important impact that political, economic, sociological, technological, legal and environmental factors have on business decisions. The module provides students with a firm base of understanding of the parameters within which organizations act. This understanding can be built upon in further units.

Summary of Learning Outcomes

On satisfactory completion of this module students are expected to be able to:

1. Identify political institutions and political issues and explain their impact on business organizations' activities in the United Kingdom and internationally.

2. Understand how the basic economic laws could impact business organizations in each type of economy, taking examples from different countries.

3. Explain the impact of economic institutions, economic forces and economic performance on business organizations in the mixed economy of the United Kingdom compared with other countries.

4. Explain how social change in the United Kingdom and internationally affects business organizations.

5. Explain how technological change affects business organizations.

Knowledge

Identify and analyse the role of the leader in setting objectives and meeting the responsibilities of an organization within its environment.

Investigate the economic, social, political and global organizational environmental information required by leaders of an organization.

Investigate the global market environment and its effect on the behaviour of organizations.

Explore the significance of international trade for Chinese businesses.

Skills

Show the ability to analyse and evaluate a range of business environment concepts.

Demonstrate the ability to apply a range of business environment concepts to contemporary business organizations and situations.

Content Synopsis:

Forms of business organizations

Organizational and business objectives

Organizational responsibilities

Stakeholder

Legislative

Ethical

The market system—prices and costs

Supply and demand

Industry and market structures

Government and markets

Rivalry and competition

The legal environment

The macro-economic environment

The political environment

The sociological environment

Environmental issues

The technological environment

The international business environment

The World Trade Organization

APEC and ASEAN

The European Union

Objectives and responsibilities of an organization

Categories of organizations: size, sector/type—private, public, voluntary, charitable; activity—primary, secondary, tertiary.

Mission, objectives and values of organizations: concept of corporate mission or vision, underlying values/philosophy, profit, market share, return on capital employed (ROCE), sales, growth, levels of service, customer/user perceptions and audits.

Stakeholders: identification of stakeholders, stakeholder groups, conflict of expectations, attitude, power-influence matrix; satisfying stakeholder objectives, measuring performance.

Responsibilities of organizations: to stakeholders, key legal responsibilities, e.g. consumer, employment, disability discrimination and equal opportunities, stakeholder pensions; wider responsibilities including ethical and environmental; ethical practice.

Economic, social and global environment

Resource issues and types of economic system: basic economic problem, effective use of resources; type of economic systems—command, free enterprise, mixed, including transitional economies, public and private sector initiatives; private finance initiatives.

Government policy: fiscal policy in the UK and China, monetary policy in the UK and China; Monetary Policy Committee (MPC—Bank of England), Bank of China, industrial policy in the UK and China; social welfare policy in the UK and China; economic growth, economic performance/indicators, influence of the Confederation of British Industries (CBI), TUC (Trades Union Council) stakeholder and interest groups, the influence of the global economy—trends, uncertainties, growth, impact on the economy, the UK and Chinese multinationals, the World Bank.

Behaviour of organizations and the market environment

Market types: perfect competition, monopoly, monopolistic competition, oligopoly, duopoly; competitive advantage, behaviour/strategies adopted by firms; role of the Competition Commission in the UK and regulatory bodies such as OFTEL, OFGAS, OFWAT.

Market forces and organizational responses: supply and demand, elasticity, customer perceptions and actions, issues relating to supply, cost and output decisions short run and long run, economies of scale, growth of organizations: reasons, methods, financing, Multi-National Corporations/Trans-National Corporations (MNCs/TNCs), joint ventures, outsourcing; core markets/skills, technology and innovation, labour market trends, cultural environment.

International trade and the European and Asian dimensions

The importance of international trade: to the UK and Chinese economy, businesses, balance of payments, patterns and trends in international trade, the World Trade Organization (WTO), the UK and Chinese trade with the European Union (EU), the USA and other countries, trading blocks throughout the world (including APEC and ASEAN), the UK membership of the EU, enlargement of the EU, direct/indirect exporting methods, trading opportunities, importance of global markets, implications for businesses of emerging markets, cultural diversity and clusters, Trans-National Corporations, the economies of Europe, Economic Monetary Union (EMU), EU budget, import duties and levies, agricultural levies, Common Agricultural Policy (CAP), Value Added Tax (VAT), competitor policy, European Single Market Act, social policy, the social chapter, tax harmonization, regional policy.

Teaching and Learning Programme

The Higher Diploma in Global Business Environment module will run over a period of 12 weeks, with an average of 3 hours formal contact time with the module leader. These hours will be divided into the following sessions:

Lectures and workshops	48 hours
Directed reading to support workshops	70 hours
Other reading	50 hours

It is essential that students attend all of the above sessions to enable satisfactory completion of assessed work. **You are required to maintain an attendance in this module of study of at least 80%.** You should provide the course leader with a doctor's medical note to cover you for any absence resulting from illness. All absences from the module should be relayed to the module or course leader on the day of absence. Any unauthorised absence will be regarded as non-attendance and will be recorded as such.

In addition to the formal contact time, students are expected to spend a further 80 hours in "self-managed" study for this module. This should include reading, preparation for seminars and completion of essays/homework.

Assessment Methods

There will be two formal assessments incorporating investigative research into an organization specified by the tutor or one chosen by the student.

Assessment 1 —Presentation: 25% weighting

Students will be assessed in a group on a PESTLE analysis. There will be a presentation of their findings.

Assessment 2 —Individual Report: 75% weighting

Produce an individual written report and other accompanying documentation. Within the report students will need to explain the underlying economic forces helping direct identified business changes.

Word count: 4,000

Table 1-7　Outline Programme（4 periods/week）

Week	Content	Credit Hours
1	Overview of unit/introduction of module guide and assessment	4
2	Types of organizations: small, middle, large organizations primary, secondary, tertiary industries sole trader, partnership corporation, company group	4
3	Objectives of organization: mission, vision, objectives and values smart principle of setting objectives	4
4	Stakeholders: identification of stakeholders, stakeholders group, conflict of expectation, power-influence matrix	4
5	Responsibilities of organization: legal, ethical and environmental responsibilities	4
6	Legal responsibilities: responsibilities to consumers, to employees, to shareholders, to suppliers	4
7	Ethical responsibilities: Ethical practice: fair, honest practice Introduction of assignment (1 period)	4
8	Organization macro-environment: political, economic, social, technological, and global environment PESTEL analysis（practice）	4

Continued

Week	Content	Credit Hours
9	Assignment 1 individual tutorials	4
10	Market forces: supply and demand, elasticity, economies of scale, price and cost	4
11	Market structure: marketing strategy, three factors deciding the degree of the competition of the market	4
12	Market types: perfect competition, monopoly, monopolistic competition, oligopoly, duopoly,	4
13	Market types: competitive advantage ; behaviours / strategies adopted by firms	4
14	The international environment The analysis of assignment 2 (1 period)	4
15	The impacts of the WTO, APEC, ASEAN, EU/EMU	4
16	Assignment 2 Assignment workshop & report submission	8
	Total	68

Course Reading/Research

It is expected that all students will read key texts and journal articles recommended during the sessions.

It is important that students do not rely solely on information from the lectures and seminars for this module.

Further reading/research of the subject area is essential to complete the module.

Study Skills/Assessment Information

To make the most of your allotted study time, do:

Get organised early. Write deadline dates in your diary and prepare well in advance.

Prepare for each session. The module guide informs you of the topic area for each week. Where possible try to come to the sessions with some background knowledge.

Attend all timetabled sessions. If you start to miss sessions you will be missing essential information for your coursework.

Read the recommended reading.

Ask questions. If you need something to be clarified then sort it out immediately before you fall behind.

Leave enough time for submitting assignment tasks.

Prepare properly for tutorial sessions by completing any tasks set.

Report Guidelines

Use text extracts to liven up your introduction, show your knowledge, don't just repeat the questions.

Include a contents page especially if you have appendices.

All pages must be numbered.

Always use double spacing.

Never submit work without appropriate number of textbook extracts, 2,000 words = 4 references.

The "Harvard" reference system should be used throughout, where the author and date are given in the text the full reference should be supplied in a general list of references at the end of your assessment.

If you use tables, figures or graphs, all should be titled and the source given. There should be a reference and explanation in the text.

Appendices should be used to support information/findings found during your research. They should be numbered and placed at the back of the essay.

Always include a conclusion. This is a summary of your main findings and their implications plus any personal views on the subject. Do not introduce new material or ideas in this section.

A word count is essential at the end of each assessment.

Always use up to the number of words requested.

All written submissions should include a title, contents, an introduction to the topic, conclusions and a list of references. Work will not be accepted without an assessment cover sheet.

Students MUST hand in ONE copy and keep a COPY for themselves.

All presentations should include an introduction, main themes and a conclusion and ONE copy of the notes handed in.

There should be full use made of visual aids.

If it is a group presentation, then all members of the group should have an equally weighted task to complete and present.

Higher Diploma In Business
Business Environment
Assignment Brief

Table 1-8　Seminar Assessment 2018—2019

Degree Programme	BA (Hons) Business
Year	1
Module Number	B119
Module Title	The Business Environment
Type of Assessment	Seminars
Weighting	25%
Deadline Date	TBC (March 2019) (for PPT slides)

Assignment Objectives

This assignment carries 25% weighting of the total mark for this unit. When preparing your work for this assignment you should remember the learning outcome assessed by this seminar:

Explain how social change in the United Kingdom and internationally affects business organizations.

You are to prepare TWO of the seminar topics listed below:

— one to present.

— one to study and to ask another group detailed questions on.

Group members will need to meet in order to discuss, plan and prepare for their seminars. An attendance record should be kept plus brief minutes (records) of meetings held. Students must not miss classes to have these meetings.

Each seminar will last up to 20 minutes and consist of a presentation and discussion. It will be delivered at a date, time and place specified by the tutor. All groups will need to submit a copy of their PowerPoint slides on the same deadline date.

Marks will only be awarded for a student's own work, so any student failing to contribute to the group's work (for any reason) will not be able to gain marks.

Marking Scheme for Seminar Presentation and Discussion

The marks represent 25% of the overall module marking and will be divided to take account of the actual seminar delivery and the relevance of the material supplied to the other students in the form of handouts and activities and your involvement in the seminars of other students.

Table 1-9 Seminar Presentation

Activity	Marks
Evidence of research work (references/quotes/statistics etc.)	20
Materials (e.g. PowerPoint slides/handouts/displays etc.)	20
Interaction with other group members (as per generic criteria)	20
Answering questions on own seminar	20
Asking questions in other groups' seminar	20
Total	100

Sociology Questions

1. Until recently in the UK relatively few young people were getting involved in politics. Should young people be encouraged to become more involved with politics? What are the benefits to any society of young people being more involved? Do young people lack the necessary experience to fully participate in public debate on issues of which they have no practical knowledge?

2. The conservation of fauna (animals) and flora (plants) is an issue of international concern. Many local and international organizations exist to raise awareness of issues and promote changes in business and government activity. To what extent should businesses accommodate environmental concerns in their decision-making? Should some form of cost-benefit analysis be completed for each significant business activity? Provide at least one detailed example to show how individuals and businesses have been affected.

3. Studies on the "smoke/vapour" produced from vaping suggest there is a significant difference in the number of carcinogens found compared to cigarette smoke. Over twenty

chemicals are found in cigarette smoke compared to only a few in the vapour. When people say they're addicted to smoking, they're actually only addicted to nicotine. Should governments and health departments promote vaping as a healthier alternative to smoking? What are the implications for government budgets? What is the effect on young people of vaping?

Table 1-10 Report

activity	Marks
Research work ((references/quotes/statistics etc.) Comments	20
Materials (e.g. PowerPoint slides/handouts/displays/samples etc.) Comments	20
Interaction with other group members (as per generic criteria) Comments	20
Answering questions on own seminar Comments	20
Asking questions in other groups' seminar Comments	20
Total	100

Table 1-11 Assessment 2018—2019

Degree Programme	BA (Hons) Business
Year	1
Module Number	B119
Module Title	The Business Environment
Type of Assessment	Assignment Report
Weighting	75%
Draft Deadline	TBC
Deadline Date	TBC
Feedback Date	TBC
Word Count	4,000 words maximum

Note to international teachers: students' work must focus on the UK practice in order to achieve the learning outcomes agreed with our university. Ample information can be obtained online and international teachers may wish to summarise this first before handing the brief to students.

Industry in general:

https://www.networkrail.co.uk/running-the-railway/looking-after-the-railway/track/

New railway lines:

https://www.networkrail.co.uk/our-railway-upgrade-plan/key-projects/

Economic contribution of rail to the UK economy.

http://oldsite.riagb.org.uk/wp-content/uploads/2014/07/The-Economic-Contribution-of-UK-Rail-Full-Report.pdf

Further support can be provided on request. Technical knowledge of the railways is not required only their contribution to the overall economy.

Assignment Objectives

This assignment carries 75% weighting of the total mark for this unit. In preparing your report for this assignment you should remember the learning outcomes that are assessed by this assignment.

1. Identify political institutions and political issues and explain their impact on business organizations' activities in the United Kingdom and internationally.

2. Understand how the basic economic laws could impact business organizations in each type of economy, taking examples from different countries.

3. Explain the impact of economic institutions, economic forces and economic performance on business organizations in the mixed economy of the United Kingdom compared with other countries.

4. Explain how technological change affects business organizations.

Assignment

You are a journalist working for a national newspaper and your editor has asked you to write a report on: **"The railway industry in 2018 in the United Kingdom"**.

To pass this assignment your report MUST be about the current industry in the UK, so NOT just historical, plus an international comparison, e.g. China.

A) The Railways in the UK

Provide information on the state of the UK railway network plus known developments or proposals (Cross rail plus HS2). You will need to provide examples of the railway network, how reliable they are, the level of fares and passenger numbers. Types and forms of ownership of the railway companies plus whether government owned. Your justified opinion on whether and where new railways should be built.

(about 800 words plus charts, diagrams and photographs)

B) The Link Between the Economy and the Railway Network

Include the supply and demand for existing and new railway travel, effect on employment (jobs) and the impact of changes in economic activity on people and goods carried (i.e. cargo or freight such as oil, coal, steel etc.). You will need to consider the customer types targeted by the industry, e.g. people commuting to work, people travelling to see family and friends, oil companies and steel companies.

(about 800 words plus graphs and tables)

C) The Impact of Technology on the UK Railway Industry

How has the Internet impacted the UK railways? Ticket sales and ticket issuance can be done by smartphone now. New signalling systems mean more trains can run on existing tracks.

(about 800 words plus diagrams)

D) Comparison with the railway industry in China.

Compare the industry in the UK with the industry in China—consider the expanding railway network, e.g. in Tibet plus the high speed railway trains. What is the impact on the economy when fast trains connect smaller cities to the Tier 1 cities?

How does China's type of economy (free market, mixed or centrally planned) help?

(about 800 words plus tables)

E) How the UK Government and its Agencies Support the UK Railway Industry.

This is about government subsidies to railway companies, planning controls and legal permission to construct and operate. You may need to check the impact on the economy, employment and any additional challenges imposed by Brexit (the UK's exit from the European Union).

(about 800 words)

Overall your article should be no more than 4,000 words (fully referenced) and should fully discuss all the key issues. Equal weighting of 20% is applied to marks for each section.

Presentation Feedback

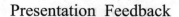

south essex college

FURTHER & HIGHER EDUCATION

Module Title: The Business Environment

Assignment (Seminar):B119

Student No. :

Assessor Comments for the Seminar Presentation:

Activity	Marks
Evidence of Research work (references/quotes/statistics etc.)	/20
Materials (e.g. PowerPoint slides/handouts/displays etc.)	/20
Interaction with other group members (as per generic criteria)	/20
Answering questions on own seminar	/20
Asking questions in other groups' seminar	/20
Total	%

Full feedback for this will be provided verbally.

All grades are provisional and may be amended up or down by an Examination Board. Grades will only be finalised at the end of each academic year, the dates for this are given in the Assessment Year Planner)

Agreed Grade Awarded (%)

Overall mark: %

Signature   Marker   _____

Print Name

Report Feedback

south essex college
FURTHER & HIGHER EDUCATION

Module Title: The Business Environment

Assignment: Report

Student No. :

Assessor comments for assessment report	
A) The Railways in the UK	
	/20
B) The Link between the Economy and the Railway Network	
	/20
C) The Impact of Technology on the UK Railway Industry	
	/20
D) Comparison with the railway industry in China.	
	/20
E) How the UK Government and its Agencies Support the UK Railway Industry	
	/20

> All grades are provisional and may be amended up or down by an Examination Board. Grades will only be finalised at the end of each academic year, the dates for this are given in the Assessment Year Planner)

Agreed Grade Awarded (%)

%

Signature   1st Marker _____   **2nd Marker** _____

Print Name

Assignment Front Sheet

Student ID No. :

Course Code No. :

Module Code:

Module Title:

Tutor:

Assignment Type/Title:

Deadline:

I confirm that in submitting this assignment:

1) The assignment is my own work and has not been previously submitted in relation to any other module.

2) I have read and understood the college regulations regarding plagiarism and academic offences and this work conform to the requirements set out in those documents.

Assignment Front Sheet

Student ID No. :

Course Code No. :

Module Code:

Module Title:

Tutor:

Assignment Type/Title:

Deadline:

I confirm that in submitting this assignment:

1)The assignment is my own work and has not been previously submitted in relation to any other module.

2) I have read and understood the college regulations regarding plagiarism and academic offences and this work conform to the requirements set out in those documents.

Part 2
Managing People

Section I Module Guide

B113 Managing People

Number of Credits

15

Module Level

4

Purpose of the Module

This module is designed to develop a basic introductory knowledge of Human Resource Management and Organizational Behaviour, and to raise and discuss issues, which are important features of this topic. It aims to provide a foundation of knowledge in Managing People in Organizations.

Aims include:

Effective verbal presentation skills: using a variety of visual and audio visual aids.

Encouragement of an understanding of an individual's role as part of an organization.

An evaluation of HR themes.

An initial development of a critical reflection on both Human Resource policy and Organizational Behaviour.

Learning Outcomes

On satisfactory completion of this module students are expected to be able to:

1. Be aware of the main areas of Human Resource knowledge—at an outline level. Link as relevant with Organizational Behaviour issues in areas like motivation/ leadership/culture / control.

2. Illustrate an awareness of issues central to the efficiency of the Human Resource function, including recruitment, selection, induction and release of staff.

3. Define explain and discuss organizational structures and relevant theories.

4. Demonstrate a broad understanding of management skills and the relevant theories.

Indicative Content

The Organization

Organizational structures

Organizational strategy

Organizational culture

Organizational objectives

Roles and responsibilities

Human Resource Management

History of the development of HRM from initial welfare concepts

Role of HRM

Role of HRD

Role of HRP

Management Skills

Management Theories

Elements of management for example decision-making, delegation and communication

Managing systems such as workflow, management information, IT, budgeting, risk and performance

Management of People

Leadership theory

Coaching

Interviewing

Disciplinary

Facilitating

Selection, recruitment, induction

Training process

Motivation theories and organizational realities

Group dynamics, formal/informal

Roles within a group

Theory and practice of change management

Empowerment

Career progression

Succession planning

Job enlargement /enrichment

Self-management including time management, priorities, self-development, assertiveness

The roles of self-management and the organization

Appraisal systems

Rewards and benefits

Legal considerations inc. health and safety, discrimination, harassment and equal opportunities

Grievance and discipline procedures

Teaching/Learning Strategy

This module will be delivered using a mixture of lectures and seminars to present the fundamentals. Underlying concepts and principles may be expounded during the more formal lectures. Seminars will be used for discussion of issues of theoretical application relative to cases and theory introduced in the lectures.

Assessment

Coursework **25%** weighting

Seminar assessment based on the input, preparation and presentation on a given topic. This could take the form of a presentation by members of the group.

Individual report **75%** weighting

To be based upon a relevant case study, to be presented in report format.

Word count: 2,500 words

Essential Reading:

Banfield, P. and Kay, R. (2012) *Introduction to Human Resource Management* (Oxford)

Indicative Reading:

Foot, M. and Hook, C. (2011) *Introducing Human Resource Management.* (Pearson)

Armstrong M. (2009) *Armstrong's Handbook of Performance Management: An Evidence-Based Guide to Delivering High Performance*

Marchington, M. and Wilkinson, A. (2005) *Human Resource Management at Work*, (CIPD)

Journals

Management Today

People Management

Quality Newspaper

Section II Assessment

south essex college

FURTHER & HIGHER EDUCATION

Assignment 2018—2019

Degree Programme	BA (Hons) Business Studies
Year	1
Module Number	B113
Module Title	Managing People
Type of Assessment	Case Study—Report
Weighting	75%
Draft Date	TBC
Deadline Date	TBC
Feedback Date	TBC

Learning Outcomes

The case study examines the following module outcomes:

1. Be aware of the main areas of Human Resource knowledge—at an outline level. Link as relevant with Organizational Behaviour issues in areas like motivation/ leadership/culture / control.

2. Define, explain and discuss organizational structures and relevant theories.

3. Demonstrate a broad understanding of management skills and the relevant theories.

Managing Human Resources in a Global Organization

Over the past 30 years the growth of globalization has been fuelled through international expansion of corporate operations through Mergers & Acquisitions (M&A), corporate partnership or the creation of new ventures. This trend continues in the early decades of the

21st century, with emerging economies seen as leading the way through outward foreign direct investment.

There are a number of motivations which drive organizations to adopt an international strategy. For enterprises from emerging economies, some of these motivations are: seeking supplies of raw materials, expanding markets, increasing efficiency and seeking strategic assets.

People are a significant asset to an organization, and have a direct impact on success or failure for multinational enterprises. Therefore, managing and developing human resources in a global context is seen as a constant challenge to multinational enterprises. The styles of human resource management required for efficient and legal, operation will vary between countries. Consequently, different approaches in advertising, selection, recruitment, deployment, training, motivation and termination will be necessary.

Required

A company based in the United Kingdom imports toys from China and sells them through retail branches in China, France and Germany and also via e-commerce to many countries around the world.

In no more than 2,500 words address the following tasks:

(1)How should this company motivate, lead and manage its staff? How will the different employment and company cultures in the UK, China, France and Germany affect its employment practices? You should include some current theories in your answer.

(25 marks)

(2) Provide an appropriate organizational structure for this toy company. Justify your choice of structure   (25 marks)

(3) How could the toy company held recruiting/ performance appraisal/ training and development for its staff? You should include some current theories in your answer.

(25 marks)

All tasks carry equal marks.

south essex college

FURTHER & HIGHER EDUCATION

Assessment 2017—2018

Degree Programme	BA (Hons.) Business Studies
Year	1
Module Number	B113
Module Title	Managing People
Type of Assessment	Case Study—Report
Weighting	75%
Draft Deadline Date	
Deadline Date	

Learning Outcomes:

1. Be aware of the main areas of Human Resource knowledge—at an outline level. Link as relevant with Organizational Behaviour issues in areas like motivation/ leadership/culture / control.

2. Illustrate an awareness of issues central to the efficiency of the Human Resource function, including recruitment, selection, induction and release of staff.

3. Demonstrate a broad understanding of management skills and the relevant theories.

Word count: 2,500 words

Managing Human Resources in A Global Organization 全球化视角管理人力资源

Over the past 30 years the growth of globalization has been fuelled through international expansion of corporate operations through Mergers & Acquisitions (M&A), corporate partnership or the creation of new ventures. This trend continues in the early decades of the 21st century, with emerging economies seen as leading the way through outward foreign direct investment.

Definition of Foreign Direct Investment (FDI) *"an activity in which an investor in one country obtains a lasting interest in, and a significant influence on management of an entity resident in another country. This may involve either creating an entirely new enterprise (so called 'greenfield site') or more typically, changing the ownership of existing enterprises (via mergers and acquisitions)"*.

Source: OECD.

It is the context of changing ownership of existing enterprises that students are asked to consider in this assignment.

There are a number of motivations which drive organizations to adopt an international strategy. In particular, for enterprises from emerging economies, among these motivations are:

- 寻找资源**Resource seeking:** Energy is the key to the development of emerging economies and much investment is made by heavy industry sectors in order to secure resources for their home manufacturing base.

- 科技发展**Technology and R&D:** Knowledge transfer is another important requirement for developing nations as they have an appetite to acquire the technological skills that have been enjoyed by western economies.

- 品牌扩张**Brand name extension:** China and India in particular have acquired some big brand corporations in recent years, e.g. Tata Motors' (India) acquisition of UK car makers Jaguar.

- 新市场开拓**New markets:** With foreign competition embedded in their home markets, looking to expand in overseas markets may be the best option.

- 风险多样化**Risk diversification:** This is quite common in the IT sector whereby some software companies acquire overseas operations in order to mitigate against failures in their home country.

- 寻求效率**Efficiency seeking:** Moving their production operations overseas can give an organization an immediate network of suppliers and customers.

By the end of 2014 China's overseas investment amounted to $870 billion according to Heritage Foundation, an American research company, who state that by the end of 2015, China's outward investment will surpass its inward investment levels.

There are many examples of both successful and failed international M&A, and a significant amount of analysis and commentary is available that discusses the appropriate examples.

Daimler (Germany) & Chrysler (USA) merged in the late 90s which was branded as a merger of equals. In 2007, Daimler sold Chrysler to a capital management company having seen significant losses over their 18 year partnership.

British Steel and Dutch Royal Hoogovens merged to form Corus Steel in 1999 to create the world's fifth largest steel maker at the time. However, lack of cultural fit saw the enterprise fail and subsequently sold to Indian steel company Tata in 2007.

People are the most significant asset to an organization, and can have a direct impact on success or failure for multinational enterprises. Therefore, managing and developing human resources in a global context is seen as a constant challenge to multinational enterprises.

Multinational or international organizations operate in more than one country and the parent company will normally take their own business approach in terms of operations, bringing their own management attitudes and leadership styles to the subsidiary organization. Thus, there is a need to develop an international human resources approach to managing the human element of the merged business.

Some topics or themes of conflict to consider:

• The variety of international organizational models.

• Variances in HRM policy and practice in different countries, often referred to as "convergence" and "divergence".

• Cultural diversity dimensions.

• The diverse approaches used to select, recruit, deploy and develop employees.

Devising an appropriate global human resource management framework is an important approach to successfully managing this element of the organization. Organizational structures, management styles, organizational cultures and approaches to change management, have to be carefully adapted to the dominant cultural attributes of the host nation, just as a careful balancing act is sought between being global whilst serving local (employee) needs.

For this assignment you are a Managing Director (MD) for an electronics company based in Tokyo where you feel it is the right time to expand into American markets. Your preferred choice is to acquire a current operation based in California, as this is relatively easily to access from your Pacific Rim location. Moreover the state of California has some excellent port operations and supply chain links to all U.S. states.

You are aware that the HR Strategy you employ at your Japanese base cannot simply be transplanted into a U.S. operation, therefore, you are going to carry out a feasibility study to ascertain what would be the best framework to adopt for your new international operation.

End of Case Study

Required

In no more than 2,500 words address the following two questions.

(1) Examine the literature on International Human Resource Management and discuss some of the key issues, especially in areas like motivation / leadership /culture /structure.

All themes should be referenced.

(50 Marks)

(2) From the issues identified in question 1, suggest how you would address these in your U.S. operation. Ensure you include the application of management skills and theory, recruitment and selection practices, induction processes and the releasing of staff.

(50 Marks)

	Characteristics of student achievement per mark band →	70%+ **Work of a distinguished quality**	60%~69% **Work of a commendable category**	50%~59% **Sound work**	40%~49% **Broadly satisfactory work**	0~39% **Work that falls short of the threshold standards**
Knowledge and understanding	Has a broad understanding of the knowledge base in a field of study and the appropriate terminology/discourse. Appreciates that some areas of this knowledge base are open to ongoing debate and reformulation.	Provides a rigorous and broad factual and conceptual knowledge base, exploring and analysing the discipline and its theory.	Provides a strong factual and/or conceptual knowledge base, exploring and analysing the discipline and its theory.	Provides a firm factual and/or conceptual base of knowledge which begins to explore and analyse the discipline and is mostly accurate with no serious omissions or inaccuracies.	Provides an adequate factual and/or conceptual base of knowledge which begins to explore the discipline. There may be some misunderstanding of key concepts and principles or omissions in understanding.	Limited knowledge base; limited understanding of discipline
Cognitive skills	Identifies principles and concepts underlying theoretical frameworks and approaches.	Demonstrates a rigorous and broad grasp of relevant principles and concepts.	Demonstrates a strong grasp of relevant principles and concepts.	Demonstrates a firm grasp of relevant principles and concepts.	Demonstrates an adequate grasp of relevant principles and concepts.	Limited grasp of relevant principles and concepts.

Continued

70%+	60%~69%	50%~59%	40%~49%	0~39%
Makes use of a range of specialized skills in the development and evaluation of problem-solving strategies. Manages information (including referencing sources), collects appropriate data from a range of sources and undertakes structured research tasks with external guidance, in a distinguished manner.	Demonstrates a commendable competence in the application of skills to the solution of a defined problem. Manages information (including referencing sources), collects appropriate data from a range of sources and undertakes structured research tasks in a commendable manner.	Demonstrates a sound competence in applying given tools and/or methods to a structured problem. Manages information (including referencing sources), collects appropriate data from a range of sources and undertakes standard research tasks in a sound manner.	Applies given tools and/or methods adequately to a well defined problem, Manages information (including referencing sources), collects appropriate data from a range of sources and undertakes standard research tasks with external guidance, in a manner that is adequate but with some limitations	Fails to display adequacy in the application of given tools and methods to a well-defined problem, fails to demonstrate an adequate ability to manage information (including referencing sources), collect appropriate data and undertake standard research tasks.
Identifies a well-defined focus for enquiry, plans investigative strategies using a limited and defined range of methods, collects data from a variety of sources, and communicates results effectively in an appropriate format				

Continued

	70%+	60%~69%	50%~59%	40%~49%	0~39%
Analyses a range of information using pre-defined principles, frameworks or criteria. Judges the reliability of data using pre-defined techniques and/or criteria.	Provides clear evidence of very strong and distinguished analysis, synthesis and evaluation.	Provides clear evidence of strong and commendable analysis, synthesis and evaluation.	Primarily standard in exposition, but provides some evidence of an ability to analyse, synthesize, evaluate and apply standard methods and techniques under guidance.	Primarily descriptive but provides occasional and broadly satisfactory analysis and evaluation. Collects and categorises ideas and information occasionally and in a predictable and standard format.	Fails to provide any adequate analysis, evaluation or synthesis.
Understands performance tasks and undertakes such tasks competently.	Demonstrates unusually complete understanding of performance tasks and demonstrates distinguished performance and high levels of competency in undertaking them.	Demonstrates complete understanding of performance tasks and demonstrates commendable performance and good competency in undertaking them.	Demonstrates understanding of performance tasks and demonstrates sound performance and competency in undertaking them.	Demonstrates base level/basic understanding of performance tasks and demonstrates satisfactory performance and competency in undertaking them.	Fails to demonstrate understanding of performance tasks and does not demonstrate performance that is competent.

Continued

	70%+	60%~69%	50%~59%	40%~49%	0~39%
Recognizes actions and behaviours appropriate to the situation and the results of actions on self and others. Uses interpersonal and communication skills and knowledge to identify and rectify problem areas.	Communicates effectively, accurately and reliably in a format appropriate to the discipline. Effective use of interpersonal skills to rectify problems.	Displays strong communication skills in a format appropriate to the discipline. Good interpersonal skills to rectify problems.	Communicate effectively in a format appropriate to the discipline. Appropriate interpersonal skills used to rectify problems.	Communicates in a broadly satisfactory manner in a format appropriate to the discipline. Satisfactory interpersonal skills.	Fails to display satisfactory interpersonal and communication skills.

south essex college

FURTHER & HIGHER EDUCATION

Seminar 2017—2018

Degree Programme	N100 BA (Hons) Business Studies
Year	1
Module Number	B113
Module Title	Managing People
Type of Assessment	Seminar—(Assignment 2)
Weighting	25%
Draft Date	TBC
Deadline Date	TBC

Learning Outcomes

The seminars examine the following module outcome:

1. Illustrate an awareness of issues central to the efficiency of the Human Resource function, including recruitment, selection, induction and release of staff.

Seminar Topics

Overview:

You will be allocated to a group by your subject tutor. You will then be allocated a seminar question from the questions below. It is possible that some groups will be working on the same seminar question.

Required:

a) Describe and explain the key procedures involved in an efficient recruitment process bearing in mind that an HRM Department needs to plan for future recruitment needs of a mid-size national organization. How can these functions be outsourced and to where?

b) Identify and critically evaluate a number of the most challenging aspects of recruiting, developing, retaining and releasing staff. Use real examples drawn from the (UK) public and private sectors. Why is it critical for HRM departments to be familiar with the UK *Equality Act 2010*?

You will need to work in a group to **write a seminar paper of around 800 words and present your conclusions** to an audience which comprises of your year cohort and selected members of the teaching team. You should support your written paper through the use of a PowerPoint presentation, or equivalent alternative.

The groups will need to meet to discuss, plan and prepare for their seminars. An attendance record of your groups' meetings should be kept as well as brief minutes (records) of meetings held. These should be submitted along with your groups' written paper. (Probably in an Appendix)

Students must not miss classes to have these meetings.

Each seminar will last up to 20 minutes and consist of a presentation and discussion. It will be delivered at a date, time and place specified by the tutor. You will need to hand in a copy of your PowerPoint slides or display material on a previous, stated date.

Marks will only be awarded for a student's own contribution, so any student unable to contribute to the group's work (for any reason) will not be able to gain marks.

Marking Scheme for Seminar Presentation and Discussion

The marks represent 25% of the overall module marking and will be divided to take account of the actual seminar delivery and the relevance of the material supplied to the other students in the form of handouts and activities and your involvement in the seminars of other students.

Activity	Marks
Evidence of research work (references/quotes/statistics etc.)	20
Materials (e.g. PowerPoint slides/handouts/displays etc.)	20
Interaction with other group members (as per generic criteria)	20
Answering questions on own seminar	20
Asking questions in other groups' seminar	20
Total	100

Activity	Marks
Research work (references/quotes/statistics etc.) Comments	20
Materials (e.g. PowerPoint slides/handouts/displays/samples etc.) Comments	20

Continued

Activity	Marks
Interaction with other group members (as per generic criteria) Comments	20
Answering questions on own seminar Comments	20
Asking questions in other groups' seminar Comments	20
Total	100

(Continued)

Generic learning outcomes	Assessment criteria by level	70%+	60%~69%	50%~59%	40%~49%	0~39%
	Characteristics of student achievement per mark band	Work of a distinguished quality	Work of a commendable category	Sound work	Broadly satisfactory work	Work that falls short of the threshold standards
Knowledge and under-standing	Has a broad understanding of the knowledge base in a field of study and the appropriate terminology/discourse. Appreciates that some areas of this knowledge base are open to ongoing debate and reformulation.	Provides a rigorous and broad factual and conceptual knowledge base, exploring and analysing the discipline and its theory.	Provides a strong factual and/or conceptual knowledge base, exploring and analysing the discipline and its theory.	Provides a firm factual and/or conceptual base of knowledge which begins to explore and analyse the discipline and is mostly accurate with no serious omissions or inaccuracies.	Provides an adequate factual and/or conceptual base of knowledge which begins to explore the discipline. There may be some misunderstanding of key concepts and principles or omissions in understanding.	Limited knowledge base; limited understanding of discipline.
Conceptual-isation and critical thinking	Identifies principles and concepts underlying theoretical frameworks and approaches.	Demonstrates a rigorous and broad grasp of relevant principles and concepts.	Demonstrates a strong grasp of relevant principles and concepts.	Demonstrates a firm grasp of relevant principles and concepts.	Demonstrates an adequate grasp of relevant principles and concepts.	Limited grasp of relevant principles and concepts.

Continued

Generic learning outcomes	Assessment criteria by level	70%+	60%~69%	50%~59%	40%~49%	0~39%
Problem solving, research and enquiry	Identifies a well-defined focus for enquiry, plans investigative strategies using a limited and defined range of methods, collects data from a variety of sources, and communicates results effectively in an appropriate format.	Makes use of a range of specialized skills in the development and evaluation of problem-solving strategies. Manages information (including referencing sources), collects appropriate data from a range of sources and undertakes structured research tasks with external guidance, in a distinguished manner.	Demonstrates a commendable competence in the application of skills to the solution of a defined problem. Manages information (including referencing sources), collects appropriate data from a range of sources and undertakes structured research tasks in a commendable manner.	Demonstrates a sound competence in applying given tools and/or methods to a structured problem. Manages information (including referencing sources), collects appropriate data from a range of sources and undertakes standard research tasks in a sound manner.	Applies given tools and/or methods adequately to a well-defined problem, manages information (including referencing sources), collects appropriate data from a range of sources and undertakes standard research tasks with external guidance, in a manner that is adequate but with some limitations.	Fails to display adequacy in the application of given tools and methods to a well-defined problem, fails to demonstrate an adequate ability to manage information (including referencing sources), collect appropriate data and undertake standard research tasks.

Continued

Generic learning outcomes	Assessment criteria by level	70%+	60%~69%	50%~59%	40%~49%	0-39%
Synthesis and creativity	Collects information to inform a choice of solutions to standard problems in familiar contexts.	Excellent management of learning resources, complemented by self-direction/ exploration. Structured/ accurate expression. Very good academic/ intellectual and team / practical/ professional skills	Good management of learning resources with some self-direction. Structured and mainly accurate expression. Good academic/ intellectual skills and team/ practical/professional skills	Satisfactory use of learning resources and input to team work. Some lack of structure/ accuracy in expression. Acceptable academic/ intellectual skills and satisfactory practical/ professional skills	Basic use of learning resources with no self-direction. Some input to team work. Some difficulty with structure and accuracy in expression. Some difficulties with academic/ intellectual skills and developing practical/ professional skills	Limited use of learning resources, No self-direction, little input to team work and difficulty with structure/ accuracy in expression. Weak academic/ intellectual skills Practical/ professional skills are not yet secure
Analysis and evaluation	Analyses a range of information using pre-defined principles, frameworks or criteria. Judges the reliability of data using pre-defined techniques and/or criteria.	Provides clear evidence of very strong and distinguished analysis, synthesis and evaluation.	Provides clear evidence of strong and commendable analysis, synthesis and evaluation.	Primarily standard in exposition, but provides some evidence of an ability to analyse, synthesise, evaluate and apply standard methods and techniques under guidance.	Primarily descriptive but provides occasional and broadly satisfactory analysis and evaluation. Collects and categorises ideas and information occasionally and in a predictable and standard format.	Fails to provide any adequate analysis, evaluation or synthesis.

Continued

Generic learning outcomes	Assessment criteria by level	70%+	60%~69%	50%~59%	40%~49%	0~39%
Team and organizational working	Recognizes the factors that affect team performance, can work effectively with others and meet obligations.	Works with others as a member of a group and meets obligations to others in a strong and distinguished manner.	Works with others as a member of a group and meets obligations to others in a strong and commendable manner.	Works with others as a member of a group and meets obligations to others in a sound manner.	Works with others as a member of a group and meets obligations to others in a manner that is broadly satisfactory.	Fails to display an adequate ability to work with others as a member of a group and meet obligations to others.
Inter-personal and communication skills	Recognizes actions and behaviours appropriate to the situation and the results of actions on self and others. Uses interpersonal and communication skills and knowledge to identify and rectify problem areas.	Communicates effectively, accurately and reliably in a format appropriate to the discipline. Effective use of interpersonal skills to rectify problems.	Displays strong communication skills in a format appropriate to the discipline. Good interpersonal skills to rectify problems.	Communicate effectively in a format appropriate to the discipline. Appropriate interpersonal skills used to rectify problems.	Communicates in a broadly satisfactory manner in a format appropriate to the discipline. Satisfactory interpersonal skills.	Fails to display satisfactory interpersonal and communication skills.

Section III Managing People

Contents

Chapter 1 The Role of Human Resources

Human Resource Management Day to Day

You have just been hired to work in the Human Resource Department of a small company. You heard about the job through a conference you attended, put on by the Society for Human Resource Management (SHRM). Previously, the owner of the company, Jennifer, had been doing everything related to Human Resource Management (HRM). You can tell she is a bit critical about paying a good salary for something she was able to juggle all on her own. On your first day, you meet the ten employees and spend several hours with the company owner, hoping to get a handle on which human resource processes are already set up.

Shortly after the meeting begins, you see she has a completely different perspective of what HRM is, and you realize it will be your job to educate her on the value of a human resource manager. You look at it as a personal challenge—both to educate her and also to show her the value of this role in the organization.

First, you tell her that HRM is a strategic process having to do with the staffing, compensation, retention, training, and employment law and policies side of the business. In other words, your job as human resources (HR) manager will be not only to write policy and procedures and to hire people (the administrative role) but also to use strategic plans to ensure the right people are hired and trained for the right job at the right time. For example, you ask her if she knows what the revenue will be in six months, and Jennifer answers, "Of course, we expect it to increase by 20 percent." You ask, "Have you thought about how many people you will need due to this increase?" Jennifer looks a bit sheepish and says, "No, I guess I haven't gotten that far." Then you ask her about the training programs the company offers, the software used to allow employees to access pay information online, and the compensation policies. She responds, "It looks like we have some work to do. I didn't know that human resources involved all of that." You smile at her and start discussing some of the specifics of the business, so you can get started right away writing the strategic Human Resource

Management plan.

The Role of Human Resources

The author introduces the chapter defining the role of Human Resource Management.

1.1 What Is Human Resources?

Learning Objectives

1. Explain the role of HRM in organizations.
2. Define and discuss some of the major HRM activities.

Every organization, large or small, uses a variety of capital to make the business work. Capital includes cash, valuables, or goods used to generate income for a business. For example, a retail store uses registers and inventory, while a consulting firm may have proprietary software or buildings. No matter the industry, all companies have one thing in common: they must have people to make their capital work for them. This will be our focus throughout the text: generation of revenue through the use of people's skills and abilities.

What is HRM?

Human Resource Management (HRM) is the process of employing people, training them, compensating them, developing policies relating to them, and developing strategies to retain them. As a field, HRM has undergone many changes over the last twenty years, giving it an even more important role in today's organizations. In the past, HRM meant processing payroll, sending birthday gifts to employees, arranging company outings, and making sure forms were filled out correctly—in other words, more of an administrative role rather than a strategic role crucial to the success of the organization. Jack Welch, former CEO of General Electric and management guru, sums up the new role of HRM: "Get out of the parties and birthdays and enrollment forms... Remember, HR is important in good times, HR is defined in hard times." (Frasch, et. al., 2010).

It's necessary to point out here, at the very beginning of this text, that every manager has some role relating to Human Resource Management. Just because we do not have the title of HR manager doesn't mean we won't perform all or at least some of the HRM tasks. For example, most managers deal with compensation, motivation, and retention of employees—

making these aspects not only part of HRM but also part of management. As a result, this book is equally important to someone who wants to be an HR manager and to someone who will manage a business.

> **Human Resource Recall**
>
> Have you ever had to work with a Human Resource Department at your job? What was the interaction like?
>
> What was the department's role in that specific organization?

The Role of HRM

Keep in mind that many functions of HRM are also tasks other department managers perform, which is what makes this information important, despite the career path taken. Most experts agree on seven main roles that HRM plays in organizations. These are described in the following sections.

Staffing

You need people to perform tasks and get work done in the organization. Even with the most sophisticated machines, humans are still needed. Because of this, one of the major tasks in HRM is staffing. Staffing involves the entire hiring process from posting a job to negotiating a salary package. Within the staffing function, there are four main steps:

Development of a staffing plan. This plan allows HRM to see how many people they should hire based on revenue expectations.

Development of policies to encourage multiculturalism at work. Multiculturalism in the workplace is becoming more and more important, as we have many more people from a variety of backgrounds in the workforce.

Recruitment. This involves finding people to fill the open positions.

Selection. In this stage, people will be interviewed and selected, and a proper compensation package will be negotiated. This step is followed by training, retention, and motivation.

Development of Workplace Policies

Every organization has policies to ensure fairness and continuity within the organization. One of the jobs of HRM is to develop the verbiage surrounding these policies. In the development of policies, HRM, and executives are involved in the process. For example, the HRM professional will likely recognize the need for a policy or a change of policy, seek opinions on the policy, write the policy, and then communicate that policy to employees. It is key to note here that HR departments do not and cannot work alone. Everything they do needs to involve all other departments in the organization. Some examples of workplace policies might be the following:

Discipline process policy

Vacation time policy

Dress code

• Human Resource Management

Ethics policy

Internet usage policy

These topics are addressed further in Chapter 5 "Compensation and Benefits", Chapter 6 "Retention and Motivation", Chapter 7 "Training and Development".

Compensation and Benefits Administration

HRM professionals need to determine that compensation is fair, meets industry standards, and is high enough to entice people to work for the organization. Compensation includes anything the employee receives for his or her work. In addition, HRM professionals need to make sure the pay is comparable to what other people performing similar jobs are being paid. This involves setting up pay systems that take into consideration the number of years with the organization, years of experience, education, and similar aspects. Examples of employee compensation include the following:

Pay

Health benefits

401(k) (retirement plans)

Stock purchase plans

Vacation time

Sick leave

Bonuses

Tuition reimbursement

Since this is not an exhaustive list, compensation is discussed further in Chapter 5 "Compensation and Benefits".

Retention

Retention involves keeping and motivating employees to stay with the organization. Compensation is a major factor in employee retention, but there are other factors as well. Ninety percent of employees leave a company for the following reasons:

Issues around the job they are performing

Challenges with their manager

Poor fit with organizational culture

Poor workplace environment

Despite this, 90 percent of managers think employees leave as a result of pay (Rivenbark, 2010). As a result, managers often try to change their compensation packages to keep people from leaving, when compensation isn't the reason they are leaving at all. Chapter 6 "Retention and Motivation" and Chapter 8 "Employee Assessment" discuss some strategies to retain the best employees based on these four factors.

Training and Development

Once we have spent the time to hire new employees, we want to make sure they not only are trained to do the job but also continue to grow and develop new skills in their job. This results in higher productivity for the organization. Training is also a key component in employee motivation. Employees who feel they are developing their skills tend to be happier in their jobs, which results in increased employee retention. Examples of training programs might include the following:

Job skills training, such as how to run a particular computer program

Training on communication

Team-building activities

Policy and legal training, such as sexual harassment training and ethics training

We address each of these types of training and more in detail in Chapter 7 "Training and Development".

Dealing with Laws Affecting Employment

Human resource people must be aware of all the laws that affect the workplace. An HRM professional might work with some of these laws:

Discrimination laws

Healthcare requirements

Compensation requirements such as the minimum wage

Worker safety laws

Labor laws

The legal environment of HRM is always changing, so HRM must always be aware of changes taking place and then communicate those changes to the entire management organization. Rather than presenting a chapter focused on HRM laws, we will address these laws in each relevant chapter.

Worker Protection

Safety is a major consideration in all organizations. Oftentimes new laws are created with the goal of setting federal or state standards to ensure worker safety. Unions and union contracts can also impact the requirements for worker safety in a workplace. It is up to the Human Resource Manager to be aware of worker protection requirements and ensure the workplace is meeting both federal and union standards. Worker protection issues might include the following:

- Chemical hazards
- Human Resource Management
- Heating and ventilation requirements
- Use of "no fragrance" zones
- Protection of private employee information

We take a closer look at these issues in Chapter 9 "Working with Labor Unions" and Chapter 13 "Safety and Health at Work".

Communication

Besides these major roles, good communication skills and excellent management skills are key to successful Human Resource Management as well as general management. We discuss these issues in Chapter 9 "Successful Employee Communication".

Awareness of External Factors

In addition to managing internal factors, the HR manager needs to consider the outside forces at play that may affect the organization. Outside forces, or external factors, are those things the company has no direct control over; however, they may be things that could positively or negatively impact human resources. External factors might include the following:

- Globalization and offshoring
- Changes to employment law
- Healthcare costs

- Employee expectations
- Diversity of the workforce
- Changing demographics of the workforce
- A more highly educated workforce
- Layoffs and downsizing
- Technology used, such as HR databases
- Increased use of social networking to distribute information to employees

For example, the recent trend in flexible work schedules (allowing employees to set their own schedules) and telecommuting (allowing employees to work from home or a remote location for a specified period of time, such as one day per week) are external factors that have affected HR. HRM has to be aware of these outside issues, so they can develop policies that meet not only the needs of the company but also the needs of the individuals. Another example is the *Patient Protection and Affordable Care Act*, signed into law in 2010. Compliance with this bill has huge implications for HR. For example, a company with more than fifty employees must provide healthcare coverage or pay a penalty. Currently, it is estimated that 60 percent of employers offer healthcare insurance to their employees (Cappelli, 2010). Because healthcare insurance will be mandatory, cost concerns as well as using health benefits as a recruitment strategy are big external challenges. Any manager operating without considering outside forces will likely alienate employees, resulting in unmotivated, unhappy workers. Not understanding the external factors can also mean breaking the law, which has a concerning set of implications as well.

An understanding of key external factors is important to the successful HR professional. This allows him or her to be able to make strategic decisions based on changes in the external environment. To develop this understanding, reading various publications is necessary.

One way managers can be aware of the outside forces is to attend conferences and read various articles on the web. For example, the website of the Society for Human Resource Management, SHRM Online, not only has job postings in the field but discusses many contemporary human resource issues that may help the manager make better decisions when it comes to people management. In Section 1.3 "Today's HRM Challenges", we go into more depth about some recent external issues that are affecting human resource management roles. In Section 1.1.2 "The Role of HRM", we discuss some of the skills needed to be successful in HRM.

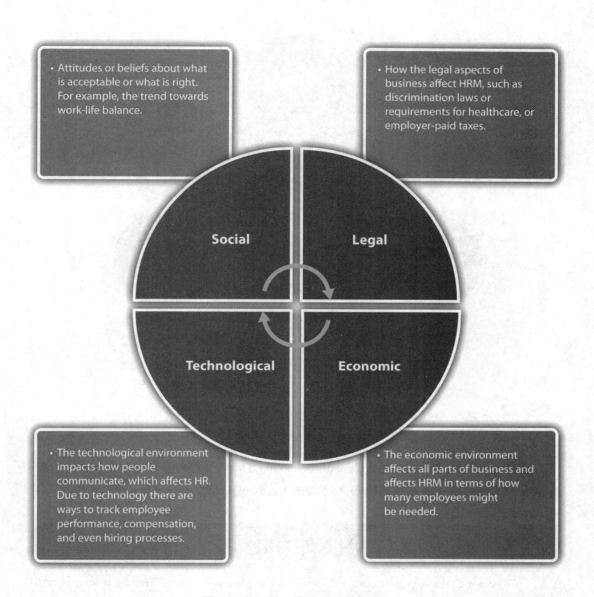

Figure 2-1 Key External Factors

Figure 2-2 External Factors

Most professionals agree that there are seven main tasks HRM professionals perform. All these need to be considered in relation to external and outside forces.

Key Takeaways

Capital includes all resources a company uses to generate revenue. Human resources or the people working in the organization are the most important resource.

Human Resource Management is the process of employing people, training them, compensating them, developing policies relating to the workplace, and developing strategies to retain employees.

There are seven main responsibilities of HRM managers: staffing, setting policies, compensation and benefits, retention, training, employment laws, and worker protection. In this book, each of these major areas will be included in a chapter or two.

In addition to being concerned with the seven internal aspects, HRM managers must keep up to date with changes in the *external environment* that may impact their employees. The trends toward flexible *schedules* and *telecommuting* are examples of external aspects.

To effectively understand how the external forces might affect human resources, it is important for the HR manager to read the HR literature, attend conferences, and utilize other ways to stay up to date with new laws, trends, and policies.

Exercises

1. State arguments for and against the following statement: there are other things more valuable in an organization besides the people who work there.

2. Of the seven tasks an HR manager does, which do you think is the most challenging? Why?

1.2 Skills Needed for HRM

Learning Objectives

1. Explain the professional and personal skills needed to be successful in HRM.

2. Be able to define Human Resource Management and the certifications that can be achieved in this profession.

One of the major factors of a successful manager or Human Resource (HR) manager is an array of skills to deal with a variety of situations. It simply isn't enough to have knowledge of HR, such as knowing which forms need to be filled out. It takes multiple skills to create and manage people, as well as a cutting-edge Human Resource Department.

The first skill needed is organization. The need for this skill makes sense, given that you are managing people's pay, benefits, and careers. Having organized files on your computer and good time-management skills are crucial for success in any job, but especially if you take on a role in human resources.

Like most jobs, being able to multitask—that is, work on more than one task at a time—

is important in managing human resources. A typical person managing human resources may have to deal with an employee issue one minute, then switch and deal with recruiting. Unlike many management positions, which only focus on one task or one part of the business, human resources focuses on all areas of the business, where multitasking is a must.

As trite as it may sound, people skills are necessary in any type of management and perhaps might be the most important skills for achieving success at any job. Being able to manage a variety of personalities, deal with conflict, and coach others are all in the realm of people management. The ability to communicate goes along with people skills. The ability to communicate good news (hiring a new employee), bad news (lay-offs), and everything in between, such as changes to policy, makes for an excellent manager and Human Resource Management (HRM) professional.

Keys to a successful career in HRM or management include understanding specific job areas, such as managing the employee database, understanding employment laws, and knowing how to write and develop a strategic plan that aligns with the business. All these skills will be discussed in this book.

A strategic mind-set as an HR professional is a key skill as well. A person with a strategic mind-set can plan far in advance and look at trends that could affect the environment in which the business is operating. Too often, managers focus on their own area and not enough on the business as a whole. The strategic HR professional is able to not only work within his or her area but also understand how HR fits into the bigger picture of the business.

Ethics and a sense of fairness are also necessary in human resources. Ethics is a concept that examines the moral rights and wrongs of a certain situation. Consider the fact that many HR managers negotiate salary and union contracts and manage conflict. In addition, HR managers have the task of ensuring compliance with ethics standards within the organization. Many HR managers are required to work with highly confidential information, such as salary information, so a sense of ethics when managing this information is essential. We discuss ethics from the organizational perspective in Chapter 1 "The Role of HRM".

Dilbert and the Evil HR Director

Human Resource Recall

Think of your current skills. Are there personal or professional skills you would like to work on?

Finally, while we can list a few skills that are important, understanding the particular business, knowing the business strategy, and being able to think critically about how HR can align itself with the strategy are ways to ensure HR departments are critical parts of the business. HR is a specialized area, much like accounting or finance. However, many individuals are placed in HR roles without having the specific knowledge to do the job. Oftentimes people with excellent skills are promoted to management and then expected (if the company is small) to perform recruiting, hiring, and compensation tasks. This is the reason we will refer to management and HR management interchangeably throughout the chapters. In addition, these skills are important for HRM professionals and managers alike.

Having said that, for those of you wanting a career in HRM, there are three exams you can take to show your mastery of HRM material:

Professional in Human Resources (PHR). To take this exam, an HR professional must have at least two years' experience. The exam is four hours long and consists of 225 multiple-choice questions in a variety of areas. Twelve percent of the test focuses on strategic management, 26 percent on workforce planning, 17 percent on human resource development, 16 percent on rewards, 22 percent on employee and labor relations, and 7 percent on risk management. The application process for taking the exam is given on the Human Resource Certification Institute website at http://www.hrci.org.

Senior Professional in Human Resources (SPHR). This exam is designed for HR professionals who focus on designing and planning, rather than actual implementation. It is recommended that the person taking this exam has six to eight years of experience and oversees and manages an HR department. In this test, the greater focus is on the strategic aspect of HRM.

Global Professional in Human Resources (GPHR). This exam is for HR professionals who perform many of their tasks on a global level and whose companies often work across borders. This exam is three hours long, with 165 multiple-choice questions. A person with two years of professional experience can take the certification test. However, because the test has the international aspect, someone who designs HR-related programs and processes to achieve business goals would be best suited to earn this certification.

The benefits of achieving certifications are great. In addition to demonstrating the abilities of the HR professional, certification allows the professional to be more marketable in a very competitive field.

Figure 2-3 GPHR

Most companies need a Human Resource Department or a manager with HR skills. The industries and job titles are so varied that it is possible only to list general job titles in human resources:

Recruiter

Compensation Analyst

Human Resources Assistant

Employee Relations Manager

Benefits Manager

Work-life Coordinator

Training and Development Manager

Human Resources Manager

Vice-president for Human Resources

This is not an exhaustive list, but it can be a starting point for research on this career path.

Key Takeaways

There are a number of skills crucial to Human Resource Management. First, being able to organize and multitask is necessary. In this job, files must be managed, and an HR manager is constantly working in different areas of the business.

Communication skills are necessary in HRM as well. The ability to present good and bad news, work with a variety of personalities, and coach employees is important in HRM.

Specific job skills, such as computer skills, knowledge of employment law, writing and developing strategic plans, and general critical-thinking skills are important in any type of management, but especially in Human Resource Management.

A sense of fairness and strong *ethics* will make for the best HR manager. Because HR works with a variety of departments to manage conflict and negotiate union contracts and salary, the HR professional needs ethics skills and the ability to maintain confidentiality.

Many people find themselves in the role of HR manager, so we will use the term HR manager throughout this book. However, many other types of managers also perform the tasks of recruiting, selecting, and compensating, making this book and the skills listed in this section applicable to all majors.

Certification exams can be taken to make you more marketable in the field of HRM. These certifications are offered by the HR Certification Institute (HRCI).

What are your perceptions of what an HR manager does on a day-to-day basis? Research this job title and describe your findings. Is this the type of job you expected?

1.3 Today's HRM Challenges

If you were to ask most business owners what their biggest challenges are, they will likely tell you that cost management is a major factor to the success or failure of their business. In most businesses today, the people part of the business is the most likely place for cuts when the economy isn't doing well.

Consider the expenses that involve the people part of any business:

Healthcare benefits

Training costs

Hiring process costs

And many more...

These costs cut into the bottom line of any business. The trick is to figure out how much, how many, or how often benefits should be offered, without sacrificing employee motivation. A company can cut costs by not offering benefits or 401(k) plans, but if its goal is to hire the best people, a hiring package without these items will most certainly not get the best people.

Containment of costs, therefore, is a balancing act. An HR manager must offer as much as he or she can attract and retain employees, but not offer too much, as this can put pressure on the company's bottom line. We will discuss ways to alleviate this concern throughout this book.

For example, there are three ways to cut costs associated with healthcare:

Shift more of the cost of healthcare to employees

Reduce the benefits offered to cut costs

Change or better negotiate the plan to reduce healthcare costs

Healthcare costs companies approximately $4,003 per year for a single employee and $9,764 for families. This equals roughly 83 percent and 73 percent of total healthcare costs for single employees and employees with families, respectively. One possible strategy for containment for healthcare plans is to implement a cafeteria plan. Cafeteria plans started becoming popular in the 1980s and have become standard in many organizations (Allen, 2010). This type of plan gives all employees a minimum level of benefits and a set amount to spend on flexible benefits, such as additional healthcare or vacation time. It creates more flexible benefits, allowing the employee, based on his or her family situation, to choose which benefits are right for them. For example, a mother of two may choose to spend her flexible benefits on healthcare for her children, while a single, childless female may opt for more vacation days. In other words, these plans offer flexibility, while saving money, too. Cost containment strategies around benefits will be discussed in Chapter 5 "Compensation and Benefits".

Another way to contain costs is by offering training. While this may seem counterintuitive, as training does cost money up front, it can actually save money in the long run. Consider how expensive a sexual harassment lawsuit or wrongful termination lawsuit might be. For example, a Sonic Drive-In was investigated by the Equal Employment Opportunity Commission (EEOC) on behalf of seventy women who worked there, and it was found that a manager at one of the stores subjected the victims to inappropriate touching and comments. This lawsuit cost the organization $2 million. Some simple training up front (costing less than the lawsuit) likely would have prevented this from happening. Training employees and management on how to work within the law, thereby reducing legal exposure, is a great way for HR to cut costs for the organization as a whole. In Chapter 7 "Training and Development", we will further discuss how to organize, set up, and measure the success of a training program.

The hiring process and the cost of turnover in an organization can be very expensive. Turnover refers to the number of employees who leave a company in a particular period of time. By creating a recruiting and selection process with cost containment in mind, HR can contribute directly to cost-containment strategies company wide. In fact, the cost of hiring an employee or replacing an old one (turnover) can be as high as $9,777 for a position that pays $60,000 (Del Monte, 2010). By hiring smart the first time, HR managers can contain costs for their organization. This will be discussed in Chapter 3 "Recruitment" and Chapter 4 "Selection". Reducing turnover includes employee motivational strategies. This will be addressed in Chapter 6 "Retention and Motivation".

In a survey reported on by the *Sales and Marketing Management* newsletter, 85 percent of managers say that ineffective communication is the cause of lost revenue. E-mail, instant messaging, text messages, and meetings are all examples of communication in business. An understanding of communication styles, personality styles, and channels of communication can help us be more effective in our communications, resulting in cost containment. In HRM, we can help ensure our people have the tools to communicate better, and contain costs and save dollars in doing so. Some of these tools for better communication will be addressed in other chapters.

One cost-containment strategy for U.S. businesses has been offshoring. Offshoring refers to the movement of jobs overseas to contain costs. It is estimated that 3.3 million U.S. jobs will be moved overseas by 2015 (Agrawal & Farrell, 2003). According to the U.S. Census Bureau, most of these jobs are Information Technology (IT) jobs as well as manufacturing jobs. This issue is unique to HR, as the responsibility for developing training for new workers and laying off domestic workers will often fall under the realm of HRM. Offshoring will be discussed in other parts, and training for new workers will be discussed in Chapter 7 "Training and Development".

Figure 2-4 Challege for Balance

Caption: One of the biggest contemporary challenges in HRM is figuring out the balance between what benefits to offer versus the impact those benefits have on employee motivation.

Of course, cost containment isn't only up to HRM and managers, but as organizations look at various ways to contain costs, human resources can certainly provide solutions.

Technology

Technology has greatly impacted human resources and will continue to do so as new technology is developed. Through use of technology, many companies have virtual workforces that perform tasks from nearly all corners of the world. When employees are not located just down the hall, management of these human resources creates some unique challenges. For example, technology creates an even greater need to have multicultural or diversity understanding. Since many people will work with individuals from across the globe, cultural sensitivity and understanding is the only way to ensure the use of technology results in increased productivity rather than decreased productivity due to miscommunications.

Technology also creates a workforce that expects to be mobile. Because of the ability to work from home or anywhere else, many employees may request and even demand a flexible schedule to meet their own family and personal needs. Productivity can be a concern for all managers in the area of flextime, and another challenge is the fairness to other workers when one person is offered a flexible schedule. Chapter 5 "Compensation and Benefits" and Chapter 6 "Retention and Motivation" will discuss flextime as a way to reward employees. Many companies, however, are going a step further and creating virtual organizations, which don't have a physical location (cost containment) and allow all employees to work from home or the location of their choice. As you can imagine, this creates concerns over productivity and communication within the organization.

The use of smartphones and social networking has impacted human resources, as many companies now disseminate information to employees via these methods. Of course, technology changes constantly, so the methods used today will likely be different one year or even six months from now.

The large variety of databases available to perform HR tasks is mind boggling. For example, databases are used to track employee data, compensation, and training. There are also databases available to track the recruiting and hiring processes. We will discuss more about technology in HR in Chapter 3 "Recruitment" through Chapter 7 "Training and Development".

Of course, the major challenge with technology is its constantly changing nature, which can impact all practices in HRM.

How Would You Handle This?

Too Many Friends,

You are the HR manager for a small company, consisting of twenty-three people plus the two owners, Steve and Corey. Every time you go into Steve's office, you see he is on Facebook. Because he is Facebook friends with several people in the organization, you have also heard he constantly updates his status and uploads pictures during work time. Then, at meetings, Steve will ask employees if they saw the pictures he recently uploaded from his vacation, weekend, or backpacking trip. One employee, Sam, comes to you with a concern about this. "I am just trying to do my job, but I feel if I don't look at his photos, he may not think I am a good employee," she says. How would you handle this?

The author discusses the "How Would You Handle This" situation in this chapter at: https://api.wistia.com/v1/ medias/1371241/embed.

Cyberloafing, a term used to describe lost productivity as a result of an employee using a work computer for personal reasons, is another concern created by technology. One study performed by Nucleus Research found that the average worker uses Facebook for fifteen minutes per day, which results in an average loss of 1.5 percent of productivity. Some workers, in fact, use Facebook over two hours per day during working hours. Restricting or blocking access to the Internet, however, can result in angry employees and impact motivation at work. Motivational factors will be discussed in Chapter 6 "Retention and Motivation".

Technology can create additional stress for workers. Increased job demands, constant change, constant e-mailing and texting, and the physical aspects of sitting in front of a computer can be not only stressful but also physically harmful to employees.

The Economy

Tough economic times in a country usually results in tough times for business, too. High unemployment and layoffs are clearly HRM and managerial issues. If a human resource manager works for a unionized company, union contracts are the guiding source when having to downsize owing to a tough economy. We will discuss union contracts in greater detail in Chapter 9 "Working with Labor Unions". Besides union restrictions, legal restrictions on who is let go and the process followed to let someone go should be on the forefront of any manager's mind when he or she is required to lay off people because of a poor economy. Dealing with performance issues and measuring performance can be considerations when it is necessary to lay off employees. These issues will be discussed in Chapter 8 "Employee Assessment".

Likewise, in a growth economy, the HR manager may experience a different kind of stress. Massive hiring to meet demand might occur if the economy is doing well. For example, McDonald's restaurants had to fill six hundred positions throughout Las Vegas and held hiring day events in 2010. Imagine the process of hiring this many people in a short period of time. The same recruiting and selection processes used under normal circumstances will be helpful in mass hiring situations. Recruiting and selection will be discussed in Chapter 3 "Recruitment" and Chapter 4 "Selection".

The Changing and Diverse Workforce

Human resources should be aware that the workforce is constantly changing. For example, in the 2010 census, the national population was 308,745,538, with 99,531,000 in 2010 working full time, down from 2008 when 106,648,000 were working full time. For full-time workers, the average weekly salary was higher the more educated the worker. See Figure 2-5 for details.

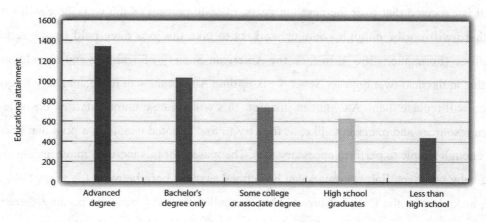

Figure 2-5 Usual Weekly Earnings of Wage and Salary Workers

Note：The average weekly earnings for workers in the United States increase with more education.

Source: Data from U.S. Bureau of Labor Statistics, "Usual Weekly Earnings of Wage and Salary Workers." Table 5, *Economic News Release,* July 20, 2010, accessed August 19, 2011, http://www.bls.gov/opub/ted/ 2010/ ted_20100726_data.htm.

Fortune **500 Focus**

Multigenerational is here to stay, and Xerox is the leader in recruiting of Generation Y talent. This age group has been moving into the labor market over the last six years, and this major demographic change, along with the retirement of baby boomers, has many companies thinking. *Fortune* 500 companies know they must find out where their new stars are coming from. In recruiting this new talent, Xerox isn't looking to old methods, because they know each generation is different. For example, Xerox developed the "Express Yourself" recruiting campaign, which is geared around a core value of this generation, to develop solutions and change. Joe Hammill, the director of talent acquisition, says, "Gen Y is very important. Xerox and other companies view this emerging workforce as the future of our organization" (Armour, 2005). Besides the new recruiting campaign, recruiters are working at what they term "core colleges"—that is, those that produce the kind of talent they need. For example, they developed recruitment campaigns with specific institutions such as the Rochester Institute of Technology because of its strong engineering and printing science programs. On their company website, they have a specific tab for the recent college graduate, emphasizing core values of this generation, including the ability to contribute, support, and build skills. With its understanding of multicultural generations, Xerox has created a talent pool for years to come.

It is expected that over the next ten years, over 40 percent of the workforce will retire, and there will not be enough younger workers to take the jobs once held by the retiring workforce (Fernandez, 2007). In fact, the American Society of Training and Development says that in the next twenty years, seventy-six million Americans will retire, and only forty-six million will replace them. As you can imagine, this will create a unique staffing obstacle for human resources and managers alike, as they try to find talented people in a pool that doesn't have enough people to perform necessary jobs. The reason for this increase in retirement is the aging baby boomers. Baby boomers can be defined as those born between the years 1946 and 1964, according to the Census Bureau. They are called the baby boomers because there was a large increase of babies born after soldiers came back from World War II. Baby boomers account for seventy-six million people in the United States in 2011, the same year in which the first of the baby boomers have started to retire.

The impact of the baby boomer generation on our country and on Human Resource Management is huge. First, the retirement of baby boomers results in a loss of a major part of the working population, and there are not enough people to fill those jobs that are left vacant. Second, the baby boomers' knowledge is lost upon their retirement. Much of this knowledge isn't formalized or written down, but it contributes to the success of business. Third, elderly people are living longer, and this results in higher healthcare costs for all currently in the workforce. It is estimated that three out of five baby boomers do not have enough money saved for retirement (Weisenthal, 2010), meaning that many of them will depend on Social Security payments to meet basic needs. However, since the Social Security system is a pay-as-you-go system (i.e., those paying into the system now are paying for current retirees), there may not be enough current workers to cover the current Social Security needs. In fact, in 1950 there were 16 workers to support each Social Security beneficiary, but today there are only 3.3 workers supporting each beneficiary (Wenning, 2010). The implications can mean that more will be paid by current workers to support retirees.

As a result of the aging workforce, human resources should keep abreast of changes in Social Security legislation and healthcare costs, which will be discussed in Chapter 5 "Compensation and Benefits". In addition, human resource managers should review current workers' skill levels and monitor retirements and skills lost upon those retirements, which is part of strategic planning. This will be discussed in Chapter 2 "Developing and Implementing Strategic HRM Plans". Having knowledge about current workers and skills, as well as predicting future workforce needs, will be necessary to deal with the challenges of an aging workforce.

> **Human Resource Recall**
>
> Have you ever worked in a multigenerational organization? What were some of the challenges in working with people who may have grown up in a different era?

Another challenge, besides lack of workers, is the multigenerational workforce. Employees between the ages of seventeen and sixty-eight have different values and different expectations of their jobs. Any manager who tries to manage these workers from varying generations will likely have some challenges. Even compensation preferences are different among generations. For example, the traditional baby boomer built a career during a time of pensions and strongly held values of longevity and loyalty to a company. Compare the benefit needs of this person to someone who is younger and expects to save through a 401(k) plan, and it is clear that the needs and expectations are different(Capezza, 2010). Throughout this book, we will discuss compensation and motivational strategies for the multigenerational workforce.

Awareness of the diversity of the workforce will be discussed in other parts, but laws regarding diversity will be discussed throughout the book. Diversity refers to age, disability, race, sex, national origin, and religion. Each of these components makes up the productive workforce, and each employee has different needs, wants, and goals. This is why it is imperative for the HRM professional to understand how to motivate the workforce, while ensuring that no laws are broken. We will discuss laws regarding diversity (and the components of diversity, such as disabilities) in Chapter 3 "Recruitment", Chapter 4 "Selection", Chapter 5 "Compensation and Benefits", and Chapter 6 "Retention and Motivation".

Ethics

A discussion of ethics is necessary when considering challenges of human resources. Much of the discussion surrounding ethics happened after the early to mid-2000s, when several companies were found to have engaged in gross unethical and illegal conduct, resulting in the loss of billions of dollars from shareholders. Consider the statistics: only 25 percent of employees trusted their CEO to tell the truth, and 80 percent of people said that employers have a moral responsibility to society. Based on these numbers, an ethical workplace is important not only for shareholder satisfaction but for employee satisfaction as well. Companies are seeing the value of implementing ethics codes within the business.

Many human resource departments have the responsibility of designing codes of ethics and developing policies for ethical decision making. Some organizations hire ethics officers to specifically focus on this area of the business. Out of four hundred companies surveyed, 48 percent had an ethics officer, who reported to either the CEO or the HR executive (McGraw, 2011). According to Steve Miranda, chief human resources officer for the Society for Human Resource Management (SHRM), "The presence of an ethics officer provides a high-level individual with positional authority who can ensure that policies, practices, and guidelines are effectively communicated across the organization". (McGraw, 2011)

For example, the insurance company Allstate recently hired a chief ethics and compliance officer (CECO) who offers a series of workshops geared toward leaders in the organization, because they believe that maintaining high ethical standards starts at the top of an organization. In addition, the CECO monitors reports of ethics complaints within the organization and trains employees on the code of ethics or code of conduct. (McGraw, 2011) A code of ethics is an outline that explains the expected ethical behavior of employees. For example, General Electric (GE) has a sixty-four-page code of conduct that outlines the expected ethics, defines them, and provides information on penalties for not adhering to the code. The code of conduct is presented below. Of course, simply having a written code of ethics does little to encourage positive behavior, so many organizations (such as GE) offer stiff penalties for ethics violations. Developing policies, monitoring behavior, and informing people of ethics are necessary to ensure a fair and legal business.

The following is an outline of GE's code of conduct:

Obey the applicable laws and regulations governing our business conduct worldwide.

Be honest, fair, and trustworthy in all your GE activities and relationships.

Avoid all conflicts of interest between work and personal affairs.

Foster an atmosphere in which fair employment practices extend to every member of the diverse GE community.

Strive to create a safe workplace and to protect the environment.

Through leadership at all levels, sustain a culture where ethical conduct is recognized, valued, and exemplified by all employees.

Key Takeaways

One of the most important aspects to productive HRM is to ensure the department adds value to the rest of the organization, based on the organization's strategic plan.

One of the major challenges of HRM is containment of costs. This can be done in several ways, for example, in the way healthcare and benefits are offered. Many companies are developing *cafeteria plans* that satisfy the employee and help contain costs.

HRM can also contain costs by developing and managing training programs and ensuring employees are well-trained to be productive in the job.

Hiring is a very expensive part of human resources, and therefore HRM should take steps to ensure they are hiring the right people for the job the first time. *Turnover* is a term used to describe the departure of an employee.

Poor communication results in wasting time and resources. We can communicate better by understanding communication channels, personalities, and styles.

Technology is also a challenge to be met by human resources. For example, employees may request alternative work schedules because they can use technology at home to get their work done.

Because technology is part of our work life, cyberloafing, or employees spending too much time on the Internet, creates new challenges for managers. Technology can also create challenges such as workplace stress and lack of work-life balance.

The economy is a major factor in Human Resource Management. HR managers, no matter what the state of the economy, must plan effectively to make sure they have the right number of workers at the right time. When we deal with a down economy, the legal and union implications of layoffs must be considered, and in an up economy, hiring of workers to meet the internal demand is necessary.

The retirement of *baby boomers* is creating a gap in the workplace, related to not only the number of people available but also the skills people have. Multigenerational companies, or companies with workers of a variety of ages, must find ways to motivate employees, even though those employees may have different needs. HR must be aware of this and continually plan for the challenge of a changing workforce. Diversity in the workplace is an important challenge in Human Resource Management. Diversity will be discussed in other part.

Ethics and monitoring of ethical behavior are also challenges in HRM. Setting ethical standards and monitoring ethical behavior, including developing a code of conduct, is a must for any successful business.

Exercises

1. Research the various generations: baby boomers, Generation X, and Generation Y (millennials). Compare and contrast five differences between the generations. How might these differences impact HRM?

2. Review news articles on the current state of the economy. Which aspects of these articles do you think can relate to HRM?

1.4　Cases and Problems

Chapter Summary

Human Resource Management is the process of employing people, training them, compensating them, developing policies relating to the workplace, and developing strategies to retain employees. Three certification exams, which are offered by the Human Resource Certification Institute, can be taken to show HRM skills and become more marketable.

Human Resource Management involves seven main areas: (1) staffing, (2) workplace policies, (3) benefits and compensation, (4) retention, (5) training, (6) employment laws, and (7) employee protection.

Human resource managers need many different types of skills. Being able to organize, multitask, and communicate effectively, as well as having specific job skills, such as how to run a particular computer program, and a sense of fairness and ethics, is crucial to a successful career in HRM.

There are many contemporary challenges associated with HRM. First, it is up to everyone in the organization to contain costs. HR managers need to look at their individual departments and demonstrate the necessity and value of their functions to the organization. HR managers can also help contain costs in several ways, such as managing benefits plans and compensation and providing training.

The fast-changing nature of technology is also a challenge in HRM. As new technologies are developed, employees may be able to implement innovative ways of working such as flextime. HR managers are also responsible for developing policies dealing with cyberloafing and other workplace time wasters revolving around technology. Employee stress and lack of work-life balance are also greatly influenced by technology.

Awareness of the changes in the economy allows the human resource manager to adequately plan for reductions and additions to the workforce.

The aging and changing workforce is our final factor. As baby boomers retire, there likely will not be enough people to replace them, and many of the skills the baby boomers have may be lost. In addition, having to work with multiple generations at once can create challenges as different expectations and needs arise from multigenerational workforces.

Chapter Case

Changes, Changes

Jennifer, the owner and manager of a company with ten employees, has hired you to take over the HRM function so she can focus on other areas of her business. During your first two weeks, you find out that the company has been greatly affected by the up economy and is expected to experience overall revenue growth by 10 percent over the next three years, with some quarters seeing growth as high as 30 percent. However, five of the ten workers are expected to retire within three years. These workers have been with the organization since the beginning and provide a unique historical perspective of the company. The other five workers are of diverse ages.

In addition to these changes, Jennifer believes they may be able to save costs by allowing employees to telecommute one to two days per week. She has some concerns about productivity if she allows employees to work from home. Despite these concerns, Jennifer has even considered closing down the physical office and making her company a virtual organization, but she wonders how such a major change will affect the ability to communicate and worker motivation.

Jennifer shares with you her thoughts about the costs of healthcare on the organization. She has considered cutting benefits entirely and having her employees work for her on a contract basis, instead of being full-time employees. She isn't sure if this would be a good choice.

Jennifer schedules a meeting with you to discuss some of her thoughts. To prepare for the meeting, you perform research so you can impress your new boss with recommendations on the challenges presented.

Point out which changes are occurring in the business that affect HRM.

What are some considerations the company and HR should be aware of when making changes related to this case study?

What would the initial steps be to start planning for these changes?

What would your role be in implementing these changes? What would Jennifer's role be?

Team Activities

In a group of two to three people, research possible career paths in HRM and prepare a PowerPoint presentation to discuss your findings.

Interview an HR manager and discuss his or her career path, skills, and daily tasks. Present your findings to your class.

Chapter 2 Developing and Implementing Strategic HRM Plans

The Value of Planning

James stumbled into his position as the human resource manager. He had been working for Techno, Inc. for three years, and when the company grew, James moved from a management position into a Human Resource Management position. Techno, Inc. is a technology and software consulting company for the music industry.

James didn't have a good handle on how to effectively run a Human Resources (HR) Department, so for much of the time he tried to figure it out as he went. When Techno started seeing rapid growth, he hired thirty people within a one-month period to meet the demand. Proud of his ability to accomplish his task of meeting the business's current needs, James was rather pleased with himself. He had spent numerous hours mulling over recruitment strategies, putting together excellent compensation plans, and then eventually sifting through résumés as a small part of the hiring process. Now the organization had the right number of people needed to carry out its projects.

Fast forward five months, however, and it turned out the rapid growth was only temporary. James met with the executives of the business who told him the contracts they had acquired were finished, and there wasn't enough new work coming in to make payroll next month if they didn't let some people go. James felt frustrated because he had gone through so much effort to hire people, and now they would be laid off. Never mind the costs of hiring and training his department had taken on to make this happen. As James sat with the executives to determine who should be laid off, he felt sad for the people who had given up other jobs just five months before, only to be laid off.

After the meeting, James reflected on this situation and realized that if he had spoken with the executives of the company sooner, they would have shared information on the duration of the contracts, and he likely would have hired people differently, perhaps on a contract basis rather than on a full-time basis. He also considered the fact that the organization could have hired an outsourcing company to recruit workers for him. As Jason mulled this over, he realized that he needed a strategic plan to make sure his department was meeting the needs of the organization. He vowed to work with the company executives to find out more about the company's strategic plan and then develop a Human Resource Management (HRM) strategic plan to make sure Techno, Inc. has the right number of workers with the right skills, at the right time in the future.

2.1 Strategic Planning

> ### Learning Objectives
>
> 1. Explain the differences between HRM and personnel management.
> 2. Be able to define the steps in HRM strategic planning.

In the past, Human Resource Management (HRM) was called the Personnel Department. In the past, the Personnel Department hired people and dealt with the hiring paperwork and processes. It is believed the first Human Resource Department was created in 1901 by the National Cash Register Company (NCR). The company faced a major strike but eventually defeated the union after a lockout. (We address unions in Chapter 9 "Working with Labor Unions".) After this difficult battle, the company president decided to improve worker relations by organizing a Personnel Department to handle grievances, discharges, safety concerns, and other employee issues. The department also kept track of new legislation surrounding laws impacting the organization. Many other companies were coming to the same realization that a department was necessary to create employee satisfaction, which resulted in more productivity. In 1913, Henry Ford saw employee turnover at 380 percent and tried to ease the turnover by increasing wages from $2.50 to $5.00, even though $2.50 was fair during this time period (Losey, 2011). Of course, this approach didn't work for long, and these large companies began to understand they had to do more than hire and fire if they were going to meet customer demand.

More recently, however, the Personnel Department has divided into Human Resource Management and Human Resource Development, as these functions have evolved over the century. HRM is not only crucial to an organization's success, but it should be part of the overall company's strategic plan, because so many businesses today depend on people to earn profits. Strategic planning plays an important role in how productive the organization is.

Table 2-1 Examples of Differences between Personnel Management and HRM

Personnel Management Focus	HRM Focus
Administering of policies	Helping to achieve strategic goals through people
Stand-alone programs, such as training	HRM training programs that are integrated with company's mission and values
Personnel Department responsible for managing people	Line managers share joint responsibility in all areas of people hiring and management
Creates a cost within an organization	Contributes to the profit objectives of the organization

Most people agree that the following duties normally fall under HRM. Each of these aspects has its own part within the overall strategic plan of the organization:

Staffing. Staffing includes the development of a strategic plan to determine how many people you might need to hire. Based on the strategic plan, HRM then performs the hiring process to recruit and select the right people for the right jobs. We discuss staffing in greater detail in Chapter 3 "Recruitment", Chapter 4 "Selection", and Chapter 5 "Compensation and Benefits".

Policies development. Development of policies to help reach the strategic plan's goals is the job of HRM. After the policies have been developed, communication of these policies on safety, security, scheduling, vacation times, and flextime schedules should be developed by the HR department. Of course, the HR managers work closely with supervisors in organizations to develop these policies. Workplace policies will be addressed throughout the book.

Compensation and benefits. In addition to paychecks, 401(k) plans, health benefits, and other perks are usually the responsibility of an HR manager. Compensation and benefits are discussed in Chapter 5 "Compensation and Benefits" and Chapter 6 "Retention and Motivation".

Retention. Assessment of employees and strategizing on how to retain the best employees is a task that HR managers oversee, but other managers in the organization will also provide input.

Training and development. Helping new employees develop skills needed for their jobs and helping current employees grow their skills are also tasks for which the HRM department is responsible. Determination of training needs and development and implementation of training programs are important tasks in any organization. Training is discussed in great detail in other parts", including succession planning. Succession planning includes handling the departure of managers and making current employees ready to take on managerial roles when a manager does leave.

Regulatory issues and worker safety. Keeping up to date on new regulations relating to employment, healthcare, and other issues is generally a responsibility that falls on the HRM Department. While various laws are discussed throughout the book, unions and safety and health laws in the workplace are covered in Chapter 9 "Working with Labor Unions".

In smaller organizations, the manager or owner is likely performing the HRM functions (De Kok & Uhlaner, 2001). They hire people, train them, and determine how much they should be paid. Larger companies ultimately perform the same tasks, but because they have more employees, they can afford to employ specialists, or human resource managers, to handle these areas of the business. As a result, it is highly likely that you, as a manager or entrepreneur, will be performing HRM tasks, hence the value in understanding the strategic components of HRM.

HRM vs. Personnel Management

Human resource strategy is an elaborate and systematic plan of action developed by a Human Resource Department. This definition tells us that an HR strategy includes detailed pathways to implement HRM strategic plans and HR plans. Think of the HRM strategic plan as the major objectives the organization wants to achieve, and the HR plan as the specific activities carried out to achieve the strategic plan. In other words, the strategic plan may include long-term goals, while the HR plan may include short-term objectives that are tied to the overall strategic plan. As mentioned at the beginning of this chapter, Human Resource Departments in the past were called Personnel Departments. This term implies that the department provided "support" for the rest of the organization. Companies now understand that the human side of the business is the most important asset in any business (especially in this global economy), and therefore HR has much more importance than it did twenty years ago. While personnel management mostly involved activities surrounding the hiring process and legal compliance, human resources involves much more, including strategic planning, which is the focus of this chapter. The Ulrich HR model, a common way to look at HRM strategic planning, provides an overall view of the role of HRM in the organization. His model is said to have started the movement that changed the view of HR; no longer merely a functional area, HR became more of a partnership within the organization. While his model has changed over the years, the current model looks at alignment of HR activities with the overall global business strategy to form a strategic partnership. (Ulrich & Brockbank, 2005) His newly revised model looks at five main areas of HR:

Strategic partner. Partnership with the entire organization to ensure alignment of the HR function with the needs of the organization.

Change agent. The skill to anticipate and respond to change within the HR function, but as a company as a whole.

Administrative expert and functional expert. The ability to understand and implement policies, procedures, and processes that relate to the HR strategic plan.

Human capital developer. Means to develop talent that is projected to be needed in the future.

Employee advocate. Works for employees currently within the organization.

According to Ulrich (Ulrich, 2011), implementation of this model must happen with an understanding of the overall company objectives, problems, challenges, and opportunities. For example, the HR professional must understand the dynamic nature of the HRM environment, such as changes in labor markets, company culture and values, customers, shareholders, and the economy. Once this occurs, HR can determine how best to meet the needs of the organization within these five main areas.

To be successful in writing an HRM strategic plan, one must understand the dynamic external environment.

HRM as a Strategic Component of the Business

David Ulrich discusses the importance of bringing HR to the table in strategic planning.

Keeping the Ulrich model in mind, consider these four aspects when creating a good HRM strategic plan.

Make it applicable. People often spend an inordinate amount of time developing plans, but the plans sit in a file somewhere and are never actually used. A good strategic plan should be the guiding principles for the HRM function. It should be reviewed and changed as aspects of the business change. Involvement of all members in the HR department (if it's a larger department) and communication among everyone within the department will make the plan better.

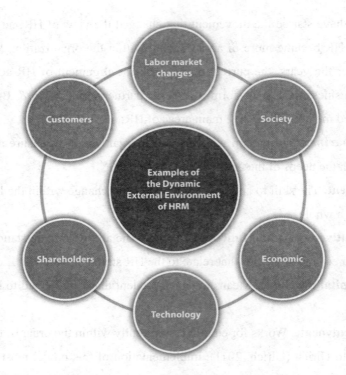

Figure 2-6　Dynamic External Environment

Be a strategic partner. Alignment of corporate values in the HRM strategic plan should be a major objective of the plan. In addition, the HRM strategic plan should be aligned with the mission and objectives of the organization as a whole. For example, if the mission of the organization is to promote social responsibility, then the HRM strategic plan should address this in the hiring criteria.

Involve people. An HRM strategic plan cannot be written alone. The plan should involve everyone in the organization. For example, as the plan develops, the HR manager should meet with various people in departments and find out what skills the best employees have. Then the HR manager can make sure the people recruited and interviewed have similar qualities as the best people already doing the job. In addition, the HR manager will likely want to meet with the Financial Department and executives who do the budgeting, so they can determine human resource needs and recruit the right number of people at the right times. In addition, once the HR Department determines what is needed, communicating a plan can gain positive feedback that ensures the plan is aligned with the business objectives.

Understand how technology can be used. Organizations oftentimes do not have the money or the inclination to research software and find budget-friendly options for implementation. People are sometimes nervous about new technology. However, the best organizations are those that embrace technology and find the right technology uses for their businesses. There are thousands of HRM software options that can make the HRM processes faster, easier, and more effective. Good strategic plans address this aspect.

HR managers know the business and therefore know the needs of the business and can develop a plan to meet those needs. They also stay on top of current events, so they know what is happening globally that could affect their strategic plan. If they find out, for example, that an economic downturn is looming, they will adjust their strategic plan. In other words, the strategic plan needs to be a living document, one that changes as the business and the world changes.

Figure 2-7   HRM Software

Human Resource Recall

Have you ever looked at your organization's strategic plan? What areas does the plan address?

The Steps to Strategic Plan Creation

As we addressed in Chapter 2 "The Steps to Strategic Plan Creation", HRM strategic plans must have several elements to be successful. There should be a distinction made here: the HRM strategic plan is different from the HR plan. Think of the HRM strategic plan as the major objectives the organization wants to achieve, while the HR plan consists of the detailed plans to ensure the strategic plan is achieved. Oftentimes the strategic plan is viewed as just another report that must be written. Rather than jumping in and writing it without much thought, it is best to give the plan careful consideration.

Conduct a Strategic Analysis

A strategic analysis looks at three aspects of the individual HRM department:

1.Understanding of the company mission and values. It is impossible to plan for HRM if one does not know the values and missions of the organization. As we have already addressed in this chapter, it is imperative for the HR manager to align department objectives with organizational objectives. It is worthwhile to sit down with company executives, management, and supervisors to make sure you have a good understanding of the company mission and values.

Another important aspect is the understanding of the organizational life-cycle. You may have learned about the life-cycle in marketing or other business classes, and this applies to HRM, too. An organizational life-cycle refers to the introduction, growth, maturity, and decline of the organization, which can vary over time. For example, when the organization first begins, it is in the introduction phase, and a different staffing, compensation, training, and labor/employee relations strategy may be necessary to align HRM with the organization's goals. This might be opposed to an organization that is struggling to stay in business and is in the decline phase. That same organization, however, can create a new product, for example, which might again put the organization in the growth phase. Table 21 "Lifecycle Stages and HRM Strategy" explains some of the strategies that may be different depending on the organizational life-cycle.

2.Understanding of the HRM department mission and values. HRM departments must develop their own departmental mission and values. These guiding principles for the department will change as the company's overall mission and values change. Often the mission statement is a list of what the department does, which is less of a strategic approach. Brainstorming about HR goals, values, and priorities is a good way to start. The mission statement should express how an organization's human resources help that organization meet the business goals. A poor mission statement might read as follows: "The Human Resource Department at Techno, Inc. provides resources to hiring managers and develops compensation plans and other services to assist the employees of our company."

A strategic statement that expresses how human resources help the organization might read as follows: "HR's responsibility is to ensure that our human resources are more talented and motivated than our competitors', giving us a competitive advantage. This will be achieved by monitoring our turnover rates, compensation, and company sales data and comparing that data to our competitors" (Kaufman, 2011). When the mission statement is written in this way, it is easier to take a strategic approach with the HR planning process.

3.Understanding of the challenges facing the department. HRM managers cannot deal with change quickly if they are not able to predict changes. As a result, the HRM manager should know what upcoming challenges may be faced to make plans to deal with those challenges better when they come along. This makes the strategic plan and HRM plan much more usable.

Table 2-2 Life-cycle Stages and HRM Strategy

Life-cycle Stage	Staffing	Compensation	Training and Development	Labor / Employee Relations
Introduction	Attract best technical and professional talent.	Meet or exceed labor market rates to attract needed talent.	Define future skill requirements and begin establishing career ladders.	Set basic employee-relations philosophy of organization.
Growth	Recruit adequate numbers and mix of qualifying workers. Plan management succession. Manage rapid internal labor market movements.	Meet external market but consider internal equity effects. Establish formal compensation structures.	Mold effective management team through management development and organizational development.	Maintain labor peace, employee motivation, and morale.
Maturity	Encourage sufficient turnover to minimize layoffs and provide new openings. Encourage mobility as reorganizations shift jobs around.	Control compensation costs.	Maintain flexibility and skills of an aging workforce.	Improve productivity and achieve flexibility in work rules. Negotiate job security and employment-adjustment policies

Continued

Life-cycle Stage	Staffing	Compensation	Training and Development	Labor / Employee Relations
Decline	Plan and implement workforce reductions and reallocations; downsizing and outplacement may occur during this stage.	Implement tighter cost control.	Implement retraining and career consulting services.	

Source: *Seattle University Presentation*, accessed July 11, 2011, http://fac-staff.seattleu.edu/gprussia/web/ mgt383/ HR%20Planning1.ppt.

Identify Strategic HR Issues

In this step, the HRM professionals will analyze the challenges addressed in the first step. For example, the department may see that it is not strategically aligned with the company's mission and values and opt to make changes to its departmental mission and values as a result of this information.

Many organizations and departments will use a strategic planning tool that identifies strengths, weaknesses, opportunities, and threats (SWOT analysis) to determine some of the issues they are facing. Once this analysis is performed for the business, HR can align itself with the needs of the business by understanding the business strategy. See Table 2-2 "Sample HR Department SWOT Analysis for Techno, Inc." for an example of how a company's SWOT analysis can be used to develop a SWOT analysis for the HR department.

Once the alignment of the company SWOT is completed, HR can develop its own SWOT analysis to determine the gaps between HR's strategic plan and the company's strategic plan. For example, if the HR manager finds that a department's strength is its numerous training programs, this is something the organization should continue doing. If a weakness is the organization's lack of consistent compensation throughout all job titles, then the opportunity to review and revise the compensation policies presents itself. In other words, the company's SWOT analysis provides a basis to address some of the issues in the organization, but it can be whittled down to also address issues within the department.

Table 2-3 Sample HR Department SWOT Analysis for Techno, Inc.

Strengths	Hiring talented people Company growth
Weaknesses	Technology implementation for business processes Excellent relationship between HRM and management/executives No strategic plan for HRM No planning for up/down cycles No formal training processes
Opportunities	Lacking of software needed to manage business processes, including go-to-market staffing strategies Development of HRM staffing plan to meet industry growth HRM software purchase to manage training, staffing, assessment needs for an unpredictable business cycle Continue development of HRM and executive relationship by attendance and participation in key meetings and decision-making processes Develop training programs and outside development opportunities to continue development of in-house marketing expertise Economy
Threats	Changing technology

Prioritize Issues and Actions

Based on the data gathered in the last step, the HRM manager should prioritize the goals and then put action plans together to deal with these challenges. For example, if an organization identifies that they lack a comprehensive training program, plans should be developed that address this need. (Training needs are discussed in Chapter 7 "Training and Development") An important aspect of this step is the involvement of the management and executives in the organization. Once you have a list of issues you will address, discuss them with the management and executives, as they may see other issues or other priorities differently than you. Remember, to be effective, HRM must work with the organization and assist the organization in meeting goals. This should be considered in every aspect of HRM planning.

Draw Up an HRM Plan

Once the HRM manager has met with executives and management, and priorities have been agreed upon, the plans are ready to be developed. Detailed development of these plans will be discussed in Section 2.2 "Writing the HRM Plan". Sometimes companies have great strategic plans, but when the development of the details occurs, it can be difficult to align the strategic plan with the more detailed plans. An HRM manager should always refer to the overall strategic plan before developing the HRM strategic plans and HR plans.

Even if a company does not have an HR department, HRM strategic plans and HR plans should still be developed by management. By developing and monitoring these plans, the organization can ensure the right processes are implemented to meet the ever-changing needs of the organization. The strategic plan looks at the organization as a whole, the HRM strategic plan looks at the department as a whole, and the HR plan addresses specific issues in the Human Resource Department.

Key Takeaways

Personnel management and *HRM* are different ways of looking at the job duties of human resources. Twenty years ago, personnel management focused on administrative aspects. HRM today involves a strategic process, which requires working with other departments, managers, and executives to be effective and meet the needs of the organization.

In general, HRM focuses on several main areas, which include staffing, policy development, compensation and benefits, retention issues, training and development, and regulatory issues and worker protection.

To be effective, the HR manager needs to utilize technology and involve others.

As part of strategic planning, HRM should conduct a strategic analysis, identify HR issues, determine and prioritize actions, and then draw up the HRM plan.

Exercises

1. What is the difference between HR plans and HRM strategic plans? How are they the same? How are they different?

2. Of the areas of focus in HRM, which one do you think is the most important? Rank them and discuss the reasons for your rankings.

2.2 Writing the HRM Plan

Learning Objective

Describe the steps in the development of an HRM plan.

As addressed in Section 2.1 "Strategic Planning", the writing of an HRM strategic plan should be based on the strategic plans of the organization and of the department. Once the strategic plan is written, the HR professional can begin work on the HR plan. This is different from the strategic plan in that it is more detailed and more focused on the short term. The six parts described here are addressed in more detail in Chapter 4 "Recruitment", Chapter 4 "Selection", Chapter 5 "Compensation and Benefits", Chapter 6 "Retention and Motivation", Chapter 7 "Training and Development".

How Would You Handle This?

Compensation Is a Touchy Subject

As the HR manager, you have access to sensitive data, such as pay information. As you are looking at pay for each employee in the marketing department, you notice that two employees with the same job title and performing the same job are earning different amounts of money. As you dig deeper, you notice the employee who has been with the company for the least amount of time is actually getting paid more than the person with longer tenure. A brief look at the performance evaluations shows they are both star performers. You determine that two different managers hired the employees, and one manager is no longer with the organization. How would you handle this?

The author discusses the "How Would You Handle" This situation in this chapter at: https://api.wistia.com/v1/ medias/1371287/embed.

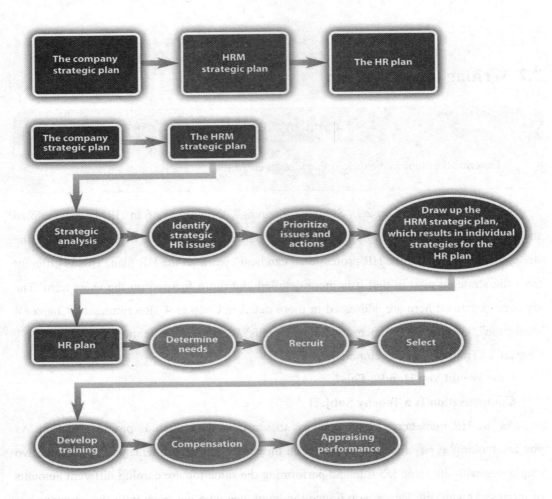

Figure 2-8 HRM Strategic Plan

As you can see from this figure, the company strategic plan ties into the HRM strategic plan, and from the HRM strategic plan, the HR plan can be developed.

The six parts of the HRM plan include the following:

Determine human resource needs. This part is heavily involved with the strategic plan. What growth or decline is expected in the organization? How will this impact your workforce? What is the economic situation? What are your forecasted sales for next year?

Determine recruiting strategy. Once you have a plan in place, it's necessary to write down a strategy addressing how you will recruit the right people at the right time.

Select employees. The selection process consists of the interviewing and hiring process.

Develop training. Based on the strategic plan, what training needs are arising? Is there new software that everyone must learn? Are there problems in handling conflict? Whatever the training topics are, the HR manager should address plans to offer training in the HRM plan.

Determine compensation. In this aspect of the HRM plan, the manager must determine pay scales and other compensation such as healthcare, bonuses, and other perks.

Appraise performance. Sets of standards need to be developed so you know how to rate the performance of your employees and continue with their development.

Each chapter of this text addresses one area of the HR plan, but the next sections provide some basic knowledge of planning for each area.

Determine Human Resource Needs

The first part of an HR plan will consist of determining how many people are needed. This step involves looking at company operations over the last year and asking a lot of questions:

Were enough people hired?

Did you have to scramble to hire people at the last minute?

What are the skills your current employees possess?

What skills do your employees need to gain to keep up with technology?

Who is retiring soon? Do you have someone to replace them?

What are the sales forecasts? How might this affect your hiring?

These are the questions to answer in this first step of the HR plan process. As you can imagine, this cannot be done alone. Involvement of other departments, managers, and executives should take place to obtain an accurate estimate of staffing needs for now and in the future. We discuss staffing in greater detail in Chapter 3 "Recruitment".

Many HR managers will prepare an inventory of all current employees, which includes their educational level and abilities. This gives the HR manager the big picture on what current employees can do. It can serve as a tool to develop employees' skills and abilities, if you know where they are currently in their development. For example, by taking an inventory, you may find out that Richard is going to retire next year, but no one in his department has been identified or trained to take over his role. Keeping the inventory helps you know where gaps might exist and allows you to plan for these gaps. This topic is addressed further in Chapter 3 "Recruitment".

HR managers will also look closely at all job components and will analyze each job. By doing this analysis, they can get a better picture of what kinds of skills are needed to perform a job successfully. Once the HR manager has performed the needs assessment and knows exactly how many people, and in what positions and time frame they need to be hired, he or she can get to work on recruiting, which is also called a staffing plan. This is addressed further in Chapter 3 "Recruitment".

Recruitment

Recruitment is an important job of the HR manager. More detail is provided in Chapter 3 "Recruitment". Knowing how many people to hire, what skills they should possess, and hiring them when the time is right are major challenges in the area of recruiting. Hiring individuals who have not only the skills to do the job but also the attitude, personality, and fit can be the biggest challenge in recruiting. Depending on the type of job you are hiring for, you might place traditional advertisements on the web or use social networking sites as an avenue. Some companies offer bonuses to employees who refer friends. No matter where you decide to recruit, it is important to keep in mind that the recruiting process should be fair and equitable and diversity should be considered.

Depending on availability and time, some companies may choose to outsource their recruiting processes. For some types of high-level positions, a head hunter will be used to recruit people nationally and internationally. A head hunter is a person who specializes in matching jobs with people, and they usually work only with high-level positions. Another option is to use an agency that specializes in hiring people for a variety of positions, including temporary and permanent positions. Some companies decide to hire temporary employees because they anticipate only a short-term need, and it can be less expensive to hire someone for only a specified period of time.

No matter how it is done, recruitment is the process of obtaining résumés of people interested in the job. In our next step, we review those résumés, interview, and select the best person for the job.

Selection

After you have reviewed résumés for a position, now is the time to work toward selecting the right person for the job. Although we discuss selection in great detail in Chapter 5 "Compensation and Benefits", it is worth a discussion here as well. Numerous studies have been done, and while they have various results, the majority of studies say it costs an average of $45,000 to hire a new manager (Herman, 1993). While this may seem exaggerated, consider the following items that contribute to the cost:

Time to review résumés

Time to interview candidates

Interview expenses for candidates

Possible travel expenses for new hire or recruiter

Possible relocation expenses for new hire

Additional bookkeeping, payroll, 401(k), and so forth

Additional record keeping for government agencies

Increased unemployment insurance costs

Costs related to lack of productivity while new employee gets up to speed

Because it is so expensive to hire, it is important to do it right. First, résumés are reviewed and people who closely match the right skills are selected for interviews. Many organizations perform phone interviews first so they can further narrow the field. The HR manager is generally responsible for setting up the interviews and determining the interview schedule for a particular candidate. Usually, the more senior the position is, the longer the interview process takes, even up to eight weeks (Crant, 2009). After the interviews are conducted, there may be reference checks, background checks, or testing that will need to be performed before an offer is made to the new employee. HR managers are generally responsible for this aspect. Once the applicant has met all criteria, the HR manager will offer the selected person the position. At this point, salary, benefits, and vacation time may be negotiated. Compensation is the next step in HR management.

Determine Compensation

What you decide to pay people is much more difficult than it seems. This issue is covered in greater detail in Chapter 5 "Compensation and Benefits". Pay systems must be developed that motivate employees and embody fairness to everyone working at the organization. However, organizations cannot offer every benefit and perk because budgets always have constraints. Even governmental agencies need to be concerned with compensation as part of their HR plan. For example, in 2011, Illinois State University gave salary increases of 3 percent to all faculty, despite state budget cuts in other areas. They reasoned that the pay increase was needed because of the competitive nature of hiring and retaining faculty and staff. The university president said, "Our employees have had a very good year and hopefully this is a good shot in the arm that will keep our morale high" (Pawlowski, 2011).

Figure 2-9 Compensation Balance

Note: Determination of compensation systems is a balancing act. Compensation should be high enough to motivate current employees and attract new ones but not so high that it breaks the budget.

The process in determining the right pay for the right job can have many variables, in addition to keeping morale high. First, as we have already discussed, the organization life-cycle can determine the pay strategy for the organization. The supply and demand of those skills in the market, economy, region, or area in which the business is located is a determining factor in compensation strategy. For example, a company operating in Seattle may pay higher for the same job than their division in Missoula, Montana, because the cost of living is higher in Seattle.

The HR manager is always researching to ensure the pay is fair and at market value. In Chapter 5 "Compensation and Benefits", we get into greater detail about the variety of pay systems, perks, and bonuses that can be offered. For many organizations, training is a perk. Employees can develop their skills while getting paid for it. Training is the next step in the HR planning process.

Develop Training

Once we have planned our staffing, recruited people, selected employees, and then compensated them, we want to make sure our new employees are successful. Training is covered in more detail in Chapter 7. One way we can ensure success is by training our employees in three main areas:

Company culture. A company culture is the organization's way of doing things. Every company does things a bit differently, and by understanding the corporate culture, the employee will be set up for success. Usually this type of training is performed at an orientation, when an employee is first hired. Topics might include how to request time off, dress codes, and processes.

Skills needed for the job. If you work for a retail store, your employees need to know how to use the register. If you have sales staff, they need to have product knowledge to do the job. If your company uses particular software, training is needed in this area.

Human relations skills. These are non-job-specific skills your employees need not only to do their jobs but also to make them all-around successful employees. Skills needed include communication skills and interviewing potential employees.

Perform a Performance Appraisal

The last thing an HR manager should plan is the performance appraisal. While we discuss performance appraisals in greater detail in Chapter 8 "Employee Assessment", it is definitely worth a mention here, since it is part of the strategic plan. A performance appraisal is a method by which job performance is measured. The performance appraisal can be called many different things, such as the following:

Employee appraisal

Performance review

360 review

Career development review

No matter what the name, these appraisals can be very beneficial in motivating and rewarding employees. The performance evaluation includes metrics on which the employee is measured. These metrics should be based on the job description, both of which the HR manager develops. Various types of rating systems can be used, and it's usually up to the HR manager to develop these as well as employee evaluation forms. The HR manager also usually ensures that every manager in the organization is trained on how to fill out the evaluation forms, but more importantly, how to discuss job performance with the employee. Then the HR manager tracks the due dates of performance appraisals and sends out e-mails to those managers letting them know it is almost time to write an evaluation.

Human Resource Recall

Have you ever been given a performance evaluation? What was the process and the outcome?

Communication Is Key in Performance Evaluations

Communication is imperative in any workplace, but especially when giving and receiving a performance evaluation.

Key Takeaways

Human resource planning is a process that is part of the strategic plan. It involves addressing specific needs within the organization, based on the company's strategic direction.

The first step in HR planning is determining current and future human resource needs. In this step, current employees, available employees in the market, and future needs are all analyzed and developed.

In the second step of the process, once we know how many people we will need to hire, we can begin to determine the best methods for recruiting the people we need. Sometimes an organization will use *head hunters* to find the best person for the job.

After the recruiting process is finished, the HR manager will begin the selection process. This involves setting up interviews and selecting the right person for the job. This can be an expensive process, so we always want to hire the right person from the beginning.

HR managers also need to work through compensation plans, including salary, bonus, and other benefits, such as healthcare. This aspect is important, since most organizations want to use compensation to attract and retain the best employees.

The HR manager also develops training programs to ensure the people hired have the tools to be able to do their jobs successfully.

Exercises

1. Of the parts of HR planning, which do you think is most difficult, and why? Which would you enjoy the most, and why?

2. Why is it important to plan your staffing before you start to hire people?

3. What is the significance of training? Why do we need it in organizations?

2.3 Tips in HRM Planning

Learning Objective

Explain the aspects needed to create a usable and successful HRM plan.

As you have learned from this chapter, human resource strategic planning involves understanding your company's strategic plan and HR's role in the organization. The planning aspect meets the needs of the strategic plan by knowing how many people should be hired, how many people are needed, and what kind of training they need to meet the goals of the organization. This section gives some tips on successful HR strategic planning.

Fortune 500 Focus

Like many *Fortune* 500 companies throughout the world, IBM in India finds that picking the best prospects for job postings isn't always easy. By using advanced analytics, however, it aims to connect the strategic plan, staffing needs, and the hiring process using a simple tool. The project was originally developed to assign people to projects internally at IBM, but IBM found this tool able to not only extract essential details like the number of years of experience but also make qualitative judgments, such as how good the person actually is for the job (Chari, 2011). This makes the software unique, as most résumé-scanning software programs can only search for specific keywords and are not able to assess the job fit or tie the criteria directly to the overall strategic plan. The project uses IBM India's spoken web technology, in which the prospective employee answers a few questions, creating the equivalent of voice résumé. Then using these voice résumés, the hiring manager can easily search for those prospects who meet the needs of the organization and the objectives of the strategic plan.

Some of the challenges noted with this software include the recognition of language and dialect issues. However, the IBM human resources solution is still one of the most sophisticated of such tools to be developed. "Services is very people-intensive. Today, there is talk of a war for talent, but attracting the right kind of people is a challenge, yet unemployment is very high. Our solution applies sophisticated analytics to workforce management," says Manish Gupta, director at IBM Research-India (Chari, 2011).

It is likely that this is only the beginning of the types of technology that allow HR professionals to tie their HR plans directly to a strategic plan with the touch of a few buttons.

Link HRM Strategic Plan to Company Plan

Understanding the nature of the business is key to being successful in creating a strategic plan for HRM. Because every business is different, the needs of the business may change, depending on the economy, the season, and societal changes in our country. HR managers need to understand all these aspects of the business to better predict how many people are needed, what types of training are needed, and how to compensate people, for example. The strategic plan that the HR manager writes should address these issues. To address these issues, the HR manager should develop the departmental goals and HR plans based on the overall goals of the organization. In other words, HR should not operate alone but in tandem with the other parts of the organization. The HRM plan should reflect this.

Figure 2-10 HRM Plan

Note: The HRM department should operate in tandem with other departments to meet the needs of the organization.

Monitor the Plan Constantly

Oftentimes a great strategic plan is written, taking lots of time, but isn't actually put into practice for a variety of reasons, such as the following:

The plan wasn't developed so that it could be useful.

The plan wasn't communicated with management and others in the HRM department.

The plan did not meet the budget guidelines of the organization.

The plan did not match the strategic outcomes of the organization.

There was lack of knowledge on how to actually implement it.

There is no point in developing a plan that isn't going to be used. Developing the plan and then making changes as necessary are important to making it a valuable asset for the organization. A strategic plan should be a living document, in that it changes as organizational or external factors change. People can get too attached to a specific plan or way of doing things and then find it hard to change. The plan needs to change constantly or it won't be of value.

Measure It

A good strategic plan and HR plan should discuss the way "success" will be measured. For example, rather than writing "Meet the hiring needs of the organization". be more specific: "Based on sales forecasts from our sales department, hire ten people this quarter with the skills to meet our ten job openings." This is a goal that is specific enough to be measured. These types of quantitative data also make it easier to show the relationship between HR and the organization, and better yet, to show how HR adds value to the bottom line. Likewise, if a company has a strategic objective to be a safe workplace, you might include a goal to "develop training to meet the needs of the organization". While this is a great goal, how will this be measured? How will you know if you did what you were supposed to do? It might be difficult to measure this with such a general statement. On the other hand, a goal to "develop a safety training workshop and have all employees complete it by the end of the year" is specific and can be measured at the end to determine success.

Human Resource Recall

What are some of your personal goals? Are these goals measureable?

Sometimes Change Is Necessary

It can be difficult to base an entire plan on forecasted numbers. As a result, an HRM department that is willing to change quickly to meet the needs of the organization proves its worthiness. Consider a sales forecast that called for fifteen new hires, but you find out months later the organization is having a hard time making payroll. Upon digging deeper, you find the sales forecasts were overexaggerated, and now you have fifteen people you don't really need. By monitoring the changes constantly (usually done by asking lots of questions to other departments), you can be sure you are able to change your strategic plan as they come.

Be Aware of Legislative Changes

One of the major challenges in HRM, as we discuss in Chapter 1 "The Role of Human Resources", is having an awareness of what is happening from a legal perspective. Because most budgets are based on certain current laws, knowing when the law changes and how it will affect department budgets and planning (such as compensation planning) will create a more solid strategic plan. For example, if the minimum wage goes up in your state and you have minimum wage workers, reworking the budget and communicating this change to your accounting team is imperative in providing value to the organization. We will discuss various legislation throughout this book.

Key Takeaways

As has been the theme throughout this chapter, any HRM plan should be directly linked to the strategic plan of the organization.

A plan should be constantly updated and revised as things in the organization change.

A good strategic plan provides tools to determine whether you met the goal. Any plan should have measureable goals so the connection to success is obvious.

Changes in a strategic plan and in goal setting are necessary as the internal and external environments change. An HR manager should always be aware of changes in forecasts, for example, so the plan can change, too.

Legislative changes may impact strategic plans and budgets as well. It's important to make sure HR managers are keeping up on these changes and communicating them.

Exercises

1. What are some ways an HR manager can keep up on legislative changes? Do a web search and list specific publications that may help keep the HR manager aware of changes.

2. Why is it important to be able to measure strategic plans? What might happen if you don't?

2.4 Cases and Problems

Chapter Summary

Human resource management was once called the personnel department. In the past, hiring people and working with hiring paperwork was this department's job. Today, the HRM department has a much broader role, and as a result, HR managers must align their strategies with the company's strategies.

Functions that fall under HRM today include staffing, creation of workplace policies, compensation and benefits, retention, training and development, and working with regulatory issues and worker protection.

Human resource strategy is a set of elaborate and systematic plans of action. The company objectives and goals should be aligned with the objectives and goals of the individual departments.

The steps to creating an HRM strategic plan include conducting a strategic analysis. This entails having an understanding of the values and mission of the organization, so you can align your departmental strategy in the same way.

The second step is to identify any HR issues that might impact the business.

The third step, based on the information from the first and second steps, is to prioritize issues and take action. Finally, the HRM professional will draw up the HRM plan.

The HRM plan consists of six steps. The first is to determine the needs of the organization based on sales forecasts, for example. Then the HR professional will recruit and select the right person for the job. HRM develops training and development to help better the skills of existing employees and new employees, too. The HR manager will then determine compensation and appraise performance of employees. Each of these parts of the HRM plan is discussed in its own separate chapter in greater detail.

As things in the organization change, the strategic plan should also change.

To make the most from a strategic plan, it's important to write the goals in a way that makes them measurable.

Chapter Case

We Merged...Now What?

Earlier this month, your company, a running equipment designer and manufacturer called Runners Paradise, merged with a smaller clothing design company called ActiveLeak. Your company initiated the buyout because of the excellent design team at ActiveLeak and their brand recognition, specifically for their MP3-integrated running shorts. Runners Paradise has thirty-five employees and ActiveLeak has ten employees. At ActiveLeak, the owner, who often was too busy doing other tasks, handled the HRM roles. As a result, ActiveLeak has no strategic plan, and you are wondering if you should develop a strategic plan, given this change. Here are the things you have accomplished so far:

Reviewed compensation and adjusted salaries for the sake of fairness. Communicated this to all affected employees.

Developed job requirements for current and new jobs.

Had each old and new employee fill out a skills inventory Excel document, which has been merged into a database.

From this point, you are not sure what to do to fully integrate the new organization.

Why should you develop an HRM strategic plan?

Which components of your HR plan will you have to change?

What additional information would you need to create an action plan for these changes?

Team Activities

1. Work in a group of three to five people. Choose a company and perform a SWOT analysis on that organization and be prepared to present it to the class.

2. Based on the SWOT analysis you performed in the first question, develop new objectives for the organization.

positions for the manag... ... TS for the office positions, ... the factory floor positions. Placed with the new ... ... the initial level in the department in accordance with the job description order.

Chapter 3 Recruitment

Keeping Up with Growth

Over the last two years, the company where Melinda works as HR manager, Dragon Enterprises, has seen plenty of growth. Much of this growth has created a need for a strategic, specific recruiting processes. In the past, Dragon Enterprises recruited simply on the basis of the applications they received, rather than actively searching for the right person for the job. The first thing Melinda did when arriving at the company was to develop a job analysis questionnaire, which she had all employees fill out using the website SurveyMonkey. The goal was to create a job analysis for each position that existed at the company. This happened to be the point where the organization started seeing rapid growth, as a result of increased demand for the types of parts the company sells. Luckily, since Melinda followed the industry closely and worked closely with management, part of her strategic outline planned for the hiring of several new positions, so she was mostly ready for it. Keeping in mind the Equal Employment Opportunity Commission (EEOC) laws and the company's position on a diverse workforce, Melinda set out to write new job descriptions for the job analysis she had performed. She knew the job analysis should be tied to the job description, and both of these should be tied to the job qualifications. Obviously, to recruit for these positions, she needed to develop a recruitment plan. Over the next year, the organization needed to hire three more floor management positions, three office positions, and fifteen factory floor positions. Next, she needed to determine a time line to recruit candidates and a method by which to accept the applications she would receive. After sharing this time line with her colleague, the chief operating officer, she went to work recruiting. She sent an e-mail to all employees asking them to refer a friend and receive a $500 bonus. Next, part of her strategy was to try to find very specialized talent in management to fill those positions. For this, she thought working with a recruiting company might be the best way to go. She also used her Twitter and Facebook accounts to broadcast the job openings. After a three-week period, Melinda had 54 applications for the management positions, 78 for the office positions, and 110 for the factory floor positions. Pleased with the way recruiting had gone, she started reviewing the résumés to continue with the selection process.

3.1 The Recruitment Process

Learning Objectives

1. Discuss the need for forecasting human resource needs and techniques for forecasting.
2. Be able to explain the steps to an effective recruitment strategy.
3. Be able to develop a job analysis and job description.

The recruitment process is an important part of Human Resource Management (HRM). It isn't done without proper strategic planning. Recruitment is defined as a process that provides the organization with a pool of qualified job candidates from which to choose. Before companies recruit, they must implement proper staffing plans and forecasting to determine how many people they will need. The basis of the forecast will be the annual budget of the organization and the short- to long-term plans of the organization—for example, the possibility of expansion. In addition to this, the organizational life-cycle will be a factor. Organization life-cycle is discussed in Chapter 2 "Developing and Implementing Strategic HRM Plans". Forecasting is based on both internal and external factors.

Internal factors include the following:

Budget constraints

Expected or trend of employee separations

Production levels

Sales increases or decreases

Global expansion plans

External factors might include the following:

Changes in technology

Changes in laws

Unemployment rates

Shifts in population

Shifts in urban, suburban, and rural areas

Competition

Once the forecasting data are gathered and analyzed, the HR professional can see where gaps exist and then begin to recruit individuals with the right skills, education, and backgrounds. This section will discuss this step in HR planning.

Recruitment Strategy

Although it might seem easy, recruitment of the right talent, at the right place and at the right time, takes skill and practice, but more importantly, it takes strategic planning. In Chapter 2 "Developing and Implementing Strategic HRM Plans", development of staffing plans is discussed. An understanding of the labor market and the factors determining the relevant aspects of the labor market is key to being strategic about your recruiting processes.

Based on this information, when a job opening occurs, the HRM professional should be ready to fill that position.

Here are the aspects of developing a recruitment strategy:

Refer to a staffing plan. This is discussed in Chapter 2 "Developing and Implementing Strategic HRM Plans"

Confirm the job analysis is correct through questionnaires

Write the job description and job specifications

Have a bidding system to recruit and review internal candidate qualifications for possible promotions

Determine the best recruitment strategies for the position

Implement a recruiting strategy

The first step in the recruitment process is acknowledgment of a job opening. At this time, the manager and/or the HRM look at the job description for the job opening (assuming it isn't a new job). We discuss how to write a job analysis and job description in Chapter 4 "Job Analysis and Job Descriptions".

Assuming the job analysis and job description are ready, an organization may decide to look at internal candidates' qualifications first. Internal candidates are people who are already working for the company. If an internal candidate meets the qualifications, this person might be encouraged to apply for the job, and the job opening may not be published. Many organizations have formal job posting procedures and bidding systems in place for internal candidates. For example, job postings may be sent to a listserv or other avenue so all employees have access to them. However, the advantage of publishing open positions to everyone in and outside the company is to ensure the organization is diverse. Diversity is discussed in other chapter. We discuss more about internal and external candidates and bidding systems in Chapter 4 "Selection".

Then the best recruiting strategies for the type of position are determined. For example, for a high-level executive position, it may be decided to hire an outside head-hunting firm. For an entry-level position, advertising on social networking websites might be the best strategy. Most organizations will use a variety of methods to obtain the best results. We discuss specific strategies in Section 3.3 "Recruitment Strategies".

Another consideration is how the recruiting process will be managed under constraining circumstances such as a short deadline or a low number of applications. In addition, establishing a protocol for how applications and résumés will be processed will save time later. For example, some HRM professionals may use software such as *Microsoft Excel* to communicate the time line of the hiring process to key managers.

Once these tasks are accomplished, the hope is that you will have a diverse group of people to interview (called the selection process). Before this is done, though, it is important to have information to ensure the right people are recruited. This is where the job analysis and job description come in. We discuss this in Chapter 4 "Job Analysis and Job Descriptions".

Job Analysis and Job Descriptions

The job analysis is a formal system developed to determine what tasks people actually perform in their jobs. The purpose of a job analysis is to ensure creation of the right fit between the job and the employee and to determine how employee performance will be assessed. A major part of the job analysis includes research, which may mean reviewing job responsibilities of current employees, researching job descriptions for similar jobs with competitors, and analyzing any new responsibilities that need to be accomplished by the person with the position. According to research by Hackman and Oldham (Hackman & Oldham, 1976), a job diagnostic survey should be used to diagnose job characteristics prior to any redesign of a job. This is discussed in Chapter 6 "Retention and Motivation".

To start writing a job analysis, data need to be gathered and analyzed, keeping in mind Hackman and Oldham's model. Figure 29 "Process for Writing the Job Analysis" shows the process of writing a job analysis. Please note, though, that a job analysis is different from a job design. Job design refers to how a job can be modified or changed to be more effective—

for example, changing tasks as new technology becomes available. We discuss job design in Chapter 6 "Retention and Motivation" and Chapter 8 "Employee Assessment".

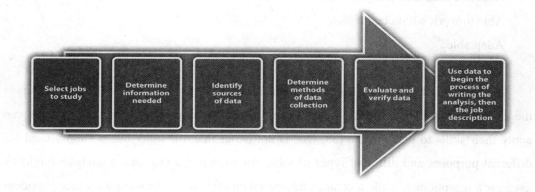

Figure 2-11   Process for Writing the Job Analysis

The information gathered from the job analysis is used to develop both the job description and the job specifications. A job description is a list of tasks, duties, and responsibilities of a job. Job specifications, on the other hand, discuss the skills and abilities the person must have to perform the job. The two are tied together, as job descriptions are usually written to include job specifications. A job analysis must be performed first, and then based on that data, we can successfully write the job description and job specifications. Think of the analysis as "everything an employee is required and expected to do".

Two types of job analyses can be performed: a task-based analysis and a competency- or skills-based analysis. A task-based analysis focuses on the duties of the job, as opposed to a competency-based analysis, which focuses on the specific knowledge and abilities an employee must have to perform the job. An example of a task-based analysis might include information on the following:

Write performance evaluations for employees

Prepare reports

Answer incoming phone calls

Assist customers with product questions

Cold call three customers a day

With task job analysis, the specific tasks are listed and it is clear. With competency based, it is less clear and more objective. However, competency-based analysis might be more appropriate for specific, high-level positions. For example, a competency-based analysis might include the following:

Able to utilize data analysis tools

Able to work within teams

Adaptable

Innovative

You can clearly see the difference between the two. The focus of task-based analyses is the job duties required, while the focus of competency-based analyses is on how a person can apply their skills to perform the job. One is not better than the other but is simply used for different purposes and different types of jobs. For example, a task-based analysis might be used for a receptionist, while a competency-based analysis might be used for a vice-president of sales position. Consider the legal implications, however, of which job analysis is used. Because a competency-based job analysis is more subjective, it might be more difficult to tell whether someone has met the criteria.

Once you have decided if a competency-based or task-based analysis is more appropriate for the job, you can prepare to write the job analysis. Of course, this isn't something that should be done alone. Feedback from managers should be taken into consideration to make this task useful in all levels of the organization. Organization is a key component to preparing for your job analysis. For example, will you perform an analysis on all jobs in the organization or just focus on one department? Once you have determined how you will conduct the analysis, a tool to conduct the analysis should be chosen. Most organizations use questionnaires (online or hard copy) to determine the duties of each job title. Some organizations will use face-to-face interviews to perform this task, depending on time constraints and the size of the organization. A job analysis questionnaire usually includes the following types of questions, obviously depending on the type of industry:

Employee information such as job title, how long in position, education level, how many years of experience in the industry

Key tasks and responsibilities

Decision-making and problem-solving: this section asks employees to list situations in which problems needed to be solved and the types of decisions made or solutions provided

Level of contact with colleagues, managers, outside vendors, and customers

Physical demands of the job, such as the amount of heavy lifting or ability to see, hear, or walk

Personal abilities required to do the job—that is, personal characteristics needed to perform well in this position

Specific skills required to do the job—for example, the ability to run a particular computer program

Certifications to perform the job

Once all employees (or the ones you have identified) have completed the questionnaire, you can organize the data, which is helpful in creating job descriptions. If there is more than one person completing a questionnaire for one job title, the data should be combined to create one job analysis for one job title. There are a number of software packages available to help human resources perform this task, such as *AutoGOJA*.

Once the job analysis has been completed, it is time to write the job description and specifications, using the data you collected. Job descriptions should always include the following components:

Job functions (the tasks the employee performs)

Knowledge, skills, and abilities (what an employee is expected to know and be able to do, as well as personal attributes)

Education and experience required

Physical requirements of the job (ability to lift, see, or hear, for example)

| | Previous View | 📧 Tell a friend about this vacancy | 🖨 Printable form |

| Server time:
01/17/2011 07:36:25 AM | Recruitment period ends:
01/24/2011 05:00 PM | **This position closes in**
7 days, 9 hours and 24 minutes |

Recruitment Bulletin
Systems Programmer I/II
Alias:
Position ID Number: 08-1116

Application Period: 01/03/2011 through 01/24/2011	Position open to: All Applicants
Department: Commerce Community & Economic Development	Division: Administrative Services
Location: Juneau	Region: Southeast
Salary: $5,026.00 Range 20 $5,745.00 Range 22 Monthly	Range: 20/22
Job Status: Full-Time	Bargaining Unit: GG

Job Description:

The Department of Commerce, Community and Economic Development (CCED) is seeking a technically skilled individual to fill a key Systems Programmer position. This position supports all aspects of the department's imaging and document repository infrastructure. The position is responsible for administering the imaging environment, including software and hardware installation, configuration, security and providing programming support to Analyst/Programmers coding applications that access and manipulate images.

Commerce's imaging environment utilizes *Oracle Content Management* and .Net applications. The successful candidate should be technically skilled and motivated to learn new technologies and processes.

Key responsibilities include:

- Administer all aspects of the department's *Oracle UCM (Universal Content Management)* servers and *Kofax* environment.
- Code custom image access and manipulation services using WSDL (web service definition language) and .Net.
- Configure, modify and update *Adobe Capture* and *UCM* inbound refinery. Develop batch classes and custom validation and release scripts.
- Install, configure and maintain high speed and flatbed scanner equipment.
- Work with users and programming staff to develop efficient physical paper workflows and practical scanning processes.
- Develop relevant scan workflows and required hardware for a variety of media such as envelopes, plain paper, and odd sizes.
- Monitor production system CPU, disk space, network utilization and error logs and make appropriate configuration changes and updates.

Figure 2-12 Sample of Job Description

Once the job description has been written, obtaining approval from the hiring manager is the next step. Then the HR professional can begin to recruit for the position. Before we discuss specific recruitment strategies, we should address the law and how it relates to hiring. This is the topic of Section 3.2 "The Law and Recruitment".

Notice how the job description includes the job function; knowledge, skills, and abilities required to do the job; education and experience required; and the physical requirements of the job.

Tips to Writing a Good Job Description

Be sure to include the pertinent information:

Title

Department

Reports to

Duties and responsibilities

Terms of employment

Qualifications needed

Think of the job description as a snapshot of the job

Communicate clearly and concisely

Make sure the job description is interesting to the right candidate applying for the job

Avoid acronyms

Don't try to fit all job aspects into the job description

Proofread the job description

Human Resource Recall

Does your current job or past job have a job description? Did it closely match the tasks you actually performed?

Key Takeaways

The recruitment process provides the organization with a pool of qualified applicants.

Description and job specifications can be written. A job description lists the components of the job, while job specifications list the requirements to perform the job.

1. Do an Internet search for "job description". Review three different job descriptions and then answer the following questions for each of the jobs:

a. What are the job specifications?

b. Are the physical demands mentioned?

c. Is the job description task based or competency based?

d. How might you change this job description to obtain more qualified candidates?

Why do the five steps of the recruitment process require input from other parts of the organization? How might you handle a situation in which the employees or management are reluctant to complete a job analysis?

3.2 The Law and Recruitment

Learning Objective

1. Explain the *Immigration Reform and Control Act (IRCA), Patriot Act*, and Equal Employment Opportunity (EEO) laws and how they relate to recruiting.

2. One of the most important parts of HRM is to know and apply the law in all activities the HR department handles. Specifically with hiring processes, the law is very clear on a fair hiring that is inclusive to all individuals applying for a job. The laws discussed here are applied specifically to the recruiting of new employees.

Immigration Reform and Control Act

The Immigration Reform and Control Act (IRCA) was adopted by Congress in 1986. This law requires employers to attest to their employees' immigration status. It also makes it illegal to hire or recruit illegal immigrants. The purpose of this law is to preserve jobs for those who have legal documentation to work in the United States. The implications for human resources lie in the recruitment process, because before entering employees into the selection process (e.g., interviewing), it is important to know they are eligible to work in the United States. This is why many application forms ask, "Are you legally able to work in the United States?" Dealing with the *IRCA* is a balancing act, however, because organizations cannot discriminate against legal aliens seeking work in the United States.

The *IRCA* relates not only to workers you hire but also to subcontractors. In a subcontractor situation (e.g., your organization hires an outside firm to clean the building after hours), your organization can still be held liable if it is determined your organization exercises control over how and when the subcontractors perform their jobs. In 2005, undocumented janitorial workers sued Walmart, arguing that the contracting company they worked for didn't pay them a minimum wage. Because the retailer controlled many of the details of their work, Walmart was considered to be a co-employer, and as a result, Walmart was held responsible not only for back wages but for the fact their subcontractor had hired undocumented workers.

HR professionals must verify both the identity and employment eligibility of all employees, even if they are temporary employees. The INS I-9 form (Employment Eligibility Verification form) is the reporting form that determines the identity and legal work status of a worker.

If an audit is performed on your company, you would be required to show I-9 forms for all your workers. If an employer hires temporary workers, it is important to manage data on when work visas are to expire, to ensure compliance. Organizations that hire illegal workers can be penalized $100 to $1,000 per hire. There is a software solution for management of this process, such as HR Data Manager. Once all data about workers are inputted, the manager is sent reminders if work authorization visas are about to expire. Employers are required to have the employee fill out the I-9 form on their first day of work, and the second section must be filled out within three days after the first day of employment. The documentation must be kept on file three years after the date of hire or for one year after termination. Some states, though, require the I-9 form be kept on file for as long as the person is employed with the organization.

In 2010, new rules about the electronic storage of forms were developed. The U.S. Department of Homeland Security said that employees can have these forms electronically signed and stored.

Patriot Act

In response to the September 11, 2001, terrorist attacks against the United States, the *Patriot Act* was signed, introducing legislative changes to enhance the federal government's ability to conduct domestic and international investigations and surveillance activities. As a result, employers needed to implement new procedures to maintain employee privacy rights while also creating a system that allowed for release of information requested by the government.

The act also amended the *Electronic Communications Privacy Act*, allowing the federal government easier access to electronic communications. For example, only a search warrant is required for the government to access voice mail and e-mail messages.

The act also amended the *Foreign Intelligence Surveillance Act*. The government is allowed to view communications if an employee is suspected of terrorism, and the government does not have to reveal this surveillance to the employer.

It is prudent for HR professionals and managers to let potential employees know of these new requirements, before the hiring process begins.

How Would You Handle This?

Wrong Job Description

Aimee, a highly motivated salesperson, has come to you with a complaint. She states that she had her performance evaluation, but all the items on her evaluation didn't relate to her actual job. In the past two years, she explains, her job has changed because of the increase of new business development using technology. How would you handle this?

The author discusses the "How Would You Handle This" situation in this chapter at: https://api.wistia.com/v1/ medias/1371475/embed.

EEO Set of Laws

We discuss Equal Employment Opportunity (EEO) laws in Chapter 3. They are worth mentioning again here in relation to the recruitment process. The Equal Employment Opportunity Commission (EEOC) is a federal agency charged with the task of enforcing federal employment discrimination laws. While there are restrictions on the type of company covered (companies with at least fifteen employees), the EEOC requires collection of data and investigates discrimination claims, again, for organizations with more than fifteen employees.

Under EEO law related to the recruitment process, employers cannot discriminate based on age (forty years or older), disability, genetic information, national origin, sex, pregnancy, race, and religion. In a job announcement, organizations usually have an EEO statement. Here are some examples:

(Company name) is fully committed to Equal Employment Opportunity and to attracting, retaining, developing, and promoting the most qualified employees without regard to their race, gender, color, religion, sexual orientation, national origin, age, physical or mental disability, citizenship status, veteran status, or any other characteristic prohibited by state or local law. We are dedicated to providing a work environment free from discrimination and harassment, and where employees are treated with respect and dignity.

(Company name) does not unlawfully discriminate on the basis of race, color, religion, national origin, age, height, weight, marital status, familial status, handicap/disability, sexual orientation, or veteran status in employment or the provision of services, and provides, upon request, reasonable accommodation including auxiliary aids and services necessary to afford individuals with disabilities an equal opportunity to participate in all programs and activities.

It is the policy of (college name), in full accordance with the law, not to discriminate in employment, student admissions, and student services on the basis of race, color, religion, age, political affiliation or belief, sex, national origin, ancestry, disability, place of birth, general education development certification (GED), marital status, sexual orientation, gender identity or expression, veteran status, or any other legally protected classification.

(College name) recognizes its responsibility to promote the principles of equal opportunity for employment, student admissions, and student services taking active steps to recruit minorities and women.

(Company name) will not discriminate against or harass any employee or applicant for employment on the basis of race, color, creed, religion, national origin, sex, sexual orientation, disability, age, marital status, or status with regard to public assistance. (Company name) will take affirmative action to ensure that all practices are free of such discrimination. Such employment practices include, but are not limited to, the following: hiring, upgrading, demotion, transfer, recruitment or recruitment advertising, selection, layoff, disciplinary action, termination, rates of pay or other forms of compensation, and selection for training.

In addition to including the EEO policy in the job announcement, HR is required to post notices of EEOC policies in a visible part of the work environment (such as the break room).

Although the EEOC laws in hiring are clear about discrimination, an exception may occur, called the Bona Fide Occupational Qualification (BFOQ). BFOQ is a quality or attribute that is reasonably necessary to the normal operation of the business and that can be used when considering applicants. To obtain a BFOQ exception, a company must prove that a particular person could not perform the job duties because of sex, age, religion, disability, and national origin. Examples of BFOQ exceptions might include the following:

A private religious school may require a faculty member to be of the same denomination.

Mandatory retirement is required for airline pilots at a certain age.

A clothing store that sells male clothing is allowed to hire only male models.

If an essence of a restaurant relies on one sex versus another (e.g., Hooters), they may not be required to hire male servers.

However, many arguments for BFOQ would not be considered valid. For example, race has never been a BFOQ, nor has customers' having a preference for a particular gender. Generally speaking, when going through the recruitment process and writing job descriptions, assuming a BFOQ would apply might be a mistake. Seeking legal council before writing a job description would be prudent.

Other aspects to consider in the development of the job description are disparate impact and disparate treatment. These are the two ways to classify employment discrimination cases. Disparate impact occurs when an organization discriminates through the use of a process, affecting a protected group as a whole, rather than consciously intending to discriminate. Some examples of disparate impact might include the following:

Requirement of a high school diploma, which may not be important to employment, could discriminate against racial groups.

A height requirement, which could limit the ability of women or persons of certain races to apply for the position.

Written tests that do not relate directly to the job.

Awarding of pay raises on the basis of, say, fewer than five years of experience, which could discriminate against people older than forty.

Disparate treatment, when one person is intentionally treated differently than another, does not necessarily impact the larger protected group as a whole, as in disparate impact. The challenge in these cases is to determine if someone was treated differently because of their race or gender or if there was another reason for the different treatment. Here are two examples:

Both a male and a female miss work, and the female is fired but the male is not.

A company does not hire people of a certain race or gender, without a BFOQ.

Human Resource Recall

Can you think of other examples of disparate impact that might affect a certain protected group of people under EEOC?

Key Takeaways

IRCA stands for *Immigration and Reform Act*. This law requires all employers to determine eligibility of an employee to work in the United States. The reporting form is called an I-9 and must be completed and kept on file (paper or electronic) for at least three years, but some states require this documentation to be kept on file for the duration of the employee's period of employment.

The *Patriot Act* allows the government access to data that would normally be considered private—for example, an employee's records and work voice mails and e-mails (without the company's consent). The HR professional might consider letting employees know of the compliance with this law.

The EEOC is a federal agency charged with ensuring discrimination does not occur in the workplace. They oversee the Equal Employment Opportunity (EEO) set of laws. Organizations must post EEO laws in a visible location at their workplace and also include them on job announcements.

Related to the EEOC, the Bona Fide Occupational Qualification (BFOQ) makes it legal to discriminate in hiring based on special circumstances—for example, requiring the retirement of airline pilots at a certain age due to safety concerns.

Disparate impact refers to a policy that may limit a protected EEO group from receiving fair treatment. Disparate impact might include a test or requirement that negatively impacts someone based on protected group status. An example is requiring a high school diploma, which may not directly impact the job. Disparate treatment refers to discrimination against an individual, such as the hiring of one person over another based on race or gender.

Exercises

1. Describe the difference between disparate treatment and disparate impact.

2. Explain a situation (other than the ones described in this section) in which a BFOQ might be appropriate. Then research to see if in the past this reasoning has been accepted as a BFOQ.

3.3 Recruitment Strategies

Learning Objective

Explain the various strategies that can be used in recruitment.

Now that we have discussed development of the job analysis, job description, and job specifications, and you are aware of the laws relating to recruitment, it is time to start recruiting. It is important to mention, though, that a recruitment plan should be in place. This plan can be informal, but you should outline where you plan to recruit and your expected time lines. For example, if one of your methods is to submit an ad to a trade publication website, you should know their deadlines. Also of consideration is to ensure you are recruiting from a variety of sources to ensure diversity. Lastly, consider the economic situation of the country. With high unemployment, you may receive hundreds of applications for one job. In an up economy, you may not receive many applications and should consider using a variety of sources.

Some companies, such as Southwest Airlines, are known for their innovative recruitment methods. Southwest looks for "the right kind of people" and are less focused on the skills than on the personality of the individual (Carey, 2011). When Southwest recruits, it looks for positive team players that match the underdog, quirky company culture. Applicants are observed in group interviews, and those who exhibit encouragement for their fellow applicants are usually those who continue with the recruitment process. This section will discuss some of the ways Southwest and many other *Fortune* 500 companies find this kind of talent.

Recruitment Videos at Zappos

Zappos has developed and posted a series of YouTube videos called *Why Do I Like Working at Zappos*? The videos show the culture of the organization and provide a great tool for recruitment.

Recruiters

Some organizations choose to have specific individuals working for them who focus solely on the recruiting function of HR. Recruiters use similar sources to recruit individuals, such as professional organizations, websites, and other methods discussed in this chapter. Recruiters are excellent at networking and usually attend many events where possible candidates will be present. Recruiters keep a constant pipeline of possible candidates in case a position should arise that would be a good match. There are three main types of recruiters:

Executive search firm. These companies are focused on high-level positions, such as management and CEO roles. They typically charge 10~20 percent of the first year salary, so they can be quite expensive. However, they do much of the upfront work, sending candidates who meet the qualifications.

Temporary recruitment or staffing firm. Suppose your receptionist is going on medical leave and you need to hire somebody to replace him, but you don't want a long-term hire. You can utilize the services of a temporary recruitment firm to send you qualified candidates who are willing to work shorter contracts.

Usually, the firm pays the salary of the employee and the company pays the recruitment firm, so you don't have to add this person to your payroll. If the person does a good job, there may be opportunities for you to offer him or her a full-time, permanent position. Kelly Services, Manpower, and Snelling Staffing Services are examples of staffing firms.

Corporate recruiter. A corporate recruiter is an employee within a company who focuses entirely on recruiting for his or her company. Corporate recruiters are employed by the company for which they are recruiting. This type of recruiter may be focused on a specific area, such as technical recruiting.

A contingent recruiter is paid only when the recruiter starts working, which is often the case with temporary recruitment or staffing firms. A retained recruiter gets paid up front (in full or a portion of the fee) to perform a specific search for a company.

While the HR professional, when using recruiters, may not be responsible for the details of managing the search process, he or she is still responsible for managing the process and the recruiters. The job analysis, job description, and job specifications still need to be developed and candidates will still need to be interviewed.

Fortune **500 Focus**

In 2009, when Amazon purchased Zappos for 10 million shares of Amazon stock (roughly $900 million in 2009), the strategic move for Amazon didn't change the hiring and recruiting culture of Zappos. Zappos, again voted one of the best one hundred companies to work for by CNN Money (Sowa, 2011) believes it all starts with the people they hire. The recruiting staff always asks, "On a scale of 1—10, how weird do you think you are?" This question ties directly to the company's strategic plan and core value number three, which is "create fun and a little weirdness". Zappos recruits people who not only have the technical abilities for the job but also are a good culture fit for the organization. Once hired, new employees go through two weeks of training. At the end of the training, newly hired employees are given "the offer". The offer is $2,000 to quit on the spot. This ensures Zappos has committed people who have the desire to work with the organization, which all begins with the recruiting process.

Campus Recruiting

Colleges and universities can be excellent sources of new candidates, usually at entry-level positions. Consider technical colleges that teach cooking, automotive technology, or cosmetology. These can be great sources of people with specialized training in a specific area. Universities can provide people that may lack actual experience but have formal training in a specific field. Many organizations use their campus recruiting programs to develop new talent, who will eventually develop into managers.

For this type of program to work, it requires the establishment of relationships with campus communities, such as campus career services departments. It can also require time to attend campus events, such as job fairs. IBM, for example, has an excellent campus recruiting program. For IBM, recruiting out of college ensures a large number of people to grow with the organization.

Setting up a formal internship program might also be a way to utilize college and university contacts. Walgreens, for example, partners with Apollo College to recruit interns; this can result in full-time employment for the motivated intern and money saved for Walgreens by having a constant flow of talent.

Professional Associations

Professional associations are usually non-profit organizations whose goal is to further a particular profession. Almost every profession has its own professional organization. For example, in the field of human resources, the Society for Human Resource Management allows companies to post jobs relating to HR. The American Marketing Association, also a professional organization, allows job postings as well. Usually, there is a fee involved, and membership in this association may be required to post jobs. Here are some examples of professional associations:

Professional Nursing Association

Society of Women Engineers

International Federation of Accountants

Institute of Management Consultants

United Professional Sales Association

National Lawyers Guild

National Organization of Minority Architects

International Federation of Journalists (union)

International Metalworkers Federation (union)

Association of Flight Attendants (union)

Labor unions can also be excellent sources of candidates, and some unions also allow job postings on their website. We will discuss unions further in Chapter 9 "Working with Labor Unions". The key to using this as a successful recruitment strategy is to identify the organizations that relate to your business and to develop relationships with members in these organizations. This type of networking can help introduce you to people in your industry who may be looking for a job or know of someone who needs a job.

Human Resource Recall

1. What do you think is the best way to determine the right set of recruitment methods for your organization?

2. What methods would be best for your current job?

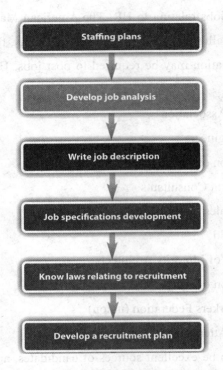

Figure 2-13 Overview of the Steps to the Recruitment Proces

Websites

If you have ever had to look for a job, you know there are numerous websites to help you do that. From the HR perspective, there are many options to place an ad, most of which are inexpensive. The downside to this method is the immense number of résumés you may receive from these websites, all of which may or may not be qualified. Many organizations, to combat this, implement software that searches for keywords in résumés, which can help combat this problem. We discuss more about this in Chapter 4 "Selection". Some examples of websites might include the following:

Your own company website

Yahoo HotJobs

Monster

CareerBuilder

JobsCentral

Social Media

Facebook, Twitter, LinkedIn, YouTube, and MySpace are excellent places to obtain a media presence to attract a variety of workers. In 2007, Sodexo, which provides services such as food service and facilities management, started using social media to help spread the word about their company culture. Since then, they have saved $300,000 on traditional recruiting methods (Sodexo, 2011). Sodexo's fifty recruiters share updates on Twitter about their excellent company culture. Use of this media has driven traffic to the careers page on Sodexo's website, from 52,000 to 181,000.

The goal of using social media as a recruiting tool is to create a buzz about your organization, share stories of successful employees, and tout an interesting culture. Even smaller companies can utilize this technology by posting job openings as their status updates. This technique is relatively inexpensive, but there are some things to consider. For example, tweeting about a job opening might spark interest in some candidates, but the trick is to show your personality as an employer early on. According to Bruce Morton of Allegis Group Services, using social media is about getting engaged and having conversations with people before they're even thinking about you as an employer (Lindow, 2011). Debbie Fisher, an HR manager for a large advertising agency, Campbell Mithun, says that while tweeting may be a good way to recruit people who can be open about their job hunt, using tools such as LinkedIn might be a better way to obtain more seasoned candidates who cannot be open about their search for a new job, because of their current employment situation. She says that LinkedIn has given people permission to put their résumé online without fear of retribution from current employers.

Creativity with a social media campaign also counts. Campbell Mithun hired thirteen interns over the summer using a unique twist on social media. They asked interested candidates to submit thirteen tweets over thirteen days and chose the interns based on their creativity.

Many organizations, including Zappos, use YouTube videos to promote the company. Within the videos is a link that directs viewers to the company's website to apply for a position in the company.

Facebook allows free job postings in Facebook Marketplace, and the company Facebook page can also be used as a recruiting tool. Some organizations decide to use Facebook ads, which are paid on a "per click" or per impression (how many people potentially see the ad) basis. Facebook ad technology allows specific regions and Facebook keywords to be targeted (Black, 2011). Some individuals even use their personal Facebook page to post status updates listing job opportunities and asking people to respond privately if they are interested.

Events

Many organizations, such as Microsoft, hold events annually to allow people to network and learn about new technologies. Microsoft's Professional Developer Conference (PDC), usually held in July, hosts thousands of web developers and other professionals looking to update their skills and meet new people.

Some organizations, such as Choice Career Fairs, host job fairs all over the country; participating in this type of job fair may be an excellent way to meet a large variety of candidates. Other events may not be specifically for recruiting, but attending these events may allow you to meet people who could possibly fill a position or future position. For example, in the world of fashion, Fashion Group International (FGI) hosts events internationally on a weekly basis, which may allow the opportunity to meet qualified candidates.

Special/Specific Interest Groups (SIGs)

Special/specific interest groups (SIGs), which may require membership of individuals, focus on specific topics for members. Often SIGs will have areas for job posting, or a variety of discussion boards where jobs can be posted. For example, the Women in Project Management SIG provides news on project management and also has a place for job advertisements. Other examples of SIGs might include the following:

Oracle Developer SIG

African American Medical Librarians Alliance SIG

American Marketing Association Global Marketing SIG

Special Interest Group for Accounting Information Systems (SIG-ASYS)

Junior Lawyer SIG

Recruiting using SIGs can be a great way to target a specific group of people who are trained in a specific area or who have a certain specialty.

Referrals

Most recruiting plans include asking current employees, "Who do you know?" The quality of referred applicants is usually high, since most people would not recommend someone they thought incapable of doing the job. E-mailing a job opening to current employees and offering incentives to refer a friend can be a quick way of recruiting individuals. Due to the success of most formalized referral programs, it is suggested that a program be part of the overall HRM strategic plan and recruitment strategy. However, be wary of using referrals as the only method for recruitment, as this can lead to lack of diversity in a workplace. Nepotism means a preference for hiring relatives of current employees, which can also lead to lack of diversity and management issues in the workplace.

For example, the University of Washington offers $1,200 any time a current employee successfully refers a friend to work at their medical centers. Usually, most incentives require the new employee to be hired and stay a specified period of time. Some examples of incentives that can be used to refer a friend might include the following:

A gift card to the employee

A financial incentive

Raffles for most referrals

These types of programs are called employee referral programs (ERPs) and tend to generate one of the highest returns on investment per hire (Lefkow, 2002). To make an ERP program effective, some key components should be put into place:

Communicate the program to existing employees.

Track the success of the program using metrics of successful hires.

Be aware of the administrative aspect and the time it takes to implement the program effectively.

Set measureable goals up front for a specialized program.

Accenture recently won the ERE Media Award for one of the most innovative ERPs. Its program has increased new hires from referrals from 14 percent to 32 percent, and employee awareness of the program jumped from just 20 percent to 99 percent (Sullivan, 2009). The uniqueness of their program lies with the reward the employee receives. Instead of offering personal financial compensation, Accenture makes a donation to the charity of the employee's choice, such as a local elementary school. Their program also seeks to decrease casual referrals, so the employee is asked to fill out an online form to explain the skills of the individual they are referring. The company has also developed a website where current employees can go to track the progress of referrals. In addition, employee referral applications are flagged online and fast-tracked through the process—in fact, every referral is acted upon. As you can see, Accenture has made their ERP a success through the use of strategic planning in the recruitment process.

Table 2-4 Advantages and Disadvantages of Recruiting Methods

Recruitment Method	Advantages	Disadvantages
Outside recruiters, executive search firms, and temporary employment agencies	Can be time saving	Expensive
Campus recruiting/ educational institutions	Can hire people to grow with the organization	Less control over final candidates to be interviewed
Professional organizations and associations	Plentiful source of talent	Time-consuming
Websites/Internet recruiting	Industry specific Networking	Only appropriate for certain types of experience levels May be a fee to place an ad
Social media	Diversity friendly Low cost	May be time-consuming to network Could be too broad
Events	Quick Inexpensive	Be prepared to deal with hundreds of résumés Time-consuming Overwhelming response
SIGs	Access to specific target markets of candidates	Can be expensive
Referrals	Industry specific	May not be the right target market
Unsolicited résumés and applications	Higher quality people	Research required for specific SIGS tied to jobs
Internet and/or traditional advertisements	Retention Inexpensive, especially with time-saving keyword résumé search software can target a specific audience	Concern for lack of diversity
Employee leasing	For smaller organizations, it means someone does not have to administer compensation and benefits, as this is handled by leasing company	Nepotism Time-consuming Can be expensive
Public employment agencies	Can be a good alternative to temporary employment if the job is permanent	Possible costs Less control of who interviews for the position

Continued

Recruitment Method	Advantages	Disadvantages
Labor unions	The potential ability to recruit a more diverse workforce no cost, since it's a government agency 2,300 points of service nationwide access to specialized skills	May receive many résumés, which can be time-consuming

Costs of Recruitment

Part of recruitment planning includes budgeting the cost of finding applicants. For example, let's say you have three positions you need to fill, with one being a temporary hire. You have determined your advertising costs will be $400, and your temporary agency costs will be approximately $700 for the month. You expect at least one of the two positions will be recruited as a referral, so you will pay a referral bonus of $500. Here is how you can calculate the cost of recruitment for the month:

cost per hire = advertising costs + recruiter costs + referral costs + social media costs + event costs.

$400 + $700 + $500 = $1600/3 = $533 recruitment cost per hire.

In addition, when we look at how effective our recruiting methods are, we can look at a figure called the yield ratio. A yield ratio is the percentage of applicants from one source who make it to the next stage in the selection process (e.g., they get an interview). For example, if you received two hundred résumés from a professional organization ad you placed, and fifty-two of those make it to the interview state, this means a 26 percent yield (52/200). By using these calculations, we can determine the best place to recruit for a particular position. Note, too, that some yield ratios may vary for particular jobs, and a higher yield ratio must also consider the cost of that method, too. For an entry-level job, campus recruiting may yield a better ratio than, say, a corporate recruiter, but the corporate recruiter may have higher cost per hires.

After we have finished the recruiting process, we can begin the selection process. This is the focus of Chapter 4 "Selection".

Key Takeaways

HR professionals must have a recruiting plan before posting any job description. The plan should outline where the job announcements will be posted and how the management of candidate materials, such as résumés, will occur. Part of the plan should also include the expected cost of recruitment.

Many organizations use recruiters. Recruiters can be executive recruiters, which means an outside firm performs the search. For temporary positions, a temporary or staffing firm such as Kelly Services might be used. Corporate recruiters work for the organization and function as a part of the HR team.

Campus recruiting can be an effective way of recruiting for entry-level positions. This type of recruiting may require considerable effort in developing relationships with college campuses.

Almost every profession has at least one professional association. Posting announcements on their websites can be an effective way of targeting for a specific job.

Most companies will also use their own website for job postings, as well as other websites such as Monster and CareerBuilder.

Social media is also a popular way to recruit. Usage of websites such as Twitter and Facebook can get the word out about a specific job opening, or give information about the company, which can result in more traffic being directed to the company's website.

Recruiting at special events such as job fairs is another option. Some organizations have specific job fairs for their company, depending on the size. Others may attend industry or job-specific fairs to recruit specific individuals.

SIGs, or special/specific interest groups, are usually very specialized. For example, female project managers may have an interest group that includes a discussion board for posting of job announcements.

Employee referrals can be a great way to get interest for a posted position. Usually, incentives are offered to the employee for referring people they know. However, diversity can be an issue, as can nepotism.

Our last consideration in the recruitment process is recruitment costs. We can determine this by looking at the total amount we have spent on all recruiting efforts compared to the number of hires. A yield ratio is used to determine how effective recruiting efforts are in one area. For example, we can look at the number of total applicants received from a particular form of media, and divide that by the number of those applicants who make it to the next step in the process (e.g., they receive an interview).

Exercises

1. Perform an Internet search on professional associations for your particular career choice. List at least three associations, and discuss recruiting options listed on their websites (e.g., Do they have discussion boards or job advertisements links?).

2. Have you ever experienced nepotism in the workplace? If yes, describe the experience. What do you think are the upsides and downsides to asking current employees to refer someone they know?

3.4 Cases and Problems

Chapter Summary

The *recruitment process* provides the organization with a pool of qualified applicants.

Some companies choose to hire internal candidates—that is, candidates who are already working for the organization. However, diversity is a consideration here as well.

A job analysis is a systematic approach to determine what a person actually does in his or her job. This process might involve a questionnaire to all employees. Based on this analysis, an accurate job description and job specifications can be written. A job description lists the components of the job, while job specifications list the requirements to perform the job.

IRCA stands for *Immigration and Reform Act*. This law requires all employers to determine eligibility of an employee to work in the United States. The reporting form is called an I-9 and must be completed and kept on file (paper or electronic) for at least three years, but some states require this documentation to be kept on file for the duration of the employee's period of employment.

The *Patriot Act* allows the government access to data that would normally be considered private, for example, an employee's records and work voice mails and e-mails (without the company's consent). The HR professional might consider letting employees know of the compliance with this law.

The Equal Employment Opportunity Commission (EEOC) is a federal agency charged with ensuring discrimination does not occur in the workplace. They oversee the EEO set of laws. Organizations must post EEO laws in a visible location at their workplace and also include them on job announcements.

Related to the EEOC, the Bona Fide Occupational Qualification (BFOQ) makes it legal to discriminate in hiring based on special circumstances, for example, requiring the retirement of airline pilots at a certain age due to safety concerns.

Disparate impact refers to a policy that may limit a protected EEO group from receiving fair treatment. Disparate impact might include a test or requirement that negatively impacts someone based on protected group status. An example is requiring a high school diploma, which may not directly impact the job. Disparate treatment refers to discrimination against an individual, such as the hiring of one person over another based on race or gender.

HR professionals must have a recruiting plan before posting any job description.

Many organizations use recruiters. Recruiters can be executive recruiters, which means an outside firm performs the search. For temporary positions, a temporary or staffing firm such as Kelly Services might be used. Corporate recruiters work for the organization and function as a part of the HR team.

Campus recruiting can be an effective way of recruiting for entry-level positions. This type of recruiting may require considerable effort in developing relationships with college campuses.

Almost every profession has at least one professional association. Posting announcements on their websites can be an effective way of targeting for a specific job.

Most companies will also use their own website for job postings, as well as other websites such as Monster and CareerBuilder.

Social media is also a popular way to recruit. Usage of websites such as Twitter and Facebook can get the word out about a specific job opening, or give information about the company, which can result in more traffic being directed to the company's website.

Recruiting at special events such as job fairs is another option. Some organizations have specific job fairs for their company, depending on the size. Others may attend industry or job specific fairs to recruit specific individuals.

SIGs or special/specific interest groups are usually very specialized. For example, female project managers may have an interest group that includes a discussion board for posting of job announcements.

Employee referrals can be a great way to get interest for a posted position. Usually, incentives are offered to the employee for referring people they know. However, diversity can be an issue, as can nepotism.

Our last consideration in the recruitment process is recruitment costs. We can determine this by looking at the total amount we have spent on all recruiting efforts compared to the number of hires. A yield ratio is used to determine how effective recruiting efforts are in one area. For example, we can look at the number of total applicants received from a particular form of media, and divide that by the number of those applicants who make it to the next step in the process (e.g., they receive an interview).

Chapter Case

Recruitment Statistics

As the assistant to the human resources director at Tally Group, you normally answer phones and set appointments for the director. You are interested in developing skills in HRM, and one day, your HR director presents you with a great opportunity for you to show what you can do. She asks you to analyze last year's recruitment data to determine which methods have worked best. As you look at the data, you aren't sure how to start, but you remember something on this from your HRM class in college. After reviewing the data in your book, you feel confident to analyze these numbers. Please go ahead and perform calculations on these numbers, then provide answers to the questions that follow.

Table 2-5 Tally Group Recruiting Numbers, 2012

Method	Total Number Recruited	Yearly Cost ($)
Temporary placement firms	8	3,200
Campus recruiting	2	1,500
Professional association ads	10	4,500
Social media/company website	33	300
Job fair	3	500
Referrals	26	26,000

Prepare a report summarizing your findings for the recruitment cost per hire and yield ratio for each type of recruiting method.

Make a recommendation to your human resource director on where the department should spend more of its time recruiting.

Team Activities

Students should be in teams of four or five. Choose a recruitment method from Table 2-5 "Tally Group Recruiting Numbers, 2012" and perform research on additional advantages and disadvantages of that method and then present ideas to the class.

Visit the *Dictionary of Occupational Titles* (http://www.occupationalinfo.org) and view the list of job titles presented on the website. Create a sample job description for a job title of your team's choice.

Chapter 4　Selection

The Interview

Many of us have or will sit in a waiting room with our best clothes on awaiting a job (or school) interview. You can feel your palms sweat and thoughts race as you wait for your name to be called. You look around at the office environment and imagine yourself walking through those doors everyday. People walk by and smile, and overall, you have a really good first impression of the organization. You hope they like you. You tell yourself to remember to smile, while recalling all your experience that makes you the perfect person for this job. A moment of self-doubt may occur, as you wonder about the abilities of the other people being interviewed and hope you have more experience and make a better impression than they do. You hear your name, stand up, and give a firm handshake to the HR manager. The interview has begun.

As she walks you back to a conference room, you think you see encouraging smiles as you pass by people. She asks you to take a chair and then tells you what the interview process will be like. She then asks the first question, "Tell me about yourself". As you start discussing your experience, you feel yourself relax, just a little bit. After the interview finishes, she asks you to take a quick cognitive test, which you feel good about. She tells you she will be doing reference checks and will let you know by early next week.

To get to this point, the hiring manager may have reviewed hundreds of résumés and developed criteria she would use for selection of the right person for the job. She has probably planned a time line for hiring, developed hiring criteria, determined a compensation package for the job, and enlisted help of other managers to interview candidates. She may have even performed a number of phone interviews before bringing only a few of the best candidates in for interviews. It is likely she has certain qualities in mind that she is hoping you or another candidate will possess. Much work goes into the process of hiring someone, with selection being an important step in that process. A hiring process done correctly is time-consuming and precise. The interviewer should already have questions determined and should be ready to sell the organization to the candidate as well. This chapter will discuss the main components to the selection process.

4.1　The Selection Process

> **Learning Objective**
>
> Be able to name and discuss the steps in the selection process.

Once you have developed your recruitment plan, recruited people, and now have plenty of people to choose from, you can begin the selection process. The selection process refers to the steps involved in choosing people who have the right qualifications to fill a current or future job opening. Usually, managers and supervisors will be ultimately responsible for the hiring of individuals, but the role of Human Resource Management (HRM) is to define and guide managers in this process. Similar to the recruitment process discussed in Chapter 3 "Recruitment", the selection process is expensive. The time for all involved in the hiring process to review résumés, weight the applications, and interview the best candidates takes away time (and costs money) that those individuals could spend on other activities. In addition, there are the costs of testing candidates and bringing them in from out of town for interviews. In fact, the U.S. Department of Labor and Statistics estimates the combined direct and indirect cost of hiring someone new can reach upwards of $40,000 (Hamm, 2011). Because of the high cost, it is important to hire the right person from the beginning and ensure a fair selection process. For example, the Austin, Texas, fire department calculated it would cost $150,000 to reinterview candidates, after the interview questions were leaked to the public, giving some candidates possibly unfair advantages in the interview process.

Figure 2-14 Interview

Note: Interviews can be nerve wracking. In this chapter, we will discuss what goes into making the best hiring decision.

The selection process consists of five distinct aspects.

Criteria development. All individuals involved in the hiring process should be properly trained on the steps for interviewing, including developing criteria, reviewing résumés, developing interview questions, and weighting the candidates.

The first aspect to selection is planning the interview process, which includes criteria development. Criteria development means determining which sources of information will be used and how those sources will be scored during the interview. The criteria should be related directly to the job analysis and the job specifications. This is discussed in Chapter 3 "Recruitment". In fact, some aspects of the job analysis and job specifications may be the actual criteria. In addition to this, include things like personality or cultural fit, which would also be part of criteria development. This process usually involves discussing which skills, abilities, and personal characteristics are required to be successful at any given job. By developing the criteria before reviewing any résumés, the HR manager or manager can be sure he or she is being fair in selecting people to interview. Some organizations may need to develop an application or a biographical information sheet. Most of these are completed online and should include information about the candidate, education, and previous job experience.

Application and résumé review. Once the criteria have been developed (step one), applications can be reviewed. People have different methods of going through this process, but there are also computer programs that can search for keywords in résumés and narrow down the number of résumés that must be looked at and reviewed.

Interviewing. After the HR manager and/or manager have determined which applications meet the minimum criteria, he or she must select those people to be interviewed. Most people do not have time to review twenty or thirty candidates, so the field is sometimes narrowed even further with a phone interview. This is discussed in other chapter.

Test administration. Any number of tests may be administered before a hiring decision is made. These include drug tests, physical tests, personality tests, and cognitive tests. Some organizations also perform reference checks, credit report checks, and background checks. Types of tests are discussed in other chapter. Once the field of candidates has been narrowed down, tests can be administered.

Making the offer. The last step in the selection process is to offer a position to the chosen candidate. Development of an offer via e-mail or letter is sometimes a more formal part of this process. Compensation and benefits will be defined in an offer. We discuss this in Chapter 5 "Compensation and Benefits".

Table 2-6 The Selection Process at a Glance

Criteria Development	Understand KSAOs Determine sources of KSAO information such as testing, interviews Develop scoring system for each of the sources of information Create an interview plan
Application and Résumé Review	Should be based on criteria developed in step one Consider internal versus external candidates
Interview	Determine types of interview(s) Write interview questions Be aware of interview bias
Test Administration	Perform testing as outlined in criteria development; could include reviewing work samples, drug testing or written cognitive and personality tests Determine which selection method will be used Compare selection method criteria
Selection	Use negotiation techniques Write the offer letter or employment agreement
Making the Offer	

We will discuss each of these aspects in detail in this chapter.

Fortune 500 Focus

In a 2010 interview (Bryant, 2010), Robert Selander, then CEO of MasterCard, cited presence as one of the most important aspects to acing an interview. He describes how, in any large organization, an employee will be expected to engage with a variety of stakeholders, from a member of Congress to a contractor replacing the carpet in the building. He says that a good employee—at any level of the organization—should be able to communicate well but also be able to communicate to a variety of stakeholders.

Candidate plans to address those weaknesses to make sure they do not become a barrier to success. He always asks the question "What can you do for us?" When asked if he could pose only one interview question, what would it be, his answer was, "Share with me two situations, work related that you are proud of, where something was achieved based on your own personal initiative and the other where the achievement was a result of the team getting something done that you could not have done alone." In other words, Selander is looking for not only personal ability but the ability to work within a team to accomplish tasks. Selander offers advice to new college grads: try to find an organization where you can be involved and see all aspects of the business and be provided training to help you with certain skills that will be needed.

Human Resource Recall

When was the last time you interviewed for a job? Did the process seem to flow smoothly? Why or why not?

Key Takeaways

The selection process refers to the steps involved in choosing someone who has the right qualifications to fill a current or future job opening.

There are five main steps in the selection process. First, criteria are developed to determine how the person will be chosen. Second is a review of the applications and résumés, often done via a computer program that can find keywords. Next is interviewing the employee. The last steps involve testing, such as a personality test or drug test, and then finally, making the offer to the right candidate.

Exercise

What components are included in the selection process? Which one do you think is the most important?

4.2 Criteria Development and Résumé Review

Learning Objectives

1. Be able to explain why criteria development is an important part of the selection process.

2. Give examples of types of criteria that can be developed.

3. Describe the advantages and disadvantages of internal and external candidates.

Before we begin to review résumés and applications, we must have a clear idea of the person we want to hire for the position. Obviously, the job specifications will help us know the minimum qualifications, such as education level and years of experience. However, additional criteria might include the attitude of the potential hire, the ability to take initiative, and other important personal characteristics and professional abilities that may not always be demonstrated in an application or résumé. A specific score on a personality test, quality of work samples, and other tools to determine qualifications should be included as part of the criteria. In other words, knowing exactly what you want before you even begin the process of looking through résumés will make this process much easier. In human resources, this is called KSAOs, or knowledge, skills, abilities, and other personal characteristics that make a person successful on the job. Some organizations, such as the United States Department of Veterans Affairs, require applicants to address each one of the KSAOs listed in the job position within their cover letter.

Criteria Development Considerations

Many HR professionals and managers develop the criteria for hiring, as well as the interview questions, before reviewing any résumés. This allows for a streamlined process with specific guidelines already set before reviewing a résumé. For example, criteria for a project management job might include the following:

Two years of experience managing a $2 million or more project budget

A bachelor's degree in business or closely related field

Ability to work on multiple projects at once

Problem-solving ability

Conflict-management ability

Ability to manage a team of five to six diverse workers

Score of at least a 70 on cognitive ability test

Score of excellent from most recent employer

By setting criteria ahead of time, the hiring team has a clear picture of exactly what qualifications they are looking for. As a result, it is easier to determine who should move forward in the selection process. For example, if someone does not have a bachelor's degree, given this is a criterion, their application materials can be filed away, perhaps for another job opening. Likewise, the HR manager can include those résumés with two or more years of experience and bachelor's degree in the interview pile and then develop interview questions that show the candidates' problem-solving, multi-tasking, and conflict-management abilities.

Résumé parsing or résumé scanning software is readily available and can make the initial screening easier. For example, *Sovren* software allows the HR manager to include keywords such as bachelor's degree or management. This software scans all received résumés and selects the ones that have the keywords. While it still may be necessary to review résumés, this type of software can save time having to look through résumés that obviously do not meet the minimum qualifications.

Validity and Reliablity

The validity refers to how useful the tool is to measure a person's attributes for a specific job opening. A tool may include any and all of the following:

Résumé-scanning software

Reference checks

Cognitive ability tests

Work samples

Credit reports

Biographical information blanks

Weighted application forms

Personality tests

Interview questions

Biographical Information Blanks (BIBs) are a useful part of the application process. A BIB is a series of questions about a person's history that may have shaped his or her behavior. The BIB can be scored in the same way as an interview or a résumé, assuming the organization knows which types of answers are predictable for success in a given job. Similarly, a weighted application form involves selecting an employee characteristic to be measured and then identifying which questions on the application predict the desired behavior. Then scores are assigned to each predictor. Of course, the development of the scoring should be determined before any résumés and application forms have been reviewed. In other words, any tool you use to determine someone's qualifications for a job should have validity to determine they are the right fit for the job.

Reliability refers to the degree in which other selection techniques yield similar data over time. For example, if you ask the same interview question of every applicant for the project management position, and the "right" answer always yields similar, positive results, such as the hiring of a successful employee every time, the question would be considered reliable. An example of an unreliable test might occur with reference checks. Most candidates would not include a reference on their résumé who might give them a poor review, making this a less reliable method for determining skills and abilities of applicants.

Fit Issues

Fit includes not only the right technical expertise, education, and experience but also fit in company culture and team culture. For example, at Facebook headquarters in Palo Alto, California, engineers are selected based on their willingness to take risks, as risk taking is nurtured at Facebook (McGirt, 2010). In addition to this component of their company culture, the company looks for the "hacker" personality, because a hacker is someone who finds ways around the constraints placed upon a system. At Zappos, profiled in Chapter 3 "Recruitment", the company culture is one focused on customer service and the willingness of people to provide the best customer service in all aspects of the business. At Amazon, the huge online retailer, a core value in their company culture is a focus on developing leaders to grow with the organization. If a potential candidate is not interested in long-term career growth, he or she might not be deemed an appropriate strategic fit with the organization. In today's organizations, most people are required to work within teams. As a result, fit within a team is as important as company culture fit. Microsoft, for example, does an immense amount of teamwork. The company is structured so that there are marketers, accountants, developers, and many others working on one product at a time. As a result, Microsoft looks for not only company culture fit but also fit with other team members.

Reviewing Résumés

Once we have developed our criteria for a specific job, we can begin the review process. Everyone prefers to perform this differently. For example, all the hiring decision makers may review all résumés, list the people they would like to meet in person, and then compare the lists. Another method might be to rate each candidate and interview only those above a certain score. This is discussed in Chapter 4 "Selection Methods". Obviously, much of the process will depend on the organization's size and the type of job. None of this process can be done fairly without first setting criteria for the job.

When looking at résumés to determine whom to interview, a manager should be concerned with the concepts of disparate impact and disparate treatment. This is discussed in Chapter 3 "Recruitment". Disparate impact is unintended discrimination against a protected group as a whole through the use of a particular requirement. Disparate impact may be present in the interviewing process, as well as other employment-related processes such as pay raises and promotions. For example, a requirement of being able to lift 110 pounds might be considered as having disparate impact on women, unless the job requires this ability. Every criteria developed should be closely considered to see if it might have disparate impact on a protected group of individuals. For example, the requirement of a certain credit score might have a negative impact on immigrants, who may not have a well-developed credit rating. However, if being able to manage money is an important requirement of the job, this requirement might not be discriminatory.

Disparate treatment in hiring might include not interviewing a candidate because of one's perception about the candidate's age, race, or gender.

The last consideration is the hiring of internal versus external candidates. An internal candidate is someone who already works within the organization, while an external candidate is someone who works outside the organization. A bidding process may occur to notify internal candidates of open positions. This is discussed in Chapter 3 "Recruitment". Generally speaking, it is best to go through a formal interview process with all candidates, even if they work within the organization. This way, an HR professional can be assured that disparate treatment does not occur because of favoritism. For example, a senior executive of your organization just left, and you believe the manager in that department is qualified to take over the position. Suppose, though, that the manager has been lobbying you for the job for some time and has even taken you out to lunch to talk about the job. While this person has maintained high visibility and lobbied for the promotion, there may be equally qualified internal candidates who did not use the same lobbying techniques. Automatically offering the position to this internal candidate might undermine others who are equally qualified. So while hiring internally can be a motivator, making assumptions about a particular person may not be a motivator to others. This is why it is best, even if you hire internally, to post a formal job announcement listing the job description and job qualifications, so everyone in the organization can have an equal opportunity to apply for the job.

Once you have completed the criteria for the particular job and narrowed down the field, you can begin the interview process.

Table 2-7 Possible Advantages and Disadvantages of Hiring an Internal versus an External Candidate

	Advantages	Disadvantages
Internal Candidates	Rewards contributions of current staff Can be cost effective, as opposed to using a traditional recruitment strategy Can improve morale Knowing the past performance of the candidate can assist in	Can produce "inbreeding", which may reduce diversity and different perspectives May cause political infighting between people to obtain the promotions Can create bad feelings if an internal candidate applies for a job and doesn't get it
External Candidates	Knowing if they meet the criteria Brings new talent into the company Can help an organization obtain diversity goals New ideas and insight brought into the company	Implementation of recruitment strategy can be expensive Can cause morale problems for internal candidates Can take longer for training and orientation

How Would You Handle This?

Poor Interviewer

As the assistant to the HR manager, one of your jobs is to help managers get ready to interview candidates. When you offer help to Johnathan, he says he has interviewed hundreds of people and doesn't need your help in planning the interview process. When you sit in the interview with him, he asks inappropriate questions that you don't feel really assess the abilities of a candidate. How would you handle this?

The author discusses the "How Would You Handle This" situation in this chapter at: https://api.wistia.com/v1/ medias/1360625/embed.

Key Takeaways

The first step in selection is to begin reviewing résumés. Even before you do this, though, it is important to develop criteria that each candidate will be measured against. This can come from the job description as well as the job qualifications.

Other tools, such as cognitive ability tests, credit checks, and personality tests, can be used to determine qualifications. When developing your criteria for interviewing, determine the level the applicant needs to meet the minimum criteria, for example, a minimum score on a personality test.

We should be concerned with validity and reliability of measurement tools. Validity refers to how valid the test is, that is, how well a test measures a candidate's abilities to do a job. Reliability refers to which selection techniques yield similar data or results over time. It is important to choose the right measurement tool used to determine whether the candidate meets the criteria.

Setting criteria before the interview process starts ensures that disparate impact or disparate treatment does not occur in the interview process.

When hiring, there is the option of internal and external candidates. Each has its own set of advantages and disadvantages. Internal candidates may be able to "hit the ground running", but external candidates may come in with new perspectives. Even if an internal candidate seems to be the best hire, it is best to still perform the process of posting the job and interviewing, since other less vocal employees might be qualified internal candidates as well. In other words, don't assume one person is the obvious choice for the promotion.

Exercises

1. Develop criteria for the position of a retail salesperson working in teams.

2. Describe the advantages and disadvantages of hiring an internal and external candidate. Give an example of when you don't think an external candidate should be considered for a position.

3. How can development of criteria or minimum standards help in a case of disparate treatment accusations?

4.3 Interviewing

Learning Objectives

1. Explain the various types of interviews and interview questions.
2. Discuss interview methods and potential mistakes in interviewing candidates.
3. Explain the interview process.

Interviewing people costs money. As a result, after candidates are selected, good use of time is critical to making sure the interview process allows for selection of the right candidate. In an unstructured interview, questions are changed to match the specific applicant; for example, questions about the candidate's background in relation to their résumé might be used. In a structured interview, there is a set of standardized questions based on the job analysis, not on individual candidates' résumés. While a structured interview might seem the best option to find out about a particular candidate, the bigger concern is that the interview revolves around the specific job for which the candidate is interviewing. In a structured interview, the expected or desired answers are determined ahead of time, which allows the interviewer to rate responses as the candidate provides answers. This allows for a fair interview process, according to the U.S. Office of Personnel Management. For purposes of this section, we will assume that all interviews you perform will be structured, unless otherwise noted.

Types of Interviews

Interview processes can be time-consuming, so it makes sense to choose the right type of interview(s) for the individual job. Some jobs, for example, may necessitate only one interview, while another may necessitate a telephone interview and at least one or two traditional interviews. Keep in mind, though, that there will likely be other methods with which to evaluate a candidate's potential, such as testing. Here are different types of interviews:

Traditional interview. This type of interview normally takes place in the office. It consists of the interviewer and the candidate, and a series of questions are asked and answered.

Telephone interview. A telephone interview is often used to narrow the list of people receiving a traditional interview. It can be used to determine salary requirements or other data that might automatically rule out giving someone a traditional interview. For example, if you receive two hundred résumés and narrow these down to twenty-five, it is still unrealistic to interview twenty-five people in person. At this point, you may decide to conduct phone interviews of those twenty-five, which could narrow the in-person interviews to a more manageable ten or so people.

Panel interview. A panel interview occurs when several people are interviewing one candidate at the same time. While this type of interview can be nerve racking for the candidate, it can also be a more effective use of time. Consider some companies who require three to four people to interview candidates for a job. It would be unrealistic to ask the candidate to come in for three or four interviews, so it makes sense for them to be interviewed by everyone at once.

Information interview. Informational interviews are usually used when there is no specific job opening, but the candidate is exploring possibilities in a given career field. The advantage to conducting these types of interviews is the ability to find great people ahead of a job opening.

Meal interviews. Many organizations offer to take the candidate to lunch or dinner for the interview. This can allow for a more casual meeting where, as the interviewer, you might be able to gather more information about the person, such as their manners and treatment of waitstaff. This type of interview might be considered an unstructured interview, since it would tend to be more of a conversation as opposed to a session consisting of specific questions and answers.

Group interview. In a group interview, two or more candidates interview at the same time. This type of interview can be an excellent source of information if you need to know how they may relate to other people in their job.

Video interviews. Video interviews are the same as traditional interviews, except that video technology is used. This can be cost saving if one or more of your candidates are from out of town. Skype, for example, allows free video calls. An interview may not feel the same as a traditional interview, but the same information can be gathered about the candidate.

Non-directive interview (sometimes called an unstructured interview). In a non-directive interview, the candidate essentially leads the discussion. Some very general questions that are planned ahead of time may be asked, but the candidate spends more time talking than the interviewer. The questions may be more open ended; for example, instead of asking, "Do you like working with customers?" you may ask, "What did you like best about your last job?" The advantage of this type of interview is that it can give candidates a good chance to show their abilities; however, the downside is that it may be hard to compare potential candidates, since questions are not set in advance. It relies on more of a "gut feeling" approach.

It is likely you may use one or more of these types of interviews. For example, you may conduct phone interviews, then do a meal interview, and follow up with a traditional interview, depending on the type of job.

Interview Questions

Most interviews consist of many types of questions, but they usually lean toward situational interviews or behavior description interviews. A situational interview is one in which the candidate is given a sample situation and is asked how he or she might deal with the situation. In a behavior description interview, the candidate is asked questions about what he or she actually did in a variety of given situations. The assumption in this type of interview is that someone's past experience or actions are an indicator of future behavior. These types of questions, as opposed to the old "tell me about yourself" questions, tend to assist the interviewer in knowing how a person would handle or has handled situations. These interview styles also use a structured method and provide a better basis for decision-making. Examples of situational interview questions might include the following:

If you saw someone stealing from the company, what would you do?

One of your employees is performing poorly, but you know he has some personal home issues he is dealing with. How would you handle complaints from his colleagues about lack of performance?

A coworker has told you she called in sick three days last week because she actually decided to take a vacation. What would you do?

You are rolling out a new sales plan on Tuesday, which is really important to ensure success in your organization. When you present it, the team is lukewarm on the plan. What would you do?

You disagree with your supervisor on her handling of a situation. What would you do?

Examples of behavior description interview questions might include the following:

Tell me about a time you had to make a hard decision. How did you handle this process?

Give an example of how you handled an angry customer.

Do you show leadership in your current or past job? What would be an example of a situation in which you did this?

What accomplishments have given you the most pride and why?

What plans have you made to achieve your career goals?

Top 36 Interview Questions and Answers

Examples of how to answer those difficult interview questions.

As you already know, there are many types of interview questions that would be considered illegal. Here are some examples:

National origin. You cannot ask seemingly innocent questions such as "That's a beautiful name, where is your family from?" This could indicate national origin, which could result in bias. You also cannot ask questions about citizenship, except by asking if a candidate is legally allowed to work in the United States. Questions about the first language of the candidate shouldn't be asked, either. However, asking "Do you have any language abilities that would be helpful in this job?" or "Are you authorized to work in the United States?" would be acceptable.

Age. You cannot ask someone how old they are, and it is best to avoid questions that might indicate age, such as "When did you graduate from high school?" However, asking "Are you over 18?" is acceptable.

Marital status. You can't ask direct questions about marital status or ages of children. An alternative may be to ask, "Do you have any restrictions on your ability to travel, since this job requires 50 percent travel?"

Religion. It's illegal to ask candidates about their religious affiliation or to ask questions that may indicate a religion-affiliated school or university.

Disabilities. You may not directly ask if the person has disabilities or recent illnesses. You can ask if the candidate is able to perform the functions of the job with or without reasonable accommodations.

Criminal record. While it is fine to perform a criminal record check, asking a candidate if they have ever been arrested is not appropriate; however, questions about convictions and guilty pleadings are acceptable.

Personal questions. Avoid asking personal questions, such as questions about social organizations or clubs, unless they relate to the job.

Besides these questions, any specific questions about weight, height, gender, and arrest record (as opposed to allowable questions about criminal convictions) should be avoided.

HR professionals and managers should be aware of their own body language in an interview. Some habits, such as nodding, can make the candidate think they are on the right track when answering a question. Also, be aware of a halo effect or reverse halo effect. This occurs when an interviewer becomes biased because of one positive or negative trait a candidate possesses. Interview bias can occur in almost any interview situation. Interview bias is when an interviewer makes assumptions about the candidate that may not be accurate (Lipschultz, 2010). These assumptions can be detrimental to an interview process. Contrast bias is a type of bias that occurs when comparing one candidate to others. It can result in one person looking particularly strong in an area, when in fact they look strong compared to the other candidates. A gut feeling bias is when an interviewer relies on an intuitive feeling about a candidate. Generalization bias can occur when an interviewer assumes that how someone behaves in an interview is how they always behave. For example, if a candidate is very nervous and stutters while talking, an assumption may be made that he or she always stutters. Another important bias called cultural noise bias occurs when a candidate thinks he or she knows what the interviewer wants to hear and answers the questions based on that assumption. Non-verbal behavior bias occurs when an interviewer likes an answer and smiles and nods, sending the wrong signal to the candidate. A similar to me bias (which could be considered discriminatory) results when an interviewer has a preference for a candidate because he or she views that person as having similar attributes as themselves. Finally, recency bias occurs when the interviewer remembers candidates interviewed most recently more so than the other candidates.

Human Resource Recall

What are the dangers of a reverse halo effect?

Figure 2-15 Halo Effect

Note: A halo effect occurs when a desirable trait makes us believe all traits possessed by the candidate are desirable. This can be a major danger in interviewing candidates.

Interview Process

Once the criteria have been selected and interview questions developed, it is time to start interviewing people.

Your interviewing plan can determine the direction and process that should be followed:

Recruit new candidates.

Establish criteria for which candidates will be rated.

Develop interview questions based on the analysis.

Set a time line for interviewing and decision-making.

Connect schedules with others involved in the interview process.

Set up the interviews with candidates and set up any testing procedures.

Interview the candidates and perform any necessary testing.

Once all results are back, meet with the hiring team to discuss each candidate and make a decision based on the established criteria.

Who doesn't know exactly the type of person and skills she is looking to hire but sets up interviews anyway. It is difficult, if not impossible, to determine who should be hired if you don't know what you are looking for in the first place. In addition, utilizing time lines for interviewing can help keep everyone involved on track and ensure the chosen candidate starts work in a timely manner. Here are some tips to consider when working with the interview process:

Make sure everyone is trained on the interviewing process. Allowing someone who has poor interviewing skills to conduct the interview will likely not result in the best candidate. In a worst-case scenario, someone could ask an illegal question, and once hired, the candidate can sue the organization. UCLA researchers (Hanricks, 2011) calculated that plaintiffs win about half of hiring discrimination cases that go to trial, sometimes because of interviewers asking illegal questions. For example, "I see you speak Spanish, where did you study it?" is a seemingly harmless question that could be indirectly asking a candidate his or her ethnic background. To avoid such issues, it's important to train managers in the proper interviewing process.

Listen to the candidate and try to develop a rapport with them. Understand how nervous they must be and try to put them at ease.

Be realistic about the job. Do not try to paint a "rosy" picture of all aspects of the job. Being honest up front helps a candidate know exactly what they will be in for when they begin their job.

Be aware of your own stereotypes and do not let them affect how you view a potential candidate.

Watch your own body language during the interview and that of the candidate. Body language is a powerful tool in seeing if someone is the right fit for a job. For example, Scott Simmons, vice-president at Crist|Kolder, interviewed someone for a CFO position. The candidate had a great résumé, but during the interview, he offered a dead-fish handshake, slouched, and fidgeted in his chair. The candidate didn't make eye contact and mumbled responses, and of course, he didn't get the job (Reeves, 2006), because his body language did not portray the expectations for the job position.

Stick to your criteria for hiring. Do not ask questions that have not been predetermined in your criteria.

Learn to manage disagreement and determine a fair process if not everyone on the interviewing team agrees on who should be hired.

Once you have successfully managed the interview process, it is time to make the decision.

Human Resource Recall

Can you think of a time when the interviewer was not properly trained? What were the results?

Key Takeaways

Traditional, telephone, panel, informational, meal, group, and video are types of interviews. A combination of several of these may be used to determine the best candidate for the job. A structured interview format means the questions are determined ahead of time, and unstructured means the questions are based on the individual applicant. The advantage of a structured interview is that all candidates are rated on the same criteria. Before interviewing occurs, criteria and questions for a structured interview should be developed.

Interview questions can revolve around situational questions or behavioral questions. Situational questions focus on asking someone what they would do in a given situation, while behavioral questions ask candidates what they have done in certain situations.

Interview questions about national origin, marital status, age, religion, and disabilities are illegal. To avoid any legal issues, it is important for interviewers to be trained on which questions cannot be asked. The halo effect, which assumes that one desirable trait means all traits are desirable, should also be avoided.

The process involved in interviewing a person includes the following steps: recruit new candidates; establish criteria for which candidates will be rated; develop interview questions based on the analysis; set a time line for interviewing and decision-making; connect schedules with others involved in the interview process; set up interviews with candidates and set up any testing procedures; interview the candidates and perform any necessary testing; and once all results are back, meet with the hiring team to discuss each candidate and make a decision based on the established criteria; then finally, put together an offer for the candidate.

Developing a rapport, being honest, and managing the interview process are tips to having a successful interview.

Exercises

1. With a partner, develop a list of five examples (not already given in the chapter) of situational and behavioral interview questions.

2. Why is it important to determine criteria and interview questions before bringing someone in for an interview?

3. Visit Monster.com and find two examples of job postings that ask those with criminal records not to apply. Do you think, given the type of job, this is a reasonable criteria?

4.4 Testing and Selecting

Learning Objectives

1. Explain the types of tests that can be administered as part of the selection process.
2. Be able to discuss the types of selection models.

Besides the interview, we can also look at several other aspects that may predict success on the job. If any test is to be criteria for measuring a candidate, this should be communicated to each person interviewing, and criteria should be developed on specific test scores and expectations before interviewing and testing begins.

Testing

A variety of tests may be given upon successful completion of an interview. These employment tests can gauge a person's KSAOs in relation to another candidate. The major categories of tests include the following:

Cognitive ability tests

Personality tests

Physical ability tests

Job knowledge tests

Work sample

A number of written tests can be administered. A cognitive ability test can measure reasoning skills, math skills, and verbal skills. An aptitude test measures a person's ability to learn new skills, while an achievement test measures someone's current knowledge. Depending on the type of job, one or both will be better suited.

A cognitive ability test measures intelligences, such as numerical ability and reasoning. The Scholastic Aptitude Test (SAT) is an example of a cognitive ability test. It is important to note that some cognitive ability tests can have disparate impact. For example, in *EEOC v. Ford Motor Co. and United Automobile Workers of America*, African Americans were rejected from an apprentice program after taking a cognitive test known as the Apprenticeship Training Selection System (ATSS). The test showed significant disparate impact on African Americans, and it was then replaced by a different selection procedure, after costing Ford $8.55 million. Some sample test categories might include the following:

Reasoning questions

Mathematical questions and calculations

Verbal and/or vocabulary skills

Aptitude tests can measure things such as mechanical aptitude and clerical aptitude (e.g., speed of typing or ability to use a particular computer program). Usually, an aptitude test asks specific questions related to the requirements of the job. To become a New York City police offer, for example, an aptitude test is required before an application will be considered. The written exam is given as a computerized test at a computerized testing center in the city. The test measures cognitive skills and observational skills (aptitude test) required for the job.

Personality tests such as Meyers-Briggs and the "Big Five" personality factors may be measured and then compared with successful employee scores. For example, The University of Missouri Health Care system recently launched a patient satisfaction initiative as part of its strategic plan. The plan includes training for current employees and personality testing for nursing, managerial, and physician candidates (Silvey, 2011). The goal of the test is to assess talent and to see if the candidate has the potential to meet the expectations of patients. They hired a private company, Talent Plus, who conducts the test via phone interviews. However, many companies administer tests themselves, and some tests are free and can be administered online.

The Big Five personality test looks at extroversion, agreeableness, conscientiousness, neuroticism, and openness.

Self-assessment statements might include the following:

I have an assertive personality.

I am generally trusting.

I am not always confident in my abilities.

I have a hard time dealing with change.

Some institutions also require physical ability tests; for example, to earn a position in a fire department, you may have to be able to carry one hundred pounds up three flights of stairs. If you use tests in your hiring processes, the key to making them useful is to determine a minimum standard or expectation, specifically related to the requirements of the job. An HR manager should also consider the legality of such tests. In the *EEOC v. Dial Corp.* case, women were disproportionately rejected for entry-level positions. Prior to the test, 46 percent of hires were women, but after implementation of the test, only 15 percent of the new hires were women. The Equal Employment Opportunity Commission (EEOC) established that the test was considerably more difficult than the job, resulting in disparate impact. Physical ability tests need to show direct correlation with the job duties.

A job knowledge test measures the candidate's level of understanding about a particular job. For example, a job knowledge test may require an engineer to write code in a given period of time or may ask candidates to solve a case study problem related to the job.

Work sample tests ask candidates to show examples of work they have already done. In the advertising business, this may include a portfolio of designs, or for a project manager, this can include past project plans or budgets.

When applying for a pharmaceutical representative position, a "brag book" might be required (Hansen, 2011). A brag book is a list of recommendation letters, awards, and achievements that the candidate shares with the interviewer. Work sample tests can be a useful way to test for KSAOs. These work samples can often be a good indicator of someone's abilities in a specific area. As always, before looking at samples, the interviewer should have specific criteria or expectations developed so each candidate can be measured fairly.

Once the interview is completed and testing occurs, other methods of checking KSAOs, including checking references, driving records, and credit history, can be performed. Some companies even use Facebook as a way of gauging the candidate's professionalism.

Reference checking is essential to verify a candidate's background. It is an added assurance that the candidate's abilities are parallel with what you were told in the interview. While employment dates and job titles can be verified with previous employers, many employers will not verify more than what can be verified in the employment record because of privacy laws. However, if you do find someone who is willing to discuss more than just dates and job titles, a list of questions is appropriate. Some of these questions might include the following:

What was the title and responsibilities of the position the candidate had while at your company?

Do you think the candidate was qualified to assume those responsibilities?

Does this person show up on time and have good attendance?

Would you consider this person a team player?

What are the three strongest and weakest characteristics of this candidate?

Would you rehire this person?

If a candidate will be driving a company car or vehicle, such as a UPS truck, driving records may be checked. Criminal background checks may also be used if the position will include interaction with the public. If the position requires handling of money, a credit check may be required, although a written notice is required to be given to the candidate before the credit check is carried out. In addition, written permission must be provided to the credit agency, and the applicants must receive a copy of the report and a copy of their rights under the *Consumer Credit Reporting Reform Act* (*CCRRA*). All these types of tests can be used to determine if someone has been honest about their past employment.

Some companies require drug testing, which causes some debate. While some organizations say this is a safety issue (and pay lower insurance premiums), others say it is an invasion of privacy. As long as drug tests are administered for a defensible reason (safety), many organizations will continue to require them. Some organizations will also require physical examinations to ensure the candidate can perform the tasks required. A final form of testing is the honesty test. A number of "what would you do" questions are asked. The challenge with this type of test is that many people know the "right" answer but may not be honest in their responses.

Table 2-8 Reasons Why Employers Acted upon Data Found on Social Networking Sites

Provocative or inappropriate photos or info	53%
Drinking or drug use	44%
Badmouthing previous employer, colleague, or client	35%
Poor communication skills	29%
Discriminatory comments	26%
Lied about qualifications	24%
Leaked confidential information about previous job	20%

Source: Kit Eaton, "If You're Applying for a Job, Censor Your Facebook Page", *Fast Company*, August 19, 2009, accessed January 27, 2011, http://www.fastcompany.com/blog/kit-eaton/technomix/if-youre-applying-job-censor-your-facebook-page.

Forty-five percent of organizations use social networking such as Facebook, Twitter, or LinkedIn to gather information about potential candidates (Eaton, 2009). See Table 2-8 "Reasons Why Employers Acted upon Data Found on Social Networking Sites" for the types of data found on social networking sites that disqualified candidates, according to an article by *Fast Company*. This can be an effective method to see the kind of image the candidate portrays in his or her personal time.

Selection Methods

Tell Me about Yourself

How to answer that famous "tell me about yourself" question in an interview.

A clinical selection approach is probably the most common selection method, and it involves all who will be making the decision to hire a candidate. The decision makers review the data and, based on what they learn from the candidate and the information available to them, decide who should be hired for a job. Because interviewers have a different perception about the strengths of a candidate, this method leaves room for error. One consideration is disparate treatment, in which one's biases may result in not hiring candidates based on their age, race, or gender. One way to handle this and limit the personal stereotypes and perceptions of the interviewers is to use a statistical method in hiring.

In the statistical method, a selection model is developed that assigns scores and gives more weight to specific factors, if necessary. For example, for some jobs, the ability to work in a team might be more important, while in others, knowledge of a specific computer program is more important. In this case, a weight can be assigned to each of the job criteria listed.

For example, if the job is a project manager, ability to work with the client might be more important than how someone dresses for the interview. So, in the example shown in Table 2-9 "Sample Selection Model, with Sample Scores and Weighting Filled In", dress is weighted 1, while being able to give bad news to a client is weighted 5. In the example, the rating is multiplied by the weight to get the score for the particular job criteria. This method allows for a fairer process and can limit disparate treatment, although it may not limit disparate impact. A statistical method may work like this: you and the hiring team review the job analysis and job description and then determine the criteria for the job. You assign weights for each area and score ranges for each aspect of the criteria, rate candidates on each area as they interview, and then score tests or examine work samples. Once each hiring manager has scored each candidate, the hiring team can compare scores in each area and hopefully hire the best person in the best way. A sample candidate selection model is included in Table 2-9 "Sample Selection Model, with Sample Scores and Weighting Filled In".

With the statistical approach, there is more objectivity than with the clinical approach. Statistical approaches include the compensatory model, multiple cutoff model, and the multiple hurdle model. In the compensatory model, a similar method of scoring is used as the weighted model but permits a high score in an important area to make up for a lower score in another area. In our Table 2-9 "Sample Selection Model, with Sample Scores and Weighting Filled In" example, ability to give bad news to a client might outweigh a test score. These decisions would be made before the interviews happen.

A multiple cutoff model requires that a candidate has a minimum score level on all selection criteria. In our Table 2-9 the candidate may be required to have a score of at least 2 out of 5 on each criteria. If this was the case, the candidate in Figure 36 scored low on "bad news to a client." meaning he or she wouldn't get the job in a multiple cutoff model. In the multiple hurdle model, only candidates with high (preset) scores go to the next stages of the selection process. For example, the expectations might be to score a 4 on at least three of the items in Table 2-9. If this were the case, this candidate might make it to the next level of the selection process, since he or she scored at least a 4 on three criteria areas.

Once the discussion on whom to hire has occurred and a person has been selected, the final phase of the process is to make an offer to the candidate. This is discussed in Section 4.5 "Making the Offer".

Table 2-9 Sample Selection Model, with Sample Scores and Weighting Filled In

Job Criteria	Rating	Weight	Total	Comments
Dress	4	1	4	Candidate dressed appropriately.
Personality	2	5	10	Did not seem excited about the job.
Interview Questions				
Give an example of a time you showed leadership.	3	3	9	Descriptive but didn't seem to have experience required.
Give an example of when you had to give bad news to a client.	0	5	0	Has never had to do this.
Tell us how you have worked well in a team	5	4	20	Great example of teamwork given.
Score on cognitive ability test.	78	5	390	Meets minimum required score of 70
			458	

*Rating system of 1—5, with 5 being the highest

**Weighting of 1—5, with 5 being the most important

Key Takeaways

Once the interview process is complete, some companies use other means of measuring candidates. For example, work samples are an excellent way of seeing how someone might perform at your company.

An aptitude test or achievement test can be given. An aptitude test measures how well someone might be able to do something, while an achievement test measures what the candidate already knows. Tests that measure cognitive ability and personality are examples.

Some organizations also perform drug tests and physical tests. A physical test might consist of being able to lift a certain amount of weight, if required for the job. Honesty tests are also given; these measure the honesty level of the candidate. However, these tests may not be reliable, since someone can guess the "right" answer.

Facebook, Twitter, and other social networking websites are also used to gather information about a candidate. Calling references is another option.

Every person interviewing the candidate should have a selection model; this method utilizes a statistical approach as opposed to a clinical approach. The selection table lists the criteria on the left and asks interviewers to provide a rating for each. This method can allow for a more consistent way of measuring candidates.

Exercises

1. Develop a sample candidate selection for your current job.

2. Visit your or another person's Facebook page. Consider the content from an interviewer's point of view. Should anything be removed or changed?

4.5 Making the Offer

Learning Objective

Explain the steps in making the offer to the candidate.

Oftentimes once the decision is made to hire a candidate, HR professionals feel their job is finished. But making the offer to the chosen candidate can be equally as important as the interview process. If the offer is not handled properly, you can lose the candidate, or if the candidates takes the job, he or she could start off on the wrong foot.

According to Paul Falcone, vice-president for human resources at the *Fortune* 500 company Time Warner, detailed information should be asked of the candidate before the offer is even made (Falcone, 2011). He says that as soon as the offer is made, power is shifted to the candidate. To handle this, he suggests asking salary questions in the interview, including the following:

"If we were to make a job offer today, when would you be in a position to accept or reject the offer?" If the candidate answers "right now", this indicates they do not have other job offers on the table or if they do, you are their first choice.

"At what point, dollar wise, would you accept our job offer and at what point, dollar wise would you reject the offer?" The advantage of using this strategy is that it gets to the point of understanding the candidate's expectations. If the interviewee does not respond right away, you can clarify by asking, "I am asking this question because I would like to gauge your interest level. Share with me the ideal salary offer versus at what point you would be willing to walk away from this opportunity."

Asking these questions can assist in qualifying candidates, based on salary expectations.

For example, if a candidate requests 20 percent more than you are able to pay for the job, this discussion can be had before the offer is even made, perhaps making this candidate no longer viable.

Once you have determined in the interview process that the salary expectation is in the range of what you can offer, the first step is to make the offer as soon as the decision is made. In a tight labor market, waiting a week or two may impact your ability to hire your first choice. You probably already have a salary range in mind and can begin to narrow down the offer based on the individual's KSAOs. Based on the range of salary you can offer, consider the following questions when making the offer to a candidate:

What is the scarcity of the particular skills set?

What are the "going" wages in your geographic area?

What are the current economic conditions?

What is the current pay for similar positions in your organization?

What is your organizational compensation strategy?

What is the fair market value of the job?

What is the level of the job within the organization?

What are your budget constraints?

How soon will the employee be productive in the organization?

Are there other candidates equally qualified that might have lower salary expectations?

What are the national and regional unemployment rates?

If you cannot pay more, can you offer other perks such as a signing bonus or flexible work schedule?

Once the offer has been made, it is reasonable to give the candidate some time to decide, but not too long, as this can result in losing other candidates should this candidate reject the job offer. It is likely the candidate may come back and ask for higher salary or benefits. Some tips to successfully negotiate are included below:

Be prepared. Know exactly what you can and can't offer.

Explain the career growth the organization can provide.

Address the benefits of the candidate's joining the organization.

Discuss the entire offer, including other benefits offered to the employee.

View the negotiation as a win-win situation.

Be able to provide salary research of similar positions and competitors for the same job title.

Use the trading technique. For example, "I cannot offer you the salary you are requesting right now, but what if we were able to review salary at your six-month performance review, assuming ____ objectives are met?"

Once the phone call is made and the candidate accepts the offer, an e-mail or formal letter should follow, outlining details of the employment agreement. The employment agreement or offer letter should include the following:

Job title

Salary

Other compensation, such as bonuses or stock options

Benefits, such as healthcare coverage, 401(k)

Non-compete agreement expectations

Additional considerations such as relocation expenses

Once the pay and benefits package has been successfully negotiated and the offer letter (or e-mail) sent, you should clarify acceptance details in writing and receive confirmation of the start date. It is not unusual for people in higher-level positions to need a month or even two to transition from their old jobs. During this period, make sure to stay in touch and even complete the new hire paperwork in the meantime.

Key Takeaways

The HR professional's job isn't finished once the selection is made. The next step is to actually make the offer. This step is important, because if it isn't done properly, you could lose the candidate or have ill feelings at the onset of the employment relationship.

Once you have made the decision to hire someone, make the offer to the candidate right away. Normally this is done through a phone call and a follow-up e-mail, outlining the details of the offer.

It is not unusual for someone to negotiate salary or benefits. Know how far you can negotiate and also be aware of how your current employees will be affected if you offer this person a higher salary.

If you are having trouble coming to an agreement, be creative in what you can offer; for example, offer flextime instead of higher pay.

Exercise

Research "salary negotiation" on the Internet. What tips are provided for job seekers? Do you think these same tips could apply to the HR professional? Why or why not?

4.6 Cases and Problems

Chapter Summary

The selection process refers to the steps involved in choosing someone who has the right qualifications to fill a current or future job opening.

There are five main steps in the selection process. First, criteria should be developed to determine how the person will be chosen. Second, a review of the applications and résumés is conducted, often via a computer program that can find keywords. Next, interview the employee. The last steps involve administering tests, such as a personality test or drug test, and making the offer to the right candidate.

The first step in selection is to review résumés. Even before you do this, though, it is important to develop criteria against which each candidate will be measured. Criteria can come from the job description as well as the job qualifications.

Other tools, such as cognitive ability tests, credit checks, or personality tests, can be used to determine qualifications. When developing your criteria for interviewing, determine the level the applicant needs to meet the minimum criteria—for example, a minimum score for a personality test.

We should be concerned with validity and reliability of measurement tools. Validity refers to how valid the test is—that is, how well a test measures a candidate's abilities to do a job. Reliability refers to which selection techniques yield similar data or results over time. It is important to choose the right measurement tool used to determine whether the candidate meets the criteria.

Use of criteria before the interview process starts is also important to make sure disparate impact or disparate treatment do not occur in the interview process.

When hiring, there is the option of internal and external candidates. Each has its own set of advantages and disadvantages. Internal candidates may be able to "hit the ground running" but external candidates may come in with new perspectives. Even if an internal candidate seems to be the best hire, it is best to still perform the process of posting the job and interviewing, since other less vocal employees might be qualified internal candidates as well. In other words, don't assume one person is the obvious choice for the promotion.

Traditional, telephone, panel, informational, meal, group, and video are types of interviews. A combination of several of these may be used to determine the best candidate for the job. A structured interview format means the questions are determined ahead of time, and unstructured means the questions are based on the individual applicant. The advantage of a structured interview is that all candidates are rated on the same criteria. Before interviewing occurs, criteria and questions for a structured interview should be developed.

Interview questions can revolve around situational questions or behavioral questions. Situational questions focus on asking someone what they would do in a given situation, while behavioral questions ask candidates what they would have done in certain situations.

Interview questions about national origin, marital status, age, religion, and disabilities are illegal. To avoid any legal issues, it is important for interviewers to be trained on which questions cannot be asked. The halo effect, which assumes that one desirable trait means all traits are desirable, should also be avoided.

The process involved in interviewing a person includes the following steps: recruit new candidates; establish criteria for which candidates will be rated; develop interview questions based on the analysis; set a time line for interviewing and decision-making; connect schedules with others involved in the interview process; set up interviews with candidates and set up any testing procedures; interview the candidates and perform any necessary testing; and once all results are back, meet with the hiring team to discuss each candidate and make a decision based on the established criteria. Finally, put together an offer for the candidate.

Developing a rapport, being honest, and managing the interview process are tips to having a successful interview.

Once the interview process is complete, some companies use other means of measuring candidates. For example, work samples are an excellent way of seeing how someone might perform at your company.

An aptitude test or achievement test can be given. An aptitude test measures how well someone might be able to do something, while an achievement test measures what the candidate already knows. Tests that measure cognitive ability and personality are examples.

Some organizations also perform drug tests and physical tests. A physical test might consist of being able to lift a certain amount of weight, if required for the job. Honesty tests are also given, which measure the honesty level of the candidate. However, these tests may not be reliable, since someone can guess the "right" answer.

Facebook, Twitter, and other social networking websites are used to gather information about a candidate. Calling references is another option.

Every person interviewing the candidate should have a selection model; this method utilizes a statistical approach as opposed to a clinical approach. The selection table lists the criteria on the left and asks interviewers to provide a rating for each. This method can allow for a more consistent way of measuring candidates.

The job of the HR professional isn't finished once the selection is made. The next step is to make the offer. This step is important, because if it isn't done properly, you could lose the candidate or have ill feelings at the onset of the employment relationship.

Once you have made the decision to hire someone, make the offer to the candidate right away. Normally this is done through a phone call and a follow-up e-mail, outlining the details of the offer.

If you are having trouble coming to an agreement, be creative in what you can offer; for example, offer flextime instead of higher pay.

Chapter Case

The Four-Fifths Rule

The four-fifths rule is a way of measuring adverse impact in selection processes of organizations. It works like this: assume your organization requires a cognitive test for employment. You set a test score of 70 as the required pass rate for the candidate to be considered for an interview. Based on our numbers, if 50 percent of men passed this test with a score of 70, then four-fifths or 40 percent of women should also be able to pass the test. You might calculate it like this:

Gender	Total Who Scored 70 or Above	Total Who Took the Test	Percent
Male	52	62	83.8% or 84% passed
Female	36	58	62.07% or 62%

If you divide the total of who scored above 70 by the total number who took the test, it shows the percentage of 84 percent passed the test. If you divide the number of women who passed by the total number of women who took the test, you come up with 62 percent. Then divide 62 percent by 84 percent (62%/84% = 73.8%). The resulting 74 percent means that it is below the 80 percent or the four-fifths rule, and this test could be considered to have disparate impact.

52%/62% = 84% of men who took the test passed the test 36%/58% = 62% of women who took the test passed the test

62%/84% = 73.8%, less than 80%, which could show disparate impact

This is only an indicator as to how the selection process works for the organization, and other factors, such as sample size, can impact the reliability of this test. Using the tables below, please calculate possible disparate impact and then answer the questions that follow.

National Origin	Passing Test Score	Total Number Taking the Test	Percent
Caucasians	56	89	
Minority groups	48	62	
Gender	Passing Test Score	Total Number Taking the Test	Percent
Male	71	82	
Female	64	85	

Please calculate the above numbers using the four-fifths rule. Based on your calculation:

a. Which group or groups might be affected negatively by this test?

b. What would be your considerations before changing any selection tools based on this data?

c. How might you change your selection process to ensure disparate impact isn't occurring at your organization?

Team Activity

1. In a team of two, take the Big Five personality test online (http://www.outofservice. com/bigfive/) and compare scores.

2. Assume you are hiring a retail salesperson and plan to administer the same Big Five personality test you took above. In your team, develop minimum percentile scores for each of the five areas that would be acceptable for your new hire.

Chapter 5　Compensation and Benefits

Matching Compensation with Core Values

As you sit down to review the compensation package your company offers, one thing that stands out is that your compensation package no longer matches the core values of your organization. When your organization merged five years ago with a similar firm that specializes in online shoe retailing, your company had to hire hundreds of people to keep up with growth. As a result—and what happens with many companies—the compensation plans are not revised and revisited as they should be. The core values your company adopted from the merging company focused on customer service, freedom to work where employees felt they could be most productive, and continuing education of employees, whether or not the education was related to the organization. The compensation package, providing the basic salary, health benefits, and 401(k) plans, seems a bit old-fashioned for the type of company yours has become.

After reviewing your company's strategic plan and your Human Resource Management (HRM) strategic plan, you begin to develop a compensation plan that includes salary, health benefits, and 401(k) plans, but you feel it might be smart to better meet the needs of your employees by making some changes to these existing plans. For example, you are considering implementing a team bonus program for high customer service ratings and coverage for alternative forms of medicine, such as acupuncture and massage. Instead of guessing what employees would like to see in their compensation packages, you decide to develop a compensation survey to assess what benefits are most important to your employees. As you begin this task, you know it will be a lot of work, but it's important to the continued recruitment, retention, and motivation of your current employees.

5.1 Goals of a Compensation Plan

> ### Learning Objective
>
> Be able to explain the goals of a compensation plan.

So far, we have discussed the process for strategic plan development and the recruitment and selection process. The next aspect of HRM is to develop compensation plans that will help in the recruitment and retention of employees. This is the topic of this chapter.

Figure 2-16 Compensation

Note: The goal of a compensation plan is not only to attract people, but to retain them.

Most of us, no matter how much we like our jobs, would not do them without a compensation package. When we think of compensation, often we think of only our paycheck, but compensation in terms of HRM is much broader. A compensation package can include pay, healthcare benefits, and other benefits such as 401(k) plans, which will all be discussed in this chapter. Before we discuss specifics, you should be aware of courses and certifications that can be earned through the WorldatWork Society of Certified Professionals, specifically related to compensation (other certifications will be discussed in their respective chapters).

WorldatWork offers several certifications in the area of compensation:

Certified Compensation Professional (CCP)

Certified Benefits Professional (CBP)

Certified Sales Compensation Professional (CSCP)

Certified Executive Compensation Professional (CECP)

These certifications involve taking a multiple-choice exam online or at one of the WorldatWork testing locations. The exams test for knowledge, experience, and skills in each of the compensation certification areas and can be a valuable asset to you when applying for HR positions.

The certifications are based on many of the aspects of this chapter, including understanding the goals of compensation packages for employees, which is our focus for this section.

First, the compensation package should be positive enough to attract the best people for the job. An organization that does not pay as well as others within the same industry will likely not be able to attract the best candidates, resulting in a poorer overall company performance.

Once the best employees and talent come to work for your organization, you want the compensation to be competitive enough to motivate people to stay with your organization. Although we know that compensation packages are not the only thing that motivates people, compensation is a key component.

Third, compensation can be used to improve morale, motivation, and satisfaction among employees. If employees are not satisfied, this can result not only in higher turnover but also in poor quality of work for those employees who do stay. A proper compensation plan can also increase loyalty in the organization.

Pay systems can also be used to reward individual or team performance and encourage employees to work at their own peak performance. In fact, in the 2011 list of the Best Companies to Work For by *Fortune* magazine, all the companies who topped the list (e.g., SAS and Boston Consulting Group) had satisfied employees—not only with their pay, but their entire benefits package.

With an appropriate pay system, companies find that customer service is better because employees are happier. In addition, having fairly compensated, motivated employees not only adds to the bottom line of the organization but also facilitates organizational growth and expansion. Motivated employees can also save the company money indirectly, by not taking sick days when the employee isn't really sick, and companies with good pay packages find fewer disability claims as well.

So far, our focus on HRM has been a strategic focus, and the same should be true for development of compensation packages. Before the package is developed for employees, it's key to understand the role compensation plays in the bottom line of the organization. For example, in 2010, the U.S. military spent 22 percent of its budget on personnel salaries. One-fifth of the total budget—or more—is not uncommon for most U.S. organizations, depending on the industry. As a result, it is easy to see why the compensation plan should be an important aspect of the overall HRM strategic plan. The next few sections will detail the aspects of creating the right compensation packages: for your organization, including legal considerations.

Human Resource Recall

If you have had or currently have a job, do you feel the compensation plan motivated you? Why or why not?

Key Takeaways

A compensation package is an important part of the overall strategic HRM plan, since much of the company budget is for employee compensation.

A compensation package can include salary, bonuses, healthcare plans, and a variety of other types of compensation.

The goals of compensation are to attract people to work for your organization and to retain people who are already working in the organization.

Compensation is also used to motivate employees to work at their peak performance and improve morale.

Employees who are fairly compensated tend to provide better customer service, which can result in organizational growth and development.

Exercise

Visit a website that gives salary information for a variety of jobs, such as http://www.salary.com. Using the search box, type in your ideal job and research salary information. What is the median salary for the job you searched? What is the lowest salary you would be willing to accept for this job? At which point would you be completely satisfied with the pay for this job?

5.2 Developing a Compensation Package

Learning Objectives

1. Be able to explain the internal and external considerations of compensation package development.

2. Know how to develop a compensation philosophy.

There are a few basic aspects of compensation packages we should discuss before moving into the specific aspects of compensation. These foundations can assist in the development of a compensation strategy that meets the goals of your organization and is in line with your strategic plan.

Before beginning work on your compensation packages, some analysis should be done to determine your organization's philosophy in regard to compensation. Before development of your compensation philosophies, there are some basic questions to address on your current compensation packages.

From the employee's perspective, what is a fair wage?

Are wages too high to achieve financial health in your organization?

Do managers and employees know and buy-into your compensation philosophy?

Does the pay scale reflect the importance of various job titles within the organization?

Is your compensation good enough to retain employees?

Are state and federal laws being met with your compensation package?

Is your compensation philosophy keeping in line with labor market changes, industry changes, and organizational changes?

Once these basic questions are addressed, we can see where we might have "holes" in our compensation package and begin to develop new philosophies in line with our strategic plan, which benefits the organization. Some possible compensation policies might include the following:

Are salaries higher or lower depending on the location of the business? For example, orthopedic surgeons are paid higher in the North Central states ($537,000) than in Hawaii ($250,000), according to the Medscape Physical report of 2011 (Miller, 2011). Reasons could include cost of living in the area and fewer qualified people in a given area, giving them leverage to ask for a higher salary.

Are salaries lower or higher than the average in your region or area? If the salary is lower, what other benefits will the employee receive to make up for this difference? For example, wages might not be as high, but offering flextime or free day care might offset the lower salary.

Should there be a specific pay scale for each position in the organization, or should salaries be negotiated on an individual basis? If there is no set pay scale, how can you ensure individual salary offers are fair and non-discriminatory?

What balance of salary and other rewards, such as bonuses, should be part of your compensation package? For example, some organizations prefer to offer a lower salary, but through bonuses and profit sharing, the employee has the potential to earn more.

When giving raises, will the employee's tenure be a factor, or will pay increases be merit based only, or a combination of both?

Let's discuss some internal and external factors in determining compensation in more detail.

Internal and External Pay Factors

One major internal factor is the compensation strategy the company has decided to use. Sixty-two percent of organizations have a written, documented compensation policy (Scott, 2011).

Some organizations choose a market compensation policy, market plus, or market minus philosophy. A market compensation policy is to pay the going rate for a particular job, within a particular market based on research and salary studies. The organization that uses a market plus philosophy will determine the going rate and add a percentage to that rate, such as 5 percent. So if a particular job category median pays $57,000, the organization with a market plus of 5 percent philosophy will pay $59,850. A market minus philosophy pays a particular percentage less than the market; so in our example, if a company pays 5 percent less, the same job would pay $54,150. The University of Arizona, for example, posts its compensation philosophy on its website:

In order to fulfill its mission, the University of Arizona shall maintain a compensation program directed toward attracting, retaining, and rewarding a qualified and diverse workforce. Within the boundaries of financial feasibility, employee compensation shall be externally competitive and internally equitable, and shall be based upon performance as recognized within the work unit.

In addition to their compensation philosophy, the university lists compensation objectives, such as "average salaries will be targeted at the average salary levels of employees in comparable positions in our various labor markets". This is an example of a market compensation policy.

An example of an organization with a market plus philosophy is Cisco Systems, listed as one of the top-paying companies on *Fortune*'s annual list. For example, they pay $131,716 for software engineers, while at Yahoo! software engineers are paid an average of $101,669, using a market philosophy. The pay at Cisco reflects its compensation philosophy and objectives:

Cisco operates in the extremely competitive and rapidly changing high-technology industry. The Board's Compensation Committee believes that the compensation programs for the executive officers should be designed to attract, motivate, and retain talented executives responsible for the success of Cisco and should be determined within a framework based on the achievement of designated financial targets, individual contribution, customer satisfaction, and financial performance relative to that of Cisco's competitors. Within this overall philosophy, the Compensation Committee's objectives are to do the following:

Offer a total compensation program that is flexible and takes into consideration the compensation practices of a group of specifically identified peer companies and other selected companies with which Cisco competes for executive talent.

Provide annual variable cash incentive awards that take into account Cisco's overall financial performance in terms of designated corporate objectives, as well as individual contributions and a measure of customer satisfaction.

Align the financial interests of executive officers with those of shareholders by providing appropriate long-term, equity-based incentives.

An example of an organization with a market minus philosophy is Whole Foods. The executive compensation for Whole Foods is a maximum of nineteen times the average store worker (or $608,000), very low by *Fortune* 500 executive pay standards, which average 343 times (Allen, 2011). According to John Mackey, Whole Foods CEO, paying on a market minus philosophy makes good business sense: "Fewer things harm an organization's morale more than great disparities in compensation. When a workplace is perceived as unfair and greedy, it begins to destroy the social fabric of the organization" (Hamner & McNichol, 2011). Another example of an organization with a market minus philosophy is Southwest Airlines. Despite the lower pay (and more hours), the organization boasts just a 1.4 percent turnover rate, which can be attributed not to pay but to the workplace culture and, as a result, loyalty to the company (Eggers, 2011).

There are many reasons why an organization would choose one philosophy over another. A market minus philosophy may tie into the company's core values, as in Whole Foods, or it may be because the types of jobs require an unskilled workforce that may be easier and less expensive to replace. A company may use a market plus philosophy because the industry's cutting-edge nature requires the best and the brightest.

Other internal pay factors might include the employer's ability to pay, the type of industry, and the value of the employee and the particular job to the organization. In addition, the presence of a union can lead to mandated pay scales.

External pay factors can include the current economic state. For example, in June 2011, the U.S. unemployment rate was 9.2 percent, which is quite high for the country. As a result of surplus workers, compensation may be reduced within organizations because of oversupply of workers. Inflation and cost of living in a given area can also determine compensation in a given market.

Once an organization has looked at the internal and external forces affecting pay, it can begin to develop a pay system within the organization. We discuss how to develop a pay system in Section 5.3 "Types of Pay Systems".

Key Takeaways

Before beginning work on a pay system, some general questions need to be answered. Important starting points include questions ranging from what is a fair wage from the employees' perspectives to how much can be paid but still retain financial health.

　　After some pay questions are answered, a pay philosophy must be developed, based on internal and external factors. Some companies implement a market compensation philosophy, which pays the going market rate for a job. Other companies may decide to utilize a market plus philosophy, which pays higher than the average. A company could decide its pay philosophy is a market minus philosophy, which pays less than the market rate. For example, an organization may decide to pay lower salaries but offer more benefits.

　　Once these tasks are done, the HR manager can then build a pay system that works for the size and industry of the organization.

Exercise

　　Think of your current organization or a past organization. What do you think their pay policy is/ was? Describe and analyze whether you think it was or is effective. If you haven't worked before, perform an Internet search on pay policies and describe/analyze the pay policy of an organization.

5.3　Types of Pay Systems

Learning Objectives

　　1. Explain types of job evaluation systems and their uses.

　　2. Be able to define and discuss the types of pay systems and factors determining the type of pay system used.

　　3. Know the laws relating to compensation.

　　Once you have determined your compensation strategy based on internal and external factors, you will need to evaluate jobs, develop a pay system, and consider pay theories when making decisions. Next, you will determine the mix of pay you will use, taking into consideration legal implications.

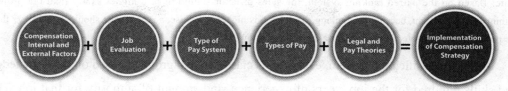

Figure 2-17 The Process for Implementing Compensation Strategy

Job Evaluation Systems

As mentioned when we discussed internal and external factors, the value of the job is a major factor when determining pay. There are several ways to determine the value of a job through job evaluation. Job evaluation is defined as the process of determining the relative worth of jobs to determine pay structure. Job evaluation can help us determine if pay is equitable and fair among our employees. There are several ways to perform a job evaluation. One of the simplest methods, used by smaller companies or within individual departments, is a job ranking system. In this type of evaluation, job titles are listed and ranked in order of importance to the organization. A paired comparison can also occur, in which individual jobs are compared with every other job, based on a ranking system, and an overall score is given for each job, determining the highest-valued job to the lowest-valued job. For example, in Table 2-10 "Example of a Paired Comparison for a Job Evaluation", four jobs are compared based on a ranking of 0, 1, or 2. Zero indicates the job is less important than the one being compared, 1 means the job is about the same, and 2 means the job is more important. When the scores are added up, it is a quick way to see which jobs are of more importance to the organization. Of course, any person creating these rankings should be familiar with the duties of all the jobs. While this method may provide reasonably good results because of its simplicity, it doesn't compare differences between jobs, which may have received the same rank of importance.

Table 2-10 Example of a Paired Comparison for a Job Evaluation

Job	Receptionist	Project Manager	Account Manager	Sales	Director
Receptionist	×	0	0	0	0= 4th
Project Administrative Assistant	1	×	0	0	1= 3rd
Account Manager	2	1	×	0	3= 2nd
Sales Director	2	2	2	×	6= 1st

Note: Based on the paired ranking system, the sales director should have a higher salary than the project administrative assistant, because the ranking for that job is higher. Likewise, a receptionist should be paid less than the project administrative assistant because this job ranks lower.

In a job classification system, every job is classified and grouped based on the knowledge and skills required for the job, years of experience, and amount of authority for that job. The U.S. military is perhaps the best known for this type of classification system. The navy, for example, has job classification codes, such as HM (hospitalman). Then the jobs are divided into specialties, such as HM-8483, the classification for surgical technologist, and HM-8451 for a hospitalman-X-ray technician. The federal government and most state governments use this type of system. Tied to each job are the basic function, characteristics, and typical work of that job classification, along with pay range data.

Another type of job evaluation system is the point-factor system, which determines the value of a job by calculating the total points assigned to it. The points given to a specific job are called compensable factors. These can range from leadership ability to specific responsibilities and skills required for the job. Once the compensable factors are determined, each is given a weight compared to the importance of this skill or ability to the organization. When this system is applied to every job in the organization, expected compensable factors for each job are listed, along with corresponding points to determine which jobs have the most relative importance within the organization. Tompkins County in New York uses a point-factor system. Some of their compensable factors include the following:

Knowledge

Autonomy

Supervision

Psychological demands

Interpersonal skills

Internal and external contacts

In this point-factor system, autonomy ranks the highest and is given a weight of twenty-nine, while knowledge is given a rate of twenty. for example, each of the compensable factors has a narrative that explains how points should be distributed for each factor. In this system, one hundred points are given for knowledge for a bachelor's degree and two to three years of experience, and eighty points are given if an employee has an associate's degree or high school diploma and two to three years of experience. The points are then multiplied by the weight (for knowledge, the weight is twenty) to give a final score on that compensable factor.

Another option for job evaluation is called the Hay profile method. This proprietary job evaluation method focuses on three factors called know-how, problem-solving, and accountability. Within these factors are specific statements such as "procedural proficiency". Each of these statements is given a point value in each category of know-how, problem-solving, and accountability. Then job descriptions are reviewed and assigned a set of statements that most accurately reflect the job. The point values for each of the statements are added for each job description, providing a quantitative basis for job evaluation and eventually, compensation. An advantage of this method is its quantitative nature, but a disadvantage is the expense of performing an elaborate job evaluation.

Pay Systems

Once you have performed a job evaluation, you can move to the third step, which we call pay grading. This is the process of setting the pay scale for specific jobs or types of jobs.

The first method to pay grade is to develop a variety of pay grade levels. Figure 2-18 "Sample Pay Scale for General Federal Jobs" shows an example. Then once the levels are developed, each job is assigned a pay grade. When employees receive raises, their raises stay within the range of their individual pay grade, until they receive a promotion that may result in a higher pay grade. The advantage of this type of system is fairness. Everyone performing the same job is within a given range and there is little room for pay discrimination to occur. However, since the system is rigid, it may not be appropriate for some organizations in hiring the best people. Organizations that operate in several cities might use a pay grade scale, but they may add percentages based on where someone lives. For example, the cost of living in Spokane, Washington, is much lower than in New York City. If an organization has offices in both places, it may choose to add a percentage pay adjustment for people living within a geographic area—for example, 10 percent higher in New York.

One of the downsides to pay grading is the possible lack of motivation for employees to work harder. They know even if they perform tasks outside their job description, their pay level or pay grade will be the same. This can incubate a stagnant environment. Sometimes this system can also create too many levels of hierarchy. For large companies, this may work fine, but smaller, more agile organizations may use other methods to determine pay structure. For example, some organizations have moved to a delayering and banding process, which cuts down the number of pay levels within the organization. General Electric delayered pay grades in the mid-1990s because it found that employees were less likely to take a reassignment that was at a lower pay grade, even though the assignment might have been a good development opportunity (Ferris, 1995). So, delayering enables a broader range of pay and more flexibility within each level. Sometimes this type of process also occurs when a company downsizes. Let's assume a company with five hundred employees has traditionally used a pay grade model but decided to move to a more flexible model. Rather than have, say, thirty pay levels, it may reduce this to five or six levels, with greater salary differentials within the grades themselves. This allows organizations to better reward performance, while still having a basic model for hiring managers to follow.

2011
Base General Schedule Pay Scale

RATES FROZEN AT 2010 LEVELS

EFFECTIVE JANUARY 2, 2011

Note: The following is a **BASE** pay scale. All U.S. locations (including Hawaii and Alaska) receive additional pay adjustments **above** the base pay ranging from **14.16%** to **35.15%**. To see the adjustment and pay scale for your location, scroll down the page and click on the location of your choice!

Grade	Step 1	Step 2	Step 3	Step 4	Step 5	Step 6	Step 7	Step 8	Step 9	Step 10	WITHIN GRADE AMOUNTS
1	17803	18398	18990	19579	20171	20519	21104	21694	21717	22269	VARIES
2	20017	20493	21155	21717	21961	22607	23253	23899	24545	25191	VARIES
3	21840	22568	23296	24024	24752	25480	26208	26936	27664	28392	728
4	24518	25335	26152	26969	27786	28603	29420	30237	31054	31871	817
5	27431	28345	29259	30173	31087	32001	32915	33829	34743	35657	914
6	30577	31596	32615	33634	34653	35672	36691	37710	38729	39748	1019
7	33979	35112	36245	37378	38511	39644	40777	41910	43043	44176	1133
8	37631	38885	40139	41393	42647	43901	45155	46409	47663	48917	1254
9	41563	42948	44333	45718	47103	48488	49873	51258	52643	54028	1385
10	45771	47297	48823	50349	51875	53401	54927	56453	57979	59505	1526
11	50287	51963	53639	55315	56991	58667	60343	62019	63695	65371	1676
12	60274	62283	64292	66301	68310	70319	72328	74337	76346	78355	2009
13	71674	74063	76452	78841	81230	83619	86008	88397	90786	93175	2389
14	84697	87520	90343	93166	95989	98812	101635	104458	107281	110104	2823
15	99628	102949	106270	109591	112912	116233	119554	122875	126196	129517	3321

Pay rates for Senior Executive Service (SES), Senior Level (SL) and Scientific & Professional (ST) positions range from $119,554 to $179,700.
NOTE: SL & ST employees receive the appropriate percentage pay adjustment for their area.

Figure 2-18 Sample Pay Scale for General Federal Jobs

Rather than use a pay grade scale, some organizations use a going rate model. In this model, analysis of the going rate for a particular job at a particular time is considered when creating the compensation package. This model can work well if market pressures or labor supply-and-demand pressures greatly impact your particular business. For example, if you need to attract the best project managers, but more are already employed (lack of supply)—and most companies are paying $75,000 for this position—you will likely need to pay the same or more, because of labor supply and demand. Many tools are available, such as salarywizard.com, to provide going rate information on particular jobs in every region of the United States.

Compensation Strategies

The president of HR That Works provides some tips on determining compensation.

Another pay model is the management fit model. In this model, each manager makes a decision about who should be paid what when that person is hired. The downside to this model may be potential discrimination, halo effects, and resentment within the organization. Of course, these factors can create morale issues, the exact thing we want to avoid when compensating employees.

In addition to the pay level models we just looked at, other considerations might include the following:

Skill-based pay. With a skill-based pay system, salary levels are based on an employee's skills, as opposed to job title. This method is implemented similarly to the pay grade model, but rather than job title, a set of skills is assigned a particular pay grade.

Competency-based pay. Rather than looking at specific skills, the competency-based approach looks at the employee's traits or characteristics as opposed to a specific skills set. This model focuses more on what the employee can become as opposed to the skills he or she already has.

Broadbanding. Broadbanding is similar to a pay grade system, except all jobs in a particular category are assigned a specific pay category. For example, everyone working in customer service, or all administrative assistants (regardless of department), are paid within the same general band. McDonald's uses this compensation philosophy in their corporate offices, stating that it allows for flexibility in terms of pay, movement, and growth of employees (McDonald's Corporation, 2011).

Variable pay system. This type of system provides employees with a pay basis but then links the attainment of certain goals or achievements directly to their pay. For example, a salesperson may receive a certain base pay but earn more if he or she meets the sales quota.

How Would You Handle This?

You have been working for your organization for five years. After lots of hard work, you are promoted to sales manager. One of your first tasks is to develop goals for your sales team, then create a budget based on these goals. First, you look at the salaries of all the sales staff to find major pay discrepancies. Some salespeople, who perform equally well, are paid much lower than some sales staff whom you consider to be non-performers. As you dig deeper, you see this is a problem throughout the sales team. You are worried this might affect motivation for your team if they find out what others are making. How would you handle this?

The author discusses the "How Would You Handle This" situation in this chapter at: https://api.wistia.com/v1/ medias/1360653/embed.

Pay Theories

Now that we have discussed pay systems, it is important to look at some theories on pay that can be helpful to know when choosing the type of pay system your organization will use.

The equity theory is concerned with the relational satisfaction employees get from pay and inputs they provide to the organization. It says that people will evaluate their own compensation by comparing their compensation to others' compensation and their inputs to others' inputs. In other words, people will look at their own compensation packages and at their own inputs (the work performed) and compare that with others. If they perceive this to be unfair, in that another person is paid more but they believe that person is doing less work, motivational issues can occur. For example, people may reduce their own inputs and not work as hard. Employees may also decide to leave the organization as a result of the perceived inequity. In HR, this is an important theory to understand, because even if someone is being paid fairly, they will always compare their own pay to that of others in the organization. The key here is perception, in that the fairness is based entirely on what the employee sees, not what may be the actual reality. Even though HR or management may feel employees are being paid fairly, this may not be the employee's belief. In HR, we need to look at two factors related to pay equity: external pay equity and internal pay equity. External pay equity refers to what other people in similar organizations are being paid for a similar job. Internal pay equity focuses on employees within the same organization. Within the same organization, employees may look at higher level jobs, lower level jobs, and years with the organization to make their decision on pay equity. Consider Walmart, for example. In 2010, Michael Duke, CEO of Walmart, earned roughly $35 million in salary and other compensation (Gomstyn,

2010), while employees earned minimum wage or slightly higher in their respective states. While Walmart contends that its wages are competitive in local markets, the retail giant makes no apologies for the pay difference, citing the need for a specialized skill set to be able to be the CEO of a *Fortune* 500 company. There are hundreds of articles addressing the issue of pay equity between upper level managers and employees of an organization. To make a compensation strategy work, the perceived inputs (the work) and outputs (the pay) need to match fairly.

The expectancy theory is another key theory in relation to pay. The expectancy theory says that employees will put in as much work as they expect to receive. In other words, if the employee perceives they are going to be paid favorably, they will work to achieve the outcomes. If they believe the rewards do not equal the amount of effort, they may not work as hard.

The reinforcement theory, developed by Edward L. Thorndike (Indiana University, 2011), says that if high performance is followed by some reward, that desired behavior will likely occur in the future. Likewise, if high performance isn't followed by a reward, it is less likely the high performance will occur in the future. Consider an extreme example of the reinforcement theory in the world of finance. On Wall Street, bonuses for traders and bankers are a major part of their salary. The average bonus in 2010 was $128,530 (Smith, 2011), which does not take into account specific commissions on trades, which can greatly increase total compensation. One interesting consideration is the ethical implications of certain pay structures, particularly commission and bonus plans. For example, after the U.S. government bailed out American International Group (AIG) with $170 billion in 2009, it was reported AIG would still provide some $165 million in bonuses to the same business unit that brought the company to near collapse, because of contractual issues. Traditionally, a bonus structure is designed to reward performance, rather than be a guaranteed part of the compensation plan, as was the case with AIG. Bonus and commission plans should be utilized to drive desired behavior and act as a reward for the desired behavior, as the reinforcement theory states.

All these theories provide us information to make better decisions when developing our own pay systems. Other considerations are discussed next.

Pay Decision Considerations

Besides the motivational aspect of creating a pay structure, there are some other considerations. First, the size of the organization and the expected expansion of the organization will be a factor. For example, if you are the HR manager for a ten-person company, you likely use a going rate or management fit model. While this is appropriate for your company today, as your organization grows, it may be prudent to develop a more formal pay structure. Ascentium Corporation, based in Seattle, Washington, found this to be the case. When the company started with fewer than fifteen employees, a management fit model was used. As the company ballooned to over five hundred employees in four cities, a pay banding model had to be put into place for fairness.

If your organization also operates overseas, a consideration is how domestic workers will be paid in comparison to the global market. One strategy is to develop a centralized compensation system, which would be one pay system for all employees, regardless of where they live. The downside to this is that the cost of living may be much less in some countries, making the centralized system possibly unfair to employees who live and work in more expensive countries. Another consideration is in what currency employees will be paid. Most U.S. companies pay even their overseas workers in dollars, and not in the local currency where the employee is working. Currency valuation fluctuations could cause challenges in this regard (Watson, 2005).

How you communicate your pay system is extremely important to enhance the motivation that can be created by fair and equitable wage. In addition, where possible, asking for participation from your employees through the use of pay attitude surveys, for example, can create a transparent compensation process, resulting in higher performing employees.

Organizations should develop market pay surveys and review their wages constantly to ensure the organization is within expected ranges for the industry.

> **Human Resource Recall**
>
> Why do you think a transparent compensation policy is so important to motivating a workforce?

Table 2-11 Types of Pay

Pay	Attributes
Salary	Fixed compensation calculated on a weekly, biweekly, or monthly basis. No extra pay for overtime work.
Hourly Wage	Employees are paid on the basis of number of hours worked.

Continued

Pay	Attributes
Piecework System	Employees are paid based on the number of items that are produced.
Types of Incentive Plans	Attributes
	An employee may or may not receive a salary but will be paid extra (e.g., a percentage for every sale made).
Commission Plans	Extra pay for meeting or beating some goal previously determined. Bonus plans can consist of monetary compensation, but also other forms such as time off or gift certificates.
Bonus Plans	Annual bonuses paid to employees based on the amount of profit the organization earned.
Profit-Sharing	When an employee is given the right to purchase company stock at a particular rate in time. Please note that a stock "option" is different from the actual giving of stock, since the option infers the employee will buy the stock at a set rate, obviously, usually cheaper than the going rate.
Plans Stock Options	Attributes
Other Types of	This can include a variety of options. Sick leave, paid vacation time, health club memberships, daycare services.
Compensation	Most organizations provide health and dental care benefits for employees. In addition, disability and life insurance benefits are offered.
Fringe Benefits Health Benefits 401(k) Plans	Some organizations provide a retirement plan for employees. The company would work with a financial organization to set up the plan so employees can save money, and often, companies will "match" a percentage of what the employee contributes to the plan.

Types of Pay

After a pay system has been developed, we can begin to look at specific methods of paying our employees. Remember that when we talk about compensation, we are referring to not only an actual paycheck but additional types of compensation, such as incentive plans that include bonuses and profit sharing. We can divide our total pay system into three categories: pay, incentives, and other types of compensation. Pay is the hourly, weekly, or monthly salary an employee earns. An incentive, often called a pay-for-performance incentive, is given for meeting certain performance standards, such as meeting sales targets. The advantage to incentive pay is that company goals can be linked directly to employee goals, resulting in higher pay for the employee and goal achievement by the organization. The following are desirable traits of incentive plans:

Clearly communicated

Attainable but challenging

Easily understandable

Tied to company goals

Most organizations use a combination of pay, incentives, and other compensation, as outlined in Table 2-11 "Types of Pay", to develop the total compensation package.

Laws Relating to Pay

As you have already guessed from our earlier chapter discussions, people cannot be discriminated against when it comes to development of pay systems. One issue hotly debated is the issue of comparable worth. Comparable worth states that people should be given similar pay if they are performing the same type of job. Evidence over the years shows this isn't the case, with women earning less than men in many industries. On average, a woman earns 79 cents for every $1.00 a man earns. For women of color, the gap is wider at 69 cents for African-American women and 59 cents for Latina women (National Organization for Women, 2011). Many publications state that women earn less than men for a few reasons:

Women work fewer hours because of family care and maternity leave.

The career path or job choice of women tends to be lower as a whole.

There is a bias favoring men as the "breadwinners", and therefore they are paid more.

Women are valued less than men in the workplace.

Women don't negotiate salaries as well as men do.

While the reasons are certainly debatable, there is evidence that young women (without children) entering the workforce actually earn more than their male counterparts, owing to higher levels of education (Dougherty, 2010). As you may remember from Chapter 3 "Diversity and Multiculturalism", the EEOC covers discrimination in the workplace, including pay discrimination based on race, color, religion, sex, and national origin. The *Equal Pay Act* of 1963 makes it illegal to pay different wages to men and women if they perform equal work in the same workplace.

More recent legislation on pay includes the *Lilly Ledbetter Fair Pay Act* of 2009, the first law signed by President Obama. This bill amends the *Civil Rights Act* stating that the 180-day statute of limitations for filing an equal pay lawsuit regarding pay discrimination resets with each discriminatory paycheck. The bill stemmed from a lawsuit against Goodyear

Tire and Rubber Company by Lilly Ledbetter, who claimed that her nineteen-year career at the company consisted of unfair pay, compared to male workers in the organization. Her complaint was time barred by the U.S. Supreme Court, and the new act addressed the time (180 days) constraint in which people have to file claims.

The *Fair Labor Standards Act*, or *FLSA*, was established in 1938 and set a minimum wage for jobs, overtime laws, and child labor laws. *FLSA* divides workers into exempt and non-exempt status, and jobs under exempt status do not fall under the *FLSA* guidelines. An exempt employee is usually paid a salary and includes executive, professional, outside sales, and administrative positions. A non-exempt employee is usually an hourly employee. For non-exempt employees, some states may implement a higher minimum wage than that established by the federal government. For example, in 2011, the minimum wage is $8.67 per hour in Washington State, while the federal minimum wage is $7.25 per hour. Obviously, as an HR manager or manager, it is your responsibility to ensure everyone is being paid the minimum wage. This law also requires overtime pay if employees work over forty hours per week. Organizations must also post the *FLSA* poster in a visible part of the workplace, outlining these laws.

Child labor also falls under *FLSA*. The goal of these laws is to protect the education of children, prohibit the employment of children in dangerous jobs, and limit the number of working hours of children during the school year and other times of the year (U.S. Department of Labor, 2011).

According to the *FLSA*, tipped employees are those earning $30 or more per month in tips, such as servers in a restaurant. Employers whose employees receive more than $30 in tips may consider tips as part of wages, but they also must pay $2.12 an hour in direct wages. They must also be able to show that the employee receives at least the applicable minimum wage. If the tips and direct wage do not meet the minimum wage, the employer must pay the difference.

Also relating to pay is the *Federal Unemployment Tax Act* (*FUTA*). *FUTA* provides for payments of unemployment compensation to workers who have lost their jobs. Most employers pay a federal and a state unemployment tax, and portions of these funds go toward unemployment benefits should the worker lose his or her job. The *Federal Employees Compensation Act* (*FECA*) provides federal employees injured in the performance of their jobs compensation benefits, such as disability. Please note that this is elective for private companies but required of federal agencies.

Key Takeaways

A job evaluation system should be used to determine the relative value of one job to another. This is the first step in setting up a pay system.

Several types of pay systems can be implemented. A pay grade system sets up specific pay levels for particular jobs, while a going rate system looks at the pay throughout the industry for a certain job title. Management fit gives maximum flexibility for managers to pay what they think someone should earn.

HR managers can also develop pay systems based on skills and competency and utilize broadbanding, which is similar to pay grades. Another option might include variable pay.

There are several motivational theories in regard to pay. First, the equity theory says that people will evaluate their own satisfaction with their compensation by comparing it to others' compensation. The expectancy theory says people will put in only as much work as they expect to receive in rewards. Finally, the reinforcement theory says if high performance is followed by a reward, high performance is likely to happen in the future.

Other pay considerations include the size of the organization, whether the company is global, and the level of communication and employee involvement in compensation. HR managers should always be aware of what others are paying in the industry by performing market surveys.

There are several laws pertaining to pay. Of course, the EEOC ensures that pay is fair for all and does not discriminate. *FLSA* sets a minimum wage and establishes standards for child labor. *FUTA* requires employers to pay unemployment taxes on employees. *FECA* ensures that federal employees receive certain benefits.

Exercises

1. Name and describe three considerations in developing a pay system. Which do you think is best?

2. Which pay theory do you think is the most important when developing your pay system? Why?

3. Visit http://www.dol.gov/dol/topic/wages/minimumwage.htm (please note that

sometimes web address change so you may need to search for the information), which publishes minimum wage data for the United States. View the map and compare your state with the federal minimum wage. Is it higher or lower? Which two states have the highest minimum wage? The lowest?

5.4 Other Types of Compensation

Learning Objective

Explain the various types of benefits that can be offered to employees.

As you already know, there is more to a compensation package than just pay. There are many other aspects to the creation of a good compensation package, including not only pay but incentive pay and other types of compensation. First, we will discuss benefits that are mandated by the federal government, and then we will discuss types of voluntary benefits, including both incentive pay and other types of compensation.

Mandated: Social Security and Medicare

The *Social Security Act* of 1935 requires employers to withdraw funds from workers' paychecks to pay for retirement benefits. This is called a payroll tax. Please note that all organizations are legally compelled to offer this benefit. After several revisions, we now call this OASDHI or the Old Age, Survivors, Disability, and Health Insurance Program. To be insured, employees must work forty quarters, with a minimum of $1,000 earned per quarter. Once this money is put aside, anyone born after 1960 will receive benefits at 67. The OASDHI tax in 2011 is 4.2 percent on earnings for employees, up to $106,800 and 6.2 percent for the employer up to the same limits. This covers both retirement income as well as medical benefits, called Medicare, once the employee reaches retirement age.

Mandated: Unemployment Insurance and Workers' Compensation

Unemployment insurance is required under the *Social Security Act* of 1935 and is also called the *Federal Unemployment Tax Act* (*FUTA*). This program's goals include providing some lost income for employees during involuntary unemployment, helping workers find a new job, incentivizing employers to continue employment, and developing worker skills if they are laid off. The majority of this plan is funded by employers' payroll taxes, which account for 8 percent per employee. The rate is actually 6.2 percent of compensation, but employers are allowed a tax credit for these payments, which results in the net 8 percent. With this benefit, employees receive unemployment benefits and/or job training when they are laid off or let go from a current job. However, employees would be ineligible to receive these benefits if they quit their job, as it must be involuntary. Just like Social Security, this payroll tax on employers is required.

Some employers also offer workers' compensation benefits. If an employee is hurt on the job, he or she would receive certain benefits, such as a percentage of pay. Jobs are classified into risk levels, and obviously the higher the risk level, the higher the cost of insurance. This is not a federally mandated program, but for some occupations in some states, it may be a requirement.

Mandated: COBRA

While the government does not require companies to provide healthcare and medical benefits to employees, the *Consolidated Omnibus Budget Reconciliation Act* (*COBRA*) requires companies to allow employees to extend their group coverage for up to thirty-six months. The restrictions for this plan include the requirement of a qualifying event that would mean a loss of benefits, such as termination or reduction in hours. For example, if an employee works forty hours a week with medical insurance, but the schedule is reduced to twenty hours, no longer qualifying him or her for benefits, *COBRA* would be an option.

Voluntary: Incentive Pay Systems

As we discussed earlier, there are several types of incentive pay systems that can be tied directly to business objectives and the employees' ability to help the company meet those objectives. They include commissions, bonuses, profit sharing, stock options, team pay, and merit pay.

Commissions are usually calculated on the basis of a percentage and earned based on the achievement of specific targets that have been agreed upon by the employee and employer. For example, many salespeople receive commissions from each item sold. Many commission incentive plans require employees to meet a minimum level of sales, who then are paid a comission on each sale beyond the minimum. A straight commission plan is one in which the employee receives no base pay and entire pay is based on meeting sales goals. Many plans, however, include a base pay and commission for each sale. Base pay is the guaranteed salary the employee earns.

Several types of bonuses can be given to employees as incentive pay. Meeting certain company goals or successfully completing a project or other objectives can be tied to a bonus, which is a one-time payment to an employee. A spot bonus is an unplanned bonus given to an employee for meeting a certain objective. These types of bonuses do not always have to be money; they can be other forms such as a gift certificate or trip. Fifty-eight percent of WorldatWork members (WorldatWork, 2000) said that they provide spot bonuses to employees for special recognition above and beyond work performance.

Some organizations choose to reward employees financially when the organization as a whole performs well, through the use of profit sharing as an incentive. For example, if an organization has a profit-sharing program of 2 percent for employees, the employees would earn 2 percent of the overall profit of the company. As you have guessed, this can be an excellent incentive for employees to both work as a team and also monitor their own personal performance so as not to let down the team. For example, in 2011, U.S. automaker General Motors gave one of its highest profit-sharing payouts ever. Forty-five thousand employees received $189 million in a profit-sharing bonus, which equaled about $4,200 per person (Bunkley, 2011). While profit sharing can be a great incentive, it can also be a large expense that should be carefully considered.

Employee ownership of the organization is similar to profit-sharing but with a few key differences. In this type of plan, employees are granted stock options, which allow the employees to buy stock at a fixed price. Then if the stock goes up in value, the employee earns the difference between what he or she paid and the value of the stock. With this type of incentive, employees are encouraged to act in the best interest of the organization. Some plans, called employee stock ownership plans, are different from stock options, in that in these plans the employee is given stock as reward for performance.

In a smaller organization, team pay or group incentives can be popular. In this type of plan, if the group meets a specified goal, such as the increase of sales by 10 percent, the entire group receives a reward, which can consist of additional pay or bonus. Please note that this is different from individualized bonuses, discussed earlier, since the incentive is a reward for the group as opposed for the individual.

Figure 2-19 Emplyee Ownership

Note: Profit-sharing and stock ownership can be a good way to motivate employees to work toward the goals of the organization.

Merit pay is a pay program that links pay to how well the employee performs within the job, and it is normally tied to performance appraisals. Merit base is normally an annual pay increase tied to performance. The problem with merit pay is that it may only be received once per year, limiting incentive flexibility. To make merit pay work, performance guidelines should be predetermined. Some organizations offer cost of living annual increases (COLAs), which is not tied to merit but is given to employees as an annual inflationary increase.

Fortune **500 Focus**

While the cost of health insurance premiums may be going up for most Americans, these premiums do not hit the individual employee's pocketbook at Microsoft. Microsoft, based in Redmond, Washington, finds itself once again on the *Fortune* 500 "Best Companies to Work For" list in several areas, including paying for 100 percent of employees' healthcare premiumS[1]. In addition to cutting this cost for employees, Microsoft also offers domestic partner benefits, one of the first *Fortune* 500 companies to do so. In 2005, Microsoft also began to offer partial coverage for transgender surgery to its existing healthcare coverage, which earned Microsoft the highest attainable score by the Human Rights Campaign (HRC) Equality Index (GLEAM, 2011). Microsoft also promotes fitness and wellness as part of its healthcare plan, providing an on-site fitness center and subsidized gym memberships.

Voluntary: Medical Insurance

According to the Bureau of Labor Statistics, 62 percent of companies in 2010 offered healthcare benefits to employees (U.S. Bureau of Labor Statistics, 2010). The yearly cost for employee medical insurance averages $9,552, according to the 2009 Towers Perrin survey (Watson, 2009). With such a significant cost to companies, it is up to HR managers to contain these costs, while not negatively affecting employee motivation. Medical insurance usually includes hospital expenses, surgical expenses, and routine healthcare visits. Most insurance plans also allow for wellness visits and other alternative care (e.g., massage and acupuncture) within the plans. Many employers also offer vision and dental care benefits as part of their benefits packages. Disability insurance is also provided by some employers as well. We will discuss each of these in detail next.

One important law to keep in mind regarding medical insurance is the *Health Insurance Portability and Accountability Act* (*HIPAA*) of 1996. It provides federal protections for personal health information held by covered entities, such as employers. In other words, employers cannot divulge or share health care information they may have on an employee.

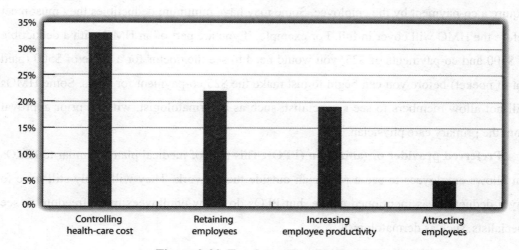

Figure 2-20 Employee Benefits Trends

Note: As you can see from MetLife's 9th annual study in 2010, cost containment is an important aspect to healthcare plans.

Source: MetLife, "9th Annual Study of Employee Benefits Trends", 2010, http://www.metlife.com/assets/ institutional/services/insights-and-tools/ebts/Employee-Benefits-Trends-Study.pdf (accessed July 23, 2011).

As the HR professional, it will likely be your responsibility to choose the healthcare plan that best meets the needs of your employees. Some options include the following:

Fee-for-service plans. In this type of plan, people pay for medical expenses out of pocket, and then are reimbursed for the benefit level. For example, if your insurance plan covers doctor visits, you could see any doctor, pay the bill, and then submit payment to your insurer for reimbursement. Most companies will have a base plan, which covers more serious issues requiring hospitalization, while the major medical part of the plan would cover routine services, such as doctor's visits. As you can imagine, the disadvantage of this type of plan can be twofold: first, the initial expense for the employee, and second, the time it may take to receive reimbursement for employees. Remember that medical insurance can help retain and motivate employees and help you recruit new employees, so consideration of the disadvantages is important.

Health maintenance organizations (HMOs). The HMO will likely have greater coverage than the fee-for-service plan, but it limits the ability of employees to see the doctors they choose. There may be a limited number of physicians and specialists for the employee to see, and going outside the plan and seeing another doctor may result in an out-of-pocket expense for the employee. Most HMOs cover a wide range of medical issues and will usually require a co-payment by the employee. Some may have minimum deductibles they must meet before the HMO will cover in full. For example, if you are part of an HMO with a deductible of $500 and co-payments of $25, you would need to see the doctor for a value of $500 (paid out of pocket) before you can begin to just make the $25 co-payment for visits. Some HMOs will not allow members to see a specialist, such as a dermatologist, without prior approval from the primary care physician.

Preferred provider organization (PPO). This type of medical plan is similar to HMOs but allows employees to see a physician outside the network. They will likely still have to pay a deductible as mentioned above, but PPOs do allow employees more freedom to see specialists, such as dermatologists.

Figure 2-21 Considerations When Choosing Medical Insurance

The cost of the plan

The type of coverage

The quality of the care

Administration of the plan

First, the cost is usually a major consideration for the HR professional. Developing a budget for healthcare costs, initiating bids from possible providers, and then negotiating those bids is a key factor in controlling this cost for employers.

Second, asking for employees' opinions about the type of coverage they would prefer is a way to ensure your plan meets the needs of your employees. Next, consider the quality of care your employees will receive, and finally, how simple will the plan be for your HR department to administer. For example, many HMO plans offer fully automated and online services for employees, making them easy to administer.

Disability insurance provides income to individuals (usually a portion of their salary) should they be injured or need long-term care resulting from an illness. Short-term disability insurance (STD) provides benefits to someone if they are unable to work for six months or less, while long-term disability insurance (LTD) covers the employee for a longer period of time. Normally, disability insurance provides income to the employee that is 60—80 percent of their normal salary.

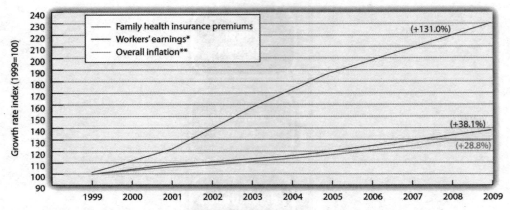

* Workers' earnings as measured by average hourly earnings for private sector production workers.
** Overall inflation as measured by the Consumer Priced Index for All Urban Consumers (CPI-U).

Figure 2-22 CPI-U

Note: One of the biggest challenges in healthcare benefits planning is to manage the growing cost of health insurance premiums for employees while still managing cost containment for the organization.

Source: Economic Policy Institute, "The State of Working America: Health Premiums", http://stateofworkingamerica. org/charts/growth-rate-of-premiums-earnings-and-inflation/ (accessed July 23, 2011).

Voluntary: 401(k) Plans

As the scenery of the workforce has changed, benefits have changed, too. One such recent change is the movement of employee pension plans to 401(k) plans. While some organizations still offer pension plans, such plans are far more rare. A pension plan is a set dollar amount an employee will receive when they retire from their organization. This type of plan was popular when most people worked their entire life at the same company. However, many pension plans have gone bankrupt, and the United States has an agency to protect people from losing pension benefits. The Pension Benefit Guaranty Corporation (PBGC) was created by the *Employee Retirement Income Security Act* (*ERISA*) to protect pension benefits in private sector pension plans. If a pension plan ends or isn't able to pay all benefits, PBGC's insurance program pays the benefit that should have been provided. Financing for this plan comes from insurance premiums paid by the companies whose plans PBGC protects.

As more mobility in the workplace has occurred, most organizations no longer offer pension plans, but instead, they offer 401(k) plans. While a pension plan can motivate employee loyalty, 401(k) plans are far more popular. According to the U.S. Bureau of Labor Statistics, employer-provided retirement plans, such as 401(k) plans, were available to 74 percent of all full-time workers in the United States (U.S. Bureau of Labor Statistics, 2010), while 39 percent of part-time workers had access to retirement benefits.

A 401(k) plan is a plan set up by the organization in which employees directly deposit money from their paycheck. The funds are tax deferred for the employee until retirement. If an employee leaves the job, their 401(k) plan goes with them. As an extra incentive, many organizations offer to match what the employee puts into the plan, usually based on a percentage. For example, an employee can sign up to contribute 5 percent of salary into a 401(k) plan, and the company will contribute the same amount. Most companies require a vesting period—that is, a certain time period, such as a year, before the employer will match the funds contributed.

Usually, 401(k) plans are easy to administer, after the initial setup has occurred. If the employer is matching employee contributions, the expense of such a plan can be great, but it also increases employee retention. Some considerations when choosing a 401(k) plan are as follows:

Is the vendor trustworthy?

Does the vendor allow employees to change their investments and account information online?

How much are the management fees?

It is first important to make sure the vendor you are considering for administration of your 401(k) plan has a positive reputation and also provides ease of access for your employees. For example, most 401(k) plans allow employees to change their address online and move investments from a stock to a bond. Twenty-four-hour access has become the expectation of most employees, and as a result, this is a major consideration before choosing a plan. Most 401(k) plans charge a fee to manage the investments of your employees. The management fees can vary greatly, so receiving a number of bids and comparing these fees is important to ensure your employees are getting the best deal.

It is important to mention the *Employee Retirement Income Security Act* (*ERISA*) here, as this relates directly to administration of your 401(k) plan. First, *ERISA* does not require employers to offer a pension or 401(k) plan, but for those who do, it requires them to meet certain standards when administering this type of plan. Some of these standards include the following:

Requires participants receive specific information about the plan, such as plan features and funding.

Sets minimum standards for participation and vesting.

Requires accountability of plan's fiduciary responsibilities.

Requires payment of certain benefits, should the plan be terminated.

Voluntary: Paid Time Off

Time off is a benefit we should address, since this type of benefit varies greatly, especially in other parts of the world. French companies, for example, are mandated by law to provide five weeks of paid vacation time to employees (Leung, 2009). In the United States, the number of days off provided is a major budget item worth considering. Here are the general types of time off.

Paid Holidays

Many companies offer a set number of paid holidays, such as New Year's Day, Memorial Day, Christmas, Independence Day, and Thanksgiving.

Sick Leave

The number of sick leave days can vary greatly among employers. The average in the United States is 8.4 paid sick days offered to employees per year (HRM Guide, 2011).

Paid Vacation

With full-time employment, many organizations also offer paid vacation to employees, and it is generally expected as part of the compensation package. According to a survey performed by Salary.com, the average number of paid vacation days in the United States is nine days for one year of service, fourteen days for five years of service, and seventeen days for ten years of service to the organization (Yang, 2011).

Organizations vary greatly in how vacation time is accrued. Some organizations give one hour for a certain number of days worked, while others require a waiting period before earning any paid time off (PTO). In addition, some organizations allow their employees to carry over unused vacation time from one year to the next, while other employees must use their vacation every year or risk losing it.

Paid Time Off (PTO)

One option is to provide a set number of days off, which can be used for vacation time, holidays, and/or sick leave.

To promote longevity, some organizations offer paid (or for example, 60 percent of salary paid) sabbaticals. For example, after five years of employment, the employee may take a paid sabbatical for one month.

A Final Note on Compensation and Benefits Strategy

When creating your compensation plan, of course the ability to recruit and retain should be an important factor. But also, consideration of your workforce needs is crucial to any successful compensation plan. The first step in development of a plan is to ask the employees what they care about. Some employees would rather receive more pay with fewer benefits or better benefits with fewer days off. Surveying the employees allows you, as the HR professional, to better understand the needs of your specific workforce. Once you have developed your plan, understand that it may change to best meet the needs of your business as it changes over time.

Once the plan is developed, communicating the plan with your employees is also essential. Inform your employees via an HR blog, e-mails, and traditional methods such as face to face. Your employees might not always be aware of the benefits cost to the company, so making sure they know is your responsibility. For example, if you pay for 80 percent of the medical insurance premiums, let your employees know. This type of communication can go a long way to allowing the employees to see their value to you within the organization.

Key Takeaways

Before beginning work on a pay system, some general questions need to be answered. Questions such as what is a fair wage from the employee's perspective and how much can be paid but still retain financial health are important starting points.

After some pay questions are answered, development of a pay philosophy must be developed. For example, an organization may decide to pay lower salaries but offer more benefits.

Once these tasks are done, the HR manager can then build a pay system that works for the size and industry of the organization.

Besides salary, one of the biggest expenses for compensation is medical benefits. These can include health benefits, vision, dental, and disability benefits.

Social Security and unemployment insurance are both required by federal law. Both are paid as a percentage of income by the employee and employer.

Depending on the state, workers' compensation might be a requirement. A percentage is paid on behalf of the employee in case he or she is hurt on the job.

A mandatory benefit, COBRA was enacted to allow employees to continue their health insurance coverage, even if they leave their job.

There are three main types of healthcare plans. A fee-for-service plan allows the insured to see any doctor and submit reimbursement after a visit. An HMO plan restricts employees to certain doctors and facilities and may require a co-payment and/or deductibles. A PPO plan is similar to the HMO but allows for more flexibility in which providers the employee can see.

Pension funds were once popular, but as people tend to change jobs more, 401(k) plans are becoming more popular, since they can move with the employee.

Profit sharing is a benefit in which employees receive a percentage of profit the organization earns. Stock ownership plans are plans in which employees can purchase stock or are granted stock and become an owner in the organization.

Team rewards are also a popular way to motivate employees. These can be in the form of compensation if a group or the company meets certain target goals.

Paid time off, or PTO, can come in the form of holidays, vacation time, and sick leave. Usually, employees earn more days as they stay with the company.

Communication with employees is key to a successful benefits strategy.

Exercises

1. Of the benefits we discussed, which ones are required by law? Which are not?

2. Research current *Federal Insurance Contributions Act* (*FICA*) tax rates and Social Security limits, as these change frequently. Write down each of these rates and be prepared to share in class.

3. Describe the considerations when developing medical benefits. Which do you think would be the most important to you as the HR manager?

4. Visit websites of three companies you might be interested in working for. Review the incentives they offer and be prepared to discuss your findings in class.

5.5 Cases and Problems

Chapter Summary

A compensation package is an important part of the overall strategic HRM plan, since much of the company budget is for employee compensation.

A compensation package can include salary, bonuses, healthcare plans, and a variety of other types of compensation.

The goals of compensation are first to attract people to work for your organization. Second, they can be used to retain people who are already working in the organization.

Compensation is also used to motivate employees to work at their peak performance and improve morale of the organization.

Employees who are fairly compensated tend to provide better customer service, which can result in organizational growth and development.

Several types of pay systems can be implemented. A pay grade system sets up specific pay levels for particular jobs, while a going rate system looks at the pay throughout the industry for a certain job title. Management fit gives maximum flexibility for managers to pay what they think someone should earn.

HR managers can also develop pay systems based on skills and competency and utilize a broadbanding approach, which is similar to pay grades. Another option might include variable pay.

There are several motivational theories in regard to pay. First, the equity theory says that people will evaluate their own satisfaction with their compensation by comparing it to others' compensation. The expectancy theory says people will put in only as much work as they expect to receive in rewards. Finally, the reinforcement theory says that if high performance is followed by a reward, high performance is likely to happen in the future.

Other pay considerations include the size of the organization, whether the company is global, and the level of communication and employee involvement in compensation. HR managers should always be aware of what others are paying in the industry by performing market surveys.

There are several laws pertaining to pay. Of course, the Equal Employment Opportunity Commission (EEOC) ensures that pay is fair for all and does not discriminate. The *Fair Labor Standards Act (FLSA)* sets a minimum wage and establishes standards for child labor. The *Federal Unemployment Tax Act (FUTA)* requires employers to pay unemployment taxes on employees. The *Federal Employees Compensation Act (FECA)* ensures that federal employees receive certain benefits.

Besides salary, one of the biggest expenses for compensation is medical benefits. These can include health benefits, vision, dental, and disability benefits.

The *Consolidated Omnibus Budget Reconciliation Act(COBRA)* was enacted to allow employees to continue their health insurance coverage, even if they leave their job.

There are three main types of healthcare plans. A fee-for-service plan allows the insured to see any doctor and submit reimbursement after a visit. An HMO plan restricts employees to certain doctors and facilities and may require a co-payment and/or deductibles. A PPO plan is similar to the HMO but allows for more flexibility in which providers the employee can see.

Pension funds were once popular, but as people tend to change jobs more, 401(k) plans are becoming more popular, since they can move with the employee.

Profit sharing is a benefit in which employees receive a percentage of profit the organization earns. Stock ownership plans are plans in which employees can purchase stock or are granted stock and become an owner in the organization.

Team rewards are also a popular way to motivate employees. These can be in the form of compensation if a group or the company meets certain target goals.

Social Security and unemployment insurance are both required by federal law. Both are paid as a percentage of income by the employee and employer.

Depending on the state, workers' compensation might be a requirement. A percentage is paid on behalf of the employee in case he or she is hurt on the job.

Paid time off, or PTO, can come in the form of holidays, vacation time, and sick leave. Usually, employees earn more days as they stay with the company.

Communication with employees is key to a successful benefits strategy. This includes communication before implementing the plan as well as communication about the plan.

Chapter Case

PTO: Too Little or Too Much?

You just finished analyzing information for the current compensation and benefits program. You find that some changes should be made, as the majority of employees (you have 120 employees) are not happy

nine years to this organization, but I receive only three days more than someone who has just started." Here is the current PTO offering:

1+ year	7 days
5+ years	10 days
10+ years	14 days

What cost considerations would you take into account when revising this part of your compensation plan?

What other considerations would you take into account when developing a new PTO plan?

Propose a new plan and estimate the cost of your plan on an Excel spreadsheet. Be prepared to present to the board of directors.

Team Activity

Work in teams of four or five. Assume your organization is expanding and wants to open a sales office overseas. What compensation factors would be a concern? Brainstorm a list and be prepared to present to the rest of the class.

Go to http://www.bls.gov/oco/ and review the information on the *Occupational Outlook Handbook* in teams of three. Pick three different jobs under the management category and record their average salary. Discuss reasons for the pay difference between the jobs you choose.

Chapter 6 Retention and Motivation

Dissatisfaction isn't Always about Pay

As an HR consultant, your job normally involves reviewing HR strategic plans and systems of small to medium size companies, then making recommendations on how to improve. Most of the companies you work with do not have large HR departments, and they find it less expensive to hire you than to hire a full-time person.

Your current client, Pacific Books, is a small online retailer with forty-seven employees. Pacific Books has had some challenges, and as the economy has improved, several employees have quit. They want you to look into this issue and provide a plan to improve retention.

Pacific Books currently has just one person managing payroll and benefits. The individual managers in the organization are the ones who handle other HR aspects, such as recruiting and developing compensation plans. As you speak with the managers and the payroll and benefits manager, it is clear employees are not happy working for this organization. You are concerned that if the company does not improve its employee retention, they will spend an excessive amount of time trying to recruit and train new people, so retention of the current employees is important.

As with most HR issues, rather than just guessing what employees want, you develop a survey to send to all employees, including management. You developed the survey on SurveyMonkey and asked employee satisfaction questions surrounding pay and benefits. However, you know that there are many other things that can cause someone to be unhappy at work, so to take this survey a step further, you decide to ask questions about the type of work employees are doing, management style, and work-life balance. Then you send out a link to all employees, giving them one week to take the survey.

When the results come in, they are astounding. Out of the forty-seven employees, forty-three selected "dissatisfied" on at least four or more areas of the five-question survey. While some employees are not happy with pay and benefits, the results say that other areas of the organization are actually what are causing the dissatisfaction. Employees are feeling micromanaged and do not have freedom over their time. There are also questions of favoritism by some managers for some employees, who always seem to get the "best" projects. When you sit down with the CEO to discuss the survey results, at first she defends the organization by saying the company offers the highest salaries and best benefits in the industry, and she doesn't understand how someone can be dissatisfied. You explain to her that employee retention and motivation is partly about pay and benefits, but it includes other aspects of the employee's job, too. She listens intently and then asks you to develop a retention and motivation plan that can improve the organization.

6.1 The Costs of Turnover

Learning Objectives

1. Be able identify the difference between direct and indirect turnover costs.
2. Describe some of the reasons why employees leave.
3. Explain the components of a retention plan.

According to the book *Keeping the People Who Keep You in Business* by Leigh Branham (Branham, 2000), the cost of losing an employee can range from 25 percent to 200 percent of that employee's salary. Some of the costs cited revolve around customer service disruption and loss of morale among other employees, burnout of other employees, and the costs of hiring someone new. Losing an employee is called turnover.

There are two types of turnover, voluntary turnover and involuntary turnover. Voluntary turnover is the type of turnover that is initiated by the employee for many different reasons. Voluntary turnover can be somewhat predicted and addressed in HR, the focus of this chapter. Involuntary turnover is where the employee has no choice in their termination—for example, employer-initiated due to non-performance.

It has been suggested that replacement of an employee who is paid $8 per hour can range upwards of $4,000 (Paiement, 2009). Turnover can be calculated by separations during the time period (month)/total number of employees midmonth × 100 = the percentage of turnover.

For example, let's assume there were three separations during the month of August and

115 employees midmonth. We can calculate turnover in this scenario by

$3/115 \times 100 = 2.6\%$ turnover rate.

This gives us the overall turnover rate for our organization. We may want to calculate turnover rates based on region or department to gather more specific data. For example, let's say of the three separations, two were in the accounting department. We have ten people in the accounting department. We can calculate that by

accounting: $2/10 \times 100 = 20\%$ turnover rate.

The turnover rate in accounting is alarmingly high compared to our company turnover rate. There may be something happening in this department to cause unusual turnover.

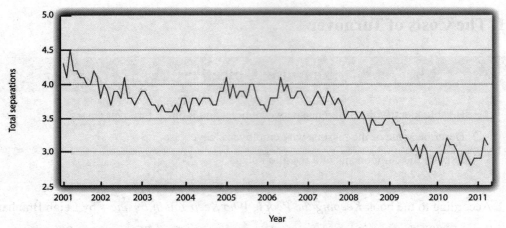

Figure 2-23 The United States Yearly Turnover Statistics, 2001—2011

Source: Data from Bureau of Labor Statistics, "Job Openings and Labor Turnover Survey", accessed August 11, 2011, http://www.bls.gov/jlt/#data.

In HR, we can separate the costs associated with turnover into indirect costs and direct costs. Direct turnover costs include the cost of leaving, replacement costs, and transition costs, while indirect turnover costs include the loss of production and reduced performance. The following are some examples of turnover costs (Maertz & Campion, 1998):

Recruitment of replacements

Administrative hiring costs

Lost productivity associated with the time between the loss of the employee and hiring of replacement

Lost productivity due to a new employee learning the job

Lost productivity associated with co-workers helping the new employee

Costs of training

Costs associated with the employee's lack of motivation prior to leaving

Sometimes, the costs of trade secrets and proprietary information shared by the employee who leaves

To avoid these costs, development of retention plans is an important function of the HR strategic plan. Retention plans outline the strategies the organization will use to reduce turnover and address employee motivation.

Table 2-12 Turnover Costs

Direct	Indirect
Recruitment costs	Lost knowledge
Advertising costs for new position	Loss of productivity while new employee is brought up to speed Cost associated with lack of motivation prior to leaving
Orientation and training of new employee Severance costs Testing costs	Cost associated with loss of trade secrets

Reasons for Voluntary Turnover

Before we discuss specific details on retention planning, it is important to address the reasons why people choose to leave an organization to begin with. One mistake HR professionals and managers make is to assume people leave solely on the basis of their unhappiness with their compensation packages.

Once we find out what can cause voluntary turnover, we can develop retention strategies to reduce turnover. Some of the common reasons employees leave organizations can include the following:

A poor match between the job and the skills of the employee. This issue is directly related to the recruitment process. When a poor match occurs, it can cause frustration for the employee and for the manager. Ensuring the recruitment phase is viable and sound is a first step to making sure the right match between job and skills occurs.

Lack of growth. Some employees feel "stuck" in their job and don't see a way to have upward mobility in the organization. Implementing a training plan and developing a clearly defined path to job growth is a way to combat this reason for leaving.

Internal pay equity. Some employees, while they may not feel dissatisfied with their own pay initially, may feel dissatisfaction when comparing their pay with others. Remember the pay equity theory discussed in Chapter 5 "Compensation and Benefits"? This theory relates to one reason why people leave.

Management. Many employees cite management as their reason for leaving. This can be attributed to overmanaging (micromanaging) people, managers not being fair or playing favorites, lack of or poor communication by managers, and unrealistic expectations of managers.

Workload. Some employees feel their workloads are too heavy, resulting in employees being spread thin and lacking satisfaction from their jobs, and possibly, lack of work-life balance as a result.

We know that some people will move or perhaps their family situation changes. This type of turnover is normal and expected. Figure 2-24 "Common Reasons for Employee Turnover" shows other examples of why people leave organizations.

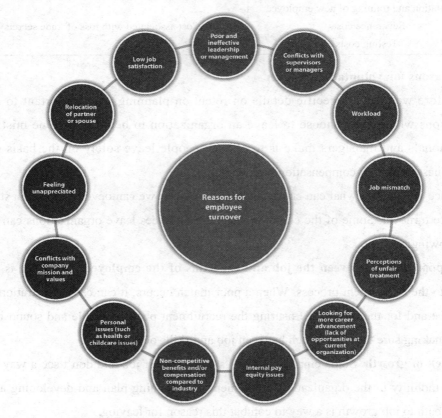

Figure 2-24　Common Reasons for Employee Turnover

As HR professionals and managers, we want to be sure we have plans in place to keep our best people. One such plan is the retention plan, which we will discuss in Section 6.2 "Retention Plans".

Human Resource Recall

Do you feel your current or past organization did a good job of reducing turnover? Why or why not?

Key Takeaways

Retaining employees is an important component to a healthy organization. Losing an employee is called turnover. Turnover can be very expensive to an organization, which is why it is important to develop retention plans to manage turnover.

Voluntary turnover is turnover that is initiated by the employee, while involuntary turnover is initiated by the organization for various reasons such as non-performance.

Direct turnover costs and indirect turnover costs can include the costs associated with employee replacement, declining employee morale, or lost customers.

Some of the reasons why employees leave can include a poor match between job and skills, no growth potential, pay inequity among employees, the fairness and communication style of management, and heavy workloads.

Exercise

Perform an Internet search of average employee turnover cost and report findings from at least three different industries or companies.

6.2 Retention Plans

Learning Objectives

1. Be able to discuss some of the theories on job satisfaction and dissatisfaction.
2. Explain the components of a retention plan.

Effective high-performance work systems (HPWS) is the name given to a set of systematic HR practices that create an environment where the employee has greater involvement and responsibility for the success of the organization. A high-performance work system is a strategic approach to many of the things we do in HR, including retention. Generally speaking, a HPWS gets employees involved in conceiving, designing, and implementing processes that are better for the company and better for the employee, which increases retention. Figure 2-25 "HR Components of a HPWS" gives an example of HR's part in creating these systems.

Figure 2-25 HR Components of a HPWS

Keeping HPWS in mind, we can begin to develop retention plans. The first step in this process is to understand some of the theories on job satisfaction and dissatisfaction. Next, we can gather data as to the satisfaction level of our current employees. Then we can begin to implement specific strategies for employee retention.

Theories on Job Dissatisfaction

There are a number of theories that attempt to describe what makes a satisfied employee versus an unsatisfied employee. While you may have learned about these theories in another class, such as organizational behavior, they are worth a review here to help us better understand employee satisfaction from an HR perspective.

Progression of Job Withdrawal

The first step to developing a retention plan is understanding some of the theories surrounding job satisfaction. One of the basic theories is the progression of job withdrawal theory, developed by Dan Farrell and James Petersen (Farrell & Petersen, 1984). It says that people develop a set of behaviors in succession to avoid their work situation. These behaviors include behavior change, physical withdrawal, and psychological withdrawal.

Within the behavior change area, an employee will first try to change the situation that is causing the dissatisfaction. For example, if the employee is unhappy with the management style, he or she might consider asking for a department move. In the physical withdrawal phase, the employee does one of the following:

Leaves the job

Takes an internal transfer

Starts to become absent or tardy

If an employee is unable to leave the job situation, he or she will experience psychological withdrawal. They will become disengaged and may show less job involvement and commitment to the organization, which can create large costs to the organization, such as dissatisfied customers.

Table 2-13　Process of Job Withdrawal

Employee becomes dissatisfied	For any number of reasons discussed earlier in this chapter
Behavior change	If unionized, increased grievances Whistle-blowing Change of conditions, such as applying for other jobs
Physical withdrawal	Leave the job Internal transfer Absenteeism Tardiness
Psychological withdrawal	Disengagement in job and/or with team members Less organizational commitment Become less productive

Hawthorne Studies

Between 1927 and 1932, a series of experiments were conducted by Elton Mayo in the Western Electric Hawthorne Works company in Illinois (Mayo, 1949; 2007). Mayo developed these experiments to see how the physical and environmental factors of the workplace, such as lighting and break times, would affect employee motivation.

This was some of the first research performed that looked at human motivation at work. His results were surprising, as he found that no matter which experiments were performed, worker output improved. His conclusion and explanation for this was the simple fact the workers were happy to receive attention from researchers who expressed interest in them. As a result, these experiments, scheduled to last one year, extended to five years to increase the knowledge base about human motivation.

The implication of this research applies to HR and managers even today. It tells us that our retention plans must include training and other activities that make the employee feel valued.

Maslow's Hierarchy of Needs

In 1943, Abraham Maslow developed what was known as the theory of human motivation (Maslow, 1999). His theory was developed in an attempt to explain human motivation. According to Maslow, there is a hierarchy of five needs, and as one level of need is satisfied, it will no longer be a motivator. In other words, people start at the bottom of the hierarchy and work their way up. Maslow's hierarchy consists of the following:

Self-actualization needs

Esteem needs

Social needs

Safety needs

Physiological needs

Physiological needs are our most basic needs, including food, water, and shelter. Safety needs at work might include feeling safe in the actual physical environment, or job security. As humans, we have the basic need to spend time with others. Esteem needs refer to the need we have to feel good about ourselves. Finally, self-actualization needs are the needs we have to better ourselves.

The implications of his research tell us, for example, that as long as an employee's physiological needs are met, increased pay may not be a motivator. Likewise, employees should be motivated at work by having all needs met. Needs might include, for example, fair pay, safety standards at work, opportunities to socialize, compliments to help raise our esteem, and training opportunities to further develop ourselves.

Herzberg Two-Factor Theory

In 1959, Frederick Herzberg published *The Motivation to Work* (Herzberg, et al., 1993), which described his studies to determine which aspects in a work environment caused satisfaction or dissatisfaction. He performed interviews in which employees were asked what pleased and displeased them about their work. From his research, he developed the motivation-hygiene theory to explain these results.

The things that satisfied the employees were motivators, while the dissatisfiers were the hygiene factors. He further said the hygiene factors were not necessarily motivators, but if not present in the work environment, they would actually cause demotivation. In other words, the hygiene factors are expected and assumed, while they may not necessarily motivate.

His research showed the following as the top six motivation factors:

Achievement

Recognition

The work itself

Responsibility

Advancement

Personal growth

The following were the top six hygiene factors:

Company policies

Supervision

Relationship with manager

Work conditions

Salary

Relationship with peers

The implication of this research is clear. Salary, for example, is on the hygiene factor list. Fair pay is expected, but it doesn't actually motivate someone to do a better job. On the other hand, programs to further develop employees, such as management training programs, would be considered a motivator. Therefore, our retention plans should be focused on the area of fair salary of course, but if they take the direction of Herzberg's motivational factors, the actual motivators tend to be the work and recognition surrounding the work performed.

McGregor

Douglas McGregor proposed the X-Y theory in his 1960 book called *The Human Side of Enterprise* (McGregor, 2006). McGregor's theory gives us a starting point to understanding how management style can impact the retention of employees. His theory suggests two fundamental approaches to managing people. Theory X managers, who have an authoritarian management style, and have the following fundamental management beliefs:

The average person dislikes work and will avoid it.

Most people need to be threatened with punishment to work toward company goals.

The average person needs to be directed.

Most workers will avoid responsibility.

Theory Y managers, on the other hand, have the following beliefs:

Most people want to make an effort at work.

People will apply self-control and self-direction in pursuit of company objectives.

Commitment to objectives is a function of expected rewards received.

People usually accept and actually welcome responsibility.

Most workers will use imagination and ingenuity in solving company problems.

As you can see, these two belief systems have a large variance, and managers who manage under the X theory may have a more difficult time retaining workers and may see higher turnover rates. As a result, it is our job in HR to provide training opportunities in the area of management, so our managers can help motivate the employees.

Training is a large part of the retention plan. This will be addressed in more detail in Section 6.3 "Implementing Retention Strategies".

Human Resource Recall

What are the disadvantages of taking a theory X approach with your employees?

Carrot and Stick

It is unknown for sure where this term was first used, although some believe it was coined in the 1700s during the Seven Years' War. In business today, the stick approach refers to "poking and prodding" to get employees to do something. The carrot approach refers to the offering of some reward or incentive to motivate employees. Many companies use the stick approach, as in the following examples:

If you don't increase your sales by 10 percent, you will be fired.

Everyone will have to take a pay cut if we don't produce 15 percent more than we are currently producing.

As you can see, the stick approach takes a punitive look at retention, and we know this may motivate for a short period of time, but not in the long-term.

The carrot approach might include the following:

If you increase sales by 10 percent, you will receive a bonus.

If production increases by 15 percent, the entire team will receive an extra day off next month.

The carrot approach takes a much more positive approach to employee motivation but still may not be effective. For example, this approach can actually demotivate employees if they do not feel the goal is achievable. Also, if organizations use this as the only motivational technique, ignoring physiological rewards such as career growth, this could be a detriment as well. This approach is used as a retention method, usually as part of a compensation plan.

Figure 2-26 Carrot Approach

Note: The carrot approach normally means some incentive will occur if expectations are met. The expectations should be attainable and shouldn't be the only method used in retention planning and turnover reduction.

All the employee satisfaction theories we have discussed have implications for the development of our retention plans and reduction of turnover. These theories can be intertwined into the specific retention strategies we will implement.

Sources of Employee Satisfaction Data

After we have an understanding of why employees leave and employee satisfaction theories, research is our next step in developing a retention plan that will work for your organization. There isn't a "one size fits all" approach to retention planning, so the research component is essential to formulate a plan that will make a difference in turnover rates.

Research can be performed in two ways. First, exit interviews of employees who are leaving the organization can provide important retention information. An exit interview is an interview performed by HR or a manager that seeks information as to what the employee liked at the organization and what they see should be improved. Exit interviews can be a valuable way to gather information about employee satisfaction and can serve as a starting point for determining any retention issues that may exist in the organization. However, the exit survey data should be reviewed over longer periods of time with several employees, so we can be sure we are not making retention plans based on the feedback of only a few people.

Sample Exit Interview Questions

1. What is your primary reason for leaving?
2. What did you like most about your job?
3. What did you like least about your job?
4. Did you feel there was room for growth in your job?
5. What incentives did you utilize while at our company?
6. Which incentives would you change and why?
7. Did you have enough training to do your job effectively?

The second way to perform research is through employee satisfaction surveys. A standardized and widely used measure of job satisfaction is the job descriptive index (JDI) survey. While JDI was initially developed in 1969 at Bowling Green State University, it has gone through extensive revisions, the most recent one in 2009. JDI looks at five aspects of job satisfaction, including present job, present pay, opportunities for promotion, supervision, and coworkers. Each of the five facets contains nine or eighteen questions; the survey can be given in whole or measure only one facet. The value of the scale is that an HR manager can measure job satisfaction over a period of time and compare current results to past results and even compare job satisfaction at their company versus their industry. This allows the HR manager to consider changes in the organization, such as a change in compensation structure, and see how job satisfaction is impacted by the change.

Any type of survey can provide information on the employee's satisfaction with their manager, workload, and other satisfaction and motivational issues. An example of a general employee satisfaction survey is shown in Figure 2-27 "A Sample Employee Satisfaction Survey". However, a few things should be considered when developing an employee satisfaction survey:

Communicate the purpose and goal of the survey.

Once the survey is complete, communicate what changes have been made as a result of the survey.

Assure employees their responses will be anonymous and private.

Involve management and leadership in the survey development.

Ask clear, concise questions that get at the root of morale issues.

Once data have been gathered and analyzed, we can formulate our retention plans. Our plan should always be tied to the strategic goals of the organization and the HPWS previously developed, and awareness of motivational theories should be coupled with the plans. Here are the components of a retention plan:

JDI survey results, other survey results, and exit interview findings.

Current retention plans, strengths, and weaknesses.

Goals of a retention plan (e.g., reduce turnover by 10 percent).

Individual strategies to meet retention and turnover reduction goals.

Budgeting. An understanding of how your retention plans will impact the payroll budget is important.

In Section 6.3 "Implementing Retention Strategies", we will discuss the implementation of specific retention strategies.

Sample Employee Satisfaction Survey/ Sample Questions for Employee Satisfaction Survey

A brief version of the larger Employee Satisfaction Survey, this questionnaire serves to obtain a brief snapshot of employee climate. Some of the topics addressed in the survey include: perception of job description, position within the company, relationships with supervisors, advancement opportunities, and overall satisfaction.

This survey asks questions about your experience working for The Company. It starts and ends with some questions about your satisfaction with various aspects of work and contains other questions about how you think and feel about The Company. Thank you for sharing your opinions.

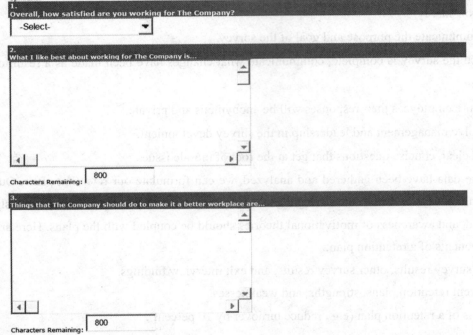

Figure 2-27 A Sample of Employee Satisfaction Survey

Source: "Sample Employee Satisfaction Surveys", Zarca Interactive, accessed August 18, 2011, http://www.zarca.com/Online-Surveys-Employee/sample-employee-surveys.html.

4.
Please indicate the extent to which you agree with the following statements:

	Disagree Completely	Strongly Disagree	Somewhat Disagree	Neither Agree Nor Disagree	Somewhat Agree	Strongly Agree	Agree Completely
(a) The company clearly conveys its mission to its employees.	○	○	○	○	○	○	○
(b) There is good communication from managers to employees.	○	○	○	○	○	○	○
(c) I have the tools and resources I need to do my job.	○	○	○	○	○	○	○
(d) I have the training I need to do my job.	○	○	○	○	○	○	○
(e) I feel underutilized in my job.	○	○	○	○	○	○	○
(f) The amount of work expected of me is reasonable.	○	○	○	○	○	○	○
(g) It is easy to get along with my colleagues.	○	○	○	○	○	○	○
(h) The morale in my department is high.	○	○	○	○	○	○	○

5.
Please indicate the extent to which you agree with the following statements.

	Disagree Completely	Strongly Disagree	Somewhat Disagree	Neither Agree Nor Disagree	Somewhat Agree	Strongly Agree	Agree Completely
(a) Overall, my supervisor does a good job.	○	○	○	○	○	○	○
(b) My supervisor promotes an atmosphere of teamwork.	○	○	○	○	○	○	○
(c) My supervisor provides me with actionable suggestions on what I can do to improve.	○	○	○	○	○	○	○
(d) When I have questions or concerns, my supervisor is able to address them.	○	○	○	○	○	○	○

6.
How satisfied are you with...

	Completely Dissatisfied	Very Dissatisfied	Somewhat Dissatisfied	Neutral	Somewhat Satisfied	Very Satisfied	Completely Satisfied
(a) your pay?	○	○	○	○	○	○	○
(b) your career progression at the company thus far?	○	○	○	○	○	○	○
(c) benefits offered by the company?	○	○	○	○	○	○	○
(d) the process used to determine annual raises?	○	○	○	○	○	○	○

Continued

7.
What is your current position?

○

Position 1

○

Position 2

○

Position 3

○

Position 4

○

Position 5

8.
In which department do you work?

○

Department 1

○

Department 2

○

Department 3

○

Department 4

○

Department 5

9.
How many years have you been with the company?

○

Less than a year

○

1－3 years

○

4－6 years

○

More than six years

Continued

Continued

10.
What is your primary work location?

○
Location 1

○
Location 2

○
Location 3

○
Location 4

○
Location 5

11.
What is your gender?

○
Male

○
Female

12.
What is your age?

○
18 – 29

○
30 – 39

○
40 – 55

○
55+ years

Sample Employee Satisfaction Survey Questions by Zarca Interactive

Key Takeaways

A high-performance work system (HPWS) is a set of systematic HR practices that create an environment where the employee has greater involvement and responsibility for the success of the organization. The overall company strategy should impact the HPWS HR develops in regard to retention.

Retention plans are developed to address employee turnover, resulting in a more effective organization.

The first step in developing a retention plan is to use exit interviews and/or surveys to find out the satisfaction level of employees. Once you have the data, you can begin to write the plan, making sure it is tied to the organizational objectives.

A standardized and widely used measure of job satisfaction is the JDI survey, or the *Job Descriptive Index*. While JDI was initially developed in 1969 at Bowling Green State University, it has gone through extensive revisions, the most recent one in 2009. JDI looks at five aspects of job satisfaction, including present job, present pay, opportunities for promotion, supervision, and coworkers.

There are many motivation theories that attempt to explain people's motivation or lack of motivation at work.

The Hawthorne studies were a series of studies beginning in 1927 that initially looked at physical environments but found that people tended to be more motivated when they felt cared about. The implications to retention are clear, in that employees should feel cared about and developed within the organization.

Maslow's theory on motivation says that if someone already has a need met, giving them something to meet more of that need will no longer motivate. Maslow divided the needs into physiological, safety, social, esteem, and self-actualization needs. Many companies only motivate based on the low-level needs, such as pay. Development of training opportunities, for example, can motivate employees on high-level self-actualization needs.

Herzberg developed motivational theories based on actual motivation factors and hygiene factors. Hygiene factors are those things that are expected in the workplace and will demotivate employees when absent but will not actually motivate when present. If managers try to motivate only on the basis of hygiene factors, turnover can be high. Motivation on both of his factors is key to a good retention plan.

McGregor's theory on motivation looked at managers' attitudes toward employees. He found that theory X managers had more of a negative view of employees, while theory Y managers had a more positive view. Providing training to the managers in our organization can be a key retention strategy based on McGregor's theory.

The carrot-and-stick approach means you can get someone to do something by prodding or by offering some incentive to motivate them to do the work. This theory implies these are the only two methods to motivate, which of course, we know isn't true. The implication of this in our retention plan is such that we must utilize a variety of methods to retain employees.

Exercises

1. What types of things will motivate you in your career? Name at least five things. Where would these fit on Maslow's hierarchy of needs and Herzberg's two-factor theory?

2. How can you apply each of these motivation techniques to motivation theories?

Training

Employee recognition programs

Bonuses

Management training for your current managers

Profit sharing

6.3 Implementing Retention Strategies

Learning Objective

Explain the strategies and considerations in development of a retention plan.

As we have addressed so far in this chapter, retention and reduction of turnover is paramount to a healthy organization. Performing research, such as calculating turnover rates, doing exit interviews, and surveying employees' satisfaction, are the first steps. Once this is done, understanding motivational theories and the application of them in the retention plan can help reduce turnover. Next, we can apply specific retention strategies to include in our plans, while keeping our budget in mind. Some of the retention strategies discussed have already or will be discussed in their own chapters, but they are certainly worth a mention here as part of the overall plan.

Salaries and Benefits

As we know from Chapter 5 "Compensation and Benefits", a comprehensive compensation plan that includes not only pay but things such as health benefits and paid time off (PTO) is the first retention strategy that should be addressed. The compensation plan should not only help in recruitment of the right people but also help retain employees. Utilizing a pay banding system, in which the levels of compensation for jobs are clearly defined, is one way to ensure fairness exists within internal pay structures.

As we know from this chapter, compensation is not everything. An employee can be well paid and have great benefits but still not be satisfied with the organization. Some of the considerations surrounding pay as a way to retain employees include the following:

Instituting a standard process. Many organizations do not have set pay plans, which can result in unfairness when onboarding (the process of bringing someone "on board" with the company, including discussion and negotiation of compensation) or offering pay increases. Make sure the process for receiving pay raises is fair and defensible, so as not to appear to be discriminatory. This can be addressed in both your compensation planning process as well as your retention plan.

A pay communication strategy. Employees deserve to know how their pay rates are being determined. Transparency in the process of how raises are given and then communicating the process can help in your retention planning process.

Paid time off. Is your organization offering competitive PTO? Consider implementing a PTO system that is based on the amount of hours an employee works. For example, rather than developing a policy based on hours worked for the company, consider revising the policy so that for every X number of hours worked, PTO is earned. This can create fairness for the salaried employee, especially for those employees who may work more than the required forty hours.

Please refer to Chapter 5 "Compensation and Benefits" for more information on pay and benefits, and analyze how your compensation plans could be negatively affecting your retention.

Training and Development

To meet our higher level needs, humans need to experience self-growth. HR professionals and managers can help this process by offering training programs within the organization and paying for employees to attend career skill seminars and programs. In addition, many companies offer tuition reimbursement programs to help the employee earn a degree. Dick's Drive-In, a local fast food restaurant in Seattle, Washington, offers $18,000 in scholarships over four years to employees working twenty hours per week. There is a six-month waiting period, and the employee must continue to work twenty hours per week. In a high turnover industry, Dick's Drive-In boasts one of the highest retention rates around.

How Would You Handle This?

You work for a small organization in the HR department. One of your web developers schedules a meeting with you, and during the meeting she says that she doesn't see any career growth for her in the organization. As a result, she confides that she is planning to leave the organization as soon as she can find another job. She is one of the best developers you have and you would hate to lose her.

The author discusses the "How Would You Handle This" situation in this chapter at: https://api.wistia.com/v1/ medias/1348713/embed.

Performance Appraisals

Chapter 8 "Employee Assessment", addresses performance appraisals. The performance appraisal is a formalized process to assess how well an employee does his or her job. The effectiveness of this process can contribute to employee retention, in that employees can gain constructive feedback on their job performance, and it can be an opportunity for the manager to work with the employee to set goals within the organization. This process can help ensure the employee's upper level self-actualization needs are met, but it also can address some of the motivational factors discussed by Herzberg, such as achievement, recognition, and responsibility.

Human Resource Recall

How important is PTO to you? How do you think the amount of PTO would affect your likelihood to accept one job over another?

Succession Planning

Succession planning is a process of identifying and developing internal people who have the potential for filling positions. As we know, many people leave organizations because they do not see career growth or potential. One way we can combat this in our retention plan is to make sure we have a clear succession planning process that is communicated to employees. Succession planning is sometimes called the talent bench, because successful companies always have talented people "on the bench" or ready to do the job should a key position become vacant. The goals of most succession plans include the following (Rothwell & Kazanas, 1999):

Identify high-potential employees capable of advancing to positions of higher responsibility.

Ensure the development of these individuals to help them be "ready" to earn a promotion into a new position.

Ensure diversity in the talent bench by creating a formal succession planning process.

Succession planning must be just that: planned. This allows clear communication to the employees on how they can further develop within the organization, and it helps them see what skills they should master before that time comes. Chapter 7 "Training and Development" will provide more information on how to develop and implement a succession plan.

Flextime, Telecommuting, and Sabbaticals

According to a Salary.com survey, the ability to work from home and flexible work schedules are benefits that would entice an employee to stay in their job. The ability to implement this type of retention strategy might be difficult, depending on the type of business. For example, a retailer may not be able to implement this, since the sales associate must be in the store to assist customers.

Some companies, such as Recreational Equipment Incorporated, based in Seattle, offer twelve weeks of unpaid leave per year (beyond the twelve weeks required under the *Family and Medical Leave Act*) for the employee to pursue volunteering or traveling opportunities. In addition, with fifteen years of service with the company, paid sabbaticals are offered, which include four weeks plus already earned vacation time.

Management Training

A manager can affect an employee's willingness to stay on the job. In a recent Gallup poll of one million workers, a poor supervisor or manager is the number one reason why people leave their jobs. Managers who bully, use the theory X approach, communicate poorly, or are incompetent may find it difficult to motivate employees to stay within the organization. While in HR we cannot control a manager's behavior, we can provide training to create better management. Training of managers to be better communicators and motivators is a way to handle this retention issue. We will discuss training further in Chapter 7 "Training and Development".

Conflict Management and Fairness

Perceptions on fairness and how organizations handle conflict can be a contributing factor to retention. Outcome fairness refers to the judgment that people make with respect to the outcomes they receive versus the outcomes received by others with whom they associate with. When people are deciding if something is fair, they will likely look at procedural justice, or the process used to determine the outcomes received. There are six main areas employees will use to determine the outcome fairness of a conflict:

Consistency. The employee will determine if the procedures are applied consistently to other persons and throughout periods of time.

Bias suppression. The employee perceives the person making the decision does not have bias or vested interest in the outcome.

Information accuracy. The decision made is based on correct information.

Correctability. The decision is able to be appealed and mistakes in the decision process can be corrected.

Representativeness. The employee feels the concerns of all stakeholders involved have been taken into account.

Ethicality. The decision is in line with moral societal standards.

For example, let's suppose Joann just received a bonus and recognition at the company party for her contributions to an important company project. Another employee, Sam, might compare his inputs and outputs and determine it was unfair that Joann was recognized because he had worked on bigger projects and not received the same recognition or bonus. When we look at how our retention strategies are developed, we want to be sure they can apply to everyone in the organization; otherwise it may cause retention problems. Some of the procedures questioned could include the following:

How time off is requested

How assignments of the "best" projects are given

Division of work

Promotion processes

Pay processes

While some of these policies may seem minor, they can make a big difference in retention. Besides development of fair policies, we should be sure that the policies are clearly communicated and any processes are communicated as well. These types of policies should be revisited yearly and addressed in the retention plan if it appears they are causing employee dissatisfaction.

In addition to a sense of fairness within the organization, there should be a specific way (process) of managing conflict. If the organization is unionized, it is likely a grievance process is already in place to handle many types of conflicts. We will discuss this process in greater detail in Chapter 9 "Working with Labor Unions". There are four basic steps to handle conflict. First, the individuals in conflict should try to handle the conflict by discussing the problem with one another. If this doesn't work, a panel of representatives from the organization should hear both sides of the dispute and make a recommendation. If this doesn't work, the organization may want to consider mediation, and in extreme cases—arbitration. In mediation, a neutral third party from outside the organization hears both sides of a dispute and tries to get the parties to come to a resolution, while in arbitration, an outside person hears both sides and makes a specific decision about how things should proceed.

Fortune 500 Focus

With over nineteen thousand employees in sixty countries, Google has seen its share of retention problems. In late 2010, Googlers left the organization En Masse to work for Facebook or Twitter (Popper, 2010). Many who left were looking for pre–initial public offering (IPO) organizations to work with, something that Google couldn't compete with, since it went IPO in April 2004. As a result of the high turnover, Google put its mathematical algorithms to work to determine which employees were most likely to leave, allowing HR to determine what departments to focus on in their retention plans. In 2011, Google gave every employee a 10 percent pay raise, and it continues to offer a variety of new and old perks, such as free food in any of its cafeterias, 20 percent of time to work on personal projects, and $175 peer spot bonuses. Google also offers free laundry services, climbing walls, tuition reimbursement, childcare centers, financial planning classes, and matching funds (up to $3,000 per employee) to non-profit organizations. For all this, Google ranked number four on *Fortune* magazine's list of 100 best companies to work for in 2015. Some say it isn't the perks, high pay, or bonuses but the company culture that Google creates. A weekly all-hands meeting with the founders, where people are encouraged to ask the founders questions, and a team focus meeting where everyone shares ideas are examples of the company culture Google creates. Google exemplifies the importance of culture in retention of employees.

Job Design, Job Enlargement, and Empowerment

As we have discussed previously, one of the reasons for job dissatisfaction is the job itself. Ensuring we are appropriately matching skills with the job when we do our initial hiring is important. Revisiting the recruitment plan and selection process should be a consideration.

Job enrichment means to enhance a job by adding more meaningful tasks to make the employee's work more rewarding. For example, if a retail salesperson is good at creating eye-catching displays, allow him or her to practice this skill and assign tasks revolving around this. Job enrichment can fulfill the higher level of human needs while creating job satisfaction at the same time. In fact, research in this area by Richard Hackman and Greg Oldham (Ford, 1969; Paul, et. al., 1969) found that employees need the following to achieve job satisfaction:

Skill variety, or many different activities as part of the job.

Task identity, or being able to complete one task from beginning to end.

Task significance, or the degree to which the job has impact on others, internally or externally.

Autonomy, or freedom to make decisions within the job.

Feedback, or clear information about performance.

In addition, job enlargement, defined as the adding of new challenges or responsibilities to a current job, can create job satisfaction. Assigning employees to a special project or task is an example of job enlargement. Be cautioned, though, that some employees may resent additional work, and job enlargement could actually be a demotivator. Otherwise, knowing the employee and his or her goals and adding work that can be an end to these goals is the best way to achieve retention through job enlargement.

Figure 2-28 Company Benifits

Note: Some companies offer unique benefits to reduce turnover. An on-site yoga class is an example of a unique, although expensive, benefit to consider including in a retention plan.

Employee empowerment involves employees in their work by allowing them to make decisions and act upon those decisions, with the support of the organization. Employees who are not micromanaged and who have the power to determine the sequence of their own work day, for example, tend to be more satisfied than those who are not empowered. Empowerment can include the following:

Encourage innovation or new ways of doing things.

Make sure employees have the information they need to do their jobs; for example, they are not dependent on managers for information in decision-making.

Use management styles that allow for participation, feedback, and ideas from employees.

Pay-for-Performance Strategies

In Chapter 5 "Compensation and Benefits", we discussed several pay-for-performance strategies we can implement to motivate our employees. A pay-for-performance strategy means that employees are rewarded for meeting preset objectives within the organization. For example, in a merit-based pay system, the employee is rewarded for meeting or exceeding performance during a given time period. Rather than a set pay increase every year, the increase is based on performance. Some organizations offer bonuses to employees for meeting objectives, while some organizations offer team incentive pay if a team achieves a specific, predetermined outcome. For example, each player on the winning team of the 2010 NFL Super Bowl earned a team bonus of $83,000 (Rovell, 2011), while the losing team of the Super Bowl took home $42,000. Players also earn money for each wild card game and payoff game. Some organizations also offer profit sharing, which is tied to a company's overall performance. Gain sharing, different from profit sharing, focuses on improvement of productivity within the organization. For example, the city of Loveland in Colorado implemented a gain-sharing program that defined three criteria that needed to be met for employees to be given extra compensation. The city revenues had to exceed expenses, expenses had to be equal to or less than the previous year's expenses, and a citizen satisfaction survey had to meet minimum requirements.

To make sure a pay-for-performance system works, the organization needs to ensure the following:

Standards are specific and measureable.

The system is applied fairly to all employees.

The system is communicated clearly to employees.

The best work from everyone in the organization is encouraged.

Rewards are given to performers versus non-performers.

The system is updated as the business climate changes.

There are substantial rewards for high performers.

As we have already addressed, pay isn't everything, but it certainly can be an important part of the employee retention plan and strategy.

Work-Life Balance

Work-life balance discussions originated during the 1960s and 1970s and pertained mostly to working mothers' meeting the demands of family and work. During the 1980s, the realization that meeting a work-life balance is important (for all, not just working mothers) resulted in companies such as IBM implementing flextime and home-based work solutions. The growing awareness of the work-life balance problem continued into the 1990s, when policies were developed and implemented but not acted upon by managers and employees, according to Jim Bird in *Employment Relations Today* (Bird, 2006). Today, work-life balance is considered an important topic, so much so that the World at Work Society offers special certifications in this area. The World at Work certification programs focus on creation of successful programs to attract, retain, and motivate employees.

Karol Rose, author of *Work Life Effectiveness* (Rose, 2006), says that most companies look at a systems approach of work-life balance, instead of a systems and individual approach. The systems approach to work-life balance includes policies and procedures that allow people flexibility, such as telecommuting and flextime options.

According to Rose, looking at the individual differences is equally as important as the systems approach. Brad Harrington, the director of Boston College's Center for Work and Family, stresses this issue: "Work-life balance comes down, not to an organizational strategy, but to an individual strategy." For example, a single parent has a different work-life balance need than someone without children. In other words, as HR professionals, we can create work-life balance systems, but we should also look at individual approaches. For example, at Recreational Equipment Incorporated (REI), they use the systems approach perspective and offer paid time off and sabbaticals, but their employee assistance program also offers access to services, referrals, and free consulting for the individual to find his or her perfect work-life balance. For this, REI receives a number nine ranking on *Fortune*'s list of best companies to work for in the area of work-life balance.

The company culture can contribute greatly to work-life balance. Some organizations have a culture of flexibility that fares well for workers who do not want to feel tethered to an office, while some workers prefer to be in the office where more informal socializing can occur. While some companies promote work-life balance on paper, upper management needs to let employees know it is OK to take advantage of the alternatives to create a positive work-life balance. For example, companies place different levels of value on work-life options such as telecommuting. An organization may have a telecommuting option, but the employees must feel it is OK to use these options. Even in a company that has work-life balance systems, a manager who sends e-mails at 10 p.m. on Saturday night could be sending the wrong message to employees about the expectations, creating an environment in which work-life balance is not practiced in reality. O'Neill, a surf gear company in California, sends a strong message to its employees by offering half-day Fridays during the summer, so employees can get a head start on the weekend.

Jim Bird, in his work-life balance article in *Employment Relations Today*, suggests implementing a work-life balance training program that is dual purpose (can serve both personal interests and professional development). In other words, implement trainings in which the employee can develop both personal skills and interests that can translate into higher productivity at work.

Besides the training program, Bird suggests creating a monthly work-life newsletter as an educational tool to show the company's commitment to work-life balance. The newsletter can include interviews from respected employees and tips on how to create a work-life balance.

Finally, training managers on the importance of work-life balance and how to create a culture that embraces this is a key way to use work-life balance as a retention strategy.

Other Retention Strategies

According to *Fortune* 's "100 Best Companies to Work For", retention strategies that are more unusual might be part of your retention plan. Some strategies from the list might include the following:

On-site daycare or daycare assistance

Gym memberships or on-site gyms

Concierge service to assist in party planning or dog grooming

On-site dry cleaning drop-off and pickup

Car care, such as oil changes, on-site once a week

On-site doggie daycare

On-site yoga or other fitness classes

"Summer Fridays", when all employees work half days on Fridays during the summer

Various support groups for cancer survivors, weight loss, or support in caring for aging parents

Allowance for fertility treatment benefits

On-site life coaches

Peer-to-peer employee recognition programs

Management recognition programs

While some of these options may not work in your organization, we must remember to be creative when our goal is to retain our best employees and reduce turnover in our organizations. The bottom line is to create a plan and make sure the plan is communicated to all employees.

Key Takeaways

Once you determine the employee's level of satisfaction through exit interviews and surveys and understand motivational theories, you can begin to develop specific retention strategies.

Of course, salary and benefits are a major component of retention strategies. Consistent pay systems and transparent processes as to how raises occur must be included in a retention plan (and compensation strategy).

Training and development meets the higher level needs of the individual. Many companies offer paid tuition programs, reimbursement programs, and in-house training to increase the skills and knowledge of the employee.

Succession plans allow employees to see how they can continue their career with the organization, and they clearly detail what employees need to do to achieve career growth, without leaving your organization.

Flextime and telecommuting options are worth considering as an addition to your retention plan. These types of plans allow the employee flexibility when developing his or her schedule and some control of his or her work. Some companies also offer paid or unpaid sabbaticals after a certain number of years with the company to pursue personal interests.

Since one of the reasons people are dissatisfied at their job is because of the relationship with their manager, providing in-house training to all management team members to help them become better communicators and better managers can trickle down to the employee level, creating better relationships and resulting in better retention and less turnover.

Reviewing company policies to ensure they are fair can contribute to better retention. For example, how projects are assigned or the process for requesting vacation time can contribute to dissatisfaction if the employee feels the processes are not fair.

Review the job design to ensure the employee is experiencing growth within their job. Changing the job through empowerment or job enlargement to help the growth of the employee can create better retention.

Other, more unique ways of retaining employees might include offering services to make the employee's life easier, such as dry cleaning, daycare services, or on-site yoga classes.

Exercise

Research two different companies you might be interested in working for. When reviewing their list of benefits, which ones are offered that might motivate someone to stay with the organization?

6.4 Cases and Problems

Chapter Summary

Retaining employees is an important component to a healthy organization. Losing an employee is called turnover.

Direct turnover costs and indirect turnover costs can include the costs associated with employee replacement, declining employee morale, or lost customers.

A high-performance work system (HPWS) is a set of systematic HR practices that create an environment where the employee has greater involvement and responsibility for the success of the organization. The overall company strategy should impact the HPWS HR develops in regard to retention.

Retention plans are developed to address employee turnover, resulting in a more effective organization.

Some of the reasons why employees leave can include a poor match between job and skills, no growth potential, pay inequity among employees, the fairness and communication style of management, and heavy workloads.

The first step in developing a retention plan is to use exit interviews and/or surveys to find out the satisfaction level of employees. Once you have the data, you can begin to write the plan, making sure it is tied to the organizational objectives.

A retention plan normally consists of survey and exit interview analysis, any current plans and strengths and weaknesses of those plans, the goal of the retention plan, and the specific strategies to be implemented.

There are many motivation theories that attempt to explain people's motivation or lack of motivation at work.

The Hawthorne studies were a series of studies beginning in 1927 that initially looked at physical environments but found that people tended to be more motivated when they felt cared about. The implications to retention are clear, in that employees should feel cared about and developed within the organization.

Maslow's theory on motivation says that if someone already has a need met, giving them something to meet more of that need will no longer motivate. Maslow divided the needs into physiological, safety, social, esteem, and self-actualization needs. Many companies only motivate based on the low-level needs, such as pay. Development of training opportunities, for example, can motivate employees on high-level self-actualization needs.

Herzberg developed motivational theories based on actual motivation factors and hygiene factors. Hygiene factors are those things that are expected in the workplace and will demotivate employees when absent but will not actually motivate when present. If managers try to motivate only on the basis of hygiene factors, turnover can be high. Motivation on both factors is key to a good retention plan.

McGregor's theory on motivation looked at managers' attitudes toward employees. He found that theory X managers had more of a negative view of employees, while theory Y managers had a more positive view. Providing training to the managers in our organization can be a key retention strategy, based on McGregor's theory.

The carrot-and-stick approach means you can get someone to do something by prodding or offering some incentive to motivate them to do the work. This theory implies these are the only two methods to motivate, which we know isn't true. The implication of this in our retention plan is such that we must utilize a variety of methods to retain employees.

Once you determine the employee's level of satisfaction through exit interviews and surveys and understand motivational theories, you can develop specific retention strategies.

Of course, salary and benefits are a major component of retention strategies. Consistent pay systems and transparent processes as to how raises occur must be included in a retention plan (and compensation strategy).

Training and development meets the higher level needs of the individual. Many companies offer paid tuition programs, reimbursement programs, and in-house training to increase the skills and knowledge of the employee.

Performance appraisals provide an avenue for feedback and goal setting. They also allow for employees to be recognized for their contributions.

Succession plans allow employees to see how they can continue their career with the organization, and they clearly detail what employees need to do to achieve career growth-without leaving your organization.

Flextime and telecommuting options are worth considering as an addition to your retention plan. These types of plans allow the employee flexibility when developing his or her schedule and some control of his or her work. Some companies also offer paid or unpaid sabbaticals after a certain number of years with the company to pursue personal interests.

Since one of the reasons people are dissatisfied at their job is because of the relationship with their manager, providing in-house training to all management team members to help them become better communicators and better managers can trickle down to the employee level, creating better relationships and resulting in better retention and less turnover.

Reviewing company policies to ensure they are fair can contribute to better retention. For example, how projects are assigned or the process for requesting vacation time can contribute to dissatisfaction if the employee feels the processes are not fair.

Other, more unique ways of retaining employees might include offering services to make the employee's life easier, such as dry cleaning, daycare services, or on-site yoga classes.

Chapter Case

Turnover Analysis

You recently completed your company's new compensation plan. You are happy with the results but know there is more to retaining the employees than just pay, and you don't currently have a retention plan. Your organization is a large staffing firm, consisting of several offices on the West Coast. The majority of employees are staffing recruiters, and they fill full-time and temporary positions for a variety of clients. One of the challenges you face is a difference in geographical areas, and as a result, there are differences in what may motivate employees.

As you initially look at turnover numbers, you have the sense that turnover has increased over the last six months. Your initial thoughts are the need for a better retention strategy, utilizing a bonus structure as well as other methods of retention. Currently, your organization pays a straight salary to employees, does not offer flextime or telecommuting options, focuses on individual performance (number of staffing placements) rather than team performance, and provides five days of vacation for every two years with the organization.

Month	Separated Employees	Total Number of Employees Midmonth
March	12	552
April	14	541
May	16	539
June	20	548
July	22	545

Calculate monthly turnover for the past six months.

What are the possible reasons for turnover in your organization and other organizations?

What steps would you take to remedy the situation?

Following is a list of some possible retention strategies. Rank each one in order of importance to you as an employee (1 being the most important), then share your rankings with classmates:

Salary

Opportunity for bonuses, profit sharing

Benefits

Opportunity to grow professionally with the organization

Team bonuses

More paid time off

Option to telecommute

Flextime scheduling

Sense of empowerment

Tuition reimbursement

Job satisfaction

Chapter 7 Training and Development

Training: Not Like it Used to Be

Imagine this: You have a pile of work on your desk and as you get started, your Outlook calendar reminds you about a sexual harassment training in ten minutes. You groan to yourself, not looking forward to sitting in a conference room and seeing PowerPoint slide after PowerPoint slide. As you walk to the conference room, you run into a colleague who is taking the same training that day and commiserate on how boring this training is probably going to be. When you step into the conference room, however, you see something very different.

Computers are set up at every chair with a video ready to start on the computer. The HR manager greets you and asks you to take a seat. When the training starts, you are introduced (via video) on each of the computers to a series of sexual harassment example scenarios. The videos stop, and there is a recorded discussion about what the videos portrayed. Your colleagues in the Washington, D.C., office are able to see the same training and via video conferencing, are able to participate in the discussions. It is highly interactive and interesting. Once the training is finished, there are assignments to be completed via specific channels that have been set up for this training. You communicate about the material and complete the assignments in teams with members of your Washington, D.C., office. If you want to review the material, you simply click on a review and the entire session or parts of the training can be reviewed. In fact, on your bus ride home from work, you access the channels on your iPhone, chatting with a colleague in your other office about the sexual harassment training assignment you have due next week. You receive an e-mail from your HR manager asking you to complete a training assessment located in a specific channel in the software, and you happily comply because you have an entirely new perspective on what training can be.

This is the training of today. No longer do people sit in hot, stuffy rooms to get training on boring content. Training has become highly interactive, technical, and interesting owing to the amount of multimedia we can use. Sun Microsystems, for example, has developed just the kind of software mentioned above, called Social Learning eXchange (SLX). This type of training allows people across the country to connect with each other, saving both money and time. In fact, Sun Microsystems received a Best Practices Award from *Training Magazine* for this innovative software in 2010. The SLX software allows training to be delivered in an interactive manner in multiple locations. The implications of this type of software are numerous. For example, SLX is used at Sun Professional Services division by delivering instructional videos on tools and software, which employees can view at their own pace. There is also a channel in the software that allows the vice-president to communicate with employees on a regular basis to improve employee communications. In another example, this software can be used to quickly communicate product changes to the sales team, who then begin the process of positioning their products to consumers. Training videos, including breakout sessions, can save companies money by not requiring travel to a session. These can even be accessed using application technology on cell phones. Employees can obtain the training they need in the comfort of their own city, office, or home. Someone is sick the day the training is delivered? No problem; they can review the recorded training sessions.

An estimated $1,400 per employee is spent on training annually, with training costs consuming 2.72 percent of the total payroll budget for the average company. With such a large amount of funds at stake, HR managers must develop the right training programs to meet the needs; otherwise, these funds are virtually wasted. This chapter is all about how to assess, develop, implement, and measure an effective training program.

7.1 Steps to Take in Training an Employee

Learning Objective

Explain the four steps involved when training an employee.

Any effective company has training in place to make sure employees can perform his or her job. During the recruitment and selection process, the right person should be hired to begin with. But even the right person may need training in how your company does things. Lack of training can result in lost productivity, lost customers, and poor relationships between employees and managers. It can also result in dissatisfaction, which means retention problems and high turnover. All these end up being direct costs to the organization. In fact, a study performed by the American Society for Training and Development (ASTD) found that 41 percent of employees at companies with poor training planned to leave within the year, but in companies with excellent training, only 12 percent planned to leave (Branham, 2005). To reduce some costs associated with not training or undertraining, development of training programs can help with some of the risk. This is what this chapter will address.

For effective employee training, there are four steps that generally occur. First, the new employee goes through an orientation, and then he or she will receive in-house training on job-specific areas. Next, the employee should be assigned a mentor, and then, as comfort with the job duties grows, he or she may engage in external training. Employee training and development is the process of helping employees develop their personal and organization skills, knowledge, and abilities.

Employee Orientation

The first step in training is an employee orientation. Employee orientation is the process used for welcoming a new employee into the organization. The importance of employee orientation is two-fold. First, the goal is for employees to gain an understanding of the company policies and learn how their specific job fits into the big picture. Employee orientation usually involves filling out employee paperwork such as I-9 and 401(k) program forms.

The goals of an orientation are as follows:

To reduce start-up costs. If an orientation is done right, it can help get the employee up to speed on various policies and procedures, so the employee can start working right away. It can also be a way to ensure all hiring paperwork is filled out correctly, so the employee is paid on time.

To reduce anxiety. Starting a new job can be stressful. One goal of an orientation is to reduce the stress and anxiety people feel when going into an unknown situation.

To reduce employee turnover. Employee turnover tends to be higher when employees don't feel valued or are not given the tools to perform. An employee orientation can show that the organization values the employee and provides tools necessary for a successful entry.

To save time for the supervisor and coworkers. A well-done orientation makes for a better prepared employee, which means less time having to teach the employee.

To set expectations and attitudes. If employees know from the start what the expectations are, they tend to perform better. Likewise, if employees learn the values and attitudes of the organization from the beginning, there is a higher chance of a successful tenure at the company.

Some companies use employee orientation as a way to introduce employees not only to the company policies and procedures but also to the staff. For an example of an orientation schedule for the day, see Figure 2-29.

Schedule

Below you find the planned schedule for New Employee Orientation. Following the topic are the beginning and ending times and the topic's duration.

Topic	Start Time	End Time	Duration
Introduction	7:30 AM	8:05 AM	35 min
Welcome Video	8:05 AM	8:20 AM	15 min
Form Completion/Oath	8:20 AM	8:55 AM	35 min
Management Welcome & Mission/Philosophy	8:55 AM	9:10 AM	15 min
Payroll	9:10 AM	9:25 AM	15 min
BREAK	9:25 AM	9:40 AM	15 min
Personnel Health (TB Test)	9:40 AM	10:10 AM	30 min
Patient Privacy Training/HIPPA	10:10AM	10:20 AM	10 min
Union	10:20 AM	10:50 AM	30 min
Police Briefing	10:50 AM	11:05 AM	15 min
ID Badges	11:05 AM	11:45 AM	40 min
LUNCH	11:45 AM	12:15 PM	30 min
Employee Responsibility and Conduct	12:15 PM	12:45 PM	30 min
Information Security	12:45 PM	1:00 PM	15 min
Benefits (*See remarks below)	1:00 PM	2:30 PM	1.5 hr
BREAK (P&R Form Completion)	2:30 PM	2:45 PM	15 min
Computer Orientation	2:45 PM	4:00 PM	1 hr 15 min
Student Programs/Career Development	2:45 PM	4:00 PM	1 hr 15 min

*All Employees **NOT** receiving Benefits will attend Computer Orientation from 1:00 PM to 2:30 PM then from 2:45 PM to 4:00 PM. Information sessions on Student Programs and Career Development are by an HR Staff member.

Beverage will be served in the morning and a box lunch will be served at lunchtime.

Figure 2-29 New Employee Orieentation Schedule

Note: Some companies have very specific orientations, with a variety of people providing information to the new hires. This can create a welcoming environment, besides giving the employee the information they need. This is an example of one such orientation.

Source: Sample schedule courtesy of Louis Stokes Cleveland VA Medical Center, http://www.cleveland.va.gov/docs/NEOSchedule.pdf, accessed September 2, 2011.

Human Resource Recall

Have you ever participated in an orientation? What was it like? What components did it have?

In-House Training

In-house training programs are learning opportunities developed by the organization in which they are used. This is usually the second step in the training process and often is ongoing. In-house training programs can be training related to a specific job, such as how to use a particular kind of software. In a manufacturing setting, in-house training might include an employee learning how to use a particular kind of machinery.

Many companies provide in-house training on various HR topics as well, meaning it doesn't always have to relate to a specific job. Some examples of in-house training include the following:

Ethics training

Sexual harassment training

Multicultural training

Communication training

Management training

Customer service training

Operation of special equipment

Training to do the job itself

Basic skills training

As you can tell by the list of topics, HR might sometimes create and deliver this training, but often a supervisor or manager delivers the training.

Mentoring

After the employee has completed orientation and in-house training, companies see the value in offering mentoring opportunities as the next step in training. Sometimes a mentor may be assigned during in-house training. A mentor is a trusted, experienced advisor who has direct investment in the development of an employee. A mentor may be a supervisor, but often a mentor is a colleague who has the experience and personality to help guide someone through processes. While mentoring may occur informally, a mentorship program can help ensure the new employee not only feels welcomed but is paired up with someone who already knows the ropes and can help guide the new employee through any on-the-job challenges.

To work effectively, a mentoring program should become part of the company culture; in other words, new mentors should receive in-house training to be a mentor. Mentors are selected based on experience, willingness, and personality. IBM's Integrated Supply Chain Division, for example, has successfully implemented a mentorship program. The company's division boasts 19,000 employees and half of IBM's revenues, making management of a mentorship program challenging. However, potential mentors are trained and put into a database where new employees can search attributes and strengths of mentors and choose the person who closely meets their needs. Then the mentor and mentee work together in development of the new employee. "We view this as a best practice," says Patricia Lewis-Burton, vice-president of human resources, Integrated Supply Chain Division. "We view it as something that is not left to human resources alone. In fact, the program is imbedded in the way our group does business." (Witt, 2005)

Figure 2-30 In-house Training

Note: In-house training occurs when someone from within the company is delivering the training information, while external training is usually delivered by someone who does not work for the company and is not physically on-site.

Some companies use short-term mentorship programs because they find employees training other employees to be valuable for all involved. Starbucks, for example, utilizes this approach. When it opens a new store in a new market, a team of experienced store managers and baristas are sent from existing stores to the new stores to lead the store-opening efforts, including training of new employees.

External Training

External training includes any type of training that is not performed in-house. This is usually the last step in training, and it can be ongoing. It can include sending an employee to a seminar to help further develop leadership skills or helping pay tuition for an employee who wants to take a marketing class. To be a Ford automotive technician, for example, you must attend the Ford ASSET Program, which is a partnership between Ford Motor Company, Ford dealers, and select technical schools.

How Would You Handle This?

To Train or Not to Train

Towanda Michaels is the human resource manager at a medium-size pet supply wholesaler. Casey Cleps is a salesperson at the organization and an invaluable member of the team. Last year, his sales brought in about 20 percent of the company revenue alone. Everybody likes Casey: he is friendly, competent, and professional.

Training is an important part of the company, and an e-mail was sent last month that said if employees do not complete the required safety training by July 1, they would be let go.

It is July 15, and it has just come to Towanda's attention that Casey has not completed the online safety training that is required for his job. When she approaches him about it, he says, "I am the best salesperson here; I can't waste time doing training. I already know all the safety rules anyway."

Would you let Casey go, as stated in the e-mail? How would you handle this?

The author discusses the "How Would You Handle This" situation in this chapter at: https://api.wistia.com/v1/ medias/1348781/embed.

Key Takeaways

Employee training and development is the framework for helping employees develop their personal and organizational skills, knowledge, and abilities. Training is important to employee retention.

There are four steps in training that should occur. Employee orientation has the purpose of welcoming new employees into the organization. An effective employee orientation can help reduce start-up costs, reduce anxiety for the employee, reduce turnover, save time for the supervisor and colleagues, and set expectations and attitudes.

An in-house training program is any type of program in which the training is delivered by someone who works for the company. This could include management or HR. Examples might include sexual harassment training or ethics training. In-house training can also include components specific to a job, such as how to use a specific kind of software. In-house training is normally done as a second and ongoing step in employee development.

A mentor form of training pairs a new employee with a seasoned employee. This is usually the third step in employee training. A mentor program for training should include a formalized program and process.

External training is any type of training not performed in-house; part of the last training step, external training can also be ongoing. It can include sending employees to conferences or seminars for leadership development or even paying tuition for a class they want to take.

Exercises

1. Why do you think some companies do not follow the four training steps? What are the advantages of doing so?

2. What qualities do you think a mentor should have? List at least five.

3. Have you ever worked with a mentor in a job, at school, or in extracurricular activities? Describe your experience.

7.2 Types of Training

Learning Objective

Be able to explain and give examples of the types of training that can be offered within an organization.

There are a number of different types of training we can use to engage an employee. These types are usually used in all steps in a training process (orientation, in-house, mentorship, and external training). The training utilized depends on the amount of resources available for training, the type of company, and the priority the company places on training. Companies such as The Cheesecake Factory, a family restaurant, make training a high priority. The company spends an average of $2,000 per hourly employee. This includes everyone from the dishwasher and managers to the servers. For The Cheesecake Factory, this expenditure has paid off. They measure the effectiveness of its training by looking at turnover, which is 15 percent below the industry average (Ruiz, 2006). Servers make up 40 percent of the workforce and spend two weeks training to obtain certification. Thirty days later, they receive follow-up classes, and when the menu changes, they receive additional training (Ruiz, 2006). Let's take a look at some of the training we can offer our employees.

As you will see from the types of training below, no one type would be enough for the jobs we do. Most HR managers use a variety of these types of training to develop a holistic employee.

Technical or Technology Training

Depending on the type of job, technical training will be required. Technical training is a type of training meant to teach the new employee the technological aspects of the job. In a retail environment, technical training might include teaching someone how to use the computer system to ring up customers. In a sales position, it might include showing someone how to use the customer relationship management (CRM) system to find new prospects. In a consulting business, technical training might be used so the consultant knows how to use the system to input the number of hours that should be charged to a client. In a restaurant, the server needs to be trained on how to use the system to process orders. Let's assume your company has decided to switch to the newest version of Microsoft Office. This might require some technical training of the entire company to ensure everyone uses the technology effectively. Technical training is often performed in-house, but it can also be administrered externally.

Quality Training

In a production-focused business, quality training is extremely important. Quality training refers to familiarizing employees with the means of preventing, detecting, and eliminating non-quality items, usually in an organization that produces a product. In a world where quality can set your business apart from competitors, this type of training provides employees with the knowledge to recognize products that are not up to quality standards and teaches them what to do in this scenario. Numerous organizations, such as the International Organization for Standardization (ISO), measure quality based on a number of metrics. This organization provides the stamp of quality approval for companies producing tangible products. ISO has developed quality standards for almost every field imaginable, not only considering product quality but also certifying companies in environmental management quality. ISO9000 is the set of standards for quality management, while ISO14000 is the set of standards for environmental management. ISO has developed 18,000 standards over the last 60 years. With the increase in globalization, these international quality standards are more important than ever for business development. Some companies, like 3M (QAI, 2011), choose to offer ISO training as external online training, employing companies such as QAI to deliver the training both online and in classrooms to employees.

Training employees on quality standards, including ISO standards, can give them a competitive advantage. It can result in cost savings in production as well as provide an edge in marketing of the quality-controlled products. Some quality training can happen in-house, but organizations such as ISO also perform external training.

Skills Training

Skills training, the third type of training, includes proficiencies needed to actually perform the job. For example, an administrative assistant might be trained in how to answer the phone, while a salesperson at Best Buy might be trained in assessment of customer needs and on how to offer the customer information to make a buying decision. Think of skills training as the things you actually need to know to perform your job. A cashier needs to know not only the technology to ring someone up but what to do if something is priced wrong. Most of the time, skills training is given in-house and can include the use of a mentor. An example of a type of skills training is from AT&T and Apple (Whitney, 2011), who in summer 2011 asked their managers to accelerate retail employee training on the iPhone 5, which was released to market in the fall.

Soft Skills Training

Our fourth type of training is called soft skills training. Soft skills refer to personality traits, social graces, communication, and personal habits that are used to characterize relationships with other people. Soft skills might include how to answer the phone or how to be friendly and welcoming to customers. It could include sexual harassment training and ethics training. In some jobs, necessary soft skills might include how to motivate others, maintain small talk, and establish rapport.

In a retail or restaurant environment, soft skills are used in every interaction with customers and are a key component of the customer experience. In fact, according to a *Computerworld* magazine survey, executives say there is an increasing need for people who have not only the skills and technical skills to do a job but also the necessary soft skills, such as strong listening and communication abilities (Hoffman, 2007). Many problems in organizations are due to a lack of soft skills, or interpersonal skills, not by problems with the business itself. As a result, HR and managers should work together to strengthen these employee skills. Soft skills training can be administered either in-house or externally.

Professional Training and Legal Training

In some jobs, professional training must be done on an ongoing basis. Professional training is a type of training required to be up to date in one's own professional field. For example, tax laws change often, and as a result, an accountant for H&R Block must receive yearly professional training on new tax codes (Silkey, 2010). Lawyers need professional training as laws change. A personal fitness trainer will undergo yearly certifications to stay up to date in new fitness and nutrition information.

Some organizations have paid a high cost for not properly training their employees on the laws relating to their industry. In 2011, Massachusetts General Hospital paid over $1 million in fines related to privacy policies that were not followed (Donnelly, 2011). As a result, the organization has agreed to develop training for workers on medical privacy. The fines could have been prevented if the organization had provided the proper training to begin with. Other types of legal training might include sexual harassment law training and discrimination law training.

Figure 2-31 Professional Training

Note: Professional training is normally given externally and is usually required for specific professions in which updates occur often, as in the accounting industry.

Team Training

Do you know the exercise in which a person is asked to close his or her eyes and fall back, and then supposedly the team members will catch that person? As a team-building exercise (and a scary one at that), this is an example of team training. The goal of team training is to develop cohesiveness among team members, allowing them to get to know each other and facilitate relationship building. We can define team training as a process that empowers teams to improve decision-making, problem-solving, and team-development skills to achieve business results. Often this type of training can occur after an organization has been restructured and new people are working together or perhaps after a merger or acquisition. Some reasons for team training include the following:

Improving communication

Making the workplace more enjoyable

Motivating a team

Getting to know each other

Getting everyone "onto the same page", including goal setting

Teaching the team self-regulation strategies

Helping participants to learn more about themselves (strengths and weaknesses)

Identifying and utilizing the strengths of team members

Improving team productivity

Practicing effective collaboration with team members

Team training can be administered either in-house or externally. Ironically, through the use of technology, team training no longer requires people to even be in the same room.

Human Resource Recall

What kind of team training have you participated in? What was it like? Do you think it accomplished what it was supposed to accomplish?

Managerial Training

After someone has spent time with an organization, they might be identified as a candidate for promotion. When this occurs, managerial training would occur. Topics might include those from our soft skills section, such as how to motivate and delegate, while others may be technical in nature. For example, if management uses a particular computer system for scheduling, the manager candidate might be technically trained. Some managerial training might be performed in-house while other training, such as leadership skills, might be performed externally.

For example, Mastek, a global IT solutions and services provider, provides a program called "One Skill a Month", which enables managers to learn skills such as delegation, coaching, and giving feedback. The average number of total training days at Mastek is 7.8 per employee and includes managerial topics and soft skills topics such as e-mail etiquette. The goal of its training programs is to increase productivity, one of the organization's core values.

Safety Training

Safety training is a type of training that occurs to ensure employees are protected from injuries caused by work-related accidents. Safety training is especially important for organizations that use chemicals or other types of hazardous materials in their production. Safety training can also include evacuation plans, fire drills, and workplace violence procedures. Safety training can also include the following:

Eye safety

First aid

Food service safety

Hearing protection

Asbestos

Construction safety

Hazmat safety

The Occupational Safety and Health Administration, or OSHA, is the main federal agency charged with enforcement of safety and health regulation in the United States. OSHA provides external training to companies on OSHA standards. Sometimes in-house training will also cover safety training.

Starbucks Training Video

This is a short video Starbucks uses to train new employees on customer service.

Please view this video at http://www.youtube.com/watch?v=OAmftgYEWqU.

Key Takeaways

There are several types of training we can provide for employees. In all situations, a variety of training types will be used, depending on the type of job.

Technical training addresses software or other programs that employees use while working for the organization.

Quality training is a type of training that familiarizes all employees with the means to produce a good-quality product. The ISO sets the standard on quality for most production and environmental situations. ISO training can be done in-house or externally.

Skills training focuses on the skills that the employee actually needs to know to perform their job. A mentor can help with this kind of training.

Soft skills training are those that do not relate directly to our job but are important. Soft skills training may train someone on how to better communicate and negotiate or provide good customer service.

Professional training is normally given externally and might be obtaining certification or specific information needed about a profession to perform a job. For example, tax accountants need to be up to date on tax laws; this type of training is often external.

Team training is a process that empowers teams to improve decision-making, problem-solving, and team-development skills. Team training can help improve communication and result in more productive businesses.

Exercises

1. Which type of training do you think is most important for an administrative assistant? What about for a restaurant server? Explain your answer.

2. Research OSHA. What are some of the new standards and laws it has recently developed? Outline a training plan for the new standards.

7.3   Training Delivery Methods

Learning Objective

Explain the types of training delivery methods.

Depending on the type of training occurring, you may choose one delivery method over another. This section discusses the types of delivery methods we can use to execute the types of training. Keep in mind, however, that most good training programs will use a variety of delivery methods.

On-the-Job Coaching Training Delivery

On-the-job coaching is one way to facilitate employee skills training. On-the-job coaching refers to an approved person training an employee on the skills necessary to complete tasks. A manager or someone with experience shows the employee how to perform the actual job. The selection of an on-the-job coach can be done in a variety of ways, but usually the coach is selected based on personality, skills, and knowledge. This type of skills training is normally facilitated in-house. The disadvantage of this training revolves around the person delivering the training. If he or she is not a good communicator, the training may not work. Likewise, if this person has "other things to do", he or she may not spend as much time required to train the person and provide guidance. In this situation, training can frustrate the new employee and may result in turnover.

Figure 2-32 OTJ Training

Note: On-the-job coaching is similar to mentoring. Think of on-the-job coaching as more skills-based training, while mentoring is usually a training delivery method that is more long-term and goes beyond just showing the employee skills to do the job.

Mentoring and Coaching Training Delivery

Mentoring is also a type of training delivery. A mentor is a trusted, experienced advisor who has direct investment in the development of an employee. Mentoring is a process by which an employee can be trained and developed by an experienced person. Normally, mentoring is used as a continuing method to train and develop an employee. One disadvantage of this type of training is possible communication style and personality conflict. It can also create overdependence in the mentee or micromanagement by the mentor. This is more different than on-the-job coaching, which tends to be short-term and focuses on the skills needed to perform a particular job.

Brown Bag Lunch Training Delivery

Brown bag lunches are a training delivery method meant to create an informal atmosphere. As the name suggests, brown bag lunch training is one in which the training occurs during lunchtime, employees bring their food, and someone presents training information to them. The trainer could be HR or management or even another employee showing a new technical skill. Brown bag lunches can also be an effective way to perform team training, as it brings people together in a more relaxed atmosphere. Some companies offer brown bag lunch training for personal development as well. For example, HR might want to bring in a specialist on 401(k) plans, or perhaps an employee provides a slide presentation on a trip he or she has taken, discussing the things learned on the trip. One disadvantage to this type of training can be low attendance and garnering enough interest from employees who may not want to "work" during lunch breaks. There can also be inconsistency in messages if training is delivered and not everyone is present to hear the message.

Human Resource Recall

What types of brown bag lunch training would employees be most willing to attend? Do you think this type of training should be required?

Web-Based Training Delivery

Web-based training delivery has a number of names. It could be called e-learning or Internet-based, computer-based, or technology-based learning. No matter what it is called, any web-based training involves the use of technology to facilitate training. There are two types of web-based learning. First, synchronous learning uses instructor-led facilitation. Asynchronous learning is self-directed, and there is no instructor facilitating the course. There are several advantages to web-based training. First, it is available on demand, does not require travel, and can be cost efficient. However, disadvantages might include an impersonal aspect to the training and limited bandwidth or technology capabilities.

Web-based training delivery lends itself well to certain training topics. For example, this might be an appropriate delivery method for safety training, technical training, quality training, and professional training. However, for some training, such as soft-skills training, job skills training, managerial training, and team training, another more personalized method may be better for delivery. However, there are many different platforms that lend themselves to an interactive approach to training, such as Sun Microsystems' Social Learning eXchange (SLX) training system, which has real-time video and recording capabilities. Hundreds of platforms are available to facilitate web-based training. DigitalChalk, for example, allows for both synchronous and asynchronous training and allows the instructor or human relations manager to track training progress and completion (DigitalChalk, 2010). Some companies use SharePoint, an intranet platform, to store training videos and materials (Microsoft SharePoint, 2010). Blackboard and Angel (used primarily by higher education institutions) allows human resource managers to create training modules, which can be moderated by a facilitator or managed in a self-paced format. In any of the platforms available, media such as video and podcasts can be included within the training.

Considerations for selecting a web-based platform include the following:

Is there a one-time fee or a per-user fee?

Do the majority of your employees use a Mac or a PC, and how does the platform work with both systems?

Is there enough bandwidth in your organization to support this type of platform?

Is the platform flexible enough to meet your training needs?

Does the software allow for collaboration and multimedia?

Is there training for the trainer in adoption of this system? Is technical support offered?

Job Shadowing Training Delivery

Job shadowing is a training delivery method that places an employee who already has the skills with another employee who wants to develop those skills. Apprenticeships use job shadowing as one type of training method. For example, an apprentice electrician would shadow and watch the journeyman electrician perform the skills and tasks and learn by watching. Eventually, the apprentice would be able to learn the skills to do the job alone. The downside to this type of training is the possibility that the person job shadowing may learn "bad habits" or shortcuts to performing tasks that may not be beneficial to the organization.

Fortune 500 Focus

It takes a lot of training for the Walt Disney Company to produce the best Mickey Mouse, Snow White, Aladdin, or Peter Pan. In Orlando at Disneyworld, most of this training takes place at Disney University. Disney University provides training to its 42,000 cast members (this is what Disney calls employees) in areas such as culinary arts, computer applications, and specific job components. Once hired, all cast members go through a two-day Disney training program called Traditions, where they learn the basics of being a good cast member and the history of the company. For all practical purposes, Traditions is a new employee orientation.

Training doesn't stop at orientation, though. While all positions receive extensive training, one of the most extensive trainings are especially for Disney characters, since their presence at the theme parks is a major part of the customer experience. To become a character cast member, a character performer audition is required. The auditions require dancing and acting, and once hired, the individual is given the job of several characters to play. After a two-week intensive training process on character history, personalities, and ability to sign the names of the characters (for the autograph books sold at the parks for kids), an exam is given. The exam tests competency in character understanding, and passing the exam is required to become hired (Hill, 2005).

While Disney University trains people for specific positions, it also offers an array of continuing development courses called Disney Development Connection. Disney says in 2010, more than 3,254,596 hours were spent training a variety of employees, from characters to management. The training doesn't stop at in-house training, either. Disney offers tuition reimbursement up to $700 per credit and pays for 100 percent of books and $100 per course for cost of other materials. In 2010, Disney paid over $8 million in tuition expenses for cast members.

Disney consistently ranks in "America's Most Admired Companies" by *Fortune* Magazine, and its excellent training could be one of the many reasons.

Job Swapping Training Delivery

Job swapping is a method for training in which two employees agree to change jobs for a period of time. Of course, with this training delivery method, other training would be necessary to ensure the employee learns the skills needed to perform the skills of the new job. Job swap options can be motivational to employees by providing a change of scenery. It can be great for the organization as well to cross-train employees in different types of jobs. However, the time spent learning can result in unproductive time and lost revenue.

Figure 2-33 Vestibule Training

Note: Vestibule training is also known as "near site" training and can work great for many types of training needs, such as team training and technical training.

Vestibule Training Delivery

In vestibule training, training is performed near the worksite in conference rooms, lecture rooms, and classrooms. This might be an appropriate method to deliver orientations and some skills-based training. For example, to become a journeyman electrician, an apprentice performs job shadowing, on-the-job training, and vestibule training to learn the law and codes related to electricity installation. During the busy holiday season, Macy's uses vestibule training to teach new hires how to use the cash register system and provides skills training on how to provide great customer service (Macy's, 2010).

Many organizations use vestibule training for technical training, safety training, professional training, and quality training. It can also be appropriate for managerial training, soft skills training, and team training. As you can tell, this delivery method, like web-based training delivery, is quite versatile. For some jobs or training topics, this may take too much time away from performing the actual "job", which can result in lost productivity.

International Assignment Training

Since we are working within a global economy, it might be necessary to provide training to employees who are moving overseas or working overseas. Up to 40 percent of international assignments are terminated early because of a lack of international training (Sullivan & Tu, 2011). Ensuring success overseas is reliant upon the local employee's learning how to navigate in the new country. The following topics might be included in this type of training:

Cultural differences and similarities

Insight and daily living in the country

Social norms and etiquette

Communication training, such as language skills

This training is best delivered by a professional in the region or area in which the employee will be working.

Key Takeaways

Training delivery methods are important to consider, depending on the type of training that needs to be performed.

Most organizations do not use only one type of training delivery method; a combination of many methods will be used.

On-the-job coaching delivery method is a training delivery method in which an employee is assigned to a more experienced employee or manager to learn the skills needed for the job. This is similar to the mentor training delivery method, except a mentor training method is less about skills training and more about ongoing employee development.

Brown bag lunch training delivery is normally informal and can involve personal development as well as specific job-related skills.

Web-based training is any type of training that is delivered using technology.

There are numerous platforms that can be used for web-based training and considerations, such as cost, when selecting a platform for use.

A synchronous training method is used for web-based training and refers to delivery that is led by a facilitator. An asynchronous training method is one that is self-directed.

Job shadowing is a delivery method consisting of on-the-job training and the employee's learning skills by watching someone more experienced.

To motivate employees and allow them to develop new skills, job swapping training delivery may be used. This occurs when two people change jobs for a set period of time to learn new skills. With this method, it is likely that other methods will also be used, too.

Vestibule training delivery is also known as "near site" training. It normally happens in a classroom, conference room, or lecture room and works well to deliver orientations and some skills-based training. Many organizations also use vestibule training for technical training, safety training, professional training, and quality training.

Exercises

1. Do an Internet search on web-based training. Discuss two of the platforms you found. What are the features and benefits?

2. Which training delivery method do you think you personally would prefer in a job and why?

3. What do you see as advantages and disadvantages to each type of training method?

7.4 Designing a Training Program

Learning Objectives

1. Be able to design a training program framework.

2. Understand the uses and applications of a career development program.

3. The next step in the training process is to create a training framework that will help guide you as you set up a training program. Information on how to use the framework is included in this section.

Training Program Framework Development

When developing your training plan, there are a number of considerations. Training is something that should be planned and developed in advance.

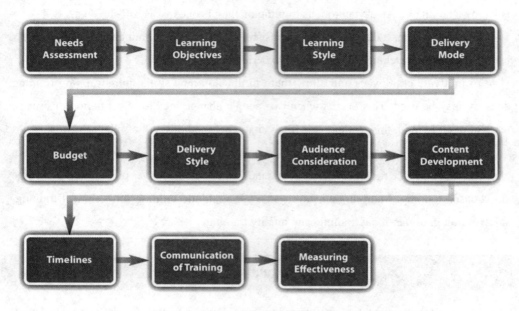

Figure 2-34　Training Program Development Model

The considerations for developing a training program are as follows:

Needs assessment and learning objectives. This part of the framework development asks you to consider what kind of training is needed in your organization. Once you have determined the training needed, you can set learning objectives to measure at the end of the training.

Consideration of learning styles. Making sure to teach to a variety of learning styles is important to development of training programs.

Delivery mode. What is the best way to get your message across? Is web-based training more appropriate, or should mentoring be used? Can vestibule training be used for a portion of the training while job shadowing be used for some of the training, too? Most training programs will include a variety of delivery methods.

Budget. How much money do you have to spend on this training?

Delivery style. Will the training be self-paced or instructor led? What kinds of discussions and interactivity can be developed in conjunction with this training?

Audience. Who will be part of this training? Do you have a mix of roles, such as accounting people and marketing people? What are the job responsibilities of these individuals, and how can you make the training relevant to their individual jobs?

Content. What needs to be taught? How will you sequence the information?

Timelines. How long will it take to develop the training? Is there a deadline for training to be completed?

Communication. How will employees know the training is available to them?

Measuring effectiveness of training. How will you know if your training worked? What ways will you use to measure this?

Human Resource Recall

1. Can you think of a time where you received training, but the facilitator did not connect with the audience?

2. Does that ever happen in any of your classes (of course not this one, though)?

Needs Assessment

The first step in developing a training program is to determine what the organization needs in terms of training. There are three levels of training needs assessment: organizational assessment, occupational (task) assessment, and individual assessment:

Organizational assessment. In this type of needs assessment, we can determine the skills, knowledge, and abilities a company needs to meet its strategic objectives. This type of assessment considers things such as changing demographics and technological trends. Overall, this type of assessment looks at how the organization as a whole can handle its weaknesses while promoting strengths.

Occupational (task) assessment. This type of assessment looks at the specific tasks, skills knowledge, and abilities required to do jobs within the organization.

Individual assessment. An individual assessment looks at the performance of an individual employee and determines what training should be accomplished for that individual.

We can apply each of these to our training plan. First, to perform an organizational assessment, we can look at future trends and our overall company's strategic plan to determine training needs. We can also see how jobs and industries are changing, and knowing this, we can better determine the occupational and individual assessments.

Researching training needs can be done through a variety of ways. One option is to use an online tool such as SurveyMonkey to poll employees on what types of training they would like to see offered.

As you review performance evaluations turned in by your managers, you may see a pattern developing showing that employees are not meeting expectations. As a result, this may provide data as to where your training is lacking.

There are also types of training that will likely be required for a job, such as technical training, safety training, quality training, and professional training. Each of these should be viewed as separate training programs, requiring an individual framework for each type of training. For example, an employee orientation framework will look entirely different from an in-house technical training framework.

Training must be tied to job expectations. Any and all training developed should transfer directly to the skills of that particular employee. Reviewing the HR strategic plan and various job analyses may help you see what kind of training should be developed for specific job titles in your organization.

Learning Objectives

After you have determined what type of training should occur, learning objectives for the training should be set. A learning objective is what you want the learner to be able to do, explain, or demonstrate at the end of the training period. Good learning objectives are performance based and clear, and the end result of the learning objective can be observable or measured in some way. Examples of learning objectives might include the following:

Be able to explain the company policy on sexual harassment and give examples of sexual harassment.

Be able to show the proper way to take a customer's order.

Perform a variety of customer needs analyses using company software.

Understand and utilize the new expense-tracking software.

Explain the safety procedure in handling chemicals.

Be able to explain the types of communication styles and strategies to effectively deal with each style.

Demonstrate ethics when handling customer complaints.

Be able to effectively delegate to employees.

Once we have set our learning objectives, we can utilize information on learning styles to determine the best delivery mode for our training.

Learning Styles

Understanding learning styles is an important component to any training program. For our purposes, we will utilize a widely accepted learning style model. Recent research has shown that classifying people into learning styles may not be the best way to determine a style, and most people have a different style depending on the information being taught. In a study by Pashler et al., the authors look at aptitude and personality as key traits when learning, as opposed to classifying people into categories of learning styles. Bearing this in mind, we will address a common approach to learning styles next.

An effective trainer tries to develop training to meet the three different learning styles:

Visual learner. A visual learner usually has a clear "picture" of an experience. A visual learner often says things such as "I can see what you are saying" or "This looks good". A visual learner is best reached using graphics, pictures, and figures.

Auditory learner. An auditory learner learns by sound. An auditory learner might say, "If I hear you right" or "What do you hear about this situation?" The auditory learner will learn by listening to a lecture or to someone explaining how to do something.

Kinesthetic learner. A kinesthetic learner learns by developing feelings toward an experience. These types of learners tend to learn by doing rather than listening or seeing someone else do it. This type of learner will often say things such as "This feels right".

Most individuals use more than one type of learning style, depending on what kinds of information they are processing. For example, in class you might be a visual learner, but when learning how to change a tire, you might be a kinesthetic learner.

Delivery Mode

Depending on the type of training that needs to be delivered, you will likely choose a different mode to deliver the training. An orientation might lend itself best to vestibule training, while sexual harassment training may be better for web-based training. When choosing a delivery mode, it is important to consider the audience and budget constrictions. For example, Oakwood Worldwide, a provider of temporary housing, recently won the Top 125 Training Award for its training and development programs. It offers in-class and online classes for all associates and constantly add to its course catalog. This is a major recruitment as well as retention tool for its employees. In fact, the company credits this program for retaining 25 percent of its workforce for ten years or more.

Budget

How much money do you think the training will cost? The type of training performed will depend greatly on the budget. If you decide that web-based training is the right delivery mode, but you don't have the budget to pay the user fee for the platform, this wouldn't be the best option. Besides the actual cost of training, another cost consideration is people's time. If employees are in training for two hours, what is the cost to the organization while they are not able to perform their job? A spreadsheet should be developed that lists the actual cost for materials, snacks, and other direct costs, but also the indirect costs, such as people's time.

Delivery Style

Taking into consideration the delivery method, what is the best style to deliver this training? It's also important to keep in mind that most people don't learn through "death by PowerPoint"; they learn in a variety of ways, such as auditory, kinesthetic, or visual. Considering this, what kinds of ice breakers, breakout discussions, and activities can you incorporate to make the training as interactive as possible? Role plays and other games can make the training fun for employees. Many trainers implement online videos, podcasts, and other interactive media in their training sessions. This ensures different learning styles are met and also makes the training more interesting.

Audience

Considering your audience is an important aspect to training. How long have they been with the organization, or are they new employees? What departments do they work in? Knowing the answers to these questions can help you develop a relevant delivery style that makes for better training. For example, if you know that all the people attending the training are from the accounting department, examples you provide in the training can be focused on this type of job. If you have a mixed group, examples and discussions can touch on a variety of disciplines.

Content Development

The content you want to deliver is perhaps one of the most important parts in training and one of the most time-consuming to develop. Development of learning objectives or those things you want your learners to know after the training makes for a more focused training. Think of learning objectives as goals—what should someone know after completing this training? Here are some sample learning objectives:

Be able to define and explain the handling of hazardous materials in the workplace.

Be able to utilize the team decision process model.

Understand the definition of sexual harassment and be able to recognize sexual harassment in the workplace.

Understand and be able to explain the company policies and structure.

After you have developed the objectives and goals, you can begin to develop the content of the training. Consideration of the learning methods you will use, such as discussion and role playing, will be outlined in your content area.

Development of content usually requires a development of learning objectives and then a brief outline of the major topics you wish to cover. With that outline, you can "fill in" the major topics with information. Based on this information, you can develop modules or PowerPoint slides, activities, discussion questions, and other learning techniques.

Timelines

For some types of training, time lines may be required to ensure the training has been done. This is often the case for safety training; usually the training should be done before the employee starts. In other words, in what time frame should an employee complete the training?

Another consideration regarding time lines is how much time you think you need to give the training. Perhaps one hour will be enough, but sometimes, training may take a day or even a week. After you have developed your training content, you will likely have a good idea as to how long it will take to deliver it. Consider the fact that most people do not have a lot of time for training and keep the training time realistic and concise.

From a long-term approach, it may not be cost effective to offer an orientation each time someone new is hired. One consideration might be to offer orientation training once per month so that all employees hired within that month are trained at the same time.

Development of a dependable schedule for training might be ideal, as in the following example:

Orientation is offered on the first Thursday of every month.

The second and third Tuesday will consist of vestibule training on management skills and communication.

Twice yearly, in August and March, safety and sexual harassment training will be given to meet the legal company requirements.

Developing a dependable training schedule allows for better communication to your staff, results in fewer communication issues surrounding training, and allows all employees to plan ahead to attend training.

Communication

Once you have developed your training, your next consideration is how you will communicate the available training to employees. In a situation such as an orientation, you will need to communicate to managers, staff, and anyone involved in the training the timing and confirm that it fits within their schedule. If it is an informal training, such as a brown bag lunch on 401(k) plans, this might involve determining the days and times that most people are in the office and might be able to participate. Because employees use Mondays and Fridays, respectively, to catch up and finish up work for the week, these days tend to be the worst for training.

Consider utilizing your company's intranet, e-mail, and even old-fashioned posters to communicate the training.

Many companies have Listservs that can relay the message to only certain groups, if need be.

Human Resource Recall

What can happen if training is not communicated to employees appropriately?

Measuring Effectiveness

After we have completed the training, we want to make sure our training objectives were met. One model to measure effectiveness of training is the Kirkpatrick model (Kirkpatrick, 2006), developed in the 1950s. His model has four levels:

Reaction: How did the participants react to the training program?

Learning: To what extent did participants improve knowledge and skills?

Behavior: Did behavior change as a result of the training?

Results: What benefits to the organization resulted from the training?

Each of Kirkpatrick's levels can be assessed using a variety of methods. We will discuss those next.

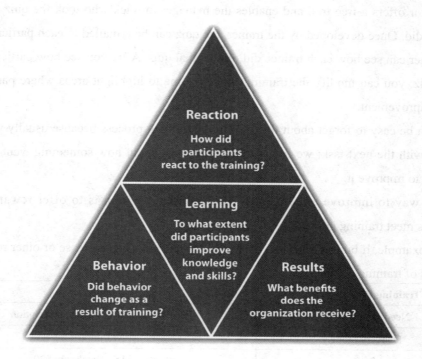

Figure 2-35 Kirkpatrick's Four Levels of Training Evaluation

Review the performance of the employees who received the training, and if possible review the performance of those who did not receive the training. For example, in your orientation training, if one of the learning objectives was to be able to request time off using the company intranet, and several employees who attended the training come back and ask for clarification on how to perform this task, it may mean the training didn't work as well as you might have thought. In this case, it is important to go back and review the learning objectives and content of your training to ensure it can be more effective in the future.

Many trainers also ask people to take informal, anonymous surveys after the training to gauge the training. These types of surveys can be developed quickly and easily through websites such as SurveyMonkey. Another option is to require a quiz at the end of the training to see how well the employees understand what you were trying to teach them. The quiz should be developed based on the learning objective you set for the training. For example, if a learning objective was to be able to follow OSHA standards, then a quiz might be developed specifically related to those standards. There are a number of online tools, some free, to develop quizzes and send them to people attending your training. For example, Wondershare

QuizCreator offers a free trial and enables the manager to track who took the quiz and how well they did. Once developed by the trainer, the quiz can be e-mailed to each participant and the manager can see how each trainee did on the final quiz. After you see how participants do on the quiz, you can modify the training for next time to highlight areas where participants needed improvement.

It can be easy to forget about this step in the training process because usually we are so involved with the next task: we forget to ask questions about how something went and then take steps to improve it.

One way to improve effectiveness of a training program is to offer rewards when employees meet training goals.

For example, if budget allows, a person might receive a pay increase or other reward for each level of training completed.

Training Framework	Plan
Needs assessment	Formalized new employee orientation
Delivery mode	Vestibule
Budget (per person)	Lunch: $15 Notebook: $20
Delivery style	Discussion. PowerPoints. Icebrea ker
Audience	New hires from all departments
Goals and learning objectives	• Be able to explain company history and structure • Understand operational company policies • Meet department heads
Timeline	4 hours for training, new employee orientation offered on the 5th and 15th of every month
Communication	E-mail to hiring managers and to new employee
Measurement method	Interactive team quiz

Training Framework	Plan
Needs assessment	Sexual harassment training
Delivery mode	Web based
Budget (per person)	User fee: $10
Delivery Style	Online modules and online assignments
Audience	Required for all employees
Goals and learning objectives	• Understand what constitutes sexual harassment • Know what to do if you are sexually harassed at work

Continued

Training Framework	Plan
Timeline	1.5 hours, offefed every Tuesday at 10:00 a.m. and every Thursday at 3:30 p.m. during the month of February
Communication	Company Listserv. announcement to department heads at weekly meeting
Measurement method	Online end-of-course quiz

Training Framework	Plan
Needs assessment	Product training
Delivery mode	Vestibule
Budget (per person)	Materials only online: $0
Delivery style	PowerPoint, roleplaying
Audience	Salespeople
Goals and learning objectives	• Understand the features of produa xx • Be able to explain the benefits of produa xx
Timeline	New product release is October lst, so training will be in September. 1 hour. Delivered during regular weekly sales meeting
Communication	E-maillist message to salespeople, work with sales manager
Measurement method	Sales figures for product xx

Figure 2-36　Training Framework

Note: Once the training framework has been developed, the training content can be developed. The training plan serves as a starting point for training development.

Career Development Programs and Succession Planning

Another important aspect to training is career development programs. A career development program is a process developed to help people manage their career, learn new things, and take steps to improve personally and professionally. Think of it as a training program of sorts, but for individuals. Sometimes career development programs are called professional development plans.

Table 2-14　Sample of Career Development Plan Developed by an Employee and Commented on by Her Manager

Today's Date	February 15, 2012
Employee	Sammie Smith

Continued

Current Job Title	Clerk, Accounts Payable
Goals	• Develop management skills • Learn accounting standards • Promoted to Accounts Payable Manager
Estimated Costs	• Management training • Peachtree accounting software Advanced training • Earn AAAS online degree in accounting • Take tax certification course • Communications training
Completion Date	Spring of 2014

Manager Notes:

In-house training offered yearly: "Reading Body Language" and "Writing Development" and "Running an Effective Meeting".

External training needed: *Peachtree* software, AAAS Degree, Tax certification Training Course

Assign Sammie to Dorothy Redgur, the CFO for mentorship

Next steps: Sammie should develop a timeline for when she plans to complete the seminars.

The budget allows us to pay up to $1,000 per year for external training for all employees. Talk with Sammie about how to receive reimbursement.

As you can see, the employee developed goals and made suggestions on the types of training that could help her meet her goals. Based on this data, the manager suggested in-house training and external training for her to reach her goals within the organization.

Career development programs are necessary in today's organizations for a variety of reasons. First, with a maturing baby-boom population, newer employees must be trained to take those jobs once baby boomers retire. Second, if an employee knows a particular path to career development is in place, this can increase motivation. A career development plan usually includes a list of short- and long-term goals that employees have pertaining to their current and future jobs and a planned sequence of formal and informal training and experiences needed to help them reach the goals. As this chapter has discussed, the organization can and should be instrumental in defining what types of training, both in-house and external, can be used to help develop employees.

To help develop this type of program, managers can consider a few components (Heller, 2005):

Talk to employees. Although this may seem obvious, it doesn't always happen. Talking with employees about their goals and what they hope to achieve can be a good first step in developing a formal career development program.

Create specific requirements for career development. Allow employees to see that if they do A, B, and C, they will be eligible for promotion. For example, to become a supervisor, maybe three years of experience, management training, and communication training are required. Perhaps an employee might be required to prove themselves in certain areas, such as "maintain and exceed sales quota for eight quarters" to be a sales manager. In other words, in career development there should be a clear process for the employees to develop themselves within the organization.

Use cross-training and job rotation. Cross-training is a method by which employees can gain management experience, even if for short periods of time. For example, when a manager is out of the office, putting an employee "in charge" can help the employee learn skills and abilities needed to perform that function appropriately. Through the use of job rotation, which involves a systematic movement of employees from job to job within an organization, employees can gain a variety of experiences to prepare them for upward movement in the organization.

Utilize mentors. Mentorship can be a great way for employees to understand what it takes to develop one's career to the next level. A formal mentorship program in place with willing mentees can add value to your career development program.

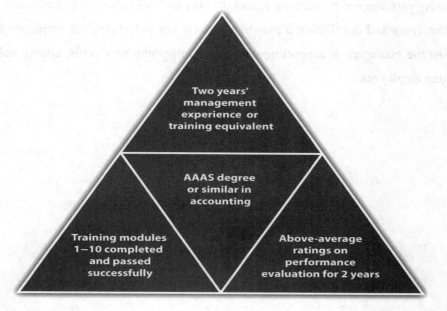

Figure 2-37 Career Development Sample Process to Become an Accounts Payable Manager

There are many tools on the web, including templates to help employees develop their own career development plans. Many organizations, in fact, ask employees to develop their own plans and use those as a starting point for understanding long-term career goals. Then hopefully the organization can provide them with the opportunities to meet these career goals. In the late 1980s, many employees felt that career opportunities at their current organizations dwindled after seeing the downsizing that occurred. It gave employees the feeling that companies were not going to help develop them, unless they took the initiative to do so themselves. Unfortunately, this attitude means that workers will not wait for career opportunities within the company, unless a clear plan and guide is put into place by the company (Capelli, 2010). Here is an example of a process that can be used to put a career development program in place (Adolfo, 2010):

Meet individually with employees to identify their long-term career interests (this may be done by human resources or the direct manager).

Identify resources within the organization that can help employees achieve their goals. Create new opportunities for training if you see a gap in needs versus what is currently offered.

Prepare a plan for each employee, or ask them to prepare the plan.

Meet with the employee to discuss the plan.

During performance evaluations, revisit the plan and make changes as necessary.

Identifying and developing a planning process not only helps the employee but also can assist the managers in supporting employees in gaining new skills, adding value, and motivating employees.

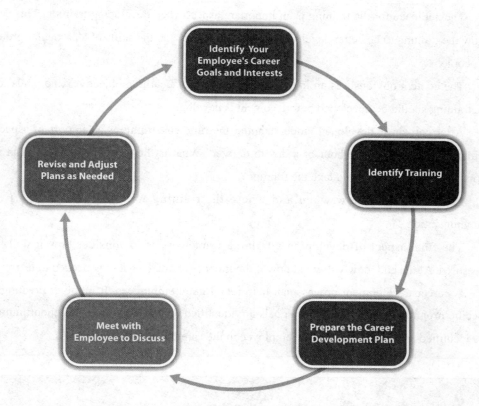

Figure 2-38 Career Development Planning Process

Key Takeaways

There are a number of key considerations in developing a training program. Training should not be handled casually but instead developed specifically to meet the needs of the organization. This can be done by a needs assessment consisting of three levels: organizational, occupational, and individual assessments.

The first consideration is the delivery mode; depending on the type of training and other factors, some modes might be better than others.

Budget is a consideration in developing training. The cost of materials, but also the cost of time, should be considered.

The delivery style must take into account people's individual learning styles. The amount of lecture, discussion, role plays, and activities are considered part of delivery style.

The audience for the training is an important aspect when developing training. This can allow the training to be better developed to meet the needs and the skills of a particular group of people.

The content obviously is an important consideration. Learning objectives and goals for the training should be developed before content is developed.

After content is developed, understanding the time constraints is an important aspect. Will the training take one hour or a day to deliver? What is the time line consideration in terms of when people should take the training?

Letting people know when and where the training will take place is part of communication.

The final aspect of developing a training framework is to consider how it will be measured. At the end, how will you know if the trainees learned what they needed to learn?

A career development process can help retain good employees. It involves creating a specific program in which employee goals are identified and new training and opportunities are identified and created to help the employee in the career development process.

Exercises

1. Develop a rough draft of a training framework using Figure 2-36 for a job you find on Monster.com.

2. Write three learning objectives you think would be necessary when developing orientation training for a receptionist in an advertising firm.

3. Why is a career development plan important to develop personally, even if your company doesn't have a formal plan in place? List at least three reasons and describe.

7.5　Cases and Problems

Chapter Summary

Employee training and development is a necessity in today's work environment. Training and development can lead to lower turnover and increased motivation.

There are four basic steps to employee training: employee orientation, in-house training, mentoring, and external training.

Different types of training can be delivered, each falling into the steps of employee training. These include technical or technology training, quality training, skills training, soft skills training, professional training, team training, managerial training, and safety training.

Within the types of training, we need to determine which method is best for the actual delivery of training. Options include on-the-job training, mentor training, brown bag lunches, web-based training, job shadowing, job swapping, and vestibule training.

Development of a training development framework is the first step in solidifying the training.

Considerations and steps to developing the training framework include determining the training needs, delivery modes, budget, delivery style, audience, content, time lines, communication of the training, and measurement of the training.

Career development programs can be an essential piece to the training puzzle. A comprehensive program or plan, either developed by employees or administered by HR, can help with motivation and fill the gap when people in the organization leave or retire. It can also be used as a motivational tool.

Chapter Case

Joann Michaels just started her job as human resources manager at In the Dog House, a retail chain specializing in dog apparel and accessories. She is a good friend of yours you met in college.

The organization has 35 stores with 250 employees in Washington, Idaho, and Oregon. As the chain has grown, the training programs have been conducted somewhat piecemeal. Upon visiting some of the stores in a three-week tour, Joann has realized that all the stores seem to have different ways of training their in-store employees.

When she digs further, she realizes even the corporate offices, which employ seventy-five people, have no formal training program. In the past, they have done informal and optional brown bag lunch training to keep employees up to date. As a result, Joann develops a survey using SurveyMonkey and sends it to all seventy-five corporate employees. She created a rating system, with 1 meaning strongly disagree and 5 meaning strongly agree. Employees were not required to answer all questions, hence the variation in the number of responses column. After this task, Joann creates a slightly different survey and sends it to all store managers, asking them to encourage their retail employees to take the survey. The results are shown here.

In the Dog House Corporate Employee Survey Results

Question	Number of Responses	Average Rating
I am paid fairly.	73	3.9
I feel my group works well as a team.	69	2.63
I appreciate the amount of soft skills training offered at In the Dog House.	74	2.1
I can see myself growing professionally here.	69	1.95
I feel I am paid fairly.	74	3.8
I have all the tools and equipment I need to do my job.	67	4.2
I feel confident if there were an emergency at the office, I would know what to do and could help others.	73	2.67
I think my direct supervisor is an excellent manager.	55	2.41
The orientation training I received was helpful in understanding the expectations of the job.	75	3.1
I would take training related to my job knowing there would be a reward offered for doing so.	71	4.24

In the Dog House Retail Employee Survey Results

Question	Number of Responses	Average Rating
I am content with the benefits I am receiving.	143	1.2
I feel my store works well as a team.	190	4.1
I appreciate the amount of product training and information offered at In the Dog House.	182	2.34
I can see myself growing professionally here.	158	1.99
I feel I am paid fairly.	182	3.2
My supervisor works with my schedule, so I work at times that are convenient for me.	172	3.67
I feel confident if I had to evacuate the store, I would know what to do and could help customers.	179	2.88

Continued

Question	Number of Responses	Average Rating
I think my store manager is a great manager.	139	3.34
The orientation training I received was helpful in understanding the expectations of the job.	183	4.3
I am content with the benefits I am receiving.	174	1.69

Based on the information Joann received from her survey, she decided some changes need to be made. Joann asks you to meet for coffee and take a look at the results. After you review them, Joann asks you the following questions. How would you respond to each?

"Obviously, I need to start working on some training programs. Which topics do you think I should start with?"

"How do I go about developing a training program that will be really useful and make people excited? What are the steps I need to take?"

"How should I communicate the training program to the corporate and retail employees? Should the new training I develop be communicated in the same way?"

"Do you think that we should look at changing pay and benefits? Why or why not?"

"Can you please help me draft a training program framework for what we have discussed? Do you think I should design one for both the corporate offices and one for the retail stores?"

Team Activity

1. In teams of three to four, outline a two-hour training program for managers to better understand motivation for their employees. Motivation is discussed in Chapter 6 "Retention and Motivation". Use the training development model discussed in this chapter. Your training should address learning objectives, delivery modes, budget, delivery style, time line, communication, and measurement. Prepare a five-minute presentation to present in class.

2. Using the same plan above, plan and deliver the content to the rest of the class.

Chapter 8 Employee Assessment

A Tough Conversation

As you wake up this morning, you think about the performance evaluation you will give one of your employees, Sean, later this morning. Sean has been with your company for two years, and over the last six months his performance has begun to slide. As the manager, it is your responsibility to talk with him about performance, which you have done on several occasions. However, the performance evaluation will make his non-performance more formalized. You know that Sean has had some personal troubles that can account for some of the performance issues, but despite this, you really need to get his performance up to par. Your goal in the performance evaluation interview today is to create an improvement plan for Sean, while documenting his non-performance.

When you arrive at work, you look over the essay rating part of Sean's evaluation. It details two client project deadlines that were missed, as well as the over-budget amounts of the two client projects. It was Sean's responsibility to oversee both aspects of this project. When Sean arrives at your office, you greet him, ask him to take a seat, and begin to discuss the evaluation with him.

"Sean, while you have always been a high performer, these last few months have been lackluster. On two of your projects, you were over budget and late. The client commented on both of these aspects when it filled out the client evaluation. As a result, you can see this is documented in your performance evaluation."

Using defensive non-verbal language, Sean says, "Missing the project deadlines and budget wasn't my fault. Emily said everything was under control, and I trusted her. She is the one who should have a bad performance review."

You say, "Ultimately, as the account director, you are responsible, as outlined in your job description. As you know, it is important to manage the accountability within your team, and in this case, you didn't perform. In fact, in your 360 reviews, several of your colleagues suggested you were not putting in enough time on the projects and seemed distracted."

"I really dislike those 360 reviews. It really is just a popularity contest, anyway," Sean says. "So, am I fired for these two mistakes?" You have worked with people who exhibited this type of defensive behavior before, and you know it is natural for people to feel like they need to defend themselves when having this type of conversation. You decide to move the conversation ahead and focus on future behavior rather than past behavior.

You say, "Sean, you normally add a lot of value to the organization. Although these issues will be documented in your performance evaluation, I believe you can produce high-quality work. As a result, let's work together to develop an improvement plan so you can continue to add value to the organization. The improvement plan addresses project deadlines and budgets, and I think you will find it helpful for your career development."

Sean agrees begrudgingly and you begin to show him the improvement plan document the company uses, so you can fill it out together.

When you head home after work, you think about the day's events and about Sean. As you had suspected, he was defensive at first but seemed enthusiastic to work on the improvement plan after you showed him the document. You feel positive that this performance evaluation was a step in the right direction to ensure Sean continues to be a high producer in the company, despite these mistakes.

8.1 Performance Evaluation Systems

Learning Objectives

1. Define the reasons for a formal performance evaluation system.
2. Explain the process to develop a performance review system.

A performance evaluation system is a systematic way to examine how well an employee is performing in his or her job. If you notice, the word systematic implies the performance evaluation process should be a planned system that allows feedback to be given in a formal—as opposed to informal—sense. Performance evaluations can also be called performance appraisals, performance assessments, or employee appraisals.

There are four reasons why a systematic performance evaluation system should be implemented. First, the evaluation process should encourage positive performance and behavior. Second, it is a way to satisfy employee curiosity as to how well they are performing in their job. It can also be used as a tool to develop employees. Lastly, it can provide a basis for pay raises, promotions, and legal disciplinary actions.

Designing a Performance Appraisal System

There are a number of things to consider before designing or revising an existing performance appraisal system. Some researchers suggest that the performance appraisal system is perhaps one of the most important parts of the organization (Lawrie, 1990), while others suggest that performance appraisal systems are ultimately flawed (Derven, 1990), making them worthless. For the purpose of this chapter, let's assume we can create a performance appraisal system that will provide value to the organization and the employee. When designing this process, we should recognize that any process has its limitations, but if we plan it correctly, we can minimize some of these.

The first step in the process is to determine how often performance appraisals should be given. Please keep in mind that managers should constantly be giving feedback to employees, and this process is a more formal way of doing so. Some organizations choose to give performance evaluations once per year, while others give them twice per year, or more. The advantage to giving an evaluation twice per year, of course, is more feedback and opportunity for employee development. The downside is the time it takes for the manager to write the evaluation and discuss it with the employee. If done well, it could take several hours for just one employee. Depending on your organization's structure, you may choose one or the other. For example, if most of your managers have five or ten people to manage (this is called span of control), it might be worthwhile to give performance evaluations more than once per year, since the time cost isn't high. If most of your managers have twenty or more employees, it may not be feasible to perform this process more than once per year. To determine costs of your performance evaluations, see Table 2-15 "Estimating the Costs of Performance Evaluations". Asking for feedback from managers and employees is also a good way to determine how often performance evaluations should be given.

Table 2-15 Estimating the Costs of Performance Evaluations

Narrow Span of Control	
Average span of control	8

Continued

Narrow Span of Control	
Average time to complete one written review	1 hour
Average time to discuss with employee	1 hour
Administrative time to set up meetings with employees	1/2 hour

8 employees × 2 hours per employee + 1/2 hour administrative time to set up times to meet with employees = 16.5 hours of time for one manager to complete all performance reviews

Wider Span of Control	
Average span of control	25
Average time to complete one written review	1 hour
Average time to discuss with employee	1 hour
Administrative time to set up meetings with employees	1 hour

25 employees × 2 hours per employee + 1 hour administrative time to set up times to meet with employees = 51 hours

Once you have the number of hours it takes, you can multiply that by your manager's hourly pay to get an estimated cost to the organization

16 hours × $50 per hour = $850

51 hours × $50 per hour = $2550

Should pay increases be tied to performance evaluations? This might be the second consideration before development of a performance evaluation process. There is research that shows employees have a greater acceptance of performance reviews if the review is linked to rewards (Bannister & Balkin, 1990).

The third consideration should include goal setting. In other words, what goals does the organization hope to achieve with the performance appraisal process?

Once the frequency, rewards, and goals have been determined, it is time to begin to formalize the process. First, we will need to develop the actual forms that will be used to evaluate each job within the organization. Every performance evaluation should be directly tied with that employee's job description.

Determining who should evaluate the performance of the employee is the next decision. It could be their direct manager (most common method), subordinates, customers or clients, self, and/or peers. Table 2-16 "Advantages and Disadvantages of Each Source for Performance

Evaluations" shows some of the advantages and disadvantages for each source of information for performance evaluations. Ultimately, using a variety of sources might garner the best results.

Table 2-16 Advantages and Disadvantages of Each Source for Performance Evaluations

Source	Advantages	Disadvantages
Manager/ Supervisor	Usually has extensive knowledge of the employee's performance and abilities Favoritism	Bias
Self	Self-analysis can help with employee growth Works well when the supervisor doesn't always directly observe the employee	In the employee's interest to inflate his or her own ratings Relationships can create bias in the review
Peer	Can bring a different perspective, since peers know the job well If confidential, may create mistrust within the organization	If evaluations are tied to pay, this can put both the employee and the peer in an awkward situation
Customer/ Client	Customers often have the best view of employee behavior Can enhance long-term relationships with the customer by asking for feedback Data garnered can include how well the manager treats employees Can determine if employees feel there is favoritism within their department	Can be expensive to obtain this feedback Possible bias Possible retaliation if results are not favorable
Subordinate	Subordinates may not understand the "big picture" and rate low as a result Can be used as a self-development tool for managers If nothing changes despite the evaluation, could create motivational issues among employees	Rating inflation If confidential, may create mistrust within the organization

A 360-degree performance appraisal method is a way to appraise performance by using several sources to measure the employee's effectiveness. Organizations must be careful when using peer-reviewed information. For example, in the *Mathewson v. Aloha Airlines* case, peer evaluations were found to be retaliatory against a pilot who had crossed picket lines during the pilot's union strike against a different airline.

Management of this process can be time-consuming for the HR professional. That's why there are many software programs available to help administer and assess 360 review feedback. Halogen 360, for example, is used by Princess Cruises and media companies such as MSNBC (Halogen Software, 2011). This type of software allows the HR professional to set criteria and easily send links to customers, peers, or managers, who provide the information requested. Then the data are gathered and a report is automatically generated, which an employee can use for quick feedback. Other similar types of software include Carbon360 and Argos.

Performance Appraisal System Errors

Before we begin to develop our performance review process, it is important to note some of the errors that can occur during this process. First, halo effects can occur when the source or the rater feels one aspect of the performance is high and therefore rates all areas high. A mistake in rating can also occur when we compare one employee to another, as opposed to the job description's standards. Sometimes halo effects will occur because the rater is uncomfortable rating someone low on a performance assessment item. Of course, when this occurs, it makes the performance evaluation less valuable for employee development. Proper training on how to manage a performance appraisal interview is a good way to avoid this.

Validity issues are the extent to which the tool measures the relevant aspects of performance. The aspects of performance should be based on the key skills and responsibilities of the job, and these should be reviewed often to make sure they are still applicable to the job analysis and description.

Reliability refers to how consistent the same measuring tool works throughout the organization (or job title). When we look at reliability in performance appraisals, we ask ourselves if two raters were to rate an employee, how close would the ratings be? If the ratings would be far apart from one another, the method may have reliability issues. To prevent this kind of issue, we can make sure that performance standards are written in a way that will make them measurable. For example, instead of "increase sales" as a performance standard, we may want to say, "increase sales by 10 percent from last year". This performance standard is easily measured and allows us to ensure the accuracy of our performance methods.

Acceptability refers to how well members of the organization, manager and employees, accept the performance evaluation tool as a valid measure of performance. For example, let's assume the current measurement tools of Blewett Gravel, Inc. are in place and show validity for each job function. However, managers don't think the tool is useful because they take too much time. As a result, they spend minimal time on the evaluation. This could mean the current process is flawed because of acceptability error.

Another consideration is the specificity, which tells employees the job expectations and how they can be met. If they are not specific enough, the tool is not useful to the employee for development or to the manager to ensure the employee is meeting expectations. Finally, after we have developed our process, we need to create a time line and educate managers and employees on the process. This can be done through formal training and communicated through company blogs or e-mails. According to Robert Kent (Kent, 2011), teaching people how to receive benefit from the feedback they receive can be an important part of the process as well.

Performance Appraisal Legal Considerations

The legality of performance appraisals was questioned in 1973 in *Brito v. Zia*, in which an employee was terminated based on a subjective performance evaluation. Following this important case, employers began to rethink their performance evaluation system and the legality of it.

The *Civil Service Reform Act* of 1978 set new standards for performance evaluation. Although these standards related only to public sector employees, the Reform Act began an important trend toward making certain performance evaluations were legal. The Reform Act created the following criteria for performance appraisals in government agencies:

All agencies were required to create performance review systems.

Appraisal systems would encourage employee participation in establishing the performance standards they will be rated against.

The critical elements of the job must be in writing.

Employees must be advised of the critical elements when hired.

The system must be based exclusively on the actual performance and critical elements of the job. They cannot be based on a curve, for example.

They must be conducted and recorded at least once per year.

Training must be offered for all persons giving performance evaluations.

The appraisals must provide information that can be used for decision-making, such as pay decisions and promotion decisions.

Early performance appraisal research can provide us a good example as to why we should be concerned with the legality of the performance appraisal process (Field & Holley,

1982). Holley and Field analyzed sixty-six legal cases that involved discrimination and performance evaluation. Of the cases, defendants won thirty-five of the cases. The authors of the study determined that the cases that were won by the defendant had similar characteristics:

Appraisers were given written instructions on how to complete the appraisal for employees.

Job analysis was used to develop the performance measures of the evaluation.

The focus of the appraisal was actual behaviors instead of personality traits.

Upper management reviewed the ratings before the performance appraisal interview was conducted.

This tells us that the following considerations should be met when developing our performance appraisal process:

Performance standards should be developed using the job analysis and should change as the job changes.

Provide the employees with a copy of the evaluation when they begin working for the organization, and even consider having the employees sign off, saying they have received it.

All raters and appraisers should be trained.

When rating, examples of observable behavior (rather than personality characteristics) should be given.

A formal process should be developed in the event an employee disagrees with a performance review.

Now that we have discussed some of the pitfalls of performance appraisals, we can begin to discuss how to develop the process of performance evaluations.

Human Resource Recall

What are the steps we should take when developing a performance review process?

Key Takeaways

A performance evaluation system is a systematic way to examine how well an employee is performing in his or her job.

The use of the term *systematic* implies the process should be planned.

Depending on which research you read, some believe the performance evaluation system is one of the most important to consider in HRM, but others view it as a flawed process, which makes it less valuable and therefore ineffective.

The first step in designing a performance appraisal process is to determine how often the appraisals will be given. Consideration of time and effort to administer the evaluation should be a deciding factor.

Many companies offer pay increases as part of the system, while some companies prefer to separate the process. Determine how this will be handled in the next step in the performance appraisal development process.

Goals of the performance evaluation should be discussed before the process is developed. In other words, what does the company hope to gain from this process? Asking managers and employees for their feedback on this is an important part of this consideration.

After determining how often the evaluations should be given, if pay will be tied to the evaluations and goals, you can now sit down and develop the process. First, determine what forms will be used to administer the process.

After you have determined what forms will be used (or developed), determine who will be the source for the information. Perhaps managers, peers, or customers would be an option. A 360 review process combines several sources for a more thorough review.

There are some errors that can occur in the process. These include halo effects or comparing an employee to another as opposed to rating employees only on the objectives. Other errors might include validity, reliability, acceptability, and specificity.

Performance evaluations should always be based on the actual job description.

Our last step in development of this process is to communicate the process and train employees and managers on the process. Also, training on how best to use feedback is the final and perhaps most important step of the process.

Exercises

1. Perform an Internet search on 360 review software. Compare at least two types of software and discuss advantages and disadvantages of each.

2. Discuss the advantages and disadvantages of each type of performance evaluation source.

8.2 Appraisal Methods

Learning Objective

Be able to describe the various appraisal methods.

It probably goes without saying that different industries and jobs need different kinds of appraisal methods. For our purposes, we will discuss some of the main ways to assess performance in a performance evaluation form. Of course, these will change based upon the job specifications for each position within the company. In addition to industry-specific and job-specific methods, many organizations will use these methods in combination, as opposed to just one method. There are three main methods of determining performance. The first is the trait method, in which managers look at an employee's specific traits in relation to the job, such as friendliness to the customer. The behavioral method looks at individual actions within a specific job. Comparative methods compare one employee with other employees. Results methods are focused on employee accomplishments, such as whether or not employees met a quota.

Within the categories of performance appraisals, there are two main aspects to appraisal methods. First, the criteria are the aspects the employee is actually being evaluated on, which should be tied directly to the employee's job description. Second, the rating is the type of scale that will be used to rate each criterion in a performance evaluation: for example, scales of 1—5, essay ratings, or yes/no ratings. Tied to the rating and criteria is the weighting each item will be given. For example, if "communication" and "interaction with client" are two criteria, the interaction with the client may be weighted more than communication, depending on the job type. We will discuss the types of criteria and rating methods next.

Graphic Rating Scale

The graphic rating scale, a behavioral method, is perhaps the most popular choice for performance evaluations. This type of evaluation lists traits required for the job and asks the source to rate the individual on each attribute. A discrete scale is one that shows a number of different points. The ratings can include a scale of 1—10; excellent, average, or poor; or meets, exceeds, or doesn't meet expectations, for example. A continuous scale shows a scale and the manager puts a mark on the continuum scale that best represents the employee's performance. For example:

Poor—Excellent

The disadvantage of this type of scale is the subjectivity that can occur. This type of scale focuses on behavioral traits and is not specific enough to some jobs. Development of specific criteria can save an organization in legal costs. For example, in *Thomas v. IBM*, IBM was able to successfully defend accusations of age discrimination because of the objective criteria the employee (Thomas) had been rated on.

Many organizations use a graphic rating scale in conjunction with other appraisal methods to further solidify the tool's validity. For example, some organizations use a mixed standard scale, which is similar to a graphic rating scale. This scale includes a series of mixed statements representing excellent, average, and poor performance, and the manager is asked to rate a "+" (performance is better than stated), "0" (performance is at stated level), or "−" (performance is below stated level). Mixed standard statements might include the following:

The employee gets along with most coworkers and has had only a few interpersonal issues.

This employee takes initiative.

The employee consistently turns in below-average work.

The employee always meets established deadlines.

An example of a graphic rating scale is shown in Figure 2-39 "Example of Graphic Rating Scale".

Essay Appraisal

In an essay appraisal, the source answers a series of questions about the employee's performance in essay form. This can be a trait method and/or a behavioral method, depending on how the manager writes the essay. These statements may include strengths and weaknesses about the employee or statements about past performance. They can also include specific examples of past performance. The disadvantage of this type of method (when not combined with other rating systems) is that the manager's writing ability can contribute to the effectiveness of the evaluation. Also, managers may write less or more, which means less consistency between performance appraisals by various managers.

Checklist Scale

A checklist method for performance evaluations lessens the subjectivity, although subjectivity will still be present in this type of rating system. With a checklist scale, a series of questions is asked and the manager simply responds yes or no to the questions, which can fall into either the behavioral or the trait method, or both. Another variation to this scale is a check mark in the criteria the employee meets, and a blank in the areas the employee does not meet. The challenge with this format is that it doesn't allow more detailed answers and analysis of the performance criteria, unless combined with another method, such as essay ratings(Figure 64). A sample of a checklist scale is provided in Figure 2-41 "Example of Checklist Scale".

Employee Performance Appraisal
XYZ Company

Employee's Name _____

Title _____

Department _____

Please put an X in the area which best describes this employee's performance.

Attribute	Above Average	Average	Below Expectations
Dependable			
Shows problem-solving ability			
Works well in a team			
Takes initiative			
Produces high quality work			
Shows leadership within department			
Communication ability			

Please provide specific comments which describe the ratings for each category.

_____
_____
_____
_____
_____
_____
_____
_____
_____

Date _____

Signature of employee _____

Signature of manager _____

Figure 2-39 Example of Graphic Rating Scale

**Employee Performance Appraisal
XYZ Company**

Employee's Name _____

Title _____

Department _____

Please write comments about the employee's performance in the space below.

Attribute	Comments
What does this employee do well?	
What aspects of his/her job performance should be improved upon?	
Describe performance challenges.	
Aspects of job to continue doing	
Aspects of job the employee should improve	

Date _____

Signature of employee _____

Signature of manager _____

Figure 2-40 Example of Essay Rating

**Employee Performance Appraisal
XYZ Company**

Employee's Name _____

Title _____

Department _____

Please select yes or no for each of the statements.

	Yes	No	Comments
This employee works well with the people on his/her team.			
He/she is well liked and respected by people on the team.			
The employee has in depth knowledge of his or her job.			
The employee needs minimum supervision in performing his or her job.			
Aspects of job the employee should improve			

Date _____

Signature of employee _____

Signature of manager _____

Figure 2-41 Example of Checklist Scale

Critical Incident Appraisals

This method of appraisal, while more time-consuming for the manager, can be effective at providing specific examples of behavior. With a critical incident appraisal, the manager records examples of the employee's effective and ineffective behavior during the time period between evaluations, which is in the behavioral category. When it is time for the employee to be reviewed, the manager will pull out this file and formally record the incidents that occurred over the time period. The disadvantage of this method is the tendency to record only negative incidents instead of postive ones. However, this method can work well if the manager has the proper training to record incidents (perhaps by keeping a weekly diary) in a fair manner. This approach can also work well when specific jobs vary greatly from week to week, unlike, for example, a factory worker who routinely performs the same weekly tasks.

Work Standards Approach

For certain jobs in which productivity is most important, a work standards approach could be the more effective way of evaluating employees. With this results-focused approach, a minimum level is set and the employee's performance evaluation is based on this level. For example, if a sales person does not meet a quota of $1 million, this would be recorded as non-performing. The downside is that this method does not allow for reasonable deviations. For example, if the quota isn't made, perhaps the employee just had a bad month but normally performs well. This approach works best in long-term situations, in which a reasonable measure of performance can be over a certain period of time. This method is also used in manufacuring situations where production is extremely important. For example, in an automotive assembly line, the focus is on how many cars are built in a specified period, and therefore, employee performance is measured this way, too. Since this approach is centered on production, it doesn't allow for rating of other factors, such as ability to work on a team or communication skills, which can be an important part of the job, too.

Ranking Methods

In a ranking method system (also called stack ranking), employees in a particular department are ranked based on their value to the manager or supervisor. This system is a comparative method for performance evaluations.The manager will have a list of all employees and will first choose the most valuable employee and put that name at the top. Then he or she will choose the least valuable employee and put that name at the bottom of the list. With the remaining employees, this process would be repeated. Obviously, there is room for bias with this method, and it may not work well in a larger organization, where managers may not interact with each employee on a day-to-day basis.

To make this type of evaluation most valuable (and legal), each supervisor should use the same criteria to rank each individual. Otherwise, if criteria are not clearly developed, validity and halo effects could be present. The *Roper v. Exxon Corp* case illustrates the need for clear guidelines when using a ranking system. At Exxon, the legal department attorneys were annually evaluated and then ranked based on input from attorneys, supervisors, and clients. Based on the feedback, each attorney for Exxon was ranked based on their relative contribution and performance. Each attorney was given a group percentile rank (i.e., 99 percent was the best-performing attorney). When Roper was in the bottom 10 percent for three years and was informed of his separation with the company, he filed an age discrimination lawsuit. The courts found no correlation between age and the lowest-ranking individuals, and because Exxon had a set of established ranking criteria, they won the case (Grote, 2005).

Another consideration is the effect on employee morale should the rankings be made public. If they are not made public, morale issues may still exist, as the perception might be that management has "secret" documents.

Fortune 500 Focus

Critics have long said that a forced ranking system can be detrimental to morale; it focuses too much on individual performance as opposed to team performance. Some say a forced ranking system promotes too much competition in the workplace. However, many *Fortune* 500 companies use this system and have found it works for their culture. General Electric (GE) used perhaps one of the most well-known forced ranking systems. In this system, every year managers placed their employees into one of three categories: "A" employees are the top 20 percent, "B" employees are the middle 70 percent, and "C" performers are the bottom 10 percent. In GE's system, the bottom 10 percent are usually either let go or put on a performance plan. The top 20 percent are given more responsibility and perhaps even promoted. However, even GE has reinvented this stringent forced ranking system. In 2006, it changed the system to remove references to the 20/70/10 split, and GE now presents the curve as a guideline. This gives more freedom for managers to distribute employees in a less stringent manner.

The advantages of a forced ranking system include that it creates a high-performance work culture and establishes well-defined consequences for not meeting performance standards. In recent research, a forced ranking system seems to correlate well with return on investment to shareholders. For example, the study (Sprenkel, 2011) shows that companies who use individual criteria (as opposed to overall performance) to measure performance outperform those who measure performance based on overall company success. To make a ranking system work, it is key to ensure managers have a firm grasp on the criteria on which employees will be ranked. Companies using forced rankings without set criteria open themselves to lawsuits, because it would appear the rankings happen based on favoritism rather than quantifiable performance data. For example, Ford in the past used forced ranking systems but eliminated the system after settling class action lawsuits that claimed discrimination (Lowery, 2011). Conoco also has settled lawsuits over its forced ranking systems, as domestic employees claimed the system favored foreign workers (Lowery, 2011). To avoid these issues, the best way to develop and maintain a forced ranking system is to provide each employee with specific and measurable objectives, and also provide management training so the system is executed in a fair, quantifiable manner.

In a forced distribution system, like the one used by GE, employees are ranked in groups based on high performers, average performers, and non-performers. The trouble with this system is that it does not consider that all employees could be in the top two categories, high or average performers, and requires that some employees be put in the non-performing category.

In a paired comparison system, the manager must compare every employee with every other employee within the department or work group. Each employee is compared with another, and out of the two, the higher performer is given a score of 1. Once all the pairs are compared, the scores are added. This method takes a lot of time and again, must have specific criteria attached to it when comparing employees.

Human Resource Recall

How can you make sure the performance appraisal ties into a specific job description?

Management by Objectives (MBO)

Management by objectives (MBOs) is a concept developed by Peter Drucker in his 1954 book *The Practice of Management* (Drucker, 2006). This method is results oriented and similar to the work standards approach, with a few differences. First, the manager and employee sit down together and develop objectives for the time period. Then when it is time for the performance evaluation, the manager and employee sit down to review the goals that were set and determine whether they were met. The advantage of this is the open communication between the manager and the employee. The employee also has "buy-in" since he or she helped set the goals, and the evaluation can be used as a method for further skill development. This method is best applied for positions that are not routine and require a higher level of thinking to perform the job. To be efficient at MBOs, the managers and employee should be able to write strong objectives. To write objectives, they should be SMART (Doran, 1981):

Specific. There should be one key result for each MBO. What is the result that should be achieved?

Measurable. At the end of the time period, it should be clear if the goal was met or not. Usually a number can be attached to an objective to make it measurable, for example "sell $1,000,000 of new business in the third quarter".

Attainable. The objective should not be impossible to attain. It should be challenging, but not impossible.

Result oriented. The objective should be tied to the company's mission and values. Once the objective is made, it should make a difference in the organization as a whole.

Time limited. The objective should have a reasonable time to be accomplished, but not too much time.

Setting MBOs with Employees

To make MBOs an effective performance evaluation tool, it is a good idea to train managers and determine which job positions could benefit most from this type of method. You may find that for some more routine positions, such as administrative assistants, another method could work better.

Behaviorally Anchored Rating Scale (BARS)

A BARS method first determines the main performance dimensions of the job, for example, interpersonal relationships. Then the tool utilizes narrative information, such as from a critical incidents file, and assigns quantified ranks to each expected behavior. In this system, there is a specific narrative outlining what exemplifies a "good" and "poor" behavior for each category. The advantage of this type of system is that it focuses on the desired behaviors that are important to complete a task or perform a specific job. This method combines a graphic rating scale with a critical incidents system. The U.S. Army Research Institute (Phillips, et. al., 2006) developed a BARS scale to measure the abilities of tactical thinking skills for combat leaders. Figure 2-42 "Example of BARS" provides an example of how the Army measures these skills.

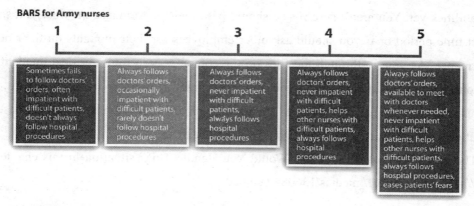

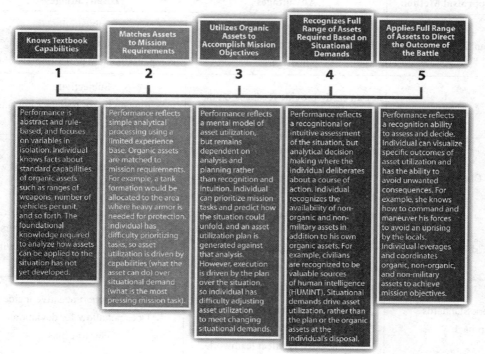

Figure 2-42 Example of BARS

How Would You Handle This?

Playing Favorites

You were just promoted to manager of a high-end retail store. As you are sorting through your responsibilities, you receive an e-mail from HR outlining the process for performance evaluations. You are also notified that you must give two performance evaluations within the next two weeks. This concerns you, because you don't know any of the employees and their abilities yet. You aren't sure if you should base their performance on what you see in a short time period or if you should ask other employees for their thoughts on their peers' performance. As you go through the files on the computer, you find a critical incident file left from the previous manager, and you think this might help. As you look through it, it is obvious the past manager had "favorite" employees and you aren't sure if you should base the evaluations on this information. How would you handle this?

The author discusses the "How Would You Handle This" situation in this chapter at: https://api.wistia.com/v1/ medias/1360849/embed.

Table 2-17 Advantages and Disadvantages of Each Performance Appraisal Method

Type of Performance		
Appraisal Method	**Advantages**	**Disadvantages**
Graphic Rating Scale	Inexpensive to develop Easily understood by employees and managers	Subjectivity Can be difficult to use in making compensation and promotion decisions
Essay	Can easily provide feedback on the positive abilities of the employee	Subjectivity Writing ability of reviewer impacts validity
Checklist scale	Measurable traits can point out specific behavioral expectations Provides specific examples time-consuming for manager	Time-consuming (if not combined with other methods)
Critical Incidents	Ability to measure specific components of the job can create a high-performance work culture	Does not allow for detailed answers or explanations (unless combined with another method)
Work Standards Approach	Validity depends on the amount of interaction between employees and manager Can negatively affect teamwork	Tendency to report negative incidents Does not allow for deviations Possible bias

Continued

Type of Performance		
Appraisal Method	Advantages	Disadvantages
Ranking	Open communication Employee may have more "buy-in"	Many only work for some types of job titles
MBOs	Focus is on desired behaviors Scale is for each specific job	Time-consuming to set up
BARS	Desired behaviors are clearly outlined	

Note: No one performance appraisal is best, so most companies use a variety of methods to ensure the best results.

Key Takeaways

When developing performance appraisal criteria, it is important to remember the criteria should be job specific and industry specific.

The performance appraisal criteria should be based on the job specifications of each specific job. General performance criteria are not an effective way to evaluate an employee.

The rating is the scale that will be used to evaluate each criteria item. There are a number of different rating methods, including scales of 1—5, yes or no questions, and essay.

In a graphic rating performance evaluation, employees are rated on certain desirable attributes. A variety of rating scales can be used with this method. The disadvantage is possible subjectivity.

An essay performance evaluation will ask the manager to provide commentary on specific aspects of the employee's job performance.

A checklist utilizes a yes or no rating selection, and the criteria are focused on components of the employee's job.

Some managers keep a critical incidents file. These incidents serve as specific examples to be written about in a performance appraisal. The downside is the tendency to record only negative incidents and the time it can take to record this.

The work standards performance appraisal approach looks at minimum standards of productivity and rates the employee performance based on minimum expectations. This method is often used for sales forces or manufacturing settings where productivity is an important aspect.

In a ranking performance evaluation system, the manager ranks each employee from most valuable to least valuable. This can create morale issues within the workplace.

An MBO or management by objectives system is where the manager and employee sit down together, determine objectives, then after a period of time, the manager assesses whether those objectives have been met. This can create great development opportunities for the employee and a good working relationship between the employee and manager.

An MBO's objectives should be SMART: specific, measurable, attainable, results oriented, and time limited.

A BARS approach uses a rating scale but provides specific narratives on what constitutes good or poor performance

Exercise

Review each of the appraisal methods and discuss which one you might use for the following types of jobs, and discuss your choices.

a. Administrative Assistant

b. Chief Executive Officer

c. Human Resource Manager

d. Retail Store Assistant Manager

8.3 Completing and Conducting the Appraisal

Learning Objectives

1. Be able to discuss best practices in performance review planning.

2. Be able to write an improvement plan for an employee.

So far, we have discussed the necessity of providing formal feedback to employees through a systematic performance evaluation system. We have stressed the importance of making sure the HR professional knows how often performance evaluations should be given and if they are tied to pay increases.

The next step is to make sure you know the goals of the performance evaluation; for example, is the goal to improve performance and also identify people for succession planning?

You will then determine the source for the performance evaluation data, and then create criteria and rating scales that relate directly to the employee's job description. Once this is done, the successful functioning of the performance evaluation system largely depends on the HR professional to implement and communicate the system to managers and employees. This will be the primary focus of our next section.

Best Practices in Performance Appraisals

The most important things to remember when developing a performance evaluation system include the following:

Make sure the evaluation has a direct relationship to the job. Consider developing specific criteria for each job, based on the individual job specifications and description.

Involve managers when developing the process. Garner their feedback to obtain "buy-in" for the process.

Consider involving the employee in the process by asking the employee to fill out a self-evaluation.

Use a variety of methods to rate and evaluate the employee.

Avoid bias by standardizing performance evaluations systems for each job.

Give feedback on performance throughout the year, not just during performance review times.

Make sure the goals of the performance evaluation tie into the organizational and department goals.

Ensure the performance appraisal criteria also tie into the goals of the organization, for a strategic HRM approach.

Review the evaluation for each job title often, since jobs and expectations change.

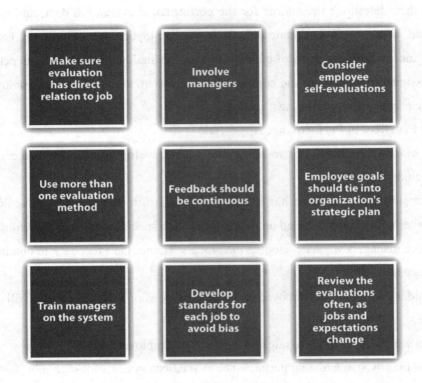

Figure 2-43 Best Practices in Performance Appraisal Systems

As you can see from Figure 2-44 "Performance Review System", the performance appraisal aspect is just one part of the total process. We can call this a performance review system. The first step of the process is goal setting with the employee. This could mean showing the employee his or her performance appraisal criteria or sitting down with the employee to develop MBOs. The basic idea here is that the employee should know the expectations and how his or her job performance will be rated.

Constant monitoring, feedback, and coaching are the next step. Ensuring the employee knows what he or she is doing well and is not doing well in a more informal manner will allow for a more productive employee.

Next, of course, is the formal performance evaluation process. Choosing the criteria, rating scale, and source of the evaluation are steps we have already discussed. The next step is to work with the employee to develop improvement plans (if necessary) and offer any rewards as a result of excellent performance. The process then begins again, setting new goals with the employee.

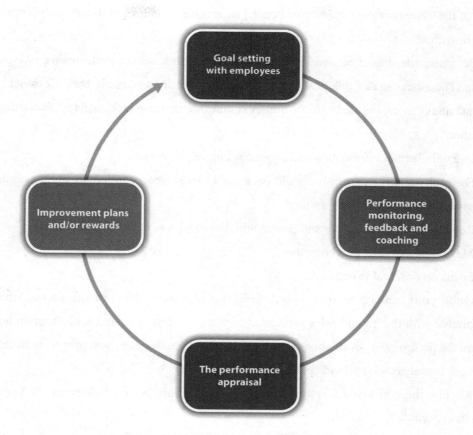

Figure 2-44 Performance Review System

Training Managers and Employees

As HR professionals, we know the importance of performance evaluation systems in developing employees, but this may not always be apparent to the managers we work with on a daily basis. It is our job to educate managers and employees on the standards for completing performance evaluation forms as well as train them on how to complete the necessary documents (criteria and ratings), how to develop improvement plans when necessary, and how to deliver the performance appraisal interview.

Employee Feedback

First, after you have developed the new performance appraisal system (or adjusted an old one), consider offering training on how to effectively use it. The training, if required, can save time later and make the process more valuable. What we want to avoid is making it seem as if the performance appraisal process is "just one more thing" for managers to do. Show the value of the system in your training or better yet, involve managers in developing the process to begin with.

Set standards should be developed for managers filling out the performance ratings and criteria. The advantage of this is accuracy of data and limiting possible bias. Consider these "ground rules" to ensure that information is similar no matter which manager is writing the evaluation:

Use only factual information and avoid opinion or perception.

For each section, comments should be at least two sentences in length, and examples of employee behavior should be provided.

Reviews must be complete and shared with the employee before the deadline.

Make messages clear and direct.

Focus on observable behaviors.

Once your managers are trained, understand how to fill out the forms, and are comfortable with the ground rules associated with the process, we can coach them on how to prepare for performance evaluations. For example, here are the steps you may want to discuss with your managers who provide performance evaluations:

Review the employee's last performance evaluation. Note goals from the previous evaluation period.

Review the employee's file and speak with other managers who interface with this person. In other words, gather data about performance.

Fill out the necessary forms for this employee's appraisal. Note which areas you want to address in the appraisal interview with the employee.

If your organization bases pay increases on the performance evaluation, know the pay increase you are able to offer the employee.

Write any improvement plans as necessary.

Schedule a time and date with the employee.

Most people feel nervous about giving and receiving performance evaluations. One way to limit this is to show the employee the written evaluation before the interview, so the employee knows what to expect. To keep it a two-way conversation, many organizations have the employee fill out the same evaluation, and answers from the employee and manager are compared and discussed in the interview. When the manager meets with the employee to discuss the performance evaluation, the manager should be clear, direct, and to the point about positives and weaknesses. The manager should also discuss goals for the upcoming period, as well as any pay increases or improvement plans as a result of the evaluation. The manager should also be prepared for questions, concerns, and reasons for an employee's not being able to meet performance standards.

Improvement plans should not be punitive, but the goal of an improvement plan should be to help the employee succeed. Improvement plans are discussed in Chapter 6 "Retention and Motivation". Coaching and development should occur throughout the employee's tenure, and he or she should know before the performance evaluation whether expectations are not being met. This way, the introduction of an improvement plan is not a surprise. There are six main components to an employee improvement plan:

Define the problem.

Discuss the behaviors that should be modified, based on the problem.

List specific strategies to modify the behavior.

Develop long- and short-term goals.

Define a reasonable time line for improvements.

Schedule "check-in" dates to discuss the improvement plan.

An employee improvement plan works best if it is written with the employee, to obtain maximum buy-in. Once you have developed the process and your managers are comfortable with it, the process must be managed.

Figure 2-45 Working Stress

Note: Just the thought of a performance review can make even the most confident person stressed out.

Organizing the Performance Appraisal Process

While it will be up to the individual manager to give performance appraisals to employees, as an HR professional, it will be up to you to develop the process (which we have already discussed) and to manage the process. Here are some things to consider to effectively manage the process:

Provide each manager with a job description for each employee. The job description should highlight the expectations of each job title and provide a sound basis for review.

Provide each manager with necessary documents, such as the criteria and rating sheets for each job description.

Give the manager instructions and ground rules for filling out the documents.

Provide coaching assistance on objectives development and improvement plans, if necessary.

Give time lines to the manager for each performance review he or she is responsible for writing.

Most HR professionals will keep a spreadsheet or other document that lists all employees, their manager, and time lines for completion of performance evaluations. This makes it easier to keep track of when performance evaluations should be given.

Of course, the above process assumes the organization is not using software to manage performance evaluations. Numerous types of software are available that allow the HR professional to manage key job responsibilities and goals for every employee in the organization. This software tracks progress on those goals and allows the manager to enter notes (critical incidents files) online. The software can track 360 reviews and send e-mail reminders when it is time for an employee or manager to complete evaluations. This type of software can allow for a smoother, more streamlined process. Of course, as with any new system, it can be time-consuming to set up and train managers and employees on how to use the system. However, many organizations find the initial time to set up software or web-based performance evaluation systems well worth the easier recording and tracking of performance goals.

No matter how the system is managed, it must be managed and continually developed to meet the ultimate goal—continuing development of employees.

Performance Appraisal Interviews

Once a good understanding of the process is developed, it is time to think about the actual meeting with the employee. A performance review process could be intricately detailed and organized, but if the meeting with the employee doesn't go well, the overall strategic objective of performance reviews may not be met. In Norman R. F. Maier's famous book *The Appraisal Interview*, he addressed three types of appraisal interview styles. The first is the tell and sell interview. In this type of interview, the manager does most of the talking and passes his or her view to the employee. In the tell and listen type of interview, the manager communicates feedback and then addresses the employee's thoughts about the interview. In the problem-solving interview, the employee and the manager discuss the things that are going well and those that are not going well, which can make for a more productive discussion. To provide the best feedback to the employee, consider the following:

Be direct and specific. Use examples to show where the employee has room for improvement and where the employee exceeds expectations, such as, "The expectation is zero accidents, and you have not had any accidents this year".

Do not be personal; always compare the performance to the standard. For example, instead of saying, "You are too slow on the production line", say the "expectations are ten units per hour, and currently you are at eight units".

Remember, it is a development opportunity. As a result, encourage the employee to talk. Understand what the employee feels he does well and what he thinks he needs to improve.

Thank the employee and avoid criticism. Instead of the interview being a list of things the employee doesn't do well (which may give the feeling of criticizing), thank the employee for what the employee does well, and work on action plans together to fix anything the employee isn't doing well. Think of it as a team effort to get the performance to the standard it needs to be.

The result of a completed performance evaluation usually means there are a variety of ramifications that can occur after evaluating employee performance:

The employee now has written, documented feedback on his or her performance.

The organization has documented information on low performance, in case the employee needs to be dismissed.

The employee has performed well and is eligible for a raise.

The employee has performed well and could be promoted.

Performance is not up to expectations, so an improvement plan should be put into place.

The employee hasn't done well, improvement plans have not worked (the employee has been warned before), and the employee should be dismissed.

In each of these cases, planning in advance of the performance appraisal interview is important, so all information is available to communicate to the employee. Consider Robin, an employee at Blewett Gravel who was told she was doing an excellent job. Robin was happy with the performance appraisal and when asked about promotion opportunities, the manager said none was available. This can devalue a positive review and impact employee motivation. The point, of course, is to use performance evaluations as a development tool, which will positively impact employee motivation.

Key Takeaways

There are many best practices to consider when developing, implementing, and managing a performance appraisal system. First, the appraisal system must always tie into organization goals and the individual employee's job description.

Involvement of managers in the process can initiate buy-in.

Consider using self-evaluation tools as a method to create a two-way conversation between the manager and the employee.

Use a variety of rating methods to ensure a more unbiased result. For example, using peer evaluations in conjunction with self- and manager evaluations can create a clearer picture of employee performance.

Be aware of bias that can occur with performance appraisal systems.

Feedback should be given throughout the year, not just at performance appraisal time.

The goals of a performance evaluation system should tie into the organization's strategic plan, and the goals for employees should tie into the organization's strategic plan as well.

The process for managing performance evaluations should include goal setting, monitoring and coaching, and doing the formal evaluation process. The evaluation process should involve rewards or improvement plans where necessary. At the end of the evaluation period, new goals should be developed and the process started over again.

It is the HR professional's job to make sure managers and employees are trained on the performance evaluation process.

Standards should be developed for filling out employee evaluations, to ensure consistency and avoid bias.

The HR professional can assist managers by providing best practices information on how to discuss the evaluation with the employee.

Sometimes when performance is not up to standard, an improvement plan may be necessary. The improvement plan identifies the problem, the expected behavior, and the strategies needed to meet the expected behavior. The improvement plan should also address goals, time lines to meet the goals, and check-in dates for status on the goals.

It is the job of the HR professional to organize the process for the organization. HR should provide the manager with training, necessary documents (such as criteria and job descriptions), instructions, pay increase information, and coaching, should the manager have to develop improvement plans.

Some HR professionals organize the performance evaluation information in an Excel spreadsheet that lists all employees, job descriptions, and due dates for performance evaluations.

There are many types of software programs available to manage the process. This software can manage complicated 360 review processes, self-evaluations, and manager's evaluations. Some software can also provide time line information and even send out e-mail reminders.

The performance evaluation process should be constantly updated and managed to ensure the results contribute to the success of the organization.

A variety of ramifications can occur, from the employee's earning a raise to possible dismissal, all of which should be determined ahead of the performance appraisal interview.

Chapter 9 Working with Labor Unions

Unhappy Employees Could Equal Unionization

As the HR manager for a two-hundred-person company, you tend to have a pretty good sense of employee morale. Recently, you are concerned because it seems that morale is low, because of pay and the increasing health benefit costs to employees. You discuss these concerns with upper-level management, but owing to financial pressures, the company is not able to give pay raises this year.

One afternoon, the manager of the marketing department comes to you with this concern, but also with some news. She tells you that she has heard talk of employees unionizing if they do not receive pay raises within the next few months. She expresses that the employees are very unhappy and productivity is suffering as a result. She says that employees have already started the unionization process by contacting the National Labor Relations Board and are in the process of proving 30 percent worker interest in unionization. As you mull over this news, you are concerned because the organization has always had a family atmosphere, and a union might change this. You are also concerned about the financial pressures to the organization should the employees unionize and negotiate higher pay. You know you must take action to see that this doesn't happen. However, you know you and all managers are legally bound by rules relating to unionization, and you need a refresher on what these rules are. You decide to call a meeting first with the CEO and then with managers to discuss strategy and inform them of the legal implications of this process. You feel confident that a resolution can be developed before the unionization happens.

9.1 The Nature of Unions

Learning Objectives

1. Be able to discuss the history of labor unions.

2. Explain some of the reasons for a decline in union membership over the past sixty years.

3. Be able to explain the process of unionization and laws that relate to unionization.

A labor union, or union, is defined as workers banding together to meet common goals, such as better pay, benefits, or promotion rules. In the United States, 11.9 percent of American workers belong to a union, down from 20.1 percent in 1983. In this section, we will discuss the history of unions, reasons for decline in union membership, union labor laws, and the process employees go through to form a union. First, however, we should discuss some of the reasons why people join unions.

People may feel their economic needs are not being met with their current wages and benefits and believe that a union can help them receive better economic prospects. Fairness in the workplace is another reason why people join unions. They may feel that scheduling, vacation time, transfers, and promotions are not given fairly and feel that a union can help eliminate some of the unfairness associated with these processes. Let's discuss some basic information about unions before we discuss the unionization process.

History and Organization of Unions

Trade unions were developed in Europe during the Industrial Revolution, when employees had little skill and thus the entirety of power was shifted to the employer. When this power shifted, many employees were treated unfairly and underpaid. In the United States, unionization increased with the building of railroads in the late 1860s. Wages in the railroad industry were low and the threat of injury or death was high, as was the case in many manufacturing facilities with little or no safety laws and regulations in place. As a result, the Borterhood of Locomotive Engineers and several other brotherhoods (focused on specific tasks only, such as conductors and brakemen) were formed to protect workers' rights, although many workers were fired because of their membership.

Labor Union AFL-CIO Perspective

The first local unions in the United States were formed in the eighteenth century, in the form of the National Labor Union (NLU).

The National Labor Union, formed in 1866, paved the way for other labor organizations. The goal of the NLU was to form a national labor federation that could lobby government for labor reforms on behalf of the labor organizations. Its main focus was to limit the workday to eight hours. While the NLU garnered many supporters, it excluded Chinese workers and only made some attempts to defend the rights of African-Americans and female workers. The NLU can be credited with the eight-hour workday, which was passed in 1862. Because of a focus on government reform rather than collective bargaining, many workers joined the Knights of Labor in the 1880s.

The Knights of Labor started as a fraternal organization, and when the NLU dissolved, the Knights grew in popularity as the labor union of choice. The Knights promoted the social and cultural spirit of the worker better than the NLU had. It originally grew as a labor union for coal miners but also covered several other types of industries. The Knights of Labor initiated strikes that were successful in increasing pay and benefits. When this occurred, membership increased. After only a few years, though, membership declined because of unsuccessful strikes, which were a result of a too autocratic structure, lack of organization, and poor management. Disagreements between members within the organization also caused its demise.

The American Federation of Labor (AFL) was formed in 1886, mostly by people who wanted to see a change from the Knights of Labor. The focus was on higher wages and job security. Infighting among union members was minimized, creating a strong organization that still exists today. In the 1930s, the Congress of Industrial Organizations (CIO) was formed as a result of political differences in the AFL. In 1955, the two unions joined together to form the AFL-CIO.

Currently, the AFL-CIO is the largest federation of unions in the United States and is made up of fifty-six national and international unions. The goal of the AFL-CIO isn't to negotiate specific contracts for employees but rather to support the efforts of local unions throughout the country.

Currently in the United States, there are two main national labor unions that oversee several industry-specific local unions. There are also numerous independent national and international unions that are not affiliated with either national union:

AFL-CIO: local unions include Airline Pilots Association, American Federation of Government Employees, Associated Actors of America, and Federation of Professional Athletes.

CTW (Change to Win Federation): includes the Teamsters, Service Employees International Union, United Farm Workers of America, and United Food and Commercial Workers.

Independent unions: Directors Guild of America, Fraternal Order of Police, Independent Pilots Association, Major League Baseball Players Association.

The national union plays an important role in legislative changes, while the local unions focus on collective bargaining agreements and other labor concerns specific to the area. Every local union has a union steward who represents the interests of union members. Normally, union stewards are elected by their peers.

A national union, besides focusing on legislative changes, also does the following:

Lobbies in government for worker rights laws.

Resolves disputes between unions.

Helps organize national protests.

Works with allied organizations and sponsors various programs for the support of unions

For example, in 2011, the national Teamsters union organized demonstrations in eleven states to protest the closing of an Ontario, California, parts distribution center. Meanwhile, Teamster Local 495 protested at the Ontario plant.

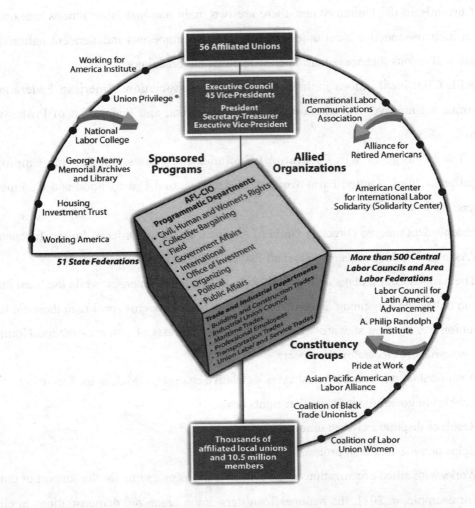

Figure 2-46 The Complicated Structure of AFL-CIO

Source: AFL-CIO.

Current Union Challenges

The labor movement is currently experiencing several challenges, including a decrease in union membership, globalization, and employers' focus on maintaining nonunion status. As mentioned in the opening of this section, the United States has seen a steady decline of union membership since the 1950s. In the 1950s, 36 percent of all workers were unionized (Friedman, 2010), as opposed to just over 11 percent today.

Human Resource Recall

When you are hired for your first job or your next job, do you think you would prefer to be part of a union or not?

Claude Fischer, a researcher from University of California Berkeley, believes the shift is cultural. His research says the decline is a result of American workers preferring individualism as opposed to collectivism (Fischer, 2010). Other research says the decline of unions is a result of globalization, and the fact that many jobs that used to be unionized in the manufacturing arena have now moved overseas. Other reasoning points to management, and that its unwillingness to work with unions has caused the decline in membership. Others suggest that unions are on the decline because of themselves. Past corruption, negative publicity, and hard-line tactics have made joining a union less favorable.

To fully understand unions, it is important to recognize the global aspect of unions. Statistics on a worldwide scale show unions in all countries declining but still healthy in some countries. For example, in eight of the twenty-seven European Union member states, more than half the working population is part of a union. In fact, in the most populated countries, unionization rates are still at three times the unionization rate of the United States (Federation of European Employers, 2011). Italy has a unionization rate of 30 percent of all workers, while the UK has 29 percent, and Germany has a unionization rate of 27 percent.

In March 2011, Wisconsin governor Scott Walker proposed limiting the collective bargaining rights of state workers to save a flailing budget. Some called this move "union busting" and said this type of act is illegal, as it takes away the basic rights of workers. The governor defended his position by saying there is no other choice, since the state is in a budget crisis. Other states such as Ohio are considering similar measures. Whatever happens, there is a clear shift for unions today.

Globalization is also a challenge in labor organizations today. As more and more goods and services are produced overseas, unions lose not only membership but union values in the stronghold of worker culture. As globalization has increased, unions have continued to demand more governmental control but have been only somewhat successful in these attempts. For example, free trade agreements such as the *North American Free Trade*

Agreement (*NAFTA*) have made it easier and more lucrative for companies to manufacture goods overseas. For example, La-Z-Boy and Whirlpool closed production facilities in Dayton and Cleveland, Ohio, and built new factories in Mexico to take advantage of cheaper labor and less stringent environmental standards. Globalization creates options for companies to produce goods wherever they think is best to produce them. As a result, unions are fighting the globalization trend to try and keep jobs in the United States.

There are a number of reasons why companies do not want unions in their organizations, which we will discuss in greater detail later. One of the main reasons, however, is increased cost and less management control. As a result, companies are on a quest to maintain a union-free work environment. In doing so, they try to provide higher wages and benefits so workers do not feel compelled to join a union. Companies that want to stay union free constantly monitor their retention strategies and policies.

Labor Union Laws

The *Railway Labor Act* (*RLA*) of 1926 originally applied to railroads and in 1936 was amended to cover airlines. The act received support from both management and unions. The goal of the act is to ensure no disruption of interstate commerce. The main provisions of the act include alternate dispute resolution, arbitration, and mediation to resolve labor disputes. Any dispute must be resolved in this manner before a strike can happen. The *RLA* is administered by the National Mediation Board (NMB), a federal agency, and outlines very specific and detailed processes for dispute resolution in these industries.

The *Norris-LaGuardia Act* of 1932 (also known as the anti-injunction bill), barred federal courts from issuing injunctions (a court order that requires a party to do something or refrain from doing something) against non-violent labor disputes and barred employers from interfering with workers joining a union. The act was a result of common yellow-dog contracts, in which a worker agreed not to join a union before accepting a job. The *Norris-LaGuardia Act* made yellow-dog contracts unenforceable in courts and established that employees were free to join unions without employer interference.

In 1935, the *Wagner Act* (sometimes called the *National Labor Relations Act*) was passed, changing the way employers can react to several aspects of unions. The *Wagner Act* had a few main aspects:

Employers must allow freedom of association and organization and cannot interfere with, restrain, or coerce employees who form a union.

Employers may not discriminate against employees who form or are part of a union, or those who file charges.

An employer must bargain collectively with representation of a union.

The National Labor Relations Board (NLRB) oversees this act, handling any complaints that may arise from the act. For example, in April 2011, the NLRB worked with employees at Ozburn-Hessey Logistics in Tennessee after they had been fired because of their involvement in forming a union. The company was also accused of interrogating employees about their union activities and threatened employees with loss of benefits should they form a union. The NLRB utilized their attorney to fight on behalf of the employees, and a federal judge ordered the company to rehire the fired employees and also to desist in other antiunion activities.

Figure 2-47 Taft-Harley Act

Note: The *Taft-Hartley Act* prevents certain types of strikes, even in unionized companies.

The *Taft-Hartley Act* also had major implications for unions. Passed in 1947, Taft-Hartley amended the *Wagner Act*. The act was introduced because of the upsurge of strikes during this time period. While the *Wagner Act* addressed unfair labor practices on the part of the company, the *Taft-Hartley Act* focused on unfair acts by the unions. For example, it outlawed strikes that were not authorized by the union, called wildcat strikes. It also prohibited secondary actions (or secondary boycotts) in which one union goes on strike in sympathy for another union. The act allowed the executive branch of the federal government to disallow a strike should the strike affect national health or security. One of the most famous injunctions was made by President Ronald Reagan in 1981. Air traffic controllers had been off the job for two days despite their no-strike oath, and Reagan ordered all of them (over eleven thousand) discharged because they violated this federal law.

The *Landrum Griffin Act*, also known as the *Labor Management Reporting and Disclosure (LMRDA) Act*, was passed in 1959. This act required unions to hold secret elections, required unions to submit their annual financial reports to the U.S. Department of Labor, and created standards governing expulsion of a member from a union. This act was created because of racketeering charges and corruptions charges by unions. In fact, investigations of the Teamsters Union found they were linked to organized crime, and the Teamsters were banned from the AFL-CIO. The goal of this act was to regulate the internal functioning of unions and to combat abuse of union members by union leaders.

Table 2-18 Major Acts Regarding Unions, at a Glance

Railway Labor Act	• Covers railroad and airlines • Alternate dispute resolution methods instead of striking for these two industries
Norris-LaGuardia Act	• As a result of yellow-dog contracts • Barred federal courts from issuing injunctions against non-violent labor disputes
Wagner Act	• Allowed for freedom to join a union without interference • May not discriminate against union employees • Set collective bargaining rules
Taft-Hartley Act	• Amended *Wagner Act* • Focus was on unfair practices by the union
Landrum-Friffing Act	• Required unions to hold secret elections • Financial reporting of unions required

The Unionization Process

There are one of two ways in which a unionization process can begin. First, the union may contact several employees and discuss the possibility of a union, or employees may contact a union on their own. The union will then help employees gather signatures to show that the employees want to be part of a union. To hold an election, the union must show signatures from over 30 percent of the employees of the organization.

Table 2-19 The Unionization Process

Employee Dissatisfaction	Union contacts employees or employees contact union
Initial Organization Meeting	Initial meeting with union to gather employee support.
Signatures	Must have 30% of employee signatures to move forward with unionization process.
Secret Ballot Election or Card Check Method	Once 30% of signatures are gathered, a secret ballot election is administered by the National Labor Relations Board (if the company does not accept the card check method).
Voting and Contract	If the vote is "yes" (51% majority), the National Labor Relations Board certifies the union as the legal bargaining representative of the employees.

Once the signatures are gathered, the National Labor Relations Board is petitioned to move forward with a secret-ballot election. An alternative to the secret-ballot election is the card check method, in which the union organizer provides the company with authorization cards signed by a simple majority (half plus one). The employer can accept the cards as proof that the employees desire a union in their organization. The NLRB then certifies the union as the employees' collective bargaining representative.

If the organization does not accept the card check method as authorization for a union, the second option is via a secret ballot. Before this method is used, a petition must be filed by the NLRB, and an election is usually held two months after the petition is filed. In essence, the employees vote whether to unionize or not, and there must be a simple majority (half plus one). The NLRB is responsible for election logistics and counting of ballots. Observers from all parties can be present during the counting of votes. Once votes are counted, a decision on unionization occurs, and at that time, the collective bargaining process begins.

Once the NLRB is involved, there are many limits as to what the employer can say or do during the process to prevent unionization of the organization. It is advisable for HR and management to be educated on what can legally and illegally be said during this process. It is illegal to threaten or intimidate employees if they are discussing a union. You cannot threaten job, pay, or benefits loss as a result of forming a union. Figure 2-48 "Things That Shouldn't Be Said to Employees during a Unionization Process" includes information on what should legally be avoided if employees are considering unionization.

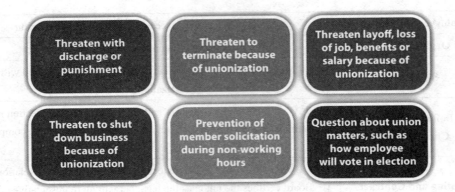

Figure 2-48 Things That Shouldn't Be Said to Employees during a Unionization Process

Obviously, it is in the best interest of the union to have as many members as possible. Because of this, unions may use many tactics during the organizing process. For example, many unions are also politically involved and support candidates who they feel best represent labor. They provide training to organizers and sometimes even encourage union supporters to apply for jobs in non-union environments to actively work to unionize other employees when they are hired. This practice is called union salting. Unions, especially on the national level, can be involved in corporate campaigns that boycott certain products or companies because of their labor practices. The United Food and Commercial Workers (UFCW), for example, has a "Wake Up Walmart Campaign" that targets the labor practices of this organization.

Strategies Companies Use to Avoid Unionization

Most organizations feel the constraints of having a union organization are too great. It affects the cost to the organization and operation efficiency. Collective bargaining at times can put management at odds with its employees and cost more to produce products and services. Ideally, companies will provide safe working conditions, fair pay, and benefits so the employees do not feel they need to form a union. There are three main phases of unionization:

Phase 1: Your organization is union free and there is little or no interest in unionizing.

Phase 2: You learn that some employees are discussing unionization or you learn about specific attempts by the union to recruit employees.

Phase 3: You receive a petition from the National Labor Relations Board filed by a union requesting a unionization vote.

Because of increased costs and operational efficiency, it is normally in a company's best interest to avoid unionization. While in phase 1, it is important to review employee relations programs including pay, benefits, and other compensation. Ensure the compensation plans are fair so employees feel fairly treated and have no reason to seek the representation of a union.

Despite your best efforts, you could hear of unionization in your organization. The goal here is to prevent the union from gaining support to ask for a National Labor Relations Board election. Since only 30 percent of employees need to sign union cards for a vote to take place, this phase to avoid unionization is very important. During this time, HR professionals and managers should respond to the issues the employees have and also develop a specific strategy on how to handle the union vote, should it get that far.

In phase 3, familiarization with all the National Labor Relations Board rules around elections and communications is important. With this information, you can organize meetings to inform managers on these rules. At this time, you will likely want to draw up an antiunion campaign and communicate that to managers, but also make sure it does not violate laws. To this end, develop specific strategies to encourage employees to vote "no" for the union. Some of the arguments that might be used include talking with the employee and mentioning the following:

Union dues are costly.

Employees could be forced to go on strike.

Employees and management may no longer be able to discuss matters informally and individually.

Unionization can create more bureaucracy within the company.

Individual issues may not be discussed.

Many decisions within a union, such as vacation time, are based on seniority only.

With unionization in decline, it is likely you may never need to handle a new union in your organization. However, organizations such as Change to Win are in the process of trying to increase union membership. This organization has four affiliated unions, with a goal to strengthen the labor movement. Teamsters, United Food and Commercial Workers, United Farm Workers, and Service Employees International Union are all unions affiliated with this organization (Change to Win, 2011). The next few years will be telling as to the fate of unions in today's organizations.

Fortune 500 Focus

Perhaps no organization is better known for its antiunion stance than Walmart. Walmart has over 3,800 stores in the United States and over 4,800 internationally with $419 billion in sales. Walmart employs more than 2 million associates worldwide. The billions of dollars Walmart earns do not immunize the company to trouble. In 2005, the company's vice-president, Tom Coughlin, was forced to resign after admitting that between $100,000 and $500,000 was spent for undeclared purposes, but it was eventually found that the money was spent to keep the United Food and Commercial Workers Union (UFCW) out of Walmart (Los Angeles Times Wire Services, 2011) (he was found guilty and sentenced to two years of house arrest).

Other claims surrounding union busting are the closing of stores, such as the Walmart Tire and Lube Express in Gatineau, Quebec (UFCW Canada, 2011), when discussions of unionization occurred. Other reports of union busting include the accusation that company policy requires store managers to report rumors of unionizing to corporate headquarters. Once the report is made, all labor decisions for that store are handled by the corporate offices instead of the store manager. According to labor unions in the United States, Walmart is willing to work with international labor unions but continues to fiercely oppose unionization in the United States. In one example, after butchers at a Jacksonville, Texas, Walmart voted to unionize, Walmart eliminated all U.S. meat-cutting departments.

A group called OUR Walmart (Organization United for Respect), financed by the United Food and Commercial Workers (UFCW) Union, has stemmed from the accusations of union busting. Walmart spokesperson David Tovar says he sees the group as a Trojan horse assembled by labor organizations to lay the groundwork for full-fledged unionization and seek media attention to fulfill their agenda. While the organization's activities may walk a fine line between legal and illegal union practices under the *Taft-Hartley Act*, this new group will certainly affect the future of unionization at Walmart in its U.S. stores.

Note: UFCW was part of the AFL-CIO until 2005 and now is an independent national union.

The Impact of Unions on Organizations

You may wonder why organizations are opposed to unions. As we have mentioned, since union workers do receive higher wages, this can be a negative impact on the organization. Unionization also impacts the ability of managers to make certain decisions and limits their freedom when working with employees. For example, if an employee is constantly late to work, the union contract will specify how to discipline in this situation, resulting in little management freedom to handle this situation on a case-by-case basis. In 2010, for example, the Art Institute of Seattle faculty filed signatures and voted on unionization. Some of the major issues were scheduling issues and office space, not necessarily pay and benefits. While the particular National Labor Relations Board vote was no to unionization, a yes vote could have given less freedom to management in scheduling, since scheduling would be based on collective bargaining contracts. Another concern about unionization for management is the ability to promote workers. A union contract may stipulate certain terms (such as seniority) for promotion, which means the manager has less control over the employees he or she can promote.

Key Takeaways

Union membership in the United States has been slowly declining. Today, union membership consists of about 11.9 percent of the workforce, while in 1983 it consisted of 20 percent of the workforce.

The reasons for decline are varied, depending on whom you ask. Some say the moving of jobs overseas is the reason for the decline, while others say unions' hard-line tactics put them out of favor.

Besides declining membership, union challenges today include globalization and companies' wanting a union-free workplace.

The United States began its first labor movement in the 1800s. This was a result of low wages, no vacation time, safety issues, and other issues.

Many labor organizations have disappeared, but the American Federation of Labor (AFL) still exists today, although it merged with the Congress of Industrial Organizations (CIO) and is now known as the AFL-CIO. It is the largest labor union and represents local labor unions in a variety of industries.

The United States has a low number of union members compared with other countries. Much of Europe, for example, has over 30 percent of their workforce in labor unions, while in some countries as much as 50 percent of the workforce are members of a labor union.

Legislation has been created over time to support both labor unions and the companies who have labor unions. The *Railway Labor Act* applies to airlines and railroads and stipulates that employees may not strike until they have gone through an extensive dispute resolution process. The *Norris-LaGuardia Act* made *yellow-dog contracts* illegal and barred courts from issuing injunctions.

The *Wagner Act* was created to protect employees from retaliation should they join a union. The *Taft-Hartley Act* was developed to protect companies from unfair labor practices by unions.

The National Labor Relations Board is the overseeing body for labor unions, and it handles disputes between companies as well as facilitates the process of new labor unions in the developing stages. Its job is to enforce both the Wagner Act and the Taft-Hartley Act.

The *Landrum Griffin Act* was created in 1959 to combat corruption in labor unions during this time period.

To form a union, the organizer must have signatures from 30 percent of the employees. If this occurs, the National Labor Relations Board will facilitate a card check to determine more than 50 percent of the workforce at that company is in agreement with union representation. If the company does not accept this, then the NLRB holds secret elections to determine if the employees will be unionized. A collective bargaining agreement is put into place if the vote is yes.

Companies prefer to not have unions in their organizations because it affects costs and operational productivity. Companies will usually try to prevent a union from organizing in their workplace.

Managers are impacted when a company does unionize. For example, management rights are affected, and everything must be guided by the contract instead of management prerogative.

Exercises

Do you agree with unionization within organizations? Why or why not? List the advantages and disadvantages of unions to the employee and the company.

Bibliography

[1] T.R.Jain, Mukesh Trehan, Ranju Trehan. Business Environment. FK Publications.

[2] Handy, C. B. (1993) Understanding Organizations. 4th ed. London: Penguin

[3] Vishwajeet Prasad. Business Environment. Gyan Publishing House, 2010

[4] BPP Professional Education. (2004) HNC/HND Business: Mandatory Unit 4: Business Environment: Course Book. London: BPP Professional Education.

[5] James P. Neelankavil, Anoop Rai . Basics of International Business. M.E. Sharpe, 2009.

[6] Neelankavil. International Business Research. M.E. Sharpe

[7] Black, T., "How to Use Social Media as a Recruiting Tool". Inc., April 22, 2010, accessed July 12, 2011, http://www.inc.com/guides/2010/04/social-media-recruiting.html.

[8] Carey, W. P., "Employees First: Strategy for Success". Knowledge @ W. P. Carey, W. P. Carey School of Business, Arizona State University, June 26, 2008, accessed July 11, 2011, http://knowledge.wpcarey.asu.edu/ article.cfm?articleid=1620.

[9] Lefkow, D., "Improving Your Employee Referral Program and Justifying Your Investment". ERE.net, February 21, 2002, accessed July 12, 2011, http://www.ere. net/2002/02/21/improving-your-employee-referral-program-and-justifying-your-investment.

[10] Lindow, A., "How to Use Social Media for Recruiting". Mashable, June 11, 2011, accessed July 12, 2011, http://mashable.com/2011/06/11/social-media-recruiting.

[11] Sodexo, "Sodexo Earns SNCR Excellent Award for Innovative Use of Social Media". news release, December 2, 2009, accessed January 17, 2011, http://www.sodexousa.com/usen/newsroom/press/press09/ sncrexcellenceaward.asp.

[12] Sowa, C., "Going Above and Beyond". America's Best, September/October 2008, accessed July 11, 2011, http://www.americasbestcompanies.com/magazine/articles/goingabove-and-beyond.aspx. Hanricks, M., "3 Interview Questions That Could Cost Your Company $1 Million". BNET, March 8, 2011, accessed August 2, 2011,

[13] Lipschultz, J., "Don't Be a Victim of Interview Bias". Career Builder, June 15, 2010, accessed July 12, 2011, http://jobs.aol.com/articles/2010/06/15/interview-bias/.

［14］Reeves, S., "Is Your Body Betraying You in Job Interviews?" Forbes, February 2006, accessed August 2, 2011, http://www.forbes.com/2006/02/15/employment-careers-interviewscx_sr_0216bizbasics.html.

［15］Dougherty, C., "Young Women's Pay Exceeds Male Peers". Wall Street Journal, September 1, 2010.

［16］Ferris, G., Handbook of Human Resource Management. Cambridge, MA: Blackwell, 1995.

［17］Gomstyn, A., "Walmart CEO Pay" .ABC News Money, July 2, 1010, accessed July 23, 2011, http://abcnews.go.com/Business/walmart-ceo-pay-hour-workers-year/ story?id=11067470.

［18］Indiana University, "Edward L. Thorndike". accessed February 14, 2011, http://www.indiana.edu/~intell/ ethorndike.shtml.

［19］Branham, L., Keeping the People Who Keep You in Business. New York: American Management Association, 2000, 6.

［20］Maertz, C. P. Jr. and M. A. Campion, "25 Years of Voluntary Turnover Research: A Review and Critique". in International Review of Industrial and Organizational Psychology, vol. 13, ed. Cary L. Cooper and Ivan T. Robertson .London: John Wiley, 1998, 49–86.

［21］Paiement, N., "It Will Cost You $4,000 to Replace Just One $8 per Hour Employee". Charity Village, July 13, 2009, accessed August 30, 2011, http://www.charityvillage.com/cv/research/rhr50.html